Paradoxes in American Criminal Justice

FIRST EDITION

Paradoxes in American Criminal Justice

EXPLORING HISTORICAL AND PHILOSOPHICAL ASPECTS
OF THE CRIMINAL JUSTICE SYSTEM

EDITED BY Tracy Tolbert

California State University, Long Beach

cognella®

SAN DIEGO

Bassim Hamadeh, CEO and Publisher
Mieka Portier, Senior Acquisitions Editor
Tony Paese, Project Editor
Emely Villavencia, Senior Graphic Designer
Alexa Lucido, Licensing Associate
Natalie Piccotti, Director of Marketing
Kassie Graves, Vice President of Editorial
Jamie Giganti, Director of Academic Publishing

cognella® | ACADEMIC PUBLISHING

3970 Sorrento Valley Blvd., Ste. 500, San Diego, CA 92121

CONTENTS

Introduction

Criminal Justice Systems in Society

The criminal justice system in America originated in the European tradition whereby the cruel spectacles of punishment gave way to the pressure and necessity of evolving into a more concrete framework of ethical standards and rational thinking. Much of this thinking emerged as the foundation of modern thought, which advanced an age of inquiry leading to major advancements in philosophy, science, and technology. By the time of the French Revolution (1750–1789), many of these ideas ushered in a social and political movement focused on the question of the efficacy of torture as a true deterrence to crime.

Through these efforts, the modern system of criminal justice emerged in a state of theoretical and philosophical perfection. Yet, despite this history, the system we know today is faltering as we rapidly devolve into practices contradictory to and reminiscent of the past.[1] Several questions come to mind. Why is this process happening? Have we lost sight of the vision, or are we affected by forces beyond our control? Questions like these and more are examined within the context of this anthology, the purpose of which is to explore what we shall call the *Paradoxes in American Criminal Justice*. From this standpoint, we want to explore the paradox constituting the current status of crime and punishment in America, as well as the empirical methods by which the success and/or failures of the system are evaluated.

---

1   According to Merriam Webster (2018), a paradox can relate to several things. For example, a paradox is often seen as a tenet contrary to received opinion. It is also a statement that is seemingly contradictory or opposed to common sense, and yet is perhaps true. It manifests also as a self-contradictory statement that at first seems true, or as an argument that apparently derives self-contradictory conclusions by valid deduction from acceptable premises. Finally, it fits the status of one (such as a person, situation, or action) having seemingly contradictory qualities or phases.

Thus, the anthology, *Paradoxes in American Criminal Justice: Exploring Historical and Philosophical Aspects of the Criminal Justice System*, presents a basic framework for this examination. The primary audience for the text is freshman students enrolled in introductory courses in criminal justice, as well as instructors wishing to take a more complex approach to the study of criminology and criminal justice in general.

Early in my career, I came to recognize what appears to be a consistent practice associated with the traditional method of teaching introductory courses in criminal justice. Specifically speaking, students were learning the material by rote, which left very little expertise in the area of critical thinking. For example, introductory instructors readily employed remedial methods such as textbook lectures, quizzes, and short response papers, which are used to measure the extent to which students are learning the material. Students, in this respect, will traditionally study the material the night before class, take a quiz or exam, and promptly forget everything as they walk out of the classroom.

I questioned the efficacy of this pedagogy and style of instruction. What have students learned about the reality of crime and the criminal justice system? Are they capable of conducting a critical analysis of these issues? Do they understand the empirical nature of cause and effect or the methodological considerations that lead to concrete answers to the questions shaping the most important issue of the day? In short, students are systematically being taught to take the test, and the textbooks used for this purpose are traditionally organized around a pedagogy designed for memorization rather than critical thinking.

I'm aware that common wisdom has it that freshman students are not academically prepared for such a high-level approach to philosophy and history in relation to the study of criminology and criminal justice. However, after seventeen years of teaching the course using the same or similar material found in this anthology, there is little doubt that students matriculating at this level are indeed capable of gaining critical thinking skills, as well as basic knowledge of the empirical process.

In this respect, the chapters are designed to facilitate knowledge of the history of the American system of criminal justice and philosophical frameworks shaping the definitions of crime and punishment in the modern and post-modern age. **Chapter 1**, for example, presents students with an overview of the institutional structure and function of the United States, and examination of how the institution of criminal justice works in tandem to form a system of *social control*, which is inherent to the success of the system. **Chapters 2–6** present the history of criminal justice in the U.S. beginning with a discussion of the original sin (i.e., *the first murder*), and impact on fairness in the current system of criminal justice; the rise of the *Inquisition* and emergence of the spectacle of punishment as an abstract form of social control; the *Age of Enlightenment* and development of a humanistic approach to crime and punishment; the *Utilitarian Reform Movement* and creation of a concrete philosophy of justice that shaped the modern world; and the *Age of Industrialization*, where we examine the emergence of the paradox as it shapes a system of justice bereft of the original intent, and one grounded more in social division and the excesses of a political economy of capitalism. **Chapters 7–13** direct attention to the more traditional aspects of the criminal justice system through discussions of the *nature of crime in America, morality and law, deviance and social control, criminology theory, law enforcement and policing, criminal court system*, and *prison systems and corrections*. **Chapter 14** provides an examination of *women and the criminal justice system*, which is essential to the overall study of criminal justice. Traditional researchers, until recently, tended to ignore the potential for women to commit violent crime, along with women's potential for success in the criminal justice system at large.

An additional feature of each chapter are the *introductions*, which are designed to give students a baseline for the material to be discussed during class lectures, including *research articles* and *essays* written by a variety of noted scholars representing the fields of *history, philosophy, criminology, criminal justice*, and *sociology*. The articles are instrumental to the anthology mainly because of the selected material, which is designed to form a framework for developing critical thinking skills relative to the *Paradoxes in American Criminal Justice*. It is not so much the task of students to know the problems we face, but to understand the empirical processes and methods by which the problems are solved. The central purpose of the anthology is to help students accomplish this task.

CHAPTER ONE

Paradoxes in American Criminal Justice

The criminal justice system in America is both a paradox and an enigma. For the most part, we think of the system through our vision of police officers who patrol the streets of our neighborhoods. We see them in our immediate vicinity, and we watch from a distance. Beyond that we have very little idea of how the criminal justice system works, mainly because most people will never experience the system firsthand. In reality, the criminal justice system is part of a much larger system of social institutions designed to integrate and operate as a framework for social control.

Social control operates on a macro level where social institutions evolved historically to form the framework through which individuals conform to the laws, norms, and values of American society. *Social control* also operates on a micro level to ensure that individuals participate in the labor market and adhere to these policies through various mediums of conformity. Five major institutions form the overarching structure of this model: *U.S. government, education, religion, marriage,* and *family*. America is also comprised of several functioning sub-institutions such as the *media, sports,* and *entertainment*, to name a few. Each of these institutions contributes greatly to the stability of this country. For the purpose of this discussion, we will focus on the U.S. government, which also encompasses the *criminal justice system,* the ultimate institution of control in American society.

The **U.S. government** is the most powerful of the five institutions, and is organized around the *executive, legislative,* and *judicial* branches of power. The **executive** branch is represented by the president, whose role as an elected official is similar to that of the CEO of an ultra-large corporation. He or she sets the philosophical framework for how the county will function over a term of four years, or eight if elected for a second term. This individual is usually thought of as the most powerful political figure in the world and represents the interests of the United States at home and abroad. The **legislature** is organized around two main entities, the *U.S. Senate* and *U.S. House of Representatives*. The role of both is to vote on legislative issues, and to set policy relating to the overall structure and function of the country. The **judiciary** is represented by the *U.S. Supreme Court*, also known as the court of last resort. The role of the individuals who serve on this court is to interpret and rule on social and political issues related to constitutional law. The court is made up of nine judges—one Chief Justice and eight Associate Justices. While the president and officials who serve within the legislative branches of government are elected, the nine justices of the U.S. Supreme Court are appointed for life.

From this model of government in America, the criminal justice system manifests through several agencies and personnel charged with the responsibility of maintaining social control. As "**agents of control**," their role and function is to represent the government and carry out a mandate of ensuring that society does not devolve into chaos, and that individuals adhere to the goals and mandates set forth by the government. These agents and agencies are traditionally represented through **law enforcement, the criminal courts**, and **corrections**. Today, we also include **victim services** as a necessary component of this structure. Each of these entities is examined throughout the anthology; however, there are several rather obvious questions about the effectiveness of this system.

At issue here, for example, is the expectation that not only do these branches of government integrate seamlessly to form a control system, but that everyone agrees with and adheres to the system. This is one way to see criminal justice as paradoxical to its structure and function in America. If people do not naturally agree with the system, and are prone to question its purpose from time to time, then how do we trust these institutions to adhere to the basic tenets of democracy, freedom, and justice for which they are responsible? Especially when history illustrates the manner in which certain groups of people have not benefitted from the system. Instead, their experiences have been anathema to the philosophical framework through which the system was formed.

In this sense, it appears that the criminal justice systems work as a system in theory, but the reality is oftentimes something quite different. We work under the assumption that all criminal justice practitioners and agencies work together to adjudicate a case from start to finish, which implies there is an actual process through which justice is served. Actually, there is such a system called "**due process**," which apparently operates as an orderly and predictable framework of clear communication between agencies and people who carefully collaborate to ensure individual rights of the defendant are protected. This would require all agencies to share a common set of goals and philosophies about what criminal justice should or should not be. Yet, it is apparent that the system is also a "**non-system**" wherein criminal justice agencies are not neatly networked into a cohesive single unit.[1] Although the system appears fairly rigid, it is important to note that the right decisions must be applied properly at every stage of the process. When considering the historical aspects of the American criminal justice system, however, agreement does not always exist about the group's goals and the proper means for achieving them. As we shall discuss throughout the anthology, this viewpoint is one of the main sources of the paradox in American criminal justice.

---

1   S. S. Owen, H. F. Fradella, T. W. Burke, and J. W. Joplin, *Foundations of Criminal Justice*, 2nd ed. (New York: Oxford University Press, 2015).

A Critical Thinking Approach to Criminal Justice

By Joycelyn Pollock

....

Chapter Preview

- What Are the Major Issues in Studying Crime Today?
- What Are the Major Issues in Policing Today?
- What Are the Major Issues in Courts Today?
- What Are the Major Issues in Corrections Today?
- What Is the Role of Criminal Justice Actors in the War on Terror?
- Focus on Data: Last Thoughts
- Critical Thinking Exercises

Throughout this book, we have modeled a critical thinking approach to the issues relevant to the various components of the criminal justice system. In this last chapter we will reiterate the approach and take a last look at a few current issues. We also will discuss the steps taken in preventing terrorist actions in this country, and discuss how that challenge overlaps with domestic criminal justice issues.

Recall that critical thinking has many definitions and no set formula, but, in general, it is an approach to problem solving that utilizes the following steps:

1. Identify and clearly formulate relevant questions or issues.

2. Gather and assess relevant information, noting the source of the information to identify any bias or vested interest.

3. Utilize data to develop well-reasoned conclusions and solutions and test them.

4. At all times be aware of assumptions that may bias your perception of data and lead to selective perception, tunnel vision, or cognitive distortion.

5. Be aware of the implications and practical consequences of findings.[1]

What are the Major Issues in Studying Crime Today?

In earlier chapters, we have noted that all three measures of crime, the Uniform Crime Reports, arrest statistics, and victim self-reports in the National Crime Victimization Survey have tracked an historic decline of crime over the last two decades. The triangulation of data makes it more likely that this decline is real. Recently, there has been an increase in homicides in some large cities. Researchers are currently trying to determine whether this trend will continue, and many complain that there are no good sources for current data. It takes six months to a year before the Uniform Crime Reports and arrest statistics are available and the NCVS findings take even longer. There is currently a partnership between the Bureau of Justice Statistics and the FBI to make these data available sooner, but until we have more current data, analysis is difficult. Cities vary, but some have extremely sophisticated data collection and analysis, and these cities have much more current data than we have available nationally. It is important, however, not to equate crime patterns of a few major cities to crime as a whole across the country since suburban and rural crime patterns are very different from the crime patterns of major cities. It is also important to wait to see if this signals a trend or is an aberration since despite the general downward trend of crime rates over the last two decades, there have been some yearly increases in some locations.

One issue with the UCR is that it does not give us much information about the crimes that many people are concerned with today—specifically, identity theft (including credit card theft), cybercrime, and other forms of white-collar crime. These crimes are not part of the **index crimes**, and they are submerged in arrest statistics under general crime categories such as forgery, fraud, embezzlement, or larceny-theft. The National Incident Based Reporting System (NIBRS) provides more information about such crimes because fraud is broken down into identity/credit card/ATM fraud, among other types of frauds, but still many forms of white-collar crime are reported as "all other offenses." NIBRS also includes a data entry for whether the offender used a computer in the crime; therefore, computer crime statistics will be more accessible as law enforcement agencies begin to report under NIBRS. The Bureau of Justice Statistics has begun to publish a report on identity theft that provides more information than we have had in the past.

For the 2014 BJS report on identity theft, go to http://www.bjs.gov/index.cfm?ty=pbdetail&iid=5408

Identity theft is obtaining and using, or attempting to use, another person's identity (name, Social Security number, address) without the owner's permission and/or the unauthorized use of a credit card or a bank account.

Figure 1.1 Identity theft affects millions of Americans every year. The NYPD Identity Theft Task Force collected this evidence, including fraudulent credit cards and drivers' licenses, during an investigation.

Source: Getty

Identity theft is both a state and a federal crime. In addition, crimes utilizing identity theft may violate federal wire-fraud and credit card fraud laws. The Bureau of Justice Statistics reports an estimated 17.6 million persons, or about 7 percent of U.S. residents age sixteen or older, were victims of at least one incident of identity theft in 2014. In 2014, the most common type of identity theft was the unauthorized misuse or attempted misuse of an existing account—experienced by 16.4 million persons. About 8.6 million victims experienced the fraudulent use of a credit card, 8.1 million experienced the unauthorized or attempted use of existing bank accounts (checking, savings, or other) and 1.5 million victims experienced other types of existing account theft, such as misuse or attempted misuse of an existing telephone, online or insurance account; some victims reported multiple types of victimization.[2]

The majority of identity theft victims did not know how the offender obtained their information, and nine in ten identity theft victims did not know anything about the offender. Two-thirds of identity theft victims reported a direct financial loss. The majority of identity theft victims (52 percent) were able to resolve any problems associated with the incident in a day or less, while about 9 percent spent more than a month. It is important to note that fewer than one in ten identity theft victims reported the incident to police. The majority (87 percent) of identity theft victims contacted a credit card company or bank to report misuse or attempted misuse of an account or personal information, while 8 percent contacted a credit bureau. More females (9.2 million) were victims of identity theft than males (8.3 million) in 2014. People in households with an annual income of $75,000 or more had the highest prevalence of identity theft (11 percent), compared to those in all other income brackets.[3]

In 2007, about 8 million households had at least one member report being a victim of this type of crime and, in 2014, 17.6 million reported being victimized. Thus, if the counting is comparable between 2007 and 2014, there was an over 100 percent increase in the prevalence of identity theft (note that these are just raw counts, not rates so we do not know how many more people there were in the population, how many more people had credit cards, or whether there were different counting methods of identity theft).

In Figure 1.2 we see the 17.6 million people who reported identity theft in 2014 can be compared to the 2.9 million who experienced burglary and the 664,210 who reported robbery in 2014.[4] Identity theft has more than doubled since 2004. In 2014, 7 percent of American households experienced some form of identity theft compared to 4 percent in 2004.[5]

Clearly, modern criminals are much less likely to use a gun or burglary tools today when they can use a computer or stolen credit card. Cases of identity theft have increased dramatically with the increasing use of computers. "**Phishing**" refers to false emails that appear to be from banks or other accounts that request the user to enter passwords and other private information. Generally, once an identity has been obtained, the offender can access and steal from bank accounts, use credit card numbers to make purchases, and/or set up credit in the victim's name and incur huge amounts of debt. Identity theft is difficult to investigate and many cases go unreported. Merchants and banks continue to improve their security devices to guard against identity theft and computer crimes, including enhanced encryption and authentication techniques, but there is no doubt that it is one of the most pervasive crime problems in America today and should be considered when discussing the crime decline.

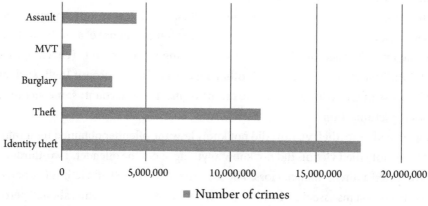

Figure 1.2 Crime Comparison

Source: E. Harrell, *Victims of Identity Theft, 2014.* Washington, DC: Bureau of Justice Statistics, 2014.

It is a paradox that the American public is so unaware of the historic low crime rates, especially of violent crime. The perception that crime is increasing, and especially violent crime, is no doubt due to pervasive media coverage. Whether homicide and other violent crime will continue to increase in major cities is a question that can be answered by accessing the available data sources. A critical thinking approach to understanding crime patterns includes using multiple data sources, e.g., FBI's Uniform Crime Reports and arrest statistics, along with NCVS data from the Bureau of Justice Statistics. Crime trends can be better understood when looking at longer periods of comparison. It is unlikely that crime rates can fall much farther since they are at historic lows. It will become important to note the factors associated with increased crime rates.

What Are the Major Issues in Policing Today?

We are in a new era where crime occurs on a worldwide platform, which means law enforcement agencies in this country must deal with narcoterrorism, drug cartels, cybercrimes, worldwide money laundering and other financial crimes, corporate criminality on a worldwide scale, and human trafficking. A recent scandal involving a Panamanian bank uncovered income tax evasion by American citizens. Often, identity theft rings steal information in the United States to be used by criminals in Africa or Eastern Europe. Other crimes include arms smuggling, counterfeiting, cyberhacking, and corporate espionage. The Russian mafia, Japanese yakuza, as well as the drug cartels, have joined older organized crime organizations in this country, and American law enforcement agencies, especially those in large cities, must respond. Each of these areas requires cooperation and involvement with Interpol and foreign law enforcement agencies. It is also important for the law enforcement and investigative agencies in the United States to work together. It is indeed a small world and the problems of Mexico or Somalia quickly become our problems as well.

One example of the international nature of crime today is human trafficking.

It is estimated that 600,000 to 2 million people are trafficked internationally each year. In many cases, there is a "willing" person who agreed to illegally enter this country for some type of work, but once they arrive they are held in jail-like conditions and work (typically in agriculture or food service) in various forms of debt bondage. In other trafficking cases, women are brought into the country to work as virtual sex slaves in brothels. Estimates are that 50 percent of trafficked persons are minors. While the victims of domestic, restaurant, and farm labor trafficking probably exceed the numbers of those trafficked in the sex industry, the most attention has been focused on sex trafficking. The Department of State indicates that approximately 14,500 to 17,500 victims are trafficked into the United States every year, although other sources estimate that 50,000 victims are trafficked into the country each year. The majority of victims seem to come from Southeast Asia, Central America, and Eastern Europe. If these women and girls are returned to their own countries, they are subject to shame and ridicule for returning home after their parents have obtained money for their services, and/or when

Figure 1.3 Although sex trafficking gets more attention, many others are forced to work on farms or in sweatshops, like these women who were among 70 immigrants freed from a garment factory in California.

Source: AP

they have been given away as a wife in return for a bride price. They face extreme challenges and hurdles in adjusting and adapting to the demands they face, even if they are rescued from a trafficking situation. The victims have no identity papers, do not speak English, and are constantly threatened with beatings, rapes, and exposure to immigration authorities who, traffickers warn, will put them in prison. Law enforcement officers sometimes have difficulty identifying victims of trafficking and treat them as criminals or immigration violators, especially because the victims are afraid to give evidence against the trafficker. If they are deported, they may fall back into the hands of the traffickers. Local law enforcement agencies may not have officers with the language skills necessary to communicate, much less gain the trust of these victims. Any investigations require the involvement of multiple state and federal agencies.

In 2000, Congress passed the Victims of Trafficking and Violence Protection Act of 2000 (VTVPA), which created or revised federal crimes targeting traffickers, including "human trafficking," "sex trafficking of children," "document servitude," and "forced labor." The Act also increased the penalties associated with these crimes. This legislation was amended four times in 2003, 2005, 2008, and 2013; it continues to be amended and ratified at different levels of government to best combat trafficking and provide services for victims. The VTVPA created agencies designed to combat trafficking both internationally, by identifying problematic countries, and domestically, by supporting task forces between federal and state agencies so that investigation and prosecution can occur more smoothly. The T-visa was created, along with other avenues, to keep the victim in this country in order to assist law enforcement and prosecution and, in some cases, the victim is granted a permanent visa in return. Trafficking is not easy to investigate or prosecute, however, and there are relatively few successful cases when compared to the scope of the problem.[6]

This is a troubling time for law enforcement. They are facing scrutiny and, in recent years, fatal attacks, spurred perhaps by the widespread perception that there have been abuses of the great power that we entrust to them. In the summer of 2016, after the killings of law enforcement officers in Dallas and Baton Rouge, many leaders spoke about the idea that when there is an attack on police, there is an attack on society itelf because they represent law and order. Critics and supporters of law enforcement have often succumbed to generalizations and bias when discussing the issues. Calm and reasoned thinking is vitally necessary to address the problems of police–community relations.

The President's Task Force on 21st Century Policing utilized a critical thinking approach in that experts (academics, community organizers, and police practitioners) came together and listened to hundreds of people from all sides in many locations across the country. They then outlined some priorities and objectives that emerged from this information. The next step in a critical thinking approach would be to implement some of the changes recommended and carefully track the results to determine effectiveness in crime prevention, community relations, and/or police officer satisfaction and health. This is currently being done.

> To read about the Task Force report, go to http://www.cops.usdoj.gov/policingtaskforce

What Are the Major Issues in Courts Today?

The Innocence Project refers to groups of attorneys and other volunteers in many states who take cases of inmates claiming innocence. It seems that every day in the news is a new case of someone being released after spending years in prison for a crime they did not commit.

Some estimates indicate that between 1 percent and 3 percent of those in prison are actually innocent or innocent of the specific charges they were convicted of; more may be factually guilty but due process was violated in the steps leading up to their conviction. To date, the Innocence Project lawyers have been instrumental in exonerating 342 inmates, usually through the use of DNA testing, and 147 true perpetrators have been identified. Some of these individuals had been incarcerated for decades, and some were days away from being executed before found to be innocent.

> To read more about the Innocence Project, go to http://www.innocenceproject.org/?gclid=CK_-vdyKy6QCFQ5O2godgy9KEg

The reasons for false convictions and imprisonment are usually a combination of eyewitness error, prosecutorial misconduct, defense attorney ineffectiveness, and false confessions (sometimes through coercion). Efforts are underway by researchers to determine the weak points in the system in

Figure 1.4 The Innocence Project works to free wrongly convicted people, like John Nolley, who served nineteen years before he was released.

Source: Getty

To read about senti-nel event research in this area, go to http://www.nij.gov/topics/justice-system/Pages/sentinelevents.aspx

To read the report of a group tracking progress in providing pre-trial justice, go to http://www.pretrial.org/download/infostop/Implementing%20the%20Recommendations%20of%20the%20National%20Symposium%20on%20Pretrial%20Justice-%20The%202013%20Progress%20Report.pdf

order to prevent wrongful convictions in the future. What these cases do show is that even with the protections mandated by our Bill of Rights and state constitutions, individuals may be falsely accused and punished when individuals subvert or ignore their duties to uphold due process. More importantly, if there are systemic problems that cause such miscarriages of justice, they need to be identified and improved.

There has been increasing concern about the lack of adequate defense for indigents. This issue is related to wrongful convictions and, perhaps, to the numbers of people in prison since someone without adequate legal assistance is more likely to be incarcerated. Another related topic is the issue of the "poverty penalty"; the fact that poor defendants get caught up in the system while those with financial means can "purchase" freedom by paying off fines, fees, and court costs. There are currently attempts underway to determine if pretrial release programs can identify those who can be released before trial without bail, but also with no risk to public safety. The prediction instruments that have been developed continue to be refined but there has to be the public will to implement them.

What Are the Major Issues in Corrections Today?

As reported in earlier chapters of this book, crime is at a thirty-year low in some categories, yet the expenditures related to criminal justice keep increasing. The current rate of increase cannot be sustained, especially as some states face billion-dollar deficits and all states are struggling with reduced budgets. The question is how to utilize correctional dollars in the most efficient way without undue risk to the public.

One of the clear issues of the day is what to do about the 700,000 individuals released from prison each year, many of whom have been in prison since the early and mid-1980s. These individuals have served long periods of time, decades even, without any meaningful programs to help them conquer addictions and adapt to their freedom on the street. Although the historic unemployment high of almost 10 percent has dropped by half it is still very difficult for ex-offenders to get jobs.

Those on probation and released from prison often go back to criminogenic communities that have pervasive social problems. These "million-dollar blocks" refer to areas of the city where more than a million dollars is spent incarcerating, returning, and revoking offenders. Typically, the communities that offenders come from and go home to are characterized by longstanding poverty from lack of jobs and business development. Schools underperform and drop-out rates are high. The residents are heavy users of government services. There is a substantial overlap between neighborhoods that are recipients of TANF (Temporary Assistance to Needy Families) and those who receive a disproportionate share of offenders (released on parole or probation).[7]

Research is beginning to show that the huge increase in incarceration that occurred since the 1980s has not necessarily been helpful to the communities hardest hit by crime. Research has found a **"tipping effect"** occurs at high rates of imprisonment where imprisonment seemed to result in more crime in certain communities.[8] Positive effects of incarceration included removal of problem family members and reducing the number of dangerous individuals in the community, but negative effects for communities included the stigma attached to returning offenders for the offender and his or her family, the financial impact of imprisonment for both the offender and his or her family, and the difficulty of maintaining interpersonal relationships through a prison sentence. High levels of incarceration reduce the number of potentially positive role models for children, result in transient populations, and affect the ability of the community to control its members through informal and affective ties.[9] Incarceration can reduce crime by the removal of criminal offenders; on the other hand, if a community experiences high levels of incarceration, it increases social mobility and social disorganization, and weakens the ability of the community to utilize parochial methods of control.[10]

Re-entry efforts have included job training/placement, drug treatment, and housing assistance, as these are identified as the major problems of those released from prison. The Second Chance Act and other state and local programs that assist ex-offenders in obtaining employment should continue to be evaluated for effectiveness. Further, programs that receive Justice Reinvestment monies should be rigorously evaluated to determine if they are meeting their mandate. This requires objective evaluators who have no stake in the outcome or can put aside their biases in implementing and conducting evaluations. Skeptical outside reviews should be welcome since they serve as a check to bias. Although it is frustrating to have contradictory evaluations, having multiple researchers or methodologies carefully evaluating how taxpayers' money is spent is an important element to a critical thinking approach to crime prevention.

Currently, there are massive changes underway in some states' sentencing structures, such as Realignment in California, that shift the correctional population to the community. Proponents of decarceration applaud such efforts while others warn that any reduction in the use of incarceration will lead to more crime. It is important, first, to note the positions of interest groups. For instance, the correctional officer union in California opposed legislative changes to the three-strikes bill that reduced the number of inmates serving long sentences and, indeed, correctional officer unions tend to oppose any legislation that would reduce prison populations. This position may be arrived at through a careful and reasoned review of the evidence or it could be colored by self-interest. Indeed, news items occur periodically describing prison workers' opposition to closing prisons. On the other side, research by advocacy groups who have a mission to reduce the number of incarcerated should

To peruse the websites of some of these groups, go to http://www.sentencing-project.org/; http://famm.org/; http://www.justice-policy.org/index.html

also be evaluated for objectivity. These non-profits have been successful at raising awareness of the problem of mass imprisonment, and their work has made data much more accessible, but a critical thinking approach requires us to not reject information outright, but also, not to accept it without scrutiny. Rather, we want to consider the data, note any potential bias, and, if possible, check multiple sources to be more sure of the facts.

What Is the Role of Criminal Justice Actors in the War on Terror?

We have, throughout this book, concentrated primarily on domestic crime and state and local responses to it. However, since 9/11, the response to terrorism has been a shared effort among all levels of law enforcement. Just as the first responders to the World Trade Towers tragedy were New York City police officers and firefighters, in any terrorist plot police play an integral role in both response and prevention.

More recently, international terrorist attacks in Brussels (March 2016), Paris (November 2015), and Nice (July 2016), and domestic attacks in San Bernadino (December 2015) and Orlando (June 2016) illustrate that local police are responsible for responding to and preventing these tragic events. In September 2016, Ahmad Khan Rahami was captured only two days after he allegedly was responsible for planting several bombs in various locations in New York City. Although at this point he is presumed innocent until proven guilty, it is a testament to the efficiency of law enforcement agencies that he was identified as the prime suspect and apprehended so quickly.

What limits should be placed on their surveillance powers? Should the 1033 program where military surplus can be given to local law enforcement, including armored vehicles and grenade launchers, be continued? What is the appropriate and legal use of robots (such as the one that was used to kill the shooter in the Dallas killings of five police officers)?

The governmental response to the threat of terrorism within the boundaries of the country has dramatically reshaped the organization and the mission of federal law enforcement. It has also created new questions for the courts to resolve and pitted federal courts against the executive branch in arguments regarding torture, renditions, executive privilege, wiretapping, civil liberties, and the security classification of government documents. Fear of crime has now been eclipsed by fear of terrorism, and new legal and ethical questions regarding the appropriate response to this threat have taken center stage in national debates.

Figure 1.5 Local police are increasingly responsible for responding to terrorist attacks, like the one at Pulse nightclub in Orlando in 2016 that left 49 people dead.

Source: Getty

Terrorism, whether domestic or with international elements, has been present from the beginning of this country's history, and so, too, have been government efforts to combat it. In earlier decades, communism was the enemy and the target of government investigation and suppression efforts. The first Alien and Sedition Acts were passed a mere twenty-two years after the birth of the United States, in 1798. The Alien Act gave the government the right to deport those thought to be a danger to the country, and the **Sedition Act** gave the government the right to punish those who spoke against the government's actions. These Acts were criticized by many prominent individuals as being contrary to the 1st Amendment and eventually disappeared; however, the Bolshevik bombings and advocacy of communism led to the Espionage Act of 1917 and the 1918 Sedition Act. The United States government, fearful that Russian immigrants would import their revolution as well, had thousands arrested. Under the Sedition Act, anyone who expressed support for communism could be arrested. Attorney General Palmer arrested 16,000 Soviet resident aliens in 1918 and 1919, and detained them without charges and without trial. The government targeted emerging labor unions, especially the Industrial Workers of the World movement, as threats to the nation, and widespread violence occurred on both sides.[11]

The next chapter in the government's campaign against communism was carried out by J. Edgar Hoover, who was appointed in 1924, and rose to prominence as director of the FBI. His continued investigation of communists eventually led to the McCarthy hearings (House Un-American Activities Committee) in the 1950s. Throughout the 1960s and 1970s, the FBI continued to infiltrate and investigate groups and individuals that were considered threats to the nation. At one point, Hoover had a card index of 450,000 people who were identified or suspected of having left-wing political views.[12]

This was during a time period when violent groups advocated and used violence, such as the Symbionese Liberation Army, which utilized kidnapping and robberies, and the Black Panthers, who used armed robbery and hijacking to advance their cause. Terrorism worldwide was on an upswing, including the horrific hostage-taking and slaying of Israeli athletes that occurred by Palestinian terrorists at the 1972 Munich Olympics, a series of IRA bombings in England, and the Baader-Meinhof (Red Army Faction) terrorist group in Germany that was responsible for a number of assassinations. However, the focus of investigations carried out by the government also included those who, objectively, did not pose a danger to the government, such as Martin Luther King Jr., Hollywood actors who espoused liberal views, and student and community groups that advocated nonviolent means of protest.

It was the abuses of the powers granted by antiterrorist legislation as well as the misuse of government intelligence by those in the Nixon administration that led to Congress dramatically curtailing the powers of federal law enforcement. The Senate created the Select Committee on Intelligence in 1976 and strengthened the Freedom of Information Act. In 1978, the Foreign Intelligence Surveillance Act (FISA) was created and it mandated procedures for requesting authorization for surveillance. A secret court was created (the Foreign Intelligence Surveillance Court—FISC), which consisted of seven federal district court judges appointed by the Supreme Court's Chief Justice. Federal law enforcement officers were required to obtain permission from the court to conduct surveillance. They had to show that their target was an agent of a foreign power and information was in furtherance of counterintelligence. FISA originally approved only electronic eavesdropping and wiretapping, but was amended in 1994 to include covert physical entries, and later in 1998 to permit "pen/trap" orders and business records.[13]

Typical search warrants are obtained only on a showing of probable cause that the target of the search will be found in the location specified, and that it is evidence or an instrumentality of a crime. However, FISA court approval may be obtained merely upon a showing that the target is a foreign power or agent and the search is relevant to a counterintelligence investigation. If the target is a U.S. citizen, there must be probable cause that their activities may involve espionage.[14]

Throughout the 1980s and 1990s, the activities and the rhetoric of the PLO, and, later, Hamas and Hezbollah, became more and more anti-American and many analysts argued that the United States, in addition to Israel, was or would become a central target of terrorist actions. The government did not sit idle, of course. President Reagan utilized national security decision directives rather than Congress to craft and employ a government response to the growing international threats. These directives established a hierarchy of authority regarding response to threats via aviation and kidnapping. Public laws were also passed, including:

- Act to Combat International Terrorism (1984), which sought international cooperation.
- Public Law 99–83 (1985), which allowed funding to be cut off to countries that supported terrorism.
- Omnibus Diplomatic Security and Antiterrorism Act (1986), which expanded the jurisdiction of the FBI to overseas when investigating acts of terrorism against U.S. citizens abroad or at home.[15]

Two of the most important pre-9/11 antiterrorist laws were passed during the Clinton administration. The Omnibus Counterterrorism Act of 1995 greatly expanded the role of the federal government over local and state law enforcement in investigating and prosecuting acts of terrorism, such as bombings, within the boundaries of the United States, and also expanded U.S. jurisdiction overseas when committed against U.S. embassies. It also criminalized fundraising for groups defined as terrorist. It expanded federal law enforcement authority to use "pen registers" and "trap-and-trace" devices, which track telephone calls. It also gave federal law enforcement the power to seek a wide range of personal and business documents with "national security letters," rather than warrants, when investigating terrorism which allowed government agents to begin surveillance while waiting for FISA approval.

This Act was replaced by the Anti-Terrorism and Effective Death Penalty Act of 1996, which incorporated most of the provisions discussed earlier, and added others, such as expanding the authority of INS to deport accused terrorists and other resident aliens, and increasing the penalties for such crimes. The other part of the Act applied to all offenders, and changed habeas corpus protections, eliminating multiple appeals and removing legal barriers to executions.[16]

Prior to 9/11, events foretold the possibility of a major attack: the 1993 bombing of the World Trade Center, the attacks on the USS *Cole* and on U.S. embassies in Africa, and the stated aim of Osama Bin Laden to "cut off the head of the snake," meaning the United States and, more specifically, U.S. economic dominance in the world. Generally, however, the FBI was largely concerned with domestic terrorism. This focus was not misplaced given the tragedy of the Oklahoma City bombing carried out by Timothy McVeigh and Terry Nichols, and the presence of other radical groups that still exist and have expressed and indicated a willingness to use violence to advance their goals. In the aftermath of the terrorist attacks on September 11, 2001, Congress enacted Public Law 107–56, which is titled Uniting and Strengthening America by Providing Appropriate Tools Required to Intercept and Obstruct Terrorism Act. This Act is known as the **USA Patriot Act** of 2001.

The Patriot Act slightly revised the definition of terrorism in the United States Code. The Act's definition included: use of weapons of mass destruction, acts of terrorism transcending national boundaries, financial transactions, providing material to terrorists, and providing material support or resources to designated foreign terrorist organizations and defined international terrorism as activities that "involve violent acts or acts dangerous to human life that are a violation of the criminal laws of the United States or of any State, or that would be a criminal violation if committed within the jurisdiction of the United States or of any State" and that appear to be intended to do one or more of the following:

1. to intimidate or coerce a civilian population
2. to influence the policy of a government by intimidation or coercion, or
3. to affect the conduct of a government by assassination or kidnapping.[17]

The Patriot Act amended that definition to include assassination or kidnapping as one of the acts that constitutes terrorism. In addition, "domestic terrorism" was included.

The Patriot Act also expanded the concept of terrorism to include the actions of individuals who attack Americans outside of the boundaries of the United States. This expansion allowed for the prosecution of John Phillip Walker Lindh, who was charged under this Act with conspiracy to murder nationals of the United States, including American military personnel and other government employees serving in Afghanistan. He was not convicted of violating the statute, but was found guilty of other offenses.[18]

The Patriot Act expanded the section that made it a crime to provide material support to terrorist groups to include anyone outside of the United States; previously it had been directed only to those who provided support within the United States. This allows legal action against anyone in the world if they provide material support to terrorists. The Patriot Act also made the President the decision maker as to which groups were determined to be terroristic.

Other elements of the Patriot Act expand federal powers of investigation. Title II, Enhanced Surveillance Procedures, substantially changed the provisions of the FISA described earlier. Specifically, the Act lowered the standard required to obtain permission to use surveillance against suspects; roving wiretaps were authorized that allowed agents to tap any phone the suspect might use; further, pen registers were allowed that followed any phone number called by the suspect. The Patriot Act also authorizes law enforcement agencies charged with investigating terrorism to share investigative information with domestic law enforcement investigators and vice versa. In summary, some of the provisions that are most controversial include:

- expanding the range of crimes trackable by electronic surveillance
- allowing the use of roving wiretaps to track any phone a suspect might use
- allowing the "sneak and peek" search (not notifying suspects of searches)
- allowing federal warrants to search records with less than probable cause

- lowering barriers of information sharing between domestic and international investigations
- creating new tools for investigating money laundering (by requiring banks to file reports on suspicious behaviors).

On March 7, 2006, Congress approved the renewal of the USA Patriot Act. Most provisions of the Act were made permanent. The bill also created a national security division in the Department of Justice. Three provisions of the Act were set to expire in 2010, but Congress voted to extend them and President Obama signed the bill in February 2010. The provisions were as follows:

- "Lone wolf" provision: allows federal agents to track and investigate a suspect with no discernible affiliation with known terrorist groups or foreign powers.
- "Business records": allows investigators access to suspect's records (i.e., telephone, financial) without his or her knowledge.
- "Roving wiretaps": allows agents to monitor phone lines or Internet accounts used by a suspect even if owned or also used by others (must receive FISA authorization).

Congress passed the Protect America Act of 2007, which was an amendment to the FISA. It basically removed any culpability for secret wiretapping that had occurred before its passage, but mandated that any future wiretapping of citizens would require authorization from the FISC. It removed the warrant requirement for non-citizens and those outside of the United States. It also protected the telecommunications companies that assisted the government in accessing private accounts from any civil liability.

President Bush created the Department of Homeland Security in March 2003. The Department of Homeland Security consolidated 22 federal agencies and more than 180,000 federal employees under one umbrella agency. It had a budget of $30 billion in 2005 and $65 billion in 2016. [19] While the CIA is not one of the agencies that has been merged into the Department of Homeland Security, the idea of a national intelligence center is at the heart of the effort, and the CIA director is no longer the titular head of the U.S. intelligence function, as that role has shifted to the Department of Homeland Security. The Immigration and Naturalization Service was dismantled and the functions distributed to two agencies, U.S. Immigration and Customs Enforcement (ICE), and the U.S. Customs and Border Protection Agency, which also subsumed and redistributed the functions of the Border Patrol and U.S. Customs. The Customs and Border Protection Agency has about 40,000 employees; together, the two agencies employ 55,000 people.

To read more about the Department of Homeland Security, go to https://www.dhs.gov/

Between 2001 and 2005, nearly 200 suspected terrorists or associates have been charged with crimes and, according to authorities, 100 terrorist plots disrupted. [20] Since then, a steady string of terrorist acts have occurred. The 2009 mass shooting at Ft. Hood by Nidal Hasan ended in thirteen deaths; a May 2010 potential bombing effort in Times Square was thwarted; the 2013 Boston Marathon bombing by the Tsarnaev brothers killed three and injured 264; the San Bernandino shooting in 2015 killed fourteen; and an attack at a Florida nightclub resulted in 49 deaths. Many other plots have been discovered and thwarted by government agents. "Self-radicalization" refers to the process by which any individual can become a terrorist, typically by interacting with terrorist groups such as ISIS via the Internet. These "lone-wolf" terrorists are much harder to track, identify, and catch before they commit acts. The major defense against them is to monitor Internet chatrooms which are becoming increasingly protected with encryption. Another source of information is tips from concerned friends and family. Indeed, one of the arguments against intemperate generalizations about Muslims and Muslim communities that seem to have spurred a rise in hate crimes directed against them is that Muslim community members are and will continue to be important sources of information for law enforcement about self-radicalized individuals in these communities.

Since 9/11, several major drug raids have uncovered ties between drug dealers and terrorist groups, such as Hezbollah, leading to the term "narcoterrorism." Opium from Afghanistan, although condemned by the Taliban, is now believed to be one of the largest sources of funding for Al Qaeda and, more recently, ISIS. Reports indicate that Mexican drug cartels may be engaged in business arrangements with Islamic terrorists, sending their "soldiers" to be trained and, in return, allowing terrorists to utilize their drug smuggling routes to secretly enter the United States.

Since 9/11, more resources have been directed to first responder training. This type of training gives law enforcement officers the skills to approach, engage, and coordinate responses to major threats, such as terrorist actions. Local police, especially those in major metropolitan areas, must assume that they will be first responders when targets of terrorist attacks are located in their city. Bridges, buildings, schools, transportation, sports complexes, other venues where there are large crowds, and nuclear reactors and power plants are the likely targets of terrorists. Actually, there are a wide range of targets that might be vulnerable to terrorist attacks. In addition to those already mentioned, the water supplies of major cities can be contaminated with toxic agents, the banking industry can be immobilized by computers, the nation's ports can be blocked with explosions, or the nation's oil and gas supplies can be sabotaged—bringing to a standstill industry, commerce, and basic services. Police are the first line of defense, both in terms of preventive observation and surveillance, as well as response and intervention.

Fusion centers employ civilian analysts to track and analyze information that might lead to uncovering terrorist plots. Joint task forces between local and federal agents have also been funded. State antiterrorism agencies have also been created to coordinate local law enforcement agencies in the state. Some cities, such as New York City, have antiterrorism units that engage in worldwide investigations.

Other smaller cities, however, may be woefully under-resourced. Their arsenal of weapons may not even match that of a well-armed militia group, the surveillance equipment may be inadequate to monitor suspected terrorists, and their communication networks may be deficient. Further, local officers may not be trained to investigate even domestic cybercrime, much less terrorists who use

Figure 1.6 Some larger cities, like New York, have dedicated counterterrorism units that conduct investigations and patrol the streets, like this officer on guard in front of the French Embassy after the terror attacks in Paris in 2015.

Source: Getty

cybertactics. Further, local agencies may not have the expertise to investigate, or training to recognize, biological threats, or even forensic accountants to track international money laundering.

To read about fusion centers, go to https://www.dhs.gov/state-and-major urban-area-fusion-centers

There is tension between national security and individual liberties played out with both federal counterterrorism agents and local law enforcement. One area of conflict is immigration control. Some cities and their police departments have refused to notify federal authorities or check the immigration status of victims or witnesses of crimes while other cities participate in the Secure Communities program whereby they partner with INS to check all people booked into jail for immigration status. Police departments that refuse to be the enforcers of federal laws argue that their role is domestic and involves only local security and crime fighting. These so-called **sanctuary cities** basically respond to crime victims or criminals, for that matter, without regard to any suspicion that the individual is an illegal alien. This issue has created a firestorm of controversy with some states (e.g., Arizona) passing laws requiring police officers to notify INS if they suspect a detainee does not have authorization to be in the country, some cities passing sanctuary city ordinances that prohibit police from doing so, and Congress threatening to withhold all federal monies from sanctuary cities. These arguments swirl around states' rights, civil liberties, and the goals and mission of law enforcement.

Local law enforcement has also been faced with difficult decisions in balancing their investigative activities against individual liberties. Federal law enforcement has sometimes taken aggressive actions in response to the threat of terrorism, especially in regard to Muslim residents and individuals of Middle Eastern descent. Immediately after 9/11, more than 5,000 resident aliens were detained without charges. Many were subsequently deported for minor immigration violations. Those who were released alleged that they were subject to illegal detention and abuse during their imprisonment. The FBI also asked local law enforcement agencies to conduct surveillance and/or question Muslims and foreign residents without any reason other than their nationality or religion. The Portland, Oregon, Police Department gained notoriety when it refused the FBI's request that it conduct interviews with all foreign students in the area. Portland police supervisors thought that they had no authority to do so because the FBI did not articulate any reasonable suspicion, the questions were in areas that were constitutionally protected, such as their religion, and did not relate to criminal matters.[21] Police and federal agents are called upon to balance civil liberties against serious threats to security in the interpretation of their powers.

We have all felt the effects of the nation's efforts to prevent terrorism. Travelers endure searches and, more recently, body scans, and a constant revision of rules concerning what can be carried onto airplanes. We learned through Edward Snowden that the National Security Agency (NSA) has been collecting "metadata"—mindboggling amounts of data on all of our electronic transmissions that it stores in semi-secret facilities in Utah and elsewhere. Whether they peek into electronic communications without warrants is a question that we cannot know the answer to since all court cases that have pushed for discovery have been dismissed on the grounds of national security.

Generally, the public has been supportive of the USA Patriot Act. In 2003, only 28 percent of those polled believed that it gave the government too much power over individual liberties, and 51 percent believed that people had to give up some individual freedom to fight terrorism.[22] However, a 2013 Gallup poll showed only 37 percent of Americans approved of the NSA's collection and storage of electronic data with 53 percent registering disapproval. Note also, though, that ideology affects our opinion about this and with all topics. Conservatives' and liberals' views have reversed from when President Bush was in office (when a majority of liberals disagreed with wiretapping) to President Obama's administration (when a majority of conservatives disagree with wiretapping).[23] Not surprisingly, even in the area of civil liberties our opinions are influenced by predispositions, in this case, political; all the more reason to practice critical thinking.

Focus on Data: Last Thoughts

Throughout this text we have modeled a critical thinking approach which means to be aware of one's biases, ask well-constructed questions, and be a critical consumer of facts. This last chapter has identified a few more current issues, but another 100 pages could be written to address more. The fact is that no textbook can comprehensively cover all current issues and, in fact, is probably already out of date in some areas by the time you read it. However, the tools to continue the exercise of critical thinking are at your disposal. The Internet is an incredible resource that instantaneously allows you to access information. Follow the path of critical thinking and you will be able to create your own Focus on Data segments or do further study on any of the issues that have been raised in this text or others that you wish had been covered.

First, identify what you want to know; phrase it as a question that can be answered. Clearly define your terms and limit your inquiry to what can be addressed with facts. Don't include presuppositions in the phrasing of your question.

Second, gather facts. The Bureau of Justice Statistics (http://www.bjs.gov/) and the FBI's Uniform Crime Reporting (https://ucr.fbi.gov/ucr) are the two most helpful sources that provide information on crime, law enforcement, courts, and corrections. The Office of Juvenile Justice and Delinquency Prevention (http://www.ojjdp.gov/) is an excellent resource for inquiries related to juvenile justice. The National Institute of Justice (http://www.nij.gov/ Pages/welcome.aspx) has funded literally hundreds of studies on a wide range of topics through the years which you can access through its website. Go to these websites and just browse the wide array of available information. You can even use the data analysis tool on the BJS website to construct your own graphs and tables of crime and victimization.

There is a myriad of other Internet sources as well. Just because a source of data may be from an advocacy group doesn't mean the information is false, but it does mean that you will want to look for alternative sources to confirm. Be careful of your own biases as well—do not ignore sources that contradict what you believe. Many of the questions that you will want answers to require sophisticated data analysis and you may not understand the methodology. Actually, many criminologists don't understand some of the data analysis done by others either. Fortunately, articles in academic peer-reviewed journals have been evaluated by those who do understand it, so you can be more confident in the findings. That is why an academic journal is a better data source than an opinion piece in a newspaper (although there still may be conflict between academic researchers that is typically presented in the article itself). The Crime and Justice Research Alliance (http://crimeandjusticeresearchalliance. org/) is a shared project between the two major academic organizations in the field, the American Criminology Society and the Academy of Criminal Justice Sciences. This webpage provides information from researchers who are experts on a range of relevant topics.

The National Academies of Science and other panels and task forces that put together numbers of researchers from different fields are also good sources of information. In effect, these panels practice a critical thinking approach because they frame a question and then bring experts in to gather and evaluate evidence. You will find that there is often still disagreement over some topical areas, which usually arises because of different methodologies resulting in conflicting findings.

If your question is a legal one, law review articles are the necessary source, along with caselaw itself. Once again, the Internet has made legal research much easier than it used to be. For Supreme Court cases, you can simply type in the case name and you will get numerous websites that provide the case holding. Several websites even provide audio or transcripts of the oral arguments before the court (e.g. https://www.oyez.org/).

The third step is to test your findings. While that may not be feasible, there are usually policy implications of the answer or answers you have arrived at. Have such policies been implemented with success? Look at your findings in a different way and determine if you can approach the issue from other data sources. Another test is to present your findings to someone who may disagree with them. Let them probe for weaknesses in your data sources or conclusion.

Critical thinking avoids generalizations, suppositions, oversimplifications, prejudicial thinking, narrow-mindedness, tunnel vision, and cognitive distortions. Done correctly, it helps us step back from any topic area (no matter how emotional) and gain a deeper understanding of the facts relevant to the issue. An accurate understanding of facts is necessary to develop and implement successful solutions. We need no less in the field of criminal justice. Hopefully, your exploration has only just begun.

Critical Thinking Exercises

1. Take any of the "Focus on Data" sections throughout the book and update it with new information gleaned either from academic journals or other sources. Rewrite it if the conclusion seems to be inconsistent with the new information.

2. Write your own section called "Current Issues in Criminal Justice." Of the topics you identify as most important, choose one and rephrase as a question, then construct a methodology that would be adequate to provide an answer to the question.

Notes

1. Adapted from The Critical Thinking Community, 6/9/2016 from http://www.criticalthinking.org/pages/our-concept-of-critical-thinking/411

2. E. Harrell, *Victims of Identity Theft, 2014* (NCJ 248991). Washington, DC: Bureau of Justice Statistics. Retrieved 12/10/2015 from http://www.bjs.gov/

3. E. Harrell, note 2.

4. J. Truman and L. Langton, *Criminal Victimization, 2014*. Washington, DC: Bureau of Justice Statistics. Retrieved from http:// www.bjs.gov/content/pub/pdf/cv14.pdf

5. K. Baum, *Identity Theft, 2014*. Washington, DC: Bureau of Justice Statistics, April 2006.

6. J. Pollock and V. Hollier, "T visas: Prosecution tool or humanitarian response?" *Women and Criminal Justice* 20 (1) (2010): 127–146; S.T. Green, "Protection for victims of child sex trafficking in the United

States: Forging the gap between U.S. immigration laws and human trafficking laws." *U.C. Davis Journal of Juvenile Law and Policy* 12 (2008): 309–379; K. Hyland, "Protecting human victims of trafficking: An American framework." *Berkeley Women's Law Journal* 16 (2001): 29–70; T. Kyckelhahn, A. Beck and T. Cohen, *Characteristics of Suspected Human Trafficking Incidents, 2007–2008*. Washington, DC: Bureau of Justice Statistics, 2009.

7. Re-entry Policy Council, *An Explanation of Justice Mapping: Three Examples, 2005*. Retrieved 12/30/2005 from www.reentry policy.org/report/justice-mapping.php.

8. T. Clear, D. Rose and J. Ryder, "Incarceration and the community: The problem of removing and returning offenders." *Crime and Delinquency* 47 (3) (2001): 335–351; T. Clear, D. Rose, E. Waring and K. Scully, "Coercive mobility and crime: A preliminary examination of concentrated incarceration and social disorganization." *Justice Quarterly* 20 (1) (2003): 33–64.

9. T. Clear, note 8.

10. J. Lynch and W. Sabol, "Assessing the effects of mass incarceration on informal social control in communities." *Criminology and Public Policy* 3 (2) (2004): 267–294.

11. J.A. Fagin, *When Terrorism Strikes Home: Defending the United States*. Boston, MA: Allyn and Bacon, 2006, p. 39.

12. J.A. Fagin, note 11, p. 51.

13. D. Cole and J. Dempsey, *Terrorism and the Constitution*. New York, NY: Free Press, 2002.

14. R. Ward, K. Kiernan and D. Mabrey, *Homeland Security: An Introduction*. Newark, NJ: LexisNexis/Matthew Bender, 2006, p. 254.

15. J.A. Fagin, note 11, p. 57.

16. J.A. Fagin, note 11, p. 62.

17. Title 18 U.S.C. § 2331

18. *United States v. Lindh*, 227 F. Supp. 2d 565 (E.D. Va. 2002).

19. DHS Budget in Brief, retrieved 7/8/2016 from https://www.dhs.gov/sites/default/files/publications/FY_2016_DHS_Bud get_in_Brief.pdf

20. Cited in Fagin, note 11, p. 127.

21. Cited in J. Fagin, note 11, p. 71.

22. Cited in J. Fagin, note 11, p. 77.

23. http://www.gallup.com/poll/163043/americans-disapprove-government-surveillance-programs.aspx

CHAPTER TWO

Historical Perspectives in Criminal Justice

The study of the ***original sin*** (i.e., ***first case of murder***), establishes a backdrop through which the issue of fairness in the criminal justice system is examined. The storyline, which involves Adam and Eve's first- and second-born sons, ***Cain and Abel***, reflects an ancient rivalry between the farmer and the nomadic shepherd.[1]

There are several issues to consider about this story that relate to the evolution of justice in America and fairness in the current system of criminal justice. For example, sibling rivalry appears to be one of the primary issues of concern, along with the criminal act of murder by Cain and the suffering of the victim, his brother Abel.[2] Also interesting is the fact that Cain denied the crime despite the overwhelming presence of forensic evidence and the act itself, which is predatory in nature. Finally, there is an issue with the subsequent punishment by exile rather than the traditional sentence of death, which seemed to be more in keeping with the time. Why did Cain murder his brother? What is the significance of banishment (i.e., exile) as a form of punishment for an act of murder in the ancient world? How has the abstract nature of this form of punishment impacted our sense of equality and fairness in the criminal justice system?

Research into this area of criminology and criminal justice is significant in that the Genesis story establishes a basic framework for an analysis of the effectiveness of the criminal justice system and manner in which variables such as ***race*** and ***social class***

---

1   Genesis 2:20–3:21, *The New American Bible.*

2   A. W. Burgess, C. Regehr, and A. Roberts, *Victimology: Theories and Applications*, 3rd ed. (Sudbury, MA: Jones and Bartlett Publishers, 2019).

impact the way we define predatory crimes and subsequent punishments. Particularly the manner in which individuals, like Cain, are able to circumvent any form of real punishment due to the unequal distribution of law, selective prosecutorial discretion, questionable adjudication processes, and uneven sentencing practices in relation to racial and social ascriptions.[3]

---

3   T. F. Tolbert, "From the Case Files of Cain and Abel: A Case/Content Analysis of the First Homicide and Historical Impact on the Definitions of Crime and Punishment in the Postmodern World of Criminal Justice" (paper presented at the 45th Annual Western Society of Criminology Conference, February 3, 2018).

The Sense of Fairness and the Emergence of Criminal Justice

By Jason Roach and Ken Pease

Introduction

We hope the last chapter clarified the role of Theory of Mind (ToM) and empathy in inclining people towards, or away from, pro-social behaviour. We need a *theory of mind* to have empathy. We need *empathy* to discern unfairness in ways which correspond to those which the direct victims of unfairness suffer. The third element which we took to be necessary for pro-social behaviour was a sense of fairness. The sense of fairness added to empathy is necessary to decide what to do to establish a system of remedies so that cooperative social functioning crucial to our ancestors' survival is maintained. In other words, empathy without some idea what to do with it is useless. The structure of televised charity appeals has three common strands:

1. The people or animals we are trying to help have thoughts and feelings like you;

2. Feel their pain;

3. It's not fair, and this is where you must send your money to make it right.

How readily do people acquire a sense of fairness? The answer is—remarkably readily. As several times before, we appeal to the reader's experience, as a product of evolution like us. One of us is a vegetarian. A few times, when meat in the fridge is about to cease to be edible and others in the family decline to eat it, he has been known to eat it himself. His justification (a technique of neutralisation as criminologists have termed it) is that it's bad enough killing the animal in the first place, but then failing to eat its meat is adding insult to injury. This justification does not save him. When anything goes wrong in the days following his lapse into carnivory (if there is such a word) he attributes it to his wickedness in eating the meat. He knows it is ridiculous, and he hates himself for it, but that is what he thinks. Rabbi Harold Kushner recounts the story of his visit to the home of a young woman who had died suddenly. The first words of the parents were 'You know, Rabbi, we didn't fast last Yom Kippur' (Kushner, 1981, p. 8). Many sufferers from obsessive–compulsive disorder (OCD) explain their compulsions as necessary actions to avoid bad consequences.

We are talking here about immanent justice, where badness automatically brings about retribution. The Swiss psychologist Jean Piaget told children stories (Piaget, 1932). For example a child steals, and later the bridge over which he is walking collapses. Many children interpret the bridge collapse as a consequence of the theft. Much research has been undertaken on how the child processes information to arrive at the idea of Nature or God taking revenge for misdeeds (Karniol, 1980). As Numbers 32:23 in the Bible threatens 'be sure your sin will find you out'.

Perhaps the most interesting is the contention that immanent justice thinking is *more* prevalent in adults than it is in children (Raman and Winer, 2004). One study with adults showed that they exhibited more immanent justice thinking when the maxim 'What goes around comes around' was included in the stories they were told. As one person reflected,

> I know that bad things happen to both good and bad people, but I believe that there is a greater chance of bad things happening to bad people. This person [in the story] was not a good person. He had cheated and lied, and he has robbed many decent people of their money. I know that illnesses like this happen to both good and bad people, but I believe serious illnesses happen at least slightly more to people who deserve them.
>
> (Raman and Winer, 2002, p. 346)

Immanent justice has been linked with the 'just world' hypothesis (Lerner, 1980), which posits that people need to believe in a world where people generally get what they deserve, which allows them to believe they inhabit a stable and orderly niche. Perhaps this is behind the notion of karmic debt, whereby suffering is a consequence of evil deeds in a previous life. By believing in karmic debt, you can believe in immanent justice, 'inexorable and relentless' in spite of the evidence before you. One can rephrase this as saying that it allows people to inhabit a world where trust, and the reputation economy, can prevail over selfishness.

> If the virtuous man who has not done any evil act in this birth suffers, this is due to some wrong act that he may have committed in his previous birth. He will have his compensation in his next birth. If the wicked man who daily does many evil actions apparently enjoys [happiness] in this birth, this is due to some good Karma he must have done in his previous birth. He will have compensation

in his next birth. He will suffer in the next birth. The law of compensation is inexorable and relentless.

(Swami Shivananda, *Practice of Karma Yoga*,
Divine Life Society, 1985, p. 102)

For scholars of the Bible, the notion of the scapegoat echoes the notion of immanent justice. Punishment for sin being inevitable (immanent justice) the burden of the sin is placed on some poor innocent goat, which is then driven into the desert.

'But the goat, on which the lot fell to be the scapegoat, shall be presented alive before the Lord, to make an atonement with him, *and* to let him go for a scapegoat into the wilderness' (Leviticus 16:10).

It was a common practice to tie a red strip of cloth to the scapegoat. The red strip represented the sin of the people which was atoned for. According to the Jewish Talmud this red strip would eventually turn white, signalling God's acceptance of the offering.[1]

Poor bloody goat.

In Christian theology, Jesus Christ was the ultimate scapegoat.

Appealing again to your own experience, what does your gut say when you read about unpleasant people winning the lottery? Do you rejoice in their good fortune, or conclude that something is wrong, that God is asleep at the switch? The tone of police frustration and malice has been evident in all press reports of such cases that we have ever encountered, such as the one in Box 2.1.

In brief, immanent justice judgements help sustain belief in a just world, which is why the reward of the undeserving and the suffering of the worthy are so troubling to us. What has all this got to do with evolution? We earlier accepted the argument that natural selection favoured groups which cooperate internally, but that within groups it favoured selfish individuals, and that this created a tension. The idea that vice will be punished *automatically*, insofar as it is believed, provides an extremely useful constraint on selfish behaviour. The important insight that immanent justice thinking *increases* with age, albeit in more sophisticated forms, suggests that, even now, we are primed to think in that way, with OCD sufferers representing the unfortunate downside of the generally pro-social belief. We introduced the notion of a meme earlier, an idea or theme (as replicator) which uses people as survival vehicles. The grandmother of one of us, dead for some fifty-five years, successfully planted the meme 'Be sure your sins will find you out' in the conscience of the still guilt-ridden second author![2]

Are we really primed to think in terms of fairness? Mark Pagel thinks we are. He writes: 'Of all the emotions associated with getting acts of reciprocity to work, our expectation for fairness is perhaps the most intriguing and explosive' (Pagel, 2012, p. 195). He cites the results of 'the ultimatum game' in support of his position. The game runs as follows. Person 1 is given a sum of money (say £100) and told he has to give some of it to Person 2 (whom he is told he will never get to meet). Person 2 knows how much money Person 1 has to give and can accept or reject the offer. If the offer is rejected, *neither person gets anything*. The rational thing for Person 1 to do is to offer a very small amount.

Sick lotto rapist Edward Putman flashed an arrogant grin as he left court after admitting a £13,000 benefits scam.

The 46-year-old now faces jail for lying about a £5 million win so he could carry on ripping off taxpayers while splashing out his fortune on fancy sports cars and a £600,000 home.

But that clearly did not seem to bother the jobless thug, who spent seven years in jail for a violent sex attack on a teenage girl more than 20 years ago.

Putman tried to hide his face under a hood and with sun specs after he admitted two counts of benefit fraud.

His payments were stopped in December 2009 after he failed to show up for a medical assessment, three months after he scooped £4.9 million on the lottery.

At the time of the win he asked for no publicity.

Prosecutor Hita Mashru told the court: 'You may see that it's very clear why. He has previous convictions and the fact that he was claiming benefits.

'Records show that in the days after winning the lottery he bought sports cars and a house. It's very calculating.'

Putman, of Kings Langley, Herts, was caught when he tried to buy his council flat for £83,000 in cash.

He had even kept his windfall from his family, St Albans magistrates heard.

Ten months later he sent a letter to the DSS begging for his benefits to be reinstated.

The conman wrote: 'I've not supported myself very well, my rent hasn't been paid, and I'm on the border of being evicted, no bills have been paid, I don't eat as my stomach will not hold it down.

'Money I have managed to get has been from selling my belongings, as I will not need them, as I expect to be evicted.'

Putman, who threatened to kill the teen he raped in Milton Keynes, Bucks, will be sentenced at St Albans crown court on July 24.

Lotto rapist number one was Iorworth Hoare, 59, of Newcastle, who won £7 million in 2004 after buying a ticket on day release from jail.

http://www.mirror.co.uk/news/uk-news/edward-putman-lottery-rapist-admits-1131857 (accessed 25 September 2012).

The rational thing for Person 2 to do is to accept whatever is offered (since something is better than nothing). Pagel reports that the game has been played with many groups in cultures around the world, and that people generally do not behave in this rational way. Person 1's typical offer is 40 per cent of the total available. Person 2 rejects offers substantially below this proportion as 'unfair', though loses out by doing so. Pagel accounts for the irrational behaviour as follows:

> You can be told the exchange is anonymous and that you will never encounter the person again, but that does not mean you can simply switch off the normal emotions that natural selection has created in us. ... The experimenters who conduct these studies are, in effect, asking their volunteers to leave behind at the door all of the evolved psychology for long-term relations.
>
> (p. 199)

Enter, Criminal Law

Sometimes the fear of immanent justice is not enough to deter people from exploitative behaviour, and groups decide collectively (or by leader dictat) to set up arrangements whereby the group as a whole sanctions those who exploit others in the group. Every sports or social club has rules whose breach leads to sanction (usually fines or expulsion). At the national or regional level, there exists criminal law. The difference between civil law and criminal law is instructive. Civil law regulates relations between citizens, the state offering its services as adjudicator as to who has wronged whom and how the wrong can be righted. In criminal law, the state and the allegedly erring citizen are the conflicting parties. In effect, the state is saying that the alleged wrongdoing is so serious that society itself rather than the individual victim is the main interested party in the conflict. Some criminologists have argued that virtually all law ought to be civil law, because conflicts are people's property, and the state is in effect stealing their conflicts from them (Christie, 1977). The counter-argument is that the overarching interest is in eliminating threats to cooperation at the group level, rather than person to person vengeance.

It is important to stress that the criminal law is designed for within-nation conflicts. Between-nation conflicts are addressed by other means, probably of different evolutionary origin. First let us state what lawyers say the criminal law is about. The American Law Institute Model Penal Code sets out the purposes succinctly:

- To forbid and prevent conduct that unjustifiably and inexcusably inflicts or threatens substantial harm to individual or public interests;
- To subject to public control persons whose conduct indicates that they are disposed to commit crimes;
- To safeguard conduct that is without fault from condemnation as criminal;
- To give fair warning of the nature of the conduct declared to be an offence;
- To differentiate on reasonable grounds between serious and minor offences.

In short, it sets out to protect citizens from other citizens, by telling them what they can't do, by acting against them when they do what they are not supposed to, by controlling them, by being proportionate in the response to offending and by protecting citizens who have done no wrong from persecution by other citizens. But the Code (and common sense) tempers justice with mercy. The Code sets out to control 'persons whose conduct indicates that they are disposed to commit crimes', not just anyone who misbehaves. An important element in the judgement of most crimes is *mens rea*, a guilty mind (Ormerod, 2011). This is true of adults but not of children. As a child grows, intention comes to the fore in judgements of wrongdoing (Piaget, 1932). This would also have made sense in the Environment of Evolutionary Adaptation (EEA). The group was important. Unintended or atypical behaviour, if sanctioned severely, may deprive a small hunting or foraging group of an important member, just as in soccer ejection of a player from the field of play handicaps a team. There is nothing in the Code which is surprising if one thinks in terms of criminal law as a second line of defence (after the fear of immanent justice) in advancing the cause of within-group solidarity. But how do students of evolutionary psychology think about the criminal law? Mostly they don't. In a 723-page tome on *The psychology and law of criminal justice processes* (Levesque, 2006) the word evolution is used once, and then not in the Darwinian sense. Owen Jones' discussion of the topic (O. Jones, 2005) characterises criminal law as 'a tool for moving human animals to behave in ways they would not otherwise behave if left to their own devices' (p. 953).

The most detailed discussion of law and criminal justice using an evolutionary perspective is that of Michael Bang Petersen and his colleagues (Petersen *et al.*, 2010), and this will be described at some length. It is particularly useful because it reconfigures concepts familiar with lawyers and criminologists in terms of evolutionary psychology.

Petersen's starting point is that the problems of exploitation as a threat to social functioning were acute in the EEA, with 'the average person situated in a world full of individuals poised to impose costs on him or her if such acts were beneficial' (p. 73). This resulted in mental programmes to 'recalibrate certain behaviour-regulating variables in the mind of the perpetrator and other potential exploiters' (p. 72). Whether this takes the form of punishment or reconciliation depends upon a number of circumstances, including whether the exploiter is a relative, the closeness of collaborative links between victim and exploiter, and the risk of counter-measures (whether the exploiter was big and strong and had loyal friends). Petersen and colleagues suggest that people have a set of internal regulatory variables (e.g. how hungry or tired am I?). Such internal regulatory variables sustain welfare-tradeoff ratios (WTRs) which are applied to the specific facts of an exploitative event. WTRs are taken to be ubiquitous. How much effort or inconvenience am I prepared to suffer to advance another's welfare by a given amount? WTRs can be thought of as person specific in two ways, which we can term personality and preference variation. As for personality, at the saintly extreme, someone is prepared to give small benefits to others (any others) at huge personal cost. At the other extreme, we find someone who would kill a person (anyone) for a few pounds. Thinking about preference, an individual may be prepared to do anything for one person, and nothing for someone else. WTRs are thus actor and other specific, and flexible in the light of new knowledge (for example a man might give a woman a seat on a bus upon learning that she is pregnant).

Simplifying somewhat, the inclination to punish or to seek reconciliation with an exploiter depends upon one's WTR in relation to him or her. So people generally inclined to have high WTRs and/or who are personally and positively linked to the exploiter will generally seek reconciliation; otherwise they are likely to seek punishment. However Petersen and colleagues make an important qualification to this by distinguishing between intrinsic and monitored WTRs. Intrinsic WTRs are those which apply when the decision will not be made public, monitored WTRs when they will. This is relevant to jury selection and witness intimidation. The decision to punish the exploiter under monitored conditions decreases if

1. The exploiter is big and strong;
2. The exploiter has big strong friends;
3. The exploiter has high social status and valued skills;
4. The exploiter is rich.

Please don't forget that we are here discussing EEA, not the present day, so what counted as rich then is more in terms of meat than banker bonuses.

Petersen continues 'fitness benefits flow from being with people who care about your welfare and attend to the welfare consequences of their actions' (p. 84). This has implications for group schism in EEA and arguably for the crime-driven decision to move home in modern times, with consequences for the creation of high crime neighbourhoods. Accordingly, across cultures, acts that indicate a low WTR are set apart, and a criminal justice system coalesces around them. There is evidence of cross-cultural consensus in the harm (signals low WTR) which is reflected in their criminalisation and differential sanction levels (Stylianou, 2003). An example of rated seriousness of a range of offences is provided as Box 2.2. You would be unusual if your ranking of seriousness deviated much from that given. It will differ somewhat because of changed values since the work was done in the mid-1980s. Check with your friends too. The agreement is real, extensive and cross-cultural (Pease et al., 1975).

It is possible to manipulate the perceived seriousness of a crime, for example by invoking the exceptional need of the exploiter (I stole to feed my children) or effects on third parties (theft of copper cable from the railway delays thousands of train travellers).

Petersen and colleagues explore in much more detail the cognitive mechanisms of the central decision about how to deal with exploiters and should be read in the original. However it is believed that the description above captures the essence of their view. We now consider how differences between the modern world and the EEA might cause problems for criminal justice arrangements. The first and central difference is that we now need a system, and a very elaborate and expensive system it is too.

> **Box 2.2   Hierarchy of crime seriousness (Taken from Pease, 1988)**
>
> Murder
> Robbery with Violence
> Sexual Offence against a child under 13
> Cruelty to children
> Indecent assault on woman
> Causing death by dangerous driving
> Manslaughter
> Fraud
> Housebreaking
> Breaking into a factory
> Stealing (without violence)
> Fighting (common assault)
> Taking away a motor vehicle without owner's consent
> Being drunk and disorderly
> Stealing by finding
> Travelling on a bus without paying the fare
> Vagrancy

When group size was limited by the Dunbar number, those with deviant WTRs would be detected by their behaviour across time, known to the group as a whole. The arrangements for sanction or reconciliation would be administered by those who knew the exploiters and their value to the group.

We cannot go back to the EEA. The next best thing is anthropological study of surviving hunter-gatherer bands. Chris Boehm (2012) has trawled the relevant literature to distinguish the kind of sanctions which are mentioned for each of the studied groups in at least one anthropologist's report. The results are shown as Table 2.1. It will be seen that there is the mixture of punishment and reconciliation tactics that Petersen assumed. It would be useful to go back to the anthropological literature and see whether the factors identified by Petersen as crucial in determining the 'recalibration' route had been noted by anthropologists.

Christopher Boehm's hunter-gatherer database contains ten groups. The cell entries are the number out of ten where at least one anthropological account mentioned the form of sanction shown in the left row.

To return to the key issue, whereas sanctions in the EEA were administered by the relatively small group of people who knew the exploiter/criminal, that is no longer the case. An impersonal apparatus

Table 2.1 Sanctions for crime

Sanction	n/10
Entire group kills culprit	6
Nominee assassinates culprit	6
Permanent expulsion from group	4
Public opinion	10
Gossip (as private expression of public opinion)	9
Ridicule	10
Direct criticism by group or spokesman	8
Group shaming	6
Other shaming	5
Spatial distancing (move or re-orient camp)	10
Group ostracism	8
Social aloofness (reduced speaking)	7
Tendency to avoid culprit	5
Total shunning (total avoidance)	5
Temporary expulsion from group	3
Nonlethal physical punishment	10
Administration of blows	5
(Boehm, 2012)	

is set up wherein the decision to proceed officially against an exploiter is taken by people who do not know him, his guilt is assessed by a jury comprising people who do not know him, and the sanction is administered by strangers. The judgements of his WTR are no longer informed by people who know the context and circumstances of the exploitation over time. Perhaps paradoxically, the group which relinquishes the exploiter to strangers is more vulnerable to his friends, fellow gang members, and so on. The only role which people who know the exploiter have in the trial by strangers is that of witness, with the endemic problem of witness intimidation in crime challenged areas. Somewhat too simply, consigning an exploiter to the criminal justice system is consigning a member of the in-group to the tender mercies of an out-group. This is what adds power to the accusation that someone is an informer, a 'grass'. This was illustrated the week before writing this. Two unarmed female police officers were murdered, having been lured to a house by a bogus phone call reporting a burglary. The killer had in the previous months killed two other people and tried to kill two more. He was a high risk person, to put it mildly. Yet those who work locally report that he was leading a pretty normal life, despite being sought by the police. The local community did not report him. On the regional news on the night of the police murders, one young man from the area explained 'Nobody likes a grass, do they?' Perhaps the evolved mechanisms of recalibration surface in the recurring attempts of localities to reclaim their right to recalibrate. This is evident in the English rural practice of 'rough music', where pots and pans were hammered outside the homes of miscreants (Thompson, 1972), commented on as follows:[3]

> Rough music belongs to a mode of life in which some part of the law belongs still to the community and is theirs to enforce. It indicates modes of social self-control and the disciplining of certain kinds of violence and anti-social offence …

It can also be seen in the parallel criminal justice system operated by paramilitary groups in Northern Ireland (Morrissey and Pease, 1982) and the local justice in South African townships including the use of petrol-filled tyres as burning necklaces to despatch wrongdoers.[4] Finally, it is evident in the wish of many sports officials to treat crimes on the field of play differently from the same actions otherwise processed by criminal law.

A double-edged sword in Petersen's characterisation of EEA justice is its flexibility. In modern criminal justice systems, actions have to be legislated as crimes. In EEA justice, the group simply has to reach a decision that a member's WTR is so out of step that action is necessary. Laws which are out of step with emerging modern sensibilities cause problems.

When Rosa Parks, a black woman, broke the law by refusing to give up her bus seat for a white passenger in Montgomery, Alabama on 1 December 1956, who you felt empathy with depended on your view of the law she was breaking. In the spirit of the place and time, many white people would feel empathy with the white folk whose exclusive rights were being denied by Rosa Parks' action. For those disgusted by discrimination, Rosa Parks was and is fêted as a heroine.[5]

It is as well not to romanticise local justice. Don't forget that women were burned as witches. Not that formal criminal justice would have saved them, as the Salem trials attest. Indeed the last woman to be convicted and branded as a witch was Helen Duncan in 1944, condemned because of her uncanny knowledge of wartime secrets.[6]

Recall the lesson of Chapter 2. Groups with too many free-riders will not do well in competition with other groups. Groups whose local justice means that their members are at each other's throats all the time will not prevail in competition with other groups or in tasks which require cooperation. There is thus a crude self-limiting factor weeding out the most brutal and inept forms of local justice. But groups like this no longer go out of existence. You can find them in crime-riven areas of our cities, consisting predominantly of young males.

Chapter Summary and Reprise

We have discussed the sense of fairness. We discussed immanent justice, whereby people have a tendency to see punishment as following automatically from misdeeds. We have discussed the mechanism by which our forebears assessed welfare and cost trade-offs of exploitative behaviour before deciding on attempts to punish or reconcile the exploiter. We discussed the mismatch between the current criminal justice system and evolved local, group-based justice.

In the next chapters we will go on to discuss the problems which have conventionally exercised criminologists, to see whether evolutionary thinking can cast new light on old problems.

Notes

1. http://www.biblehistory.net/newsletter/scapegoat.htm (accessed 25 September 2012).

2. The first author recalls one of his grandparents saying something to the same effect but was insulated from any guilt on the grounds that he wasn't listening properly.

3. http://obscenedesserts.blogspot.co.uk/2006/08/ep-thompson-uncommon.html (accessed 25 September 2012).

4. http://news.bbc.co.uk/1/hi/world/africa/2115644.stm (accessed 25 September 2012).

5. http://www.achievement.org/autodoc/page/par0bio-1 (accessed (appropriately) on 4 July 2012).

6. http://www.guardian.co.uk/uk/2007/jan/13/secondworldwar.world (accessed 25 September 2012).

References

Boehm, C. (2012). *Moral origins: the evolution of virtue, altruism, and shame.* New York: Basic Books.

Christie, N. (1977). Conflicts as Property. *British Journal of Criminology*, 17 (1), 1–15.

Jones, O. (2005). Evolutionary psychology and the law. In (ed.) D. Buss. *The handbook of evolutionary psychology*, pp. 953–74. Hoboken, NJ: Wiley.

Karniol, R. (1980). A conceptual analysis of immanent justice responses in children. *Child Development*, 51 (1), 118–30.

Kushner, H. (1981). *When bad things happen to good people.* New York: Avon.

Lerner, M. (1980). *The belief in a just world: a fundamental delusion.* New York: Plenum.

Levesque, R. (2006). *The psychology and law of criminal justice processes.* New York: Nova.

Morrissey, M., and Pease, K. (1982). The black criminal justice system in west Belfast. *Howard Journal of Criminal Justice*, 21 (1–3), 159–66.

Ormerod, D. (2011). *Smith and Hogan's criminal law*, 13th edn. Oxford: Oxford University Press.

Pagel, M. (2012). *Wired for culture.* London: Allen Lane.

Pease, K. (1988). *Judgements of crime seriousness: findings from the 1984 British crime survey.* London: Home Office.

Pease, K., Ireson, J., and Thorpe, J. (1975). Modified crime indices for eight countries. *The Journal of Criminal Law and Criminology*, 66 (2), 209–14.

Petersen, M., Sell, A., Tooby, J., and Cosmides, L. (2010). Evolutionary psychology and criminal justice: a recalibrational theory of punishment and reconciliation. In (ed.) H. Høgh-Olesen. *Human morality and sociality*, pp. 73–131. New York: Palgrave Macmillan.

Piaget, J. (1932). *The moral judgment of the child.* London: Kegan Paul.

Raman, L., and Winer, G. (2002). Children's and adults' understanding of illness: evidence in support of a coexistence model. *Genetic, Social, and General Psychology Monographs*, 128 (4), 325–55.

Raman, L., and Winer, G. (2004). Evidence of more immanent justice responding in adults than children: a challenge to traditional developmental theories. *British Journal of Developmental Psychology*, 22 (2), 255–74.

Stylianou, S. (2003). Measuring crime seriousness perceptions: what have we learned and what else do we want to know? *Journal of Criminal Justice*, 31 (1), 37–56.

Thompson, E. (1972). Rough music: the English charivari. *Annales*, 27, 285–312.

CHAPTER THREE

The Inquisition and the Spectacle of Punishment

The criminal justice system in America originated in the European tradition whereby the cruel spectacles of punishment provided the framework for social control grounded in abstract systems of thought and a form of cruelty consistent with the doctrines surrounding the original sin. This strategy of control is seen in the manner in which the Roman Catholic Church consolidated power in the early Middle Ages. As a result, behavioral patterns were regulated through a social structure of corruption, power, and homicidal control over the state. Definitions of crime and punishment were grounded in superstition, mysticism, and subjective thinking as opposed to concrete thinking.

One of the chief architects of this system is Pope Gregory IX, who instituted the Papal Inquisition (1231) for the apprehension and trial of heretics.[1] The term *inquisition* is derived from the Latin verb *inquiro* (to inquire into), which appears benign in every respect. An inquiry, in this sense, reflects a situation in which an individual may be questioned by authorities with the greater potential of a benign outcome. In reality, the Inquisition is something quite different and much more sinister. Heresy, for example, was defined by law as a deliberate denial of an article of truth as defined by the Catholic Church. The heretic is considered an enemy of the state, and thus a threat to social order and control.[2]

An examination of the doctrines supporting arrests, criminal trials, and subsequent punishments reveals much about this system of control. It raises significant questions pertaining to the defining structure of crime in the period, significance of the spectacle

---

1   "The Catholic Bible," *Wikipedia*, accessed May 6, 2012, https://en.wikipedia.org/wiki/Pope_Gregory_IX.

2   Also see: H. Kramer and J. Springer, *The Malleus Maleficarum* (New York: Dover Publication, Inc., 1971).

of punishment in obscuring the reality of the political economy, and ultimate need for church leaders to control individuals and groups who would challenge the authority of the state.

The Inquisition and Iniquity

Burning Heretics or History?

By Selwyn Duke

The Inquisition, used by atheists to revile Christians, was not a Catholic killing machine, but a fairly successful attempt to save lives from secular "justice."

I f Napoleon Bonaparte was right, history is but "a series of agreed upon myths." We probably shouldn't be quite that cynical, yet skepticism is always in order when dealing with human beings, who are always likely to view and portray matters through the prism of their own prejudices. But this provides a clue as to how to penetrate any veil of untruths: Understand the characteristic prejudices of your age and place, and you'll know what the myths are likely to be.

Some myths are innocent, such as a young George Washington having replied when asked about cutting down the cherry tree, "I cannot tell a lie." Others reflect the technique of the Big Lie. And when the Nazis promulgated the myth of "positive Christianity," which portrayed Jesus as a Nordic character fighting a Jewish establishment, it was to be expected from a group preaching Aryan superiority and Judaic persecution. Likewise, when Barack Obama's erstwhile Trinity United Church taught Black Liberation Theology and that Jesus was a black rebel fighting an oppressive white Roman establishment, it also was to be expected from a group preaching black superiority and white persecution.

Yet while the latter is believed by only a small group, this isn't because the lie isn't big but because its sympathetic subculture is small. But when the issue is the spirit of our age—which is militant secularism—it's a different matter. Thus do millions of educated people believe that Pope Pius XII was a Nazi collaborator, even though Jewish sources credit him with saving more than 800,000 Jews from the Holocaust.[1] And thus is it a modern narrative that the Crusades were efforts by rapacious knights and imperialistic popes to convert a peaceful Muslim world, even though we know that they were defensive actions designed to stave off Islamic aggression.[2] Big lies have big bases of believers when they attack the secular world's favorite whipping boy: Christianity.

But while the Crusades and Pius myths are merely cats-o'-nine-tales designed for this purpose, there may be an even taller tale. Because recent scholarship tells us that the dark stories of the Inquisitions—those medieval church entities charged with investigating heresy—are themselves more fiction than fact.

Such an assertion may shock many. Like "McCarthyism," "inquisition" has become a term that epitomizes intolerance, tyranny, and the squelching of free expression. Moreover, stories of Inquisition barbarity date back much further than the Crusade myth, whose seeds weren't sown till the 19th century. For instance, a man writing under the pseudonym Reginaldus Gonzalvus Montanus described the Spanish Inquisition thus in his 1567 document *A Discovery and Plain Declaration of Sundry and Subtill Practices of the Holy Inquisition of Spain*: "A court without allegiance to any earthly authority, a bench of monks without appeal. There is nothing else in the world to go beyond them in their most devilish examples of tyranny. Indeed, they do so far exceed all barbarousness, a man cannot more aptly liken them than to that they most closely resemble and from whence they proceed: their sire, Satan himself." Now, this certainly is a thorough condemnation, but is it perhaps a bit too thorough? Does it seem a bit too infused with a fervor that could lend itself to fiction making? And given that

---

1   See the March 15, 2010 TNA article "Pope Pius XII: Hero in the Unmaking."
2   See the February 15, 2010 TNA article "When Christendom Pushed Back."

subsequent Inquisition histories were strongly influenced by Montanus' claims, that its imagery has colored all Inquisitions—and that the narrative now aligns perfectly with our militant-secular spirit of the age—we perhaps should wonder if it is more agreed-upon myth than matter of fact.

Critical of Catholicism

The first myth that should be addressed is the notion that Inquisitions were a purely Catholic phenomenon. In point of fact, there were Protestant Inquisitions after the Reformation, and both Luther and Calvin maintained that the state had a right to protect society by ridding it of false religion. Nor were such efforts a solely Christian, medieval, or European phenomenon. As *The Dublin Review* wrote in its chapter "The Inquisition" in 1850:

> Plato, in his tenth book on Laws, lays it down as one of the duties of the magistrate to punish all blasphemers and unbelievers of the national religion. Charondas, of Catana, the celebrated lawgiver of Thurium, enacted a similar law. Diopithes introduced an equally stringent enactment at Athens. ...
>
> It was the same in Rome, even in its most advanced stage of enlightenment and intellectual cultivation. ... One of the laws of the Twelve Tables, prohibited the worship of foreign gods without public authority. A similar law is recited by Cicero ... and Cicero lays it down as an indisputable principle, that the ceremonies and dogmas of religion are to be maintained by the arm of the law, even through the infliction of capital punishment.

Judge, jury, and clergy? While anti-Inquisition propaganda labeled inquisitors "a bench of monks without appeal," they were at least as likely to be lawyers as churchmen and adhered to strict rules of jurisprudence.

This is why the Athenian Socrates was forced to drink the hemlock for, in part, "mocking the gods." It is part of the reason why the Romans persecuted Christians and suppressed Judaism as well. And the same intolerant spirit could be seen in every belief set, from Hinduism to Zoroastrianism to communism, the last of which made Torquemada—the first Grand Inquisitor—seem a font of tolerance. But now back to the Inquisitions of popular lore and gore, the Catholic ones.

The first clue as to the truth here may be found in a discrepancy between claims against the Inquisitions and the timing of the latter's inception. After all, we're told that the Catholic Church was bent on persecuting heretics, yet it took her until 1184—more than 1,000 years after her birth—to institute the first Inquisition (which was in southern France). And it wasn't as if heretics were previously in short supply. In the fifth century, for instance, Arian Christian Vandals began conquering Roman and Catholic North Africa, persecuting Catholics in the process and sometimes giving them the choice of conversion or death (church father Augustine of Hippo died during the Vandal siege of his city in 430). And even when Roman Emperor Justinian reconquered North Africa in 534, the church saw no need for an Inquisition to root out closet Arians. So what happened 600 years later? Did heretics become such a problem that the church felt compelled to act?

In point of fact, heretics were already taking it on the chin—from the state. Heresy was generally a capital offense under secular law. St. Louis University history professor Thomas F. Madden explained why in his article "The Real Inquisition: Investigating the Popular Myth," writing:

> To understand the Inquisition we have to remember that the Middle Ages were, well, medieval. We should not expect people in the past to view the world and their place in it the way we do today. (You try living through the Black Death and see how it changes your attitude.) For people who lived during those times, religion was not something one did just at church. It was science, philosophy, politics, identity, and hope for salvation. It was not a personal preference but an abiding and universal truth. Heresy, then, struck at the heart of that truth. It doomed the heretic, endangered those near him, and tore apart the fabric of community.

Consequently, writes Madden, "Heresy was a crime against the *state*. Roman law in the Code of Justinian made it a capital offense. Rulers, whose authority was believed to come from God, had no patience for heretics. Neither did common people, who saw them as dangerous outsiders who would bring down divine wrath."

In other words, heresy was somewhat analogous to treason. And who judged traitors? The government did. And this is precisely what happened to those accused of heresy in medieval times: They would be brought before the local lord for judgment. You can imagine the problems this presented. Not only might nobles be reluctant to devote the time necessary to assess a case fairly, but they had little if any theological training and were often arbitrary, capricious, and heavy-handed; they were hardly suited to judge whether a person really was a heretic or some hapless soul accused by enemies seeking revenge. The result was that many innocent people were tortured and killed.

So the church didn't have to worry about heretics, as the secular authorities were already suppressing them with vigor. But the church was worried about heretics—about their being treated unfairly.

Have Mercy

The startling fact—the Big Truth hidden by the Big Lie—is that Inquisitions were initially instituted as works of *mercy* designed to stop unjust punishments and executions. As Madden explains, while secular powers viewed heretics as "traitors to God and the king" who "deserved death," to the church they were simply "lost sheep who had strayed from the flock." As such, the pope and bishops had an obligation to be good shepherds and provide them with the opportunity to avoid severe punishment and continued community ostracism.

It should be emphasized again here that heresy was a capital offense only under the state, *not the church*. The church's goal was to seek the truth behind accusations. This is why the institutions

The minds of men: The medieval "Inquisition" torture chamber is a frightening image—and this is precisely why it was used as propaganda. Modern scholars now know that it never existed.

developed for that purpose wore a label with the root "inquire," which means "to ask"; and why, as the *Online Etymology Dictionary* tells us, *inquisitor* is a Latin word meaning "'searcher, examiner,' in law, 'an investigator, collector of evidence.'"

This isn't what you generally learn in schools, hear from the media, or see portrayed on television, but the proof is in the pudding. The aforementioned *Dublin Review* made this case already 163 years ago, and Henry Kamen of the Higher Council for Scientific Research in Barcelona, Spain, did so even more thoroughly in his groundbreaking 1965 book *The Spanish Inquisition*. And with the investigation of Spanish Inquisition files in the 1990s and the opening of Vatican records in 1998, eyes have been opened further. Note here that, unlike lords who might sentence an accused heretic to death and then eat dinner, inquisitors kept meticulous files; in fact, every single case handled by the Spanish Inquisition in its 350-year history has its own file on record. And what do those open eyes see? An 800-page study of the Vatican files compiled in 1998 by 60 historians and other experts from around the world concluded that when compared to secular courts of its day, the Inquisition was positively benign. Contrary to myth, most accused heretics were not executed, but, rather, were acquitted or had their sentences suspended. And most of those found guilty were allowed to do penance and integrate themselves back into society. As Italian history professor and the editor of the study, Agostino Borromeo, explained, writes the *Catholic News Agency*:

> "For a long time, judgments were confused with death sentences, and it was said that 100,000 were executed [during the Spanish Inquisition]—a figure completely unreal. Although some were sentenced to prison or to the galleys, most were given spiritual sentences: pilgrimages, penances, prayers, etc."
>
> Asked about the punishment used by Inquisitions in other countries, Borromeo said that "between 1551 and 1647, it [sic] Italian court of Aquileia condemned only 0.5% of accused to death. On the other hand, the Portuguese Inquisition between 1450 and 1629 condemned to death 5.7% of its 13,255 cases."
>
> Borromeo added that the total number of cases in the entire history of the Inquisition which resulted in death sentences is around 2%.

The notorious Spanish Inquisition, by the way, comes in at just about the average: 1.8 percent.

Yet even more perspective is needed. It must be reiterated that the church did not rate heresy a capital crime—the state did. So contrary to Hollywood fiction. Inquisitions did not burn heretics. And a good case in point is that of Jacques de Molay, the last Grand Master of the Knights Templar, who, along with the rest of his order, was accused of heresy (it's likely that their only sin was lending King Philip IV of France more money than he was willing to pay back). The king had him burned at the stake in 1314 without the bishops' and pope's approval—by way of an Inquisition or otherwise—and despite their lobbying for leniency.

Inquisitions, however, were far more professional operations whose task was to assess evidence and render judgments. And while inquisitors would no doubt have spared Molay, if a heretic was unbending and obstinate, he would have to be excommunicated and released to the government. Nonetheless, as Madden puts it, "The simple fact is that the medieval Inquisition *saved* uncounted thousands of innocent (and even not-so-innocent) people who would otherwise have been roasted by secular lords or mob rule."

Tortured Truth

But what of torture? It's true that inquisitors would occasionally resort to it to extract information. But before providing specifics, perspective is again necessary. As the BBC (hardly a font of Christian piety or conservative ideological purity) stated in its 1994 documentary *The Myth of the Spanish Inquisition* (MSI), "During the same [Inquisition] time period in the rest of Europe, hideous physical cruelty was commonplace. In England you could be executed for damaging shrubs in public gardens. If you returned to Germany from banishment, you could have your eyes gouged out. In France, you could be disemboweled for sheep stealing." In fact,

Fate versus forgiveness; Jacques de Molay's fate illustrated well the church-state divide over punishment. The Templar Grand Master was executed by King Philip IV despite calls for leniency by bishops and the pope.

even Enlightenment giant Thomas Jefferson, much later in history, prescribed draconian measures. As he wrote in *A Bill for Proportioning Crimes and Punishments,* "Whosoever shall be guilty of Rape, Polygamy, or Sodomy with man or woman shall be punished, if a man, by castration, if a woman, by cutting thro' the cartilage of her nose a hole of one half inch diameter at the least."

Despite this, it was perhaps in the Inquisitions that torture was used least. As Henry Kamen said when appearing in the MSI, "We find that comparing the Inquisition, merely in Spain with other tribunals, that the Inquisition used torture less than other tribunals. And if you compare the Inquisition with tribunals in other countries, we find that the Inquisition has a [very clean] record with respect to torture." The MSI elaborated:

> The Inquisition used none of these [torture] methods [prevalent among secular authorities]. They had a rulebook ... which specified what could and could not be done; those breaking the rules were sacked. So the Inquisition did not, as alleged, roast their victims' feet, or brick them up [encase them in a wall] to languish for all eternity, or smash their joints with hammers, or flail them on wheels. They never used the iron maiden. ... The inquisitors didn't ravish their female victims. ... In fact, the inquisitorial torture chamber of popular myth never existed, even though this image [of a torture chamber presented in the documentary] was reprinted hundreds of times. And it was not only the use of torture that was falsified; stories were also fabricated about the gruesome conditions in which prisoners were kept.

Kamen expanded on this last point, saying:

> Ironically, the Inquisition had probably the best jails in Spain, ... Let me take a quotation from the inquisitors in Barcelona in the middle of the 16th century, when they were asked to report on the state of their prisons and they said, "Our prisons are full." But then they complained to their bosses in Madrid, "We don't know where to send the leftover prisoners we have; we cannot send them to the city jails because the city jails are overcrowded, and there they are dying at the rate of 20 a week."

In fact, so superior were Inquisition jails that there were "instances of prisoners in secular criminal courts blaspheming in order to get into the Inquisition prison to escape the maltreatment they received in the secular prison," said another MSI-featured expert, Northern Illinois University history professor Stephen Haliczer.

Inquisition jurisprudence was superior as well. Just consider how the Roman Inquisition, established in 1588 by Pope Sixtus V, started to bring modernity to the Middle Ages. As scholar John Tedeschi points out in *The Prosecution of Heresy: Collected Studies on the Inquisition in Early Modern Italy*, the Roman Inquisition gave the accused a right to counsel and would even provide him an attorney, and a notarized copy of the charges would be available so that a defense could be formulated in advance. Secular courts at the time offered none of these rights and protections. In fact, so ahead of its time was the Roman Inquisition that, Tedeschi writes, "It may not be an exaggeration to claim ... that in several respects the Holy Office was a pioneer in judicial reform."

This brings us to the next myth. While Montanus and others portrayed inquisitors as shadowy robed monks devilishly chanting Latin in gothic halls, this was more Hollywood than hellacious reality. The truth is that the average inquisitor was an administrator and legal expert. Kamen explained, "They were career men who didn't even have to be priests. In the early period of the Inquisition, we have examples of some who were not even priests; they were simply lawyers trained at the university. And they would use the Inquisition merely as a career that maybe could be a stepping stone to another career." But, as the MSI put it, "Bureaucrats make boring copy."

They make for bad propaganda, too.

Perhaps the silliest myth is that Jews and Muslims feared the wrath of inquisitors bent on converting them. But the fact is that Inquisitions' role was to try those accused of heresy, which is defined as the denial of some of the doctrines of *one's own faith.* Thus, if you're a member of a different faith, you cannot be a heretic. Of course, governments at various times might have decided to expel or persecute those of minority religions, but this wouldn't have been within an Inquisition's scope. For it is clear what a person of a different faith is—and there is no need for inquisition when there is nothing to "inquire" about. Yet it is important to understand where the idea that Inquisitions persecuted Jews came from, and this brings us to the matter of the *conversos* of Spain.

Suppression of heresy has been history's norm. In fact, Martin Luther himself joined Plato, Cicero, and countless other figures in teaching that false religion should be purged from society.

Spain Inflamed

Spain was unique among European nations. It had been invaded by the Muslim Moors in 711, and most of Iberia (the peninsula comprising Spain and Portugal) was under their control by 750. Christians and Jews then lived in Islamic Iberia as the second-class citizens known as *dhimmis,* a situation that became far worse in 1172 when fundamentalist Muslims known as Almohads largely took control and gave the *dhimmis* a choice between conversion and death, causing many of them to emigrate. By this time, however, the Christian effort to reclaim their lands, the *reconquista,* had been progressing, and it was mostly complete by the late medieval period. This didn't mean Spain was united, however. Muslims still controlled Granada in the 15th century, and the Christians themselves were divided politically.

This began to change with the marriage of King Ferdinand II of Aragon and Queen Isabella I of Castile in October 1469. Being part of a marriage that initiated the unification of their two regions, the monarchs were no doubt intensely focused on eliminating division. Thus did they not only plan to complete the *reconquista* by retaking Granada, but they also resolved to eliminate internal religious division as well, believing it an impediment to political unity. This is where the *converses*—Jews who had converted to Christianity—enter the picture. Suspicious that they were "Judaizing" (practicing Judaism secretly), the monarchs instituted the Spanish Inquisition in 1478. And the rest is history—albeit often the twisted variety.

In other words, unlike earlier Inquisitions, the Spanish Inquisition wasn't a response to unjust adjudication of heresy accusations by secular authorities, but was animated by religious suspicion. Kamen claims that one reason for this was the *conversos*' failure to assimilate, a phenomenon which he says Spain's Muslim community exhibited as well. I would add that if you had been occupied wholly or in part by Muslims for 781 years, it's entirely possible you might be just a tad paranoid about alien religious influence on your soil. And these feelings no doubt only intensified, as the Spanish government expelled the nation's remaining Jews (not the *conversos*) in 1492 and its last Muslims in 1609. Again, however, while this might have been motivated by the same spirit that created the Spanish Inquisition, it was not the work of the tribunal.

Given the true nature of the Inquisitions, what explains the Montanus myths? Well, note here that when the Spanish Inquisition was first instituted, the rest of Europe congratulated Spain for finally becoming Christian; as the MSI put it, "A new age of Christian unity was said to be dawning." But this lasted for only about 30 years, until that great fissure in Christianity: the Reformation.

Obviously, emotions were running high on both sides after the Reformation in 1517, and the fur was flying. This not only took the form of armed conflict, such as the Battle of Muhlberg in 1547, but also a war of words. And with the Guttenberg printing press having been invented in 1448, it could be waged like never before. Knowing this, Montanus—widely believed to be Spanish Protestant Antonio del Corro—and others used the technology to wage what was perhaps the first truly modern propaganda campaign, spreading a big lie through the first big media.

Yet there were geo-political motivations as well. Not only had the Battle of Muhlberg pitted Spanish Imperial forces against northern European ones, but English-Spanish conflict in the 1580s was running high, causing King Philip II of Spain to plan an invasion of England and leading to the defeat of his armada in 1588. All these conflicts and events—religious and national—occurring at roughly the same time, amounted to a perfect storm of anti-Spanish sentiment in northern European countries. The result was, among other things, the embrace of the Montanus-disgorged "Black Legend," as the

A whispering war: Hot Reformation conflict, such as the Battle of Muhlberg, was followed by a cold war of words that led to anti-Inquisition propaganda such as the "Black Legend."

myth of the Spanish Inquisition came to be known. And via guilt by association, it came to tarnish other Inquisitions as well.

Yet as time wore on, anti-Spanish sentiment diminished, and the prejudices became more generalized. "The Inquisition" legend would grow and be advanced by anti-Christian movements and entities ranging from the French Revolution (its instigators tried to institute 10-day weeks that omitted Sundays) to the ideologically similar but short-lived Roman Republic of 1849 to today's militant secularists.

Having said this, it's inevitable that some will call this exposition a whitewash, averring that Inquisition transgressions are many but my examples of them few. And, of course, Inquisitions did have different characters in different places, and so did inquisitors. As Johns Hopkins history professor Richard L. Kagan complained in a *New York Times* review of Kamen's book, Kamen said little about how inquisitors "were not faceless bureaucrats but law graduates with varying interests and career aims" and about the "ploys, like bribes and pleas of insanity" used by defendants. All right, fair enough. But what are we to say about these failings? How is it much different from our legal system today?

And that really is the point. If all critics can respond with is that the Inquisitions were guilty of faults that ever plague man, I can rest my case. Of course, there is still the matter of torture, whose even occasional use we find abhorrent. Yet not only were the inquisitors quite civilized for their time in that area, whatever they did, they didn't employ euphemisms such as "coercive interrogation."

It also bears mention that the very cultural relativists who would whitewash human-sacrificing Aztecs as noble savages demonstrate no such charity in their very absolutist attitude toward that age's Europeans, whom they convict under our "values," forgetting, to again quote Thomas Madden, that the "Middle Ages were, well, medieval." But even this misses the mark, as it implies a perhaps unjustified sense of superiority. Note that medieval Christians would no doubt be aghast at our age's rampant abortion, sexual promiscuity, denial of sin, lack of piety, and communist killing fields, not to mention our hate-speech laws—enforced by "inquisitions" called Human Rights Tribunals—used to punish today's "heretics." And, if they could consider our trespasses, perhaps the best we might hope for is that a few of them would shake their heads and say that modernity is, well, modernistic.

But most of all, modernity is of man, with the unchanging nature that implies. So we can be sure that we'll continue to burn inconvenient pages from our history books—and that the Inquisition myth will be agreed upon for a very, very long time to come.

CHAPTER FOUR

The Age of Enlightenment

The cruel spectacle of punishment gave way to the pressure and necessity of evolving into a more concrete framework of ethical standards and rational thinking. Much of this thinking emerged as the foundation of modern thought, which advanced an age of inquiry leading to major advancements in philosophy, science, and technology. By the time of the French Revolution (1750–1789), many of these ideas ushered in a social and political movement focused on the question of the efficacy of torture as a true deterrence to crime.

This change in perspective is generally known as the *Enlightenment or Age of Reason*, which originated in the late seventeenth century (1650) and continued through the French Revolution (1789). The Enlightenment is thought to be largely a European phenomenon. The Enlightenment scholars, who are primarily associated with England, France, Spain, Russia, and Germany, also contributed to the ideology of early American democratic ideals and social policy. The *Declaration of Independence*, for example, is grounded in the basic concept of the Enlightenment, which argues that each individual has the right to choose and speak their own religious, political, moral, and philosophical beliefs as well as to pursue happiness and lead a life they think is right. These ideas are considered revolutionary in that they shape the *central demand of modern philosophy*, which pertains to the idea of the autonomy of the individual person.[1]

Each of us has the ability to ascertain what is true and right through our own thinking and experience, without a singular dependence on outside authority. Whether you believe in God or not must be decided by your own reason and argumentation, which you can

---

1   John Christman, "Autonomy in Moral and Political Philosophy," in *The Stanford Encyclopedia of Philosophy*, ed. Edward N. Zalta. Article published Spring 2018, https://plato.stanford.edu/archives/spr2018/entries/autonomy-moral/>.

formulate and examine for yourself. The idea of individual autonomy thus created a major shift in the social order, with the criminal justice system being largely affected as well. The method in which this shift takes place will be discussed in the following chapter. The ideas put forth by Enlightenment philosophers, as powerful as they are, also give rise to several significant questions pertaining to the potential for these ideas to benefit everyone in society. Particularly since indigenous people, men of color, women, and poor people were not included in the documentation, within the theoretical and philosophical frameworks used to create these ideas, nor within the promise of enlightenment itself.

Race and the Copernican Turn

By Deborah K. Heikes

....

The Enlightenment is said to be an era of moral equality, but the historical evidence suggests that few men, and even fewer women, were ever actually equal. The racism and sexism evident throughout much of modern philosophy has been ignored or dismissed as unfortunate but are, in fact, relevant to central philosophical claims of the period. Despite the hope that such offensive attitudes are simply a product of their authors' personal biases, good reasons exist to believe that modern racist attitudes are as much an outgrowth of the epistemic difficulties those philosophers encountered and are, consequently, grounded in core philosophical doctrines. The Cartesian turn inward toward ideas of the mind creates a situation in which epistemic objectivity is necessarily grounded in a radical subjectivism. As a result, philosophers such as Hume and Kant find it necessary to grant epistemic authority only to those who reason according to proper methodologies, which, in turn, has consequences for moral agency. The result is that, by the end of the Enlightenment, rationality and personhood are no longer the possession of every human being.

Keywords: Kant, Hume, race

The Age of Enlightenment is also known as an Age of Equality. It is the era in which we find the first assertions of the equality of men. It is also the era in which some of the very same philosophers who argue for the universality of moral rights exwplicitly deny women's equality and disparage non-Whites. Well known are the principle ideas of the Enlightenment: all men (literally,

Deborah K. Heikes, "Race and the Copernican Turn," *The Journal of Mind and Behavior*, vol. 36, no. 3-4, pp. 139-163. Copyright © 2015 by Institute of Mind & Behavior. Reprinted with permission. Provided by ProQuest LLC. All rights reserved.

men) are born equal; objective truth is obtainable; man is capable of perfecting himself through the use of reason; the path to knowledge requires freeing oneself from ignorance and superstition. This list may not be complete, but it should be familiar. What is missing, however, is an explicit statement of how narrowly these ideas apply. For example, Thomas Jefferson, the very same person who found men's equality to be self-evident, himself owned slaves. Of course, this hypocritical stance is not unique to Jefferson; in fact, it is the rule rather than the exception. Throughout the Enlightenment, many of the people who are central in arguing the moral and political equality of men are the very same people who explicitly denigrate women and non-Whites, denying them rights and denying them the status of persons. The most egregious example is Kant, who champions the ultimate worth of each rational agent and who nevertheless speaks of "the fair sex" and of "negroes" in less than glowing terms. This repeated and pervasive disconnect is anything but accidental.

Of course, feminist philosophers have for decades been raising concerns about Enlightenment philosophical concepts. Genevieve Lloyd (1984) points out that during this period reason comes to be not simply "a distinguishing feature of human nature, but … an achievement—a skill to be learned, a distinctively methodical way of thinking, sharply differentiated from other kinds of thought." She goes on to add that "something happened here which proved crucial for the development of stereotypes of maleness and femaleness" (p. 39). Something also happened which proved crucial for the development of stereotypes of race. This "something" is the modern epistemological turn inward. As reason comes to be understood as a faculty dependent only upon itself, as epistemological justifications come to be dependent solely on internal ideas and cognitive structures, the threat of subjectivism looms large. The domain of reason comes to be circumscribed so tightly as to exclude anyone conceived to be different in epistemically relevant ways. And, unfortunately, skin color (as well as having female body parts) comes to be an epistemically relevant feature, albeit inferentially. The connection between the rise of racism and the Enlightenment's pursuit of universal knowledge and moral equality is not accidental—and between them lies the modern concept of reason.

The significance of race is surely tied to the attitudes and biases of the philosophers who develop the concept, but this significance also arises out of theoretical concerns with the subjectivism inherent in the Copernican turn. Descartes originates this turn by transforming the focus of philosophy away from the world and toward the inner realm of the mind. Kant then completes the turn and formally establishes that knowledge can be had only through very human ways of cognizing. Because this shift is well understood, I begin with merely a brief overview of its Cartesian origins and the ways in which Humean and Kantian conceptions of reason respond to its subjectivist implications. These responses hold the key to understanding why racist remarks during that time are not simply incidental to core philosophical theses. What Hume and Kant understand is that if reason can rely on nothing outside of itself, then it is either capable of justifying its own processes or it is not. Each grabs an opposite horn of this dilemma: Hume largely denies the authority of reason while Kant asserts it with a vengeance. However, with respect to race, each ends up in a similar place, defending the superiority of Whites.

This happens as each makes epistemic and moral moves intended to ground objective knowledge in the subjectivity of internal ideas, but these moves also serve as a theoretical basis for their racist attitudes. As it turns out, the theoretical ground Kant offers for his understanding of race is far more developed than is Hume's, but Hume's attitude stems equally from his core philosophical beliefs. In the end, the racist remarks of both these philosophers are tied to central philosophical doctrines developed in response to the threat of subjectivism. Even if Kant's attitude toward race is on more solid theoretical ground than is Hume's, both philosophers diminish the capacity of non-Whites to achieve epistemic and moral standing.

To make the case, I begin with an overview of the paradox created when modern philosophers place the ground of objective knowledge within a subjective realm of ideas. Specifically, I consider the responses of Hume and Kant to this paradox, arguing that the way each cuts off the threat of subjectivism provides the conditions necessary for a theoretical ground of racism. Given these epistemic concerns, I then discuss their relevance to Hume's discussion of a standard of taste. Even though his empiricism cannot establish the necessity of a racial heirarchy, he nevertheless seeks to establish a universal standard accessible only to certain sorts of people (most notably, those who are White and European). Kant, on the other hand, can and does allow for the necessary inferiority of non-Whites and non-males, arguing quite explicitly that skin color and body parts affect one's capacity to act according to principles. Finally, I consider the quite serious moral implications of the Enlightenment's epistemological concerns, namely the ways in which the concept of humanity is decoupled from the concepts of rationality and personhood. The unfortunate outcome is that the Copernican turn originated by Descartes and completed by Kant narrows the domain of personhood and restricts the application of so-called universal moral concepts such as equality and justice only to those who reason in the right sort of way.

Modernism's Subjective Paradox

During the Enlightenment, rationality comes to be an acquired skill, one that requires following a specific procedure for obtaining knowledge. To follow this procedure means that one is capable of freeing oneself from bias, prejudice, and unfounded belief, thereby assuring objective knowledge, particularly with respect to the natural world. As the spotlight of epistemology turns inward, reason requires a detachment from material and emotional aspects of the world and a rigorous commitment to understanding the logical structure of the world. The result is that individual minds become autonomous arbiters of truth, provided they follow a method that dissects and analyzes internal operations of mind according to certain rules. With the notable exception of Hume, whom I will discuss shortly, philosophers of the modern era assert thoroughly authoritative, procedural accounts of rationality as not simply a luxury but as a necessity. Why? Because at the heart of modern philosophy lies a paradox in which the path to knowledge of the world is through an exclusive focus on the ideas in one's own mind: radical objectivity comes to be intelligible and accessible only through radical subjectivity (see Taylor, 1989, pp. 175–176). And because the origin of all knowledge is suddenly subjective, philosophers must explain how human beings come to be devoid of subjectivity. As Wittgenstein (1958, §293) was to highlight a couple of centuries later, when we each look inward toward the ideas in our own minds, we need some assurance that each of us is starting with the same ideas and procedures for relating and connecting those ideas; otherwise, we lack any basis for objective knowledge. While Wittgenstein externalizes this assurance through practices and language-games, the moderns take the individual knowing subject to have precedence in the generation of knowledge. If subjects cannot be counted on to be identical to one another in all relevant respects, then we lose any guarantee of objective knowledge. What counts as a "relevant respect" is an open question, but we all know that, contrary to their oft stated position, Enlightenment philosophers do take material conditions like skin color or body parts to be relevant to one's ability to achieve rationality.

This story of modern reason has been told and retold, as has the story of how such procedurally governed concept invokes "images of domination, oppression, repression, patriarchy, sterility, violence, totality, totalitarianism, and even terror" (Bernstein, 1986, p. 187). As postmodernists, feminists, and other critics of the Enlightenment have repeatedly argued, the Enlightenment is not all sunshine and light. The story, however, that is less well told is how this transformation in our understanding of reason motivates an exclusive—and exclusionary—account of reason. In other words, we recognize what Enlightenment reason is and we understand the destruction it wreaks for many; what is often overlooked, however, is how the very development of the modern concept demands marginalization, at least if the objectivity of knowledge is to be sufficiently defended. The question is, why?

The emphasis on subjectivity comes with a radical, if artificially conceived, skepticism. What makes Cartesian skepticism so transformative is the insistence on doubting reason itself. Aristotle may ask for a level of precision appropriate to the area of inquiry, but Descartes asks for certainty: pure, simple, and beyond all doubt whatsoever. As Étienne Gilson (1930) summarizes,

> From the point of view of medieval philosophy, someone who plays the role of the *indisciplinatus* takes pride in insisting on the same degree of certainty in every discipline, no matter how inappropriate. In a word, he [Descartes] no longer recognizes an intermediary between the true and the false; his philosophy radically eliminates the notion of "the probable." (p. 235)[1]

The result is a quest for certainty that adopts an all-or-nothing approach which in turn diminishes any way of thinking that fails to achieve this peculiar kind of certainty. For Stephen Toulmin (2001), Descartes' exclusive emphasis on "the rigor of theoretical arguments ... [and] the need for technical terminology based on abstractions" (p. 32) causes reason to become unbalanced. Yet Descartes needs

---

1   Translation mine.

this exclusive emphasis. Alternative procedures would undermine the confidence we can have in *our* ways of reasoning. The result is not simply that Cartesian rationality shuts down the possibility of alternative ways of thinking but that it must do so. The light of reason, which guides all our reflections, "cannot in any way be open to doubt" (Descartes, 1641/1984, p. 27).

By contrast, Greek rationality was always able to remain largely unthreatened by conceptual diversity since whatever account of the world one wanted to come up, it ultimately had to face the tribunal of an ontologically real and independent reality. The same is not at all true for the moderns. As the connection between the realm of inner ideas and the realm of objects in the world becomes more tenuous, the need for cognition to have a strictly logical order becomes more evident because we have only our own wits upon which to depend. The subjectivist implications of this leaves philosophers with two obvious choices: give up the authority of reason (i.e., Hume) or assert it with a vengeance (i.e., Kant). Hume and Kant both discern the tension between asserting infallible access to internal ideas and the necessity of grounding those ideas in a world beyond the ideas themselves. Both understand that the loss of metaphysics puts the veracity of our representations into doubt. But each responds in a different manner, and each response entails a narrowing of epistemology and value theory in ways that ultimately reflect on race. Epistemologically, Hume is entirely honest about the implications of Cartesianism for an empiricist: reason must be less an authoritative faculty and more a natural instinct. Aesthetically, Hume is less honest. When it comes to matters of taste, he seeks universal principles that are unattainable for some. Kant, on the other hand, accepts the force of Hume's empirical arguments, but he also understands that if experience worked along Humean lines, we would have little hope of ever surmounting the problem of explaining how the world hangs together in some orderly and objective way. Thus, Hume must be leaving out something important. The authority of reason must have an a priori source, both epistemically and morally.

By the time Hume arrives on the scene, representational epistemologies have precious little to re-present. He recognizes that a commitment to sensation and reflection as the only sources of knowledge means that the connection between our ideas and an external world is essentially unknowable. He recognizes that even though philosophers attempt to distinguish fleeting perceptions from objects with continued existence, the attempt to do so is "only a palliative remedy" (1738/1978, p. 211). For Hume, we can never establish that our sensory impressions are grounded in stable, external objects for "it follows that we may observe a conjunction or a relation of cause and effect between different perceptions, but can never observe it between perceptions and objects" (1738/1978, p. 212). The order among our ideas must come from internal operations of our minds. In fact, more than any other Enlightenment philosopher, Hume understands that we can't get outside the system and see what the world is like independently of what we think it is like. And this lack of outside constraint on cognition means that our justifications of epistemic norms must actually presuppose those very norms.

Again, all this is familiar and appears entirely disconnected from any sort of racist observation. Quite to the contrary, it may very well seem that a philosophical theory based on empirical principles allows for more openness to difference. After all, cognitive principles are for Hume (1738/1978) merely probabilistic: "reason must be consider'd as a kind of cause, of which truth is the natural effect; but such-a-one as by the irruption of other causes, and by the inconstancy of our mental powers, may frequently be prevented. By this means all knowledge degenerates into probability" (p. 180). He further explains that reason can offer only subjective assurances: "'Tis not solely in poetry and music, we must follow our taste and sentiment, but likewise in philosophy. ... When I give the preference to one set of arguments above another, I do nothing but decide from my feeling concerning the superiority of their influence" (1738/1978, p. 103). Not exactly the authoritativeness Descartes had in mind when he introduced a methodological account of reason. And not exactly the words one would expect from someone who denies civilization among non-Whites. What is left out in these remarks, however, is a further commitment to the uniformity and regularity of reason and taste, which guides us through the world of experience. Even though the only assurance we can have of the universality of reason is through empirical observation, it is an assurance on which Hume ultimately relies. It is also an assurance that uneasily grounds his observations concerning race. For now, I turn to Kant.

Given the strong and thoroughgoing skepticism Hume expresses concerning the nature of reason, it is little wonder that Kant awakens from his dogmatic slumber. However, rather than reject Hume's conclusions outright, he acknowledges this powerful motivation for skepticism, then attempts to overcome it. He may consider it a scandal that metaphysics is dead, but he also understands the epistemological shift in which the governing principles of the world are henceforth to be found only within reason itself. Ultimately, what he objects to are not Hume's arguments concerning the nature of empirical knowledge but the incompleteness of these arguments in providing a satisfactory explanation for the regularity of experience. As a result, Kant seeks to reestablish the authority of reason through the discovery of a priori principles of cognition. But in removing contingency, he also lays the seeds for a much more virulent form of racism than could ever be established through empirical arguments grounded in taste or sentiment.

To reestablish the epistemic authority of reason, Kant builds an a priori foundation for Hume's a posteriori edifice. What Hume misses, says Kant, is the importance of a transcendental structure for experience. Consider the A-Deduction of the first *Critique* (which begins at 1781/1929, p. A120). In it we are told that perceptions are appearances conjoined with consciousness and that these perceptions are atomistically isolated, requiring cognitive activity to bring them together into an "object of knowledge." We are told that it is impossible for us to produce a connection of impressions "were it not that there exists a subjective ground which leads the mind to reinstate a preceding perception alongside the subsequent perception to which it has passed, and so to form whole series of perceptions" (Kant, 1781/1929, p. A121). In other words, the connection among perceptions follows subjective principles. Nothing in this tale of mental activity thus far distinguishes the Kantian from the Humean story. In fact, Kant's summary reflects Hume's claim that "there is a principle of connexion between the different thoughts or ideas of the mind, and that in their appearance to the memory or imagination, they introduce each other with a certain degree of method and regularity" (Hume, 1748/1975, p. 23). By the end of the argument, however, Kant makes a quite non-Humean declaration: the principles that allow for the connection among ideas cannot all be subjective. Where Hume offers, at best, universality through empirical observation, Kant (1781/1929) claims that we must "also [have] an objective ground which makes it impossible that appearances should be apprehended by the imagination otherwise than under the condition of a possible synthetic unity of this apprehension" (p. A121). Stated plainly: reason itself provides a necessary structure for how the world hangs together, and this necessity allows for the possibility of objective experience because it is, well, necessary. Since reason must operate according to this structure, Kant thereby dissolves the threat of subjectivism and Humean skepticism, at least in theory.

Epistemologically, this result may appear quite comforting. We need not worry that experience will be cohesive and regular because the nature of cognition itself guarantees a systematic unity. We can rest assured that nature operates according to regular principles that we can discover; after all, these principles stem from reason itself. Nevertheless, such epistemological contentment is gained at the expense of alternative conceptual schemes, a result that philosophers have, over the past century, been quite eager to point out. Less noticeable are the moral implications of such a narrow and methodological conception of reason. These implications have been, and still are, anything but comforting for those who fail to reason in the "right way."

When it comes to morality, Hume and Kant both accept the division between reason and some variation of sentiment or desire. And they both recognize that conforming the will to moral principle is quite different from knowing the difference between right and wrong. That is, becoming moral is as much of an achievement as is becoming rational. Of course, the significance each accords these distinctions is quite different. Still, Kant and Hume do agree on one thing: any connection between moral law and will must be shown to be necessary. Says Hume (1738/1978),

> 'Tis one thing to know virtue, and another to conform the will to it. In order, therefore, to prove, that the measures of right and wrong are eternal laws, oblig-atory on every rational mind, 'tis not sufficient to shew the relations upon which they are founded: We must also point out the connexion betwixt the relation and the will; and must prove that this connexion is so necessary, that in every well-disposed mind, it must take place and have its influence; tho' the difference betwixt these minds be in other respects immense and infinite. (p. 465)

Of course, Hume rejects the possibility of such a necessary connection while Kant embraces it. In the case of Hume, passions are not conformable to reason, so morality becomes a matter not of intellect but of taste, the very same taste which lies at the heart of some key remarks on race. Reason is to be distinguished from taste insofar as "the former conveys the knowledge of truth and falsehood:

the latter gives sentiment of beauty and deformity, vice and virtue" (Hume, 1738/1978, p. 294). Hence, morality and taste stand in opposition to reason; morality is "more properly felt than judged of" (p. 470). And in a line that must have made Kant absolutely cringe, "reason alone can never be a motive to any action of the will" (p. 413).

Kant, by contrast, insists that reason does guide us toward the satisfaction of our desire, if only unreliably. That is, he stands with Hume insofar as emotions can be heteronomous influences on action (see Kant, 1785/1996, p. 51). Yet Kant simply cannot accept Hume's skepticism toward the power of reason. The heteronomy of emotion should be no obstacle to reason in its a priori function, for reason must be the motive toward an action of the will if that action is to have moral worth. Reason acts freely only when it excludes desires as relevant considerations for choice and operates solely according to principle. In making this move to radicalize autonomy, Kant asserts the authority of reason to act independently of desires, which, in turn, eliminates subjectivity from the realm of morality. Unlike Hume, he need not assume everyone shares the same sentiments. Because moral motivation can never stem from sentiment or desire but must come instead from the necessity of acting according to a law that reason gives itself, Kant can establish an objective ground for a morality based solely on principle.

In articulating regular and uniform principles, Hume and Kant eliminate the subjectivity of emotion, desire, and perception in their value theory as much as they do in their epistemology. They, like all good Enlightenment philosophers, have faith in reason's ability to provide objective knowledge of the world. Yet the tensions of this faith are quite evident in their work. They are, after all, fully aware of the need, both epistemically and morally, to articulate explicitly the connection between mind and world, as well as the connection between reason, emotion, and will. Because secret springs and principles escape empirical notice, Hume is reduced to denying the power of reason, claiming that, in the end, only a fool or a madman would deny experience to be an indispensable guide to human life. Somewhat magically, "regular conjunction has been universally acknowledged among mankind, and has never been the subject of dispute" (Hume, 1748/1975, p. 88). Conversely, Kant accepts that secret springs and principles cannot be had empirically, but he maintains that we still have recourse to regulative principles, of the kind that can be had a priori. These are indeed capable of providing necessity, unity, and purposiveness. Whether empirically or transcendentally, Enlightenment philosophers share a desire to seek universal principles, and they do this, at least in part, to overcome the difficulties inherent in a subjectively grounded representationalism. For those who can reason correctly, objective knowledge can be had.

The difficulty, of course, is that not everyone can reason correctly. Kant's moral theory, for example, requires acting according to rational principle. An obvious question, albeit one that has not been obvious until very recently, is: Who is indeed capable of such severely principled action? The answer Kant (1764/1960) gives is quite specific: he "hardly believe[s] that the fair sex is capable of principles" and adds that "these are also extremely rare in the male" (p. 81). By all appearances, the ability to act according to principles is a rather uncommon trait. It is not universally achievable. Yet anyone who knows anything about Kantian ethics understands the enormous importance of acting from principles. Without this, genuine moral worth is impossible. After all, morality is all about reason and about laws that we autonomously give ourselves. The result is that when we start to take seriously these philosophers' comments on race, it seems that rationality (and taste) become a whole lot less achievable and a whole lot less universal than Enlightenment dogma would have us believe. The need to limit the proper methodology for cognition may not require the exclusion of those who appear different, but the manner in which the concept is constructed, combined with the obvious prejudice of many key Enlightenment thinkers, practically guarantees such exclusion. The result is the imposition of limitations on rationality and moral equality that actually offer something far, far less than the universalism promised by Enlightenment thinkers. I turn first to Hume and consider the epistemic anxieties evident in his comments on race. In the following section, I address Kant and reflect on how his critical response to subjectivist threats provides a foundation for his racial theory.

Hume on the Standard of Race

What has left many contemporary philosophers confused, or even incredulous, is the oppression and exclusion that go hand in hand with Enlightenment moral concepts such as equality, justice, and freedom. How is it that philosophers who defend these concepts can own slaves or make disparaging remarks about non-Whites?[2] Whether or not various Enlightenment philosophers are genuinely racist is a matter of much discussion and debate.[3] What is not a matter of debate is that Hume and Kant both make some especially reprehensible statements about non-Whites (and about women). However much we contemporary philosophers might wish to minimize and diminish the significance of these remarks, their comments are deliberate and grounded in their theoretical responses to the threat of subjectivism. In other words, the racist overtones of their works are far from ancillary.

When it comes to the topic of race, Hume has less to say than Kant. Yet what Hume has to say is no less objectionable. The most infamous of passages in Hume's (1758) work is the following:

> I am apt to suspect the negroes and in general all other species of men (for there
> are four or five different kinds) to be naturally inferior to the whites. There
> never was a civilized nation of any other complexion than white, nor even any

2   Beyond the remarks of Hume and Kant discussed here, Berkeley owned slaves, and Locke invested in the slave trade. Bernasconi points out that the word "power" in *The Fundamental Constitutions of Carolina* is written in Locke's hand. The result is a document that reads, "Every Freeman of Carolina shall have absolute power and Authority over his Negro slaves" (Bernasconi, 2003, p. 14).

3   See, for example, Bernasconi, 2001, 2002, 2003; Eze, 1997, 2000; Hill and Boxill, 2001; Immerwahr, 1992; Kleingeld, 2007; Larrimore, 2008; Lind, 1994; Louden, 2000; Mills, 2002, 2005; Reiss, 2005; and Zack, 2002.

individual eminent either in action or speculation. No ingenious manufactures
amongst them, no arts, no sciences. (p. 125)[4]

Whether or not this sort of comment is indicative of a deeper racist attitude, it is far from an unreflective remark. As John Immerwahr points out, Hume edits this remark quite deliberately to direct his attack more narrowly against Blacks. In the edited version, he writes: "I am apt to suspect the negroes to be naturally inferior to the whites. There scarcely ever was a civilized nation of that complexion, nor even any individual eminent either in action or speculation" (Hume, 1757/1964a, p. 252). In this latter version, Hume may be more charitable toward the three or four remaining kinds of men, but we can take him at his word with respect to Blacks; otherwise, he would not have precised his comment in the way he did. As objectionable as this passage is, however, nothing foundational to Humean philosophy hangs on this one comment. Nothing specific to his response to subjectivism is implicated. Still, this is not the only reference Hume makes to non-Whites. In Hume's other famously racist passage, that concerning the lack of aesthetic appreciation for wine, his attitude stems from much deeper roots and from a clear worry that there must be a single standard of taste.

Compared to other philosophers of his day, Hume is noticeably less insistent upon universalizable principles. Still, he is not entirely insensitive to their power to overcome subjectivity and, hence, to their worth. The clearest expression of Hume's concern for universality comes in his aesthetics, where he offers an explicit appeal to a universal standard as a means of subverting subjectivity in matters of taste. Hume (1757/1964b) believes that "certain qualities in objects ... are fitted by nature to produce those particular feelings" (p. 273). Yet to know which qualities fit with which feelings, we must consider the responses that fall under the heading of "delicacy of taste." Says Hume (1757/1964b),

> Where the organs are so fine, as to allow nothing to escape them; and at the same time so exact, as to perceive every ingredient in the composition: This we call delicacy of taste. ... Here then the general rules of beauty are of use. ... And if the same qualities, in a continued composition, and in a smaller degree, affect not the organs with a sensible delight or uneasiness, we exclude the person from all pretensions to this delicacy. (p. 273)

Intriguingly, he does not adopt his normal skeptical stance in this circumstance. In the epistemological case, he is content to reject the authority of reason in favor of "a species of natural instinct" (which turns out by lucky chance to be universal). In matters of taste, he asserts general rules that, it seems,

---

4   This remark is often dismissed since it is merely a footnote and not part of the main text. However, Immerwahr (1992), Eze (2000), and Zack (2002) argue that it is far from being an offhand remark. Immerwahr makes a scholarly argument for the deliberateness of this remark; Eze believes it is quite carefully placed and grounded in Hume's theory of human nature; and Zack argues that it implies an essentialism concerning racial divisions.

not everyone has the ability to discern. "Naturally," non-Whites emerge as less capable in aesthetic judgments.

> A Laplander or Negro has no notion of the relish of wine. And though there are few or no instances of a like deficiency in the mind, where a person has never felt or is wholly incapable of a sentiment or passion that belongs to his species; yet we find the same observation to take place in a less degree. ... It is readily allowed, that other beings may possess many senses of which we can have no conception; because the ideas of them have never been introduced to us in the only manner by which an idea can have access to the mind, to wit, by the actual feeling and sensation. (Hume, 1748/1975, p. 20)

Hume does charitably admit that it is possible that others have senses we do not, but given the entirety of his view, it seems unlikely that he would find a white European male deficient in the same way as the Negro, who lacks civilization.

Now, the philosophical problem here is not so much Hume's racist remarks, although they are deeply problematic; rather, the problem is that he is not allowed the universality of taste against which he judges the Laplander and Negro lacking. He needs this universality of taste if he is to avoid taste becoming merely a subjective judgment, but the only means empiricists have for establishing such universality of taste is observation and reflection. And herein lies the difficulty. Marcia Lind (1994) notices in both Hume's aesthetics and ethics, an illegitimate assumption (one I believe is also evident in his epistemology): the assumption of an underlying similarity of all people. In the moral case, he needs to establish some uniformity of human action and volition in the face of seeming "caprice and inconstancy," but as with induction, Hume (1748/1975) maintains "the conjunction between motives and voluntary actions is ... regular and uniform ... [and] has been universally acknowledged among mankind" (p. 88). Echoing his remarks from "Of the Standard of Taste," Hume (1748/1975) says in the first *Enquiry*, "it is universally acknowledged that there is a great uniformity among the actions of men, in all nations and ages, and that human nature remains still the same in its principles and operations" (p. 83). Thus, in both the epistemic and moral cases, Hume assumes that cognition operates along the same lines regardless of who the cognizer is, as long as the cognizer is White and male.

The issue for Lind, however, is something different, namely, that Hume fails to establish a uniformity among humans as a matter of fact. Instead, he simply states his claim. But, says Lind (1994), "distortions" do exist in our perceptions and judgments, so the universality of taste (and of judgment) can only be had by "artificially constructing agreement among critics by limiting who was party to the agreement" (p. 57). That is, on the basis of an unsupported generalization, Hume limits who can be considered to possess delicacy of taste, and we should note that "exposure to 'superior' beauties is not just *any* sort of education, with any sort of range, but a *classical* education" (p. 57). Clearly, not everyone has access to a classical education, especially in the eighteenth century. Although Lind herself argues that Hume's wider moral theory can overcome this limitation (p. 62), objectivity in matters of taste is clearly obtained by excluding those who do not share the right biases. To legitimize *his* judgment as correct, a critic

> must preserve his mind free from all prejudice, and allow nothing to enter into his consideration but the very object which is submitted to his examination. We may observe, that every work of art, in order to produce its due effect on the mind, must be surveyed in a certain point of view, and cannot be fully relished by persons, whose situation, real or imaginary, is not conformable to that which is required by the performance. (Hume, 1757/1964b, p. 276)

Aesthetically, there is a difference between right and wrong, and the only way to "get it right" is to focus on the object from the correct point of view.

Despite the passing nature of his remarks, Hume is indeed reflective in his disparagement of the abilities of non-Whites. Even while asserting that human perception and cognition is governed by a uniform standard, especially when it comes to delicacy of taste, he also maintains that the appropriate application of this standard lies beyond the capacity of some. Now, Hume might be defended insofar as he does not explicitly state non-Whites fail to achieve rationality, but recall that reason is distinguished from taste insofar as "the latter gives sentiment of beauty and deformity, vice and virtue" (Hume, 1748/1975, p. 294). Non-Whites may (or may not) be sufficiently able to determine matters of truth and falsehood, but because they are lacking in taste, they will, by implication, also be lacking in virtue. Even though Humean empiricism cannot support the assumption of uniformity of rational principles and moral sentiments, that does not diminish the fact that Hume uses this assumption to disparage those who are different. Nor does it help Hume that the assumption of uniform and regular principles is not ad hoc; not only is it a central aspect of his wider philosophical views, it is also specifically used to assert the superiority of non-Whites. Hume may not (or may) exhibit a sufficiently theoretical racism, but his racist remarks are not philosophically accidental. Kant, on the other hand, appears to have a theory which is seriously, intrinsically racist.

Kant on the Purposiveness of Race

Whatever their differences in value theory, Kant shares Hume's sense that aesthetic judgments are universal and that they are closely linked to moral judgment. In the aesthetic case, Kant (1790/1987) states:

> Taste is basically an ability to judge the [way in which] moral ideas are made sensible ... ; the pleasure that taste declares valid for mankind as such and

not just for each person's private feeling must indeed derive from this [link] and from the resulting increase in our receptivity for the feeling that arises from moral ideas. Plainly, then, the propaedeutic that will truly establish our taste consists in developing our moral ideas and in cultivating [*Kultur*] moral feeling. (p. 356)

Correct judgments on matters of taste are not only universally valid but also grounded in correct moral belief. One possible implication of this is that failures in judgments of taste may very well be indicative of failures in moral reasoning as well. And moral failures are not to be taken lightly for Kant. Where Hume claims non-Whites exhibit failures of taste, Kant ups the ante. His approach to race, and to the inequalities among the various races, goes deeper than mere aesthetic judgments. Kant is theoretically committed to an epistemological and moral essentialism that diminishes the personhood of non-Whites and non-males.

That Kant is an essentialist about race is not a new argument, but it is a controversial one. Interpreters of Kant disagree on the significance of his racial remarks for his critical work. Philosophers like Emmanuel Eze (1997) and Charles Mills (2002, 2005) argue that Kant's core philosophical doctrines are infected by his racist anthropology. Philosophers like Thomas Hill and Bernard Boxill (2001) argue that while the racism is unfortunate, it can be safely set aside, leaving Kant's epistemology and morality intact. My own sympathies lie with the former interpretation, and my concern is that this essentialism underpins an unsustainable moral hierarchy within deontology. My argument echoes one originated by Eze (1997), who asserts that "what Kant settled upon as the 'essence' of humanity, that which one ought to become in order to deserve human dignity, sounds very much like Kant himself: 'white,' European, and male" (p. 130). What Hill and Boxill (2001) find lacking in this view is that Eze "says nothing to suggest that Kant believed that these [racist] passages were any more than empirical a posteriori claims that could be falsified by experience" (p. 455). Instead, they argue that the racist bits of Kant are not central to his core philosophical views. More to the point, they hold that we cannot support the conclusion that Kant denies the humanity of non-Whites. Now, Kant does accept Buffon's rule and allows that "all human beings anywhere on earth belong to the same natural genus because they always produce fertile children with one another even if we find great dissimilarities in their form" (Kant, 1777/2000, p. 9). This, however, does not entail that his racist passages are merely empirically falsifiable claims. While Hill and Boxill maintain that Kant's remarks do not imply that "non-whites lack dignity, in the sense that they lack the capacity to act morally" (2001, p. 455), the highly structural and architectonic nature of all of Kant's work makes their position highly unlikely. Whether or not Eze makes the case, a case can be made that Kant's racism and sexism go far deeper than simply empirical observations. Robert Bernasconi agrees. He finds suspect the strategy of segregating the "basic" aspects of Kant's theory from the "separable" parts and to jettison what is not necessarily connected to the theory (2003, p. 16). When we more fully examine Kant's work on race, it becomes more difficult to deny that what he actually says is grounded in core aspects of his critical theory.

Unlike Hume, whose objectionable remarks appear (but only appear) to be made in passing, Kant writes elaborately on the topic of race.[5] Kant is surely the staunchest defender of individual rights and moral dignity in the philosophical tradition; however, he is also one of the most offensive of all Enlightenment philosophers in his attitudes toward both non-Whites and non-males. Put differently, he makes plenty of objectionable, yet empirically falsifiable, claims. In a particularly odious remark, he states that the difference between races is so "fundamental" that it "appears to be as great in regard to mental capacities as in colour" and that being "quite black from head to foot" is "clear proof that what he said was stupid [*dumm*]" (Kant, 1764/1960, pp. 111, 113). In addition, he explicitly says, without "any prejudice on behalf of the presumptuously greater perfection of one color," that Whites more closely resemble the original stem stock from which all humans descend (Kant, 1775/2013a p. 54). Later he adds that "humanity is at its greatest perfection in the race of whites" (Kant 1804/1997, p. 62). These are anything but mere empirically determined remarks. This perfection—this epistemic, moral, and aesthetic racial superiority—emerges from a unifying concept that goes far beyond what can be empirically discovered. It arises out of a specifically *purposive* unity, a concept that lies at the heart of Kant's critical theory.

The argument for purposiveness in racial hierarchy begins innocently enough with Kant acknowledging the humanness of all humans insofar as the mark of species membership is the ability to produce offspring. Over time, the "special seeds or natural dispositions" all humans originally possessed came to be developed differently in different peoples. The reason for the divergence is innocent enough: we are forced by our climate or environment to adapt to different conditions in order to survive. More specifically, race emerges from living in climates in which conditions such as air and sun alter the "original seeds" humans once shared. This view may sound somewhat simplistic, but it does not sound inherently racist. Continuing on, within the original lineal stem stock of humans are "seeds" which are "*purposively suited for the first general populating <of the earth> ...*" (Kant, 1788/2013b, p. 181).[6] Original humans contain all possible endowments, but nature, in its purposive wisdom, sees fit to adapt these natural dispositions over time (1788/2013b, pp. 178–181). The ostensive reason for this change is to better adapt us to survival, but there is more to it than that: "Any possible change with the potential for replicating itself must instead have already been present in the reproductive power so that chance development appropriate to the circumstances might take place according to a previously determined plan" (Kant, 1777/2000, p. 14). A central task of Kant's anthropology is to discover, through observation, which traits persist over generations, but as Mark Larrimore (2008) notes, "classification of human varieties is never innocent" (p. 342). Kant's "scientific" discussion of

---

5   See Eze, 1997; Mills, 2005; and Kleingeld, 2007.
6   See again Kant, 1777/2000, p. 9.

race quickly transitions into considerations of dissimilarities and deviations that ultimately undermine the personhood and moral dignity of non-Whites—and all because these differences are purposive.[7]

Given the centrality of purposiveness to Kant's critical work, it is important to understand the role played by this concept. In the section on Transcendental Dialectic in his first *Critique*, Kant (1781/1929) makes perhaps his strongest statement of the necessity of purposive unity as a regulative concept:

> The law of reason which requires us to seek for this unity, is a necessary law, since without it we should have no reason at all, and without reason no coherent employment of the understanding, and in the absence of this no sufficient criterion of empirical truth. (p. A651/B679)[8]

Purposive unity saves us from Humean skepticism for it offers an assurance that all the individual pieces of experience will fit together into a coherent whole. It guarantees that nature will indeed conform to our faculties. When we find systematic unity in experience we rejoice "as if it were a lucky chance favoring our design," but it is far from simple luck—it is something that we must assume, else we should have no reason at all (Kant, 1790/2001, p. 184). Furthermore, in the absence of this unity, we lack any assurance of a connection between the realms of nature and freedom. In fact, Kant (1788/2013b) argues that a purposive unity is essential to nature and freedom:

> Nature must consequently also be capable of being regarded in such a way that in the conformity to law of its form it at least harmonizes with the possibility of the ends to be effectuated in it according to the laws of freedom.—There must, therefore, be a ground of the unity of the superpersensible that lies at the basis of nature, with what the concept of freedom contains in a practical way, and although the concept of this ground neither theoretically nor practically attains to a knowledge of it, and so has no peculiar realm of its own, still it renders possible the transition from the mode of thought according to the principles of the one to that according to the principles of the other. (p. 176)

While purposive unity assures that the laws of nature will conform to the systematic unity of the necessary conditions for thought, it also explains how nature effects the ends of freedom and of morality. This is because the purposiveness of material nature is ultimately determined by our moral nature (see Kant, 1790/2001, p. xxvii). Purposiveness speaks to the worth of humans—but not all humans turn out to have equal worth.

---

7   He does much the same with non-males, but Kant's view on women is a subject for a different paper. For more on this see Heikes, 2010, pp. 53–68, and see Woolwine and Dadlez, 2015.

8   Also see Kant, 1781/1929, pp. A815–16/B843–44.

Purposiveness is the glue that holds together Kant's architechtonic, but it also undergirds the Kantian distinction among races. In his 1788 article, "On the Use of Teleological Principles in Philosophy," Kant (1788/2013b) reiterates a point he makes more notably in the first *Critique*: "Where <experience> comes to an end and we have to begin with material forces we have personally invented <that operate> according to unheard of laws incapable of proof, we are already beyond natural science" (p. 189). Albeit stated in slightly different language, Kant (1781/1929) is asking, "what and how much can the understanding and reason know apart from all experience?" (p. xvii). The answer given in the first *Critique* is rather straightforward: experience requires a presumption that there is a knowable, unified order to the world and this presumed unity must be a priori. The point is one oft repeated in Kant: metaphysical explanations must supplement merely physical–mechanical ones. In other words, the way we make up for the deficiencies and limitations of merely naturalistic explanations is through an appeal to ultimate purposes that can be determined by a priori reason. When he makes this point in his writings on race, however, the claim becomes sinister: humans may all be human, but we are subject to metaphysical explanation that ultimately shows some of us to be less than persons.

Because not everything about nature can be explained using natural methods, Kant (1788/2013b) attempts, "in a little essay on the human races to demonstrate a similar warrant, indeed, a need, to proceed from a teleological principle where theory forsakes us" (p. 173). The argument of this "little essay," "On the Different Human Races," is that race must be more than just an accidental feature of mere appearance. Kant is always more concerned with the structure lying beneath appearances than with the appearances themselves. According to him, "it is easily without doubt certain that nothing purposive would ever be found <in nature> by means of purely empirical groping about without a guiding principle that might direct one's search: for *to observe* just means to engage experience methodically" (Kant, 1777/2000, p. 174). Yet the mere fact of variation among human races is not his predominate interest. His predominate interest is why this variation exists. What is the underlying metaphysical cause? And there is a metaphysical cause. After all, determinate principles are a precondition for the possibility of observation. Kant (1777/2000) attempts "to examine the entire human genus as it can be found all over the earth and to specify purposive causes to account for the appearance of deviations in those cases where natural causes are not readily discernable" (p. 14). The study of racial variations, then, has the normative goal of obtaining a greater understanding of "purposiveness [*Zweckmäßigkeit*] and fitness [*Angemessenheit*]" (Kant, 1788/2013b, p. 178). What Kant "discovers" is that variations within the human species are not a matter of chance. In the case of race, once nature has modified a group of people, these traits infallibly reproduce over generations. And the purposive unity of nature assures this will have a metaphysical ground. Empirical generalizations, even ones concerning skin color, are indicative of a transcendental teleology, one that favors Whites over non-Whites.[9]

---

9   Zack (2002) deals more empirically with the issue of skin color in Kant, but even she recognizes that although Kant essentialized skin color, "he knew something weightier than skin color would have to be at work in order to sustain the kinds of differences implied by racial taxonomy" (p. 22).

The significance of Kant's insistence upon underlying purposes is this: where Hume notes not "a single example in which a Negro has shown talents," Kant (1764/1960, p. 111) takes such so-called evidence as something far more than a mere empirical observation. As a result, he is confident in claiming that Africans are incapable of "the feeling of the beauty and worth of human nature" (Kant, 1764/1960, p. 51), not simply accidentally but as a matter of metaphysical necessity. Yet, that Africans lack a feeling for the worth of human nature is no small claim since this very worth is linked to moral dignity. For Kant (1764/1960) "true virtue can be grafted only upon principles ... [that are] the consciousness of a feeling that lives in every human breast. ... [It] is the feeling of the beauty and dignity of human nature" (p. 60). Hill and Boxill tell us that Kant does not deny the humanity of non-Whites, but here Kant himself tells us that a certain feeling lives in every human breast—just not in the breast of Africans. Are we not being told that a significant moral component comes into play as races are separated by the transformation of original possibilities?

Going back to Buffon's rule, Kant never explicitly denies the humanity of non-Whites, but humanity is not what confers dignity. As Eze (1997) explains, our "developmental expression of rational-moral 'character'" is what undergirds our freedom and our dignity and is what distinguishes humans from animals (p. 120). He adds that "if non-white peoples lack 'true' rational character ... and therefore lack 'true' feeling and moral sense, then they do not have 'true' worth, or dignity" (p. 121). This is a conclusion that, upon reflection, is difficult to refute, despite Hill and Boxill's attempts to save Kant from himself. Aside from the issues I have already discussed, the difficulty of separating the so-called essential from non-essential aspects of Kant's writing is that he takes moral character to be a distinctive constitution or peculiar property of the will, and he says that the will "is to make use of gifts of nature" such as talents of mind or qualities of temperament (Kant, 1785/1996, p. 49). What this means, according to Allan Gibbard (1990), is that Kant "insists that morally good character is the place to start" (p. 310n). Felicitas Munzel (1999) adds that "character" may not imply acting according to habituated dispositions that appropriately respond to and influence inclination, but it can be "a moral task definitive of our vocation as members of humanity" (p. 2). Only moral beings possess dignity, and morality requires the capacity to act autonomously according to principles. But when it comes to non-Whites and non-males, Kant often disparages their ability to properly make use of "natural gifts," to have feelings of beauty and dignity, and to act according to principles. As a result, it is, at best, unclear whether non-Whites or women are even capable of developing the right sort of moral character.

The shift in Kant's thinking, and it is a subtle one, is to link moral worth not to humanity but to rationality. Dignity requires principles. What gives one moral standing is being able to act autonomously, meaning solely according to principles one gives oneself. That is, what makes one a person (in the technical sense of that term) deserving of respect is the ability to rationally formulate moral principles, which is a rare quality in non-Whites and non-males. Humans who are perceived to be incapable of principles, as are non-males and non-Whites, hardly appear capable of acquiring moral standing. Thus, even though Kant's moral theory provides a decidedly strong account of equality and dignity, his account does not allow those lacking in the right sort of reason to count as moral agents.

Perhaps surprisingly, women are lacking in reason much more explicitly than non-Whites for they lack the capacity for a "deep understanding" (i.e., one based on principles). Concerning women, Kant (1764/1960) says,

> Deep meditation and a long-sustained reflection are noble but difficult, and do not well befit a person in whom unconstrained charms should show nothing else than a beautiful nature. Laborious learning or painful pondering, even if a woman should greatly succeed in it, destroy the merits that are proper to her sex, and because of her rarity they can make of her an object of cold admiration. (p. 78)

In the end, a woman's philosophy "is not to reason, but to sense" (p. 79). The exclusion is straightforward: the real worth of a human being is found in reasoning according to principles, and women sense rather than reason according to principles. In the case of Blacks, Kant surely views their reasoning as inferior, but the denial of principled reasoning is less direct. As with women, Blacks have, at best, a lesser moral standing. Why? Because to lack the ability to act according to principle is to fall short morally; to fall short morally is to lack in dignity; to lack in dignity is to fail to be someone to whom we can be directly morally obligated or to fail to be someone whom we must treat as an end-in-itself. When one acts according to sensation, the action cannot be truly moral since morality is about acting autonomously according to laws one gives oneself and doing so from the a priori motivation of duty. Because women lack duty, compulsion, obligation, they must, by logical inference, lack moral standing. So, too, with non-Whites. To repeat Eze (1997), "If non-white peoples lack 'true' rational character ... and therefore lack 'true' feeling and moral sense, then they do not have 'true' worth, or dignity" (p. 121). He concludes that for Kant, "European humanity is the humanity *par excellence*" (p. 121). Perhaps more accurately: male European humanity is the standard.

Now, when it comes to the actual moral characterization of non-males and non-Whites, Kant at least allows European women some measure of virtue, albeit only a "beautiful virtue," which is of a different sort than a man's "noble virtue" (1764/1960, p. 81). When it comes to non-Whites, such a charitable interpretation is not as readily available. In the *Observations*, Kant (1764/1960) says, "The mental characters of people are most discernible by whatever in them is moral, on which account we will yet take under consideration their different feelings in respect to the sublime and beautiful ... " (pp. 99–100). Immediately following he adds in an unusual and short lived display of sensitivity, "In each folk the finest part contains praiseworthy character of all kinds" (p. 100).[10] Such a sympathetic observation is undercut, however, when he goes on to add that "The Negroes of Africa have by nature

---

10   In discussing Kant's version of cosmopolitanism, Mendieta (2009) argues that Kant cannot allow that other races have an excellence or that other cultures are capable of contributing to human accomplishments (p. 248).

no feeling that rises above the trifling" (Kant, 1764/1960, p. 110). Women may not be capable of feeling with respect to the sublime, but at least they are capable of feeling with respect to the beautiful. Africans cannot even achieve that. In addition, Kant (1788/2013b) explains that even those non-Whites who migrate to Europe get no benefit from doing so for "those exiled into <northern lands> ... have in their descendants never wanted to serve as a stock useful to settled farmers or craftsmen" (pp. 186–187). Taking this passage, Kleingeld (2007) argues that Kant is linking his physical race theory to a "moral characterization" of races:

> His claim that the different races do not change, once they have differentiated out from the *Stammgattung*, is given a teleological interpretation, *viz* in terms of purposive design; and he connects this claim with the assumption that some races are not just different, but inferior. ... What is important in the present context, however, is that Kant's comment about the "Indians" ("Gypsies") and "Negroes" makes clear that his assumption that the non-white races have inferior mental capacities (including capacities for agency) plays a crucial role. (p. 581)

Kant may say that he has no prejudice when it comes to identifying the greater perfection of one color skin over others, but this claim is somewhat incredulous given the sum of his writings on race. According to Eze (1997), "Kant's position manifests an inarticulate subscription to a system of thought which assumes that what is different, especially that which is 'black,' is bad, evil, inferior, or a moral negation of 'white,' light, and goodness" (p. 117). He adds that Kant uncritically assumes that "the particularity of European existence is *the* empirical as well as ideal model of ... *universal* humanity, so that others are more or less human or civilized ... as they approximate the European ideal" (p. 117). In other words, Kant's racial theory is not simply hierarchical but also contains within it both moral and aesthetic judgments.

Eze is correct in stating that Kant associates beauty with the good. In a completely different, non-racial context, A.C. Genova (1970) considers the way in which the *Critique of Judgment* bridges the gap between the realms of nature and of freedom and asserts that Kant's "analysis is that beauty becomes the symbol of the good, and sublimity of moral dignity" (p. 465). When the connection of beauty with the good is linked to Kant's remarks on race, his prejudice against non-Whites appears even more dramatic. For Kant (1788/2013b), Pacific islanders can be distinguished from Negroes "partly because of their skin color ... partly because of their head and beard hair, which, contrary to the attributes of the Negro, can be combed out to a presentable length" (p. 188). "Beauty," which clearly reflects a classical ideal, can be approximated by the Pacific Islander, who is thereby "more presentable." And this is not the only occasion when Kant makes this sort of claim. Elsewhere he states, "The inhabitant of the temperate parts of the world ... has a more beautiful body, works harder, is more jocular, more controlled in his passions, more intelligent than any other race of people in the world" (Kant, 1804/1997, p. 64). The beauty that Whites achieve far more readily is indicative of superior moral properties. Of course, we should remember that standards of taste are, for Hume as well as for Kant (1790/1987), declared *valid for mankind as such and not just for each person's private feeling* (p. 356). Nevertheless, the standards of aesthetic and moral evaluation that European thinkers such as Kant use, somehow explicitly favor Whites over every other identified racial group. Within Kant's work specifically, the standard is not ancillary or merely empirical but is a central aspect of his architectonic. In other words, the superiority of Whites is part of a purposive nature. This purposiveness is regulative, necessary, and integral to both the theoretical and practical philosophy.

Regardless of what sort of defense one constructs, Kant's own words speak against him again and again and again, although this does not stop even his critics from offering some defense on his behalf. Kleingeld (2007) maintains that Kant's moral principles are formulated in a race neutral manner, even though they are ultimately infected with his racist attitudes (p. 584). But even if we can allow that Kantian morality is itself race neutral, his larger architectonic is not because the purposiveness of nature demands the heritable differences among humans signify a moral difference. And this insight does come out in Kleingeld. She admits that even though Kant's "own *definition* of race as such is formulated merely in terms of heritable differences in physical appearance, he nevertheless connects his understanding of race with a hierarchical account according to which the races *also* vary greatly in their capacities for agency and their powers of intellect" (p. 574). The hesitancy I have with even this admission is that it does not take seriously enough how philosophically insistent Kant is about requiring these heritable differences to mark essential, metaphysical differences. Truly remarkable in all this is how the same philosopher who insists that rational beings have intrinsic worth is the very same philosopher who finds a man's skin color to be indicative of his "stupidity" and who agrees with Hume that "negroes and in general all other species of [non-white] men ... to be naturally inferior to whites." Evidently, "negroes and in general all other species of non-white men," lack some sort of moral standing; otherwise, they could not be "inferior."

Modern Reason and Moral Personhood

The Enlightenment is indeed an Age of Equality, albeit only for a narrowly specified domain of European men capable of the appropriate sort of objectivity within cognition. Whether such narrowness should have been visible to philosophers of that time is an open question. What is no longer an open question is whether such a perspective is truly universal. Toulmin (1972) explains that in "philosophical epistemology, especially since Kant, the existence of some fundamental and unchanging framework of concepts and principles, which forms the universal and compulsory skeleton for all more technical and empirical 'world-pictures,' has widely been taken for granted" (p. 413). Yet to recognize alternative ways of reasoning immediately raises questions of cultural relativism or subjectivism, which is precisely what Hume understood in his remarks on taste. And it is precisely why he was unwilling to allow non-Whites a delicacy of taste. Hume and Kant both understand the dilemma: recognize as legitimate different methods of reasoning (e.g., of Africans, of women, and so on) or to exclude from the domain of reason these different ways of things, these alternative conceptual schemes. Both these philosphers also understand the necessity of compulsory skeletons for cutting of cultural relativism and salvaging the objectivity of knowledge. Their task becomes to restrict rationality—and consequently to restrict personhood—only to those who could properly *achieve* it. The result is that some humans fail to count as persons possessing dignity. But this means that concepts dependent upon these skeletons—for instance, justice, freedom, dignity, autonomy—cannot allow for a diversity within rational methodologies, at least not without different grounds provided by a less narrow and exclusive account of reason.

This is the problem for modern thinkers: both epistemically and morally, the tools of modernism demand privileging of a particular point of view. The conception of a procedural rationality that makes invisible perspective and bias is the ground for Enlightenment moral concepts, and as a result, personhood comes to be "universally conferred" only upon those who are seen as conforming to the prescribed methods and standards for cognition. Difference, subjectivity, emotion, particularity, narrative—these all become difficult to see during the Enlightenment. And this, in turn, has detrimental consequences for those who fall outside the domain of reason. Lynda Lange (1998) points out that Europeans of this time perceived indigenous peoples in the Americas in an entirely self-referential way:

> they literally did not perceive the "other" as "other," but rather as deficient examples of "the same. ... Spanish selfreferentiality [sic] was so strong that even the dazzling evidence of urban development among the Aztecs and Incans that was superior to what the Spanish would have known in Europe failed to suggest to them that these peoples might be best thought of as simply different from them, rather than inferior to them." (p. 135)

As rationality comes to be associated with a particular methodology, people who seem not to conform to this method lack the full status of moral persons.

Thus, while all humans may be human, not all are persons—and the reason goes directly back to the threat of subjectivism created with Descartes' origination of the Copernican turn. Hume and Kant become key players in the subtle and effective decoupling of personhood from humanity, a decoupling which largely goes unnoticed because modern philosophers still presume humans are rational animals. However harsh Kant's notion of morality can sound, he always understands that in our actions toward non-persons (i.e., animals, small children, those suffering dementia) we are still bound by some duties, even if these duties are indirect. Of course, that is the rub. Personhood, with its ties to rationality, lies at the heart of deontological ethics, and moral concepts such as equality, liberty, and justice apply to all persons—but only to persons in the technical sense of that term. Duties cannot be directly owed to those incapable of formulating and acting according to principles. As a result, Kant cannot assure that we are morally required to treat all humans equally. All he can offer is the equal treatment of persons, that is, rational agents who are autonomous lawgivers to themselves and other rational beings. Even in the strictest case of Kantian ethics, universality fails to be truly universal.

For all their talk of objectivity, universality, and equality, Enlightenment philosophers quietly mask a shift toward narrow, uniform, methodological understandings of reason. The domain of the rational comes to be demarcated by a particular, scientifically determined model of investigation which does not and cannot allow for differing methods. Richard Rorty (1979) sees this clearly for he tells us that "Once consciousness and reason are separated out ..., then personhood can be seen for what I claim it is—a matter of decision rather than knowledge, an acceptance of another being into fellowship rather than a recognition of a common essence" (p. 38). Anything that falls outside of the model established by standards of fellowship is dismissed, ignored, and made invisible. "Person," says Mills (2002), "is really a technical term of art, referring to a status whose attainment requires more than simple humanity" (p. 8). By the time of Kant, personhood is clearly not attributed to all humans, only to humans of the right sort, but, of course, what constitutes a "person of the right sort" is never adequately or explicitly articulated. The definition of "person" must be reverse engineered from what we are told about the failures of women and non-Whites to achieve rationality.

When the concept of personhood becomes linked to a modern account of reason, the status of "person" comes to be unattainable for many. The Enlightenment concept of reason makes rationality an achievement of which non-Whites and non-males are largely incapable. But the arguments for this are, within the framework of modernism, much stronger than many contemporary philosophers care to admit. It is much easier for us to dismiss the racism of the mighty dead than it is to acknowledge how deeply held and theoretically defensible are their beliefs. Racism itself may not be essential to modernist thinking, but neither is it accidental. Given the threat of subjectivism, allowing for differing points of view, ways of thinking, or conceptual schemes would undermine the objectivity of any knowledge claims, including those of the new science. In cutting off this threat, philosophers also cut off the capacity for fully rational cognitive activity in anyone who fails to think or perceive in the so-called right way. The Copernican turn in philosophy takes objects to conform to human ways of cognizing, but only if you are a certain type of human.

References

Bernasconi, R. (2001). Who invented the concept of race? Kant's role in the Enlightenment construction of race. In R. Bernasconi (Ed.), *Race* (pp. 11–36). Oxford: Blackwell.

Bernasconi, R. (2002). Kant as an unfamiliar source of racism. In T. Lott and J. Ward (Eds.), *Philosophers on race* (pp. 145–166). Oxford: Oxford University Press.

Bernasconi, R. (2003). Will the real Kant please stand up—The challenge of Enlightenment racism to the study of the history of philosophy. *Radical Philosophy, 117*, 13–22.

Bernstein, R. (1986). The rage against reason. *Philosophy and Literature, 10*, 186–210.

Descartes, R. (1984). *Meditations on first philosophy*. In J. Cottingham, R. Stoothoof, and D. Murdoch [Trans.], *The philosophical writings of Descartes*, Vol. 2 (pp. 17–62). Cambridge: Cambridge University Press. (Originally published 1641)

Eze, E.C. (1997). The color of reason: The idea of "race" in Kant's anthropology. In E. C. Eze (Ed.), *Postcolonial African philosophy: A critical reader* (pp. 103–140). Cambridge, Massachusetts: Black-well Publishing.

Eze, E. C. (2000). Hume, race, and human nature. *Journal of the History of Ideas, 61*, 691–698.

Genova, A. C. (1970). Kant's complex problem of reflective judgment. *The Review of Metaphysics, 23*, 452–480.

Gibbard, A. (1990). *Wise choices, apt feelings: A theory of normative judgment*. Cambridge, Massachu-setts: Harvard University Press.

Gilson, É. (1930). *Études sur le role de la pensée médiévale dans la formation du système cartésien*. Paris: Vrin.

Heikes, D. (2010). *Rationality and feminist philosophy*. New York: Continuum.

Hill, T., and Boxill, B. (2001). Kant and race. In B. Boxill (Ed.), *Race and racism* (pp. 448–471). Oxford: Oxford University Press.

Hume, D. (1758). Of national characters. In *Essays and treatises on several subjects* (pp. 119–129). London: A. Miller.

Hume, D. (1964a). Of national characters. In T. H. Green and T.H. Grose (Eds.), *Essays: Moral, political, and literary*, Volume 1 (pp. 244–257). Darmstadt: Scientia Verlog Aalen. (Originally published 1757)

Hume, D. (1964b). Of the standard of taste. In T.H. Green and T.H. Grose (Eds.), *Essays: Moral, political, and literary*, Volume I (pp. 266–286). Darmstadt: Scientia Verlag Aalen. (Originally published 1757)

Hume, D. (1975). *Enquiries concerning human understanding and concerning the principles of morals* (L.A. Selby-Bigge, Ed.). Oxford: Clarendon Press. (Originally published 1748)

Hume, D. (1978). *A treatise of human nature* (L.A. Selby-Bigge, Ed.). Oxford: Clarendon Press. (Originally published 1738)

Immerwahr, J. (1992). Hume's revised racism. *Journal of the History of Ideas, 53*, 481–486.

Kant, I. (1929). *Critique of pure reason* [N. K. Smith, Trans.]. New York: St. Martin's Press. (Originally published 1781)

Kant, I. (1960). *Observations on the feeling of the beautiful and sublime* [J. Goldthwait, Trans.]. Berkeley: University of California Press. (Originally published 1764)

Kant, I. (1987). *Critique of judgment* [W. Pluhar, Trans.]. Indianapolis: Hackett Publishing. (Originally published 1790)

Kant, I. (1996). *Groundwork of the metaphysics of morals*. In M. Gregor [Trans. and Ed.], *Immanuel Kant: Practical philosophy* (pp. 37–108). Cambridge: Cambridge University Press. (Originally published 1785)

Kant, I. (1997). Physical geography. In E. C. Eze (Ed.), *Race and the Enlightenment: A reader* (pp. 62–64). Oxford: Blackwell. (Originally published 1804)

Kant, I. (2000). Of the different human races. In R. Bernasconi and T. Lott (Eds.), *The idea of race* (pp. 8–22). Indianapolis: Hackett Publishing. (Originally published 1777)

Kant, I. (2001). *Critique of the power of judgment* [P. Guyer and E. Matthews, Trans.]. Cambridge: Cambridge University Press. (Originally published 1790)

Kant, I. (2013a). Of the different human races. In J. Mikkelsen [Trans. and Ed.], *Kant and the concept of race* (pp. 41–54). Albany: SUNY Press. (Originally published 1775)

Kant, I. (2013b). On the use of teleological principles in philosophy. In J. Mikkelsen [Trans. and Ed.], *Kant and the concept of race* (pp. 169–194). Albany: SUNY Press. (Originally published 1788)

Kleingeld, P. (2007). Kant's second thoughts on race. *The Philosophical Quarterly, 57,* 573–592.

Lange, L. (1998). Burnt offerings to rationality: A feminist reading of the construction of indigenous peoples in Enrique Dussel's theory of modernity. *Hypatia, 13,* 132–145.

Larrimore, M. (2008). Antinomies of race: Diversity and destiny in Kant. *Patterns of Prejudice, 42,* 341–363.

Lind, M. (1994). Indians, savages, peasants, and women. In B. A. Bar-On (Ed.), *Modern engenderings* (pp. 51–67). Albany: SUNY Press.

Lloyd, G. (1984). *The man of reason.* Minneapolis: University of Minnesota Press.

Louden, R. (2000). *Kant's impure ethics.* Oxford: Oxford University Press.

Mendieta, E. (2009). From imperial to dialogical cosmopolitanism. *Ethics and Global Politics, 2,* 241–258.

Mills, C. (2002, October). Kant's *Untermenschen.* Paper presented at the Thirty-sixth Annual University of North Carolina at Chapel Hill Colloquium in Philosophy (pp. 1–34). University of North Carolina: Chapel Hill, North Carolina.

Mills, C. (2005). Kant's *Untermenschen.* In A. Valls (Ed.), *Race and racism in modern philosophy* (pp. 169–193). Ithaca, New York: Cornell University Press.

Munzel, G. F. (1999). *Kant's conception of moral character: The "critical" link of morality, anthropology, and reflective judgment.* Chicago: University of Chicago Press.

Reiss, T. (2005). Descartes's silences on slavery and race. In A. Valls (Ed.), *Race and racism in modern philosophy* (pp. 16–42). Ithaca, New York: Cornell University Press.

Rorty, R. (1979). *Philosophy and the mirror of nature.* Princeton: Princeton University Press.

Taylor, C. (1989). *Source of the self: The making of the modern identity.* Cambridge, Massachusetts: Harvard University Press.

Toulmin, S. (1972). *Human understanding: The collective use and evolution of concepts.* Princeton: Princeton University Press.

Toulmin, S. (2001). *Return to reason.* Cambridge, Massachusetts: Harvard University Press. Wittgenstein, L. (1958). *Philosophical investigations* [G.E.M. Anscombe, Trans.]. New York: Macmillan Publishing.

Woolwine, S., and Dadlez, E. M. (2015). Gender and moral virtue. *Southwest Philosophy Review, 31,* 109–118.

Zack, N. (2002). *Philosophy of science and race.* New York: Routledge.

CHAPTER FIVE

The Utilitarian Reform Movement

Following the Age of Reason, the ideas of the Enlightenment ushered in a social movement, where scholars and political reformers constituting a variety of academic disciplines questioned the efficacy of torture as a true deterrence to crime.[1][2] These new ideas are based on Enlightenment principles, which emphasized *rationalism* and *humanitarianism* in contrast to the turmoil and disorder created by harsh and barbaric punishments.

This shift in philosophical development emerged in the work of scholars associated with the Classical School, which set out to study the relationship of citizens to the state's legal structure. The main emphasis here was on reforming the state's antiquated, ineffective, and cruel systems of administering crime and punishment. The result of which gave rise to an increase in the legitimacy of the state and its rule of law, influenced in part by the related logic of two new doctrines—*the social contract* and the notion of *free will*. Within this doctrine, reason and experience, rather than faith and superstition, replaced the excesses and corruption used to give legitimacy to the spectacle of punishment and gave rise to new definitions of crime along with the modern system of punishment.

As suggested in chapter four, the method in which this shift takes place is questionable as the ideas put forth by utilitarian philosophers, as powerful as they are, also give rise to several issues pertaining to the potential for these ideas to benefit everyone in society.

---

1   J. Bentham, *An Introduction to the Principles of Morals and Legislation* (New York: Hafner Publishing Company, 1948).

2   C. Beccaria, *On Crimes and Punishment* (Indianapolis. IN: Hackett Publishing Company, 1986).

Deterrence

By Thom Brooks

Introduction

Deterrence has traditionally been understood as the primary alternative to retributivism. Both have been at loggerheads for literally centuries. It is easy to see why. Retributivists give special attention to a criminal's desert for a past injustice: it is primarily a backward-looking theory of punishment. Deterrence is primarily a forward-looking theory of punishment: deterrence proponents give special attention to deterring future criminality. Therefore, deterrence offers us a very different focus and understanding of the purpose of punishment. This chapter will clarify the leading theories of deterrence to determine their promise and potential problems.

What is deterrence?

Deterrence theories of punishment claim that the general justification of punishment is deterrence. Deterrence proponents argue that a key feature of punishment should be its ability to make crime less frequent, if not end. Punishment that merely harmed criminals and lacked any clear beneficial effects may even be seen as cruel. Instead, punishment may be justified on account of the good consequences that it makes possible. These may include deterrence of criminality.

Deterrence proponents have traditionally argued that people are deterred by the threat of punishment. Many classic defenders of deterrence have been utilitarians. Generally speaking, utilitarians argue that we seek pleasure and avoid pain. The threat of punishment is a pain to be avoided. Punishment deters because we want to avoid the pains of punishment. For example, David Hume argues:

'Tis indeed certain, that as all human laws are founded on rewards and punishments, 'tis suppos'd as a fundamental principle, that these motives have an influence on the mind, and both produce the good and prevent the evil actions.[1]

Utilitarians often assume that individuals are naturally selfish. We are influenced by external influences, not least social influences including the threat of punishment. The idea is that punishment may have a deterrent effect upon us because we are naturally selfish and we would normally choose to avoid the pain of punishment. We choose to be law abiding after making a rational choice calculus: the burdens of potential punishment outweigh the benefits from crime.

Deterrent punishment helps realize an important good. The political community has enacted a criminal law. If the criminal law is just, then it is right that we encourage others to act in accordance with it and avoid criminality. Punishment can play a positive role in protecting the security of us all in deterring potential criminals.[2] This idea has its roots in Plato's writings:

> It is appropriate for everyone who is subject to punishment rightly inflicted by another either to become better and profit from it, or else be made an example to others, so that when they see him suffering whatever it is he suffers, they may be afraid and become better.[3]

This defence of deterrence is shared by a great many today. For example, Ted Honderich argues that punishment 'may be acceptable simply because it deters'.[4] Acceptance of deterrence may lie in the beneficial consequences it might produce.

Deterrent punishments can take several forms, such as general or specific deterrence. General deterrence is often understood as the public threat of punishment and specific deterrence as the individual's experience of punishment. An alternative view of this distinction is between *macro-deterrence* (general deterrence) and *microdeterrence* (specific deterrence).[5] Macrodeterrence concerns society in general. It asks how we might best construct deterrent punishments for society at large. This analysis focuses on the crime and steps that could be taken to deter persons from crime. Macrodeterrence judges success on the basis of how well punishment acts as a general deterrence.

Microdeterrence focuses on the criminal. It asks how we might deter an individual from crime. This view finds expression in a brief essay by John Stuart Mill: 'You do not punish one person in order that another may be deterred. The other is deterred, not by the punishment of the first, but by the expectation of being punished himself'.[6] Microdeterrence judges success on the basis of how well punishment acts as a specific deterrent for particular individuals.

Macrodeterrence and microdeterrence offer different perspectives on how we might approach the construction of deterrent punishments. However, these different perspectives need not translate into conflicting viewpoints. Instead, the two should be understood as working together in approaching the same project from different angles. Furthermore, they may overlap so that general and specific deterrence may be achieved together.

The way we construct deterrent punishments may take several forms, such as fear, incapacitation, and reform. The first form is the traditional understanding of deterrence. Deterrent punishments are public threats: individuals are deterred from criminality by the fear of threatened punishment if they engage in criminality. This fear of threatened pain is what motivates individuals to remain law abiding. If the public is sufficiently afraid of threatened punishment, then the public will not offend.

The second form of constructing deterrent punishments is incapacitation. This view, first argued for by William Paley, has a long history as well.[7] The incapacitation approach argues that the criminal can be said to be deterred from criminality by virtue of his becoming imprisoned. For example, the idea is that all potential criminals have something in common: they are not imprisoned. Whatever prison's deterrent effects upon the general public, prison has an undeniable deterrent effect on imprisoned criminals: they cannot commit crimes while imprisoned. The incapacitation approach does suffer from at least two serious problems. The first is that it may compel us to imprison everyone. If our desired goal is to deter as much crime as we can and no imprisoned person can commit crime, then we can deter more crime by imprisoning more people. Moreover, we can deter all crime when we imprison (virtually) everyone.[8]

This position is highly objectionable because incapacitation is not reducible to punishment, nor vice versa.[9] Recall that we should understand punishment as a response to crime: punishment must be of a person for breaking the law. The first problem for incapacitation is that it might justify the imprisonment of innocent persons in order to prevent future crime. The second problem is that criminality does not stop at the prison gate: criminals can and do (and perhaps always have) committed crimes within prisons. Such crimes include assaults and abuse of controlled substances. Not only might incapacitation insufficiently guard against objectionable implications, but it rests on a mistake about *the geography of crime*, namely, that crimes are not confined to public places or private homes, but they may take place in prisons as well. Criminality is possible both within and outside prisons. A deterrent theory of punishment must recognize this fact about the geography of crime, a feature too often overlooked and unnoticed.[10]

A final form that deterrence might take is reform. Future criminality might be deterred because criminals have become reformed. I will highlight this further understanding of deterrence as reform in the next chapter.

Deterrence and crime reduction

Deterrence is about crime reduction, but not all crime reduction is evidence of deterrence. This is because deterrence is one approach amongst many to reduce crime. One method of crime reduction may be the rehabilitation of offenders. Rehabilitated offenders are reformed and refrain from future criminality, which assists crime reduction efforts. But this is not deterrence. Deterrence theories aim to reduce crime by deterring potential criminal offenders. They are deterred where they choose against crime because they desire to avoid punishment. Crime reduction may be a result of deterrence, but deterrence is not the only method for achieving crime reduction. It is important to recognize that deterrence is one of many penal strategies for achieving crime reduction because it highlights that there may be significant differences in how we approach crime reduction. So if there was evidence that crime has been reduced over a period of time, then this is not necessarily evidence that crime reduction was a result of deterrence. Deterrence may always aim at crime reduction, but not all crime reduction is a result of deterrence.

Deterrence and desert

The problem most commonly associated with deterrence is the problem of punishing the innocent: deterrence should be rejected because it could justify the punishment of innocent persons. This problem is frequently used by retributivists to argue that retribution should be preferred over deterrence because only retribution takes criminal desert seriously. Let me explain this debate further.

Retributivists argue–in what we might call *the standard view*–that punishment should be distributed only where it is deserved. Retribution is a deontological theory in that punishment is not justified by its effects, but desert. Deterrence is instead a consequentialist theory whereby punishment is justified where it has specific consequences, such as a deterrent effect. This difference gives rise to a disagreement about how we justify the punishment of criminals. One criticism of deterrence is that, as Hegel argues, 'to justify punishment in this way is like raising one's stick at a dog; it means treating a human being like a dog instead of respecting his honour and freedom'.[11] For critics like Hegel, deterrence fails to honour people in failing to offer them reasons for good citizenship and avoidance of criminality.

We might respond that this criticism misses its target. Deterrence does offer reasons to citizens to refrain from criminality: if citizens engage in crime, the state threatens to impose punishment. Nor need this be problematic where citizens believe. Deterrence proponents might also claim that retributivists are no better. Both declare that criminals will be punished in advance. One important difference is that deterrence proponents believe that the threat of punishment may have a deterrent effect. We should expect potential criminals to reconsider participating in criminal activity to avoid the possibility of punishment. Retributivists may accept a similar analysis. While retributivists might argue that the severity of punishment is not set with a view of any future deterrent effect, retributivists may still claim that the *wrongness* of a crime should weigh on the conscience of potential criminals and contribute to their reconsidering any criminal activity. Deterrence proponents are mistaken to believe that the only deterrent effect to be found is in the threat of punishment and not the gravity of a crime's wrongfulness.

Deterrence proponents might reply that its aim is to reduce criminal activity by rendering it sufficiently unattractive. One relevant factor will be the threat of punishment, but a second factor will be the criminal act itself. Citizens may find criminal activity unattractive because they wish to avoid the possibility of punishment, but also because they agree with the laws governing their relations. Cesare Beccaria says:

> What are the true and most effective laws? They are those pacts and conventions that everyone would observe and propose while the voice of private interest, which one always hears, is silent or in agreement with the voice of the public interest.[12]

The result is that perhaps deterrence does aim to manipulate the incentive structure for citizens in order to reduce crime. No plausible theory of punishment claims that criminal activity is desirable or good. If punishment could be used to reduce crime by winning the agreement of citizens and deterring potential criminals, then these should be compelling arguments in its favour.

This raises a deeper concern often raised by retributivists against deterrence. Let us accept that the reduction of crime is desirable or even good. The traditional argument against deterrence is that it might permit the punishment, or even execution, of the innocent. The objection is as follows. Deterrence proponents believe that punishment is justified, at least in part, by its deterrent effects. If these effects were obtained by punishing the innocent, then punishment would be justified because it would have a deterrent effect. If deterring potential criminals is what matters, then this does not rule out our only punishing criminals. The objection is that we should never punish the innocent for crimes they did not commit. Deterrence is an objectionable penal aim because it might justify punishing innocent people.

This concern is not lost on leading proponents of deterrence. In fact, it is difficult to find any major figure who accepts the possibility of punishing the innocent under any circumstances: the worry that deterrence approaches would lead to the punishment of the innocent is largely a criticism about deterrence approaches and not a policy that deterrence proponents espouse. All place clear limits on how deterrence should be pursued. Examples abound. Plato argues that the criminal should receive 'due punishment for the wrongdoing he commits'.[13] Fichte similarly claims that 'in a well-governed state, no innocent person should ever be punished'.[14] Bentham likewise rejects the punishment of the innocent.[15] Beccaria is a possible exception. He argues it is necessary to execute an innocent person if his death was 'the *only* real way of restraining others from committing crimes'.[16] However, this is not much of a concession to critics of deterrence approaches if we believed that such cases might be so rare as to be virtually non-existent.

We might then argue that deterrence theories are at best impure. Each would appear to accept some retributivist core that punishment must first be deserved before it can be punished and never imposed on the innocent. The difference would then appear to be that deterrence theories link the severity of punishment with expected future effects rather than the gravity of a crime's wrongfulness. If true, then these deterrent theories might be understood as *negative retributivist* theories of punishment. Negative retributivists argue that desert is necessary, but not sufficient for punishment. Punishment is distributed where other non-desert factors obtain.[17]

Deterrence proponents need not accept that their 'deterrence' theories are in fact a species of retributivism. Another compelling perspective is the following.[18] The state issues threats: if citizens perform a crime, then they will be punished for it. The state then punishes those persons who have failed to heed such threats.[19] So the state only punishes those persons who have failed to obey its threats and, thus, the state aims to deter without punishing the innocent. The state punishes to make good on its original threat to punish crimes: these threats would lack substance if the state failed to make good on its promise. Only those who break the law are subject to punishment: 'The threat is addressed to each individually, and each is punished because he, individually, chose to ignore the threat; the others, and their potential behaviour, are irrelevant'.[20] This understanding of deterrence punishes only the guilty, but not on grounds of desert. Deterrence theories can avoid justifying the punishment of innocent people.

One final consideration is criminals who resist deterrence: *the problem of the undeterrable*. Retributivists, on the standard view, would punish the undeterrable because punishment is deserved. Future consequences are irrelevant. This is untrue for deterrence, where future consequences take centre stage. The undeterrable are not a major problem for theories of macrodeterrence: while some may not be deterred, punishment may be justified where it leads to reductions in crime for the general population. The situation is different with the microdeterrence of an individual offender. If a person is genuinely resistant to changing his behaviour in response to any deterrent efforts, then specific deterrence would fail in like cases. The problem of undeterrable criminals raises an important difficulty for microdeterrence accounts. If certain persons cannot be deterred, then punishment is not justified because it will not have any deterrent effect on them. Punishment might only be justified on grounds of macro-deterrence were it possible to have a deterrent effect on others, or the deterrable.

Deterrence and difference

Deterrence theories of punishment aim to deter potential criminals from criminality. Our focus is on constructing a suitable deterrent for members of a political community. This is a consequentialist approach: the deterrent proponent aspires to secure a particular consequence, namely, reduced criminality. The target is the political community and this raises several potential problems concerning *the problem of difference*.

The first potential problem is that we cannot hope to find any single punishment that might have the same deterrent effect for everyone everywhere. A penal threat may have a greater effect upon you than me. There are several reasons why this is the case. One reason is that deterrence is specific to local social conditions: what works as a deterrent in one political community may lack a similar effect in other communities. So a punishment may have a different deterrent effect or none at all in different political communities. Furthermore, this problem may not merely exist between political communities, but it may also exist within political communities. Call this *the problem of domestic difference*. Some social groups within the same political community may respond differently to the same deterrent threats. A second reason why deterrent punishments may differ between communities is that deterrence is linked with particular crimes and these crimes may differ from one community to the next. Therefore, deterrent punishments for crimes may not hold universally where there is disagreement between different political communities on what is included within the criminal law. This is only a problem for a global theory of deterrent punishment: deterrence may only be a genuine possibility within a political community.

The second potential problem is that what may deter today may not deter tomorrow. This is *the problem of time and changing effects*. Whatever knowledge we have of deterrent effects is always knowledge of the past: the owl of Minerva takes flight at dusk.[21] The fact that some were deterred last year or even yesterday may be no guarantee that we can expect a similar number to be deterred today or next month. The deterrent power of punishment constantly changes over time in response to social conditions. Therefore, the deterrent potential of any punishment is always in flux and subject to constant change. One problem is that this potential may only be known after the fact; the deterrent potential of present punishments is always a matter of guesswork to some degree. We can never say that any one punishment is always best to maximize the deterrence of potential criminals for any crime. This is because we can only guess at likely future effects and these effects are subject to constant revision.

The use of the same punishment may have different deterrent effects in different communities and be subject to constant change over time. These issues highlight the deep complexity associated with deterrence and the challenges for presenting global theories of deterrence. These concerns do not entail that we cannot know whether there are deterrent effects from the threat of punishment, but rather that such knowledge is complex and difficult to acquire.

The data on deterrence

Deterrence proponents offer a theory of punishment linked to empirical claims. They argue not only *that* punishment should be designed to bring about deterrence, but that punishment *has* a deterrent effect. Deterrence is an evidence-based approach to criminal justice. So what do the data reveal?

The big problem for deterrence theories is that punishment does not appear to have much, if any, confirmed deterrent effect.[22] There is much disagreement about the best measures of deterrence and indications of success or failure, but several conclusions have become established in recent years concerning criminals who have been imprisoned. Many reoffend upon release. For example, most criminals who are imprisoned receive sentences of 12 months or less. Approximately 60 per cent will reoffend and often within weeks of release.[23] One study of American prisoners released since 1994 found that two-thirds were arrested for a serious misdemeanour or felony within three years, and half of these were reconvicted for new crimes. The study concluded that 'no evidence was found that spending more time in prison raises the recidivism rate'.[24]

These results have been confirmed in several international studies which have also cast doubt on whether there is any link between time served and reoffending.[25] For example, the British Prime Minister's Strategy Unit has concluded that 'there is no convincing evidence that further increases in the use of custody would significantly reduce crime'.[26] Increasing prison sentences may be popular with the public, but the evidence is that such policies place greater pressures on taxpayers for no substantive improvements upon recidivism rates. The public may often support 'tough on crime' policies whereby penal tariffs rise ever higher, but such support lacks sufficient evidence that it works. The main consequence is much higher costs without improvements in crime reduction.[27]

Perhaps surprisingly, even threats of severe punishment have not been conclusively shown to possess a deterrent effect, and decreased offending has not been strongly linked with increasing the severity of punishments.[28] One example is California's so-called 'Three Strikes and You're Out' law. This motto refers to baseball where a batter is 'out' after receiving three strikes. Anyone convicted of a third strike-eligible crime faces a minimum 25 year imprisonment. This is irrespective of the seriousness of the crimes committed. It might be expected that –even if an unreasonable policy–such a high penal tariff would have some clear deterrent effect, but the findings are surprising. The deterrent effect appears small and is estimated at about 2 per cent or less.[29] The policy has led to an explosion in the prison population and contributed to the further problem of prison overcrowding.[30] Thus, even fairly severe threats of punishment have not conclusively demonstrated a clear deterrent effect, but these penal experiments have contributed to ever higher costs for little, if any, public benefit.

A common criticism is that imprisoning criminals makes them better criminals. For example, criminals may be thought to become transformed into *criminal labourers* through imprisonment: the 'professional' thief, for example. Some claim that imprisonment may even be *criminogenic* because it may contribute to more crime and not less.[31] The contributing problems are that imprisonment often leads to offenders 'losing their jobs, their homes and their families'.[32] While we would expect those with the longest prison sentences to be most likely to reoffend, this is not supported by most evidence. Most released prisoners will reoffend, but these persons often serve sentences of less than one year. Recidivism rates drop for all criminals serving more than one year in prison: the longer a criminal is imprisoned, the less likely he is to reoffend upon release. This may have more to do with the crimes associated with longer sentences and the greater professional support these inmates can expect to receive, as well as the age of offenders upon release. It is worth noting that criminals given suspended sentences and community sentences reoffend less often than criminals imprisoned for under a year.[33] If our aim is to reduce crime rates, then the use of prison may be counterproductive. This may be counterintuitive: we might expect the burdens of imprisonment to deter better than community service, but deterrence proponents must support policies that best meet their preferred penal goals. If alternatives to prison work best, then these alternatives should be endorsed.

None of this need deny that crime rates have ever fallen. Instead, the issue is that where we find lower crime rates there are often non-deterrence factors to account for such changes.[34] For example, there is evidence that crime rates may be linked to the number of males aged between 15 and 24 years: the greater the number of males, the higher the expected crime rates.[35] There is also evidence that increased economic insecurity leads to both rising crime rates and a greater public fear of crime. It has been claimed that 'individuals who are worried about their economic stability may be more likely to fear criminals, who could further threaten their increasingly tenuous economic positions'.[36] Furthermore, Steven Levitt and Stephen Dubner argue:

> It is true that a stronger job market may make certain crimes relatively less attractive. But that is only the case for crimes with a direct financial motivation— burglary, robbery, and auto theft—as opposed to violent crimes like homicide, assault, and rape. Moreover, studies have shown that an unemployment decline of 1 percentage point accounts for a 1 percent drop in nonviolent crime.[37]

One clear result is that a strong job creation strategy ensuring low unemployment rates is not only good economics, but a good criminal justice policy leading to lower crime rates and lower public fear of crime.

Not all studies have failed to find substantive deterrent effects. However, these studies often conclude that these effects are modest at best. For example, the results often reveal that the effects of deterrence upon crime rates is at most between about a 2 to 5 per cent decrease in crime following a 10 per cent increase in the prison population.[38] If this is true, then prison may have an identifiable deterrent effect. However, the effects do not appear large and come at a significant cost to taxpayers.

Judging success

Discussions about the data on deterrence inevitably raise important questions about what constitutes 'success' for any deterrence theory of punishment. We have at least three options:

1. Deterrent theories of punishment aim for any deterrent effect.
2. Deterrent theories of punishment aim for any substantial effect.
3. Deterrent theories of punishment aim for a complete effect.

The first option is too weak and the third is too strong. The first option claims that the aims of deterrent punishment are satisfied where *any* deterrent effect may be identified. This is too weak.

Suppose we have two different punishments. The difference between them is that one punishment is known to deter a small handful and the other punishment lacks any known effect. The deterrence proponent would seem compelled to prefer a punishment with *any* deterrent effect over an alternative that *lacked* any effect. But would this remain true if a very small effect were only made possible by way of inflicting great pain? The deterrence proponent is not a retributivist: she does not link a punishment's severity with what is deserved, but rather what has a deterrent effect. But this is not quite right. Deterrence proponents argue that deterrence is a central justification of punishment. Therefore, deterrence should not have a mere negligible presence, but it should play a clearer role in punishing. If deterrence is the justification of punishment, then it must also play some clear –and not merely tangential–role. Deterrence is *reductivist*: its goal is the reduction of crime. A deterrent approach that can promise no more than little, if any, reduction in crime is not much worth its name.

The third option is too strong. While we may hope that a great many will be deterred from criminality, we cannot expect our hope will be realized. There is a little appreciated fact about crime that I call *the fact of crime in society*. It is a fact that any society will have crime if it has a criminal law. This fact is not always recognized by proponents of deterrence. For example, Johann Gottlieb Fichte argues:

> Punishment is not an absolute end ... Punishment is a means for achieving the state's end, which is public security; and its only purpose is to prevent offenses by threatening to punish them. The end of penal law is to render itself unnecessary. The threat of punishment aims to ... never be necessary.[39]

However noble its aim of seeing punishment wither on the vine one day, it is pure fantasy to believe that crime will ever disappear so long as we are governed by the rule of law.[40] Laws are not made to be broken, but are broken inevitably nonetheless by carelessness as well as design. There is little point in creating *a utopia of crimelessness*, but much promise in aspiring to restrict the fact of crime in society as best as is possible. Penal theorists may disagree on the ultimate justification of punishment, but they should all prefer less crime and lower recidivism.

The fact that crime is ever present does not mean we should accept crime however it is found. Deterrence proponents should not be satisfied with punishments with negligible deterrent effects nor aspire to full or 'perfect' deterrence. Instead, deterrence proponents defend deterrence as a substantial consequence of justified punishment. This leads us to endorse the second option. A successful deterrence theory is one that can demonstrate a substantial deterrent effect. So what would such an effect look like? It is difficult to pinpoint any specific figure, but surely 2–5 per cent falls far below any plausible indication of a 'substantial deterrent effect'. Nevertheless, our knowledge about the deterrence effects, if any, for any crime is 'exceedingly thin'.[41]

Deterrence, intuitions, and knowledge limits

Many deterrence proponents naturally assume that punishment has a deterrent effect notwithstanding contrary findings by existing studies. For example, James Q. Wilson says:

> People are governed in their daily lives by rewards and penalties of every sort
> ... To assert that 'deterrence doesn't work' is tantamount to either denying the
> plainest facts of everyday life or claiming that would-be criminals are utterly
> different from the rest of us.[42]

It is assumed that we, the community, know the laws that govern us. Ignorance of the law is no defence from future punishment.[43] It is also assumed that the burdens of punishment should outweigh expected benefits from possible criminal activity. Where this obtains, individuals engaged in a cost-benefit analysis will rationally choose to avoid crime. It would be irrational to commit a crime where the costs outweigh expected benefits. The deterrent effect of punishment is intuitively true. Evidence to the contrary is opposed to our most basic intuitions about criminal justice. Or so deterrence proponents may argue.

There are many reasons why this intuitive justification of deterrence is problematic. First, there is little evidence to suggest that criminals weigh costs and benefits in the way many deterrence models assume.[44] Criminals appear to rely on little more than guesswork about their possible likelihood of arrest and conviction.[45] But this is not all. In short, deterrence may assume too much. Michael Davis says: '"Deterrent" does not have any relation to actual or probable crime without assumptions about the rationality of criminals, the efficiency of police, the likelihood that the penalty will not itself make the crime glamorous, and so on'.[46] How many people would have stolen a car last week, if the laws had been different? How many people were deterred from any crime because of any specific legislation? If punishment deters criminals, then it might be possible to have some idea about how to answer these questions. Yet, such answers remain elusive.[47]

For example, deterrence presupposes knowledge about crimes, possible sanctions, the likelihood of arrest and conviction. There are many reasons to believe these articles of faith do not cohere with reality. First, only a few citizens will have knowledge about even a majority of crimes and perhaps no one knows them all. If citizens are to conduct a rational choice assessment weighing the costs and burdens of criminal activity, then they must have satisfactory knowledge about what counts as criminal activity. Most lack this knowledge. Punishment fails to serve its deterrent function where citizens do not know what is criminalized. Perhaps punishment might have a more limited deterrent function on a crime-by-crime basis. For example, many may be unaware about the full range of property crimes, but many will know that murder is criminalized. Punishment may only have a deterrent function for those crimes that citizens have sufficiently satisfactory knowledge about. The problem is that citizens lack such knowledge about most crimes.[48] Citizens cannot be deterred from crimes that they are unaware of.

Second, citizens lack knowledge about most crimes *and* they lack knowledge about possible sanctions for most crimes. This is perhaps a more serious problem than the first. While citizens may not know all crimes, they might still identify a plentiful core acknowledging arson, burglary, murder, and theft amongst others. However, their knowledge of what possible sanctions would relate from a conviction for any of these crimes is even worse. I have lectured on criminal law and punishment in several countries and before many distinguished audiences: not once has anyone been able to correctly identify the tariff for arson for any jurisdiction.[49] Can you? This is despite the fact that all recognize arson as a serious crime. If academics, lawyers, and policymakers are unsure about how arson might be punished, then there is reason to believe the lay public would perform no better. The problem is that punishment cannot have a deterrent effect where citizens do not know how their crimes might be punished.

Third, suppose we possess satisfactory knowledge about crimes and their possible punishments. We would still require satisfactory knowledge *in addition to this* about the likelihood of our arrest and conviction. The facts are startling: the majority of crimes are unsolved. Murders have the highest detection rates, but these are often no better than about 80 per cent. Do you know the likelihood of your being arrested or convicted for benefit fraud or illegal trading? Or for any crime? Punishment cannot have a deterrent effect where citizens do not know crimes, how their crimes might be punished, the likelihood of arrest for crimes, nor the likelihood of punishment.

There is a further issue concerning imprisonment. Many prisoners remain imprisoned beyond their official release date. There are an estimated 2,500 prisoners in the UK alone in this position. The justification is that they remain imprisoned because they have been found to remain a threat to the general public.[50] It is unclear whether or not this improves future deterrence for crimes that may involve imprisonment. On the one hand, this may be relatively unknown by persons potentially affected and so not enter into risk calculations about engaging in crime. On the other hand, the possibility that a prison sentence represents a minimal term and may be for life could have a potential deterrent effect if it is communicated effectively to persons potentially affected. It is perhaps shocking how little effort governments expend on informing the public about possible criminal sanctions. Whatever the reality of deterrence, there is a clear need for improved communication between governments and their citizens to better educate them about criminal punishment.

Many deterrence proponents claim that it is at least intuitively true that punishment has a deterrent effect. We have seen that few studies have shown any substantial deterrent effect. Furthermore, there is little reason to believe that citizens could be deterred by punishment for most crimes. This is because citizens lack sufficient relevant knowledge necessary for deterrence to obtain. Citizens do not know most crimes, know less about possible punishments for crimes, and know little, if anything, about the likelihood for arrest and conviction. It is clear that there is a need for greater communication about such matters with the general public to improve their knowledge in these areas. The intuitive evidence for deterrence seems limited to persons with perfect information about crimes, punishments, and other factors that no one has in fact. The conclusion to be drawn is not that deterrence is impossible, but rather that it is substantially more difficult to determine and perceive than we may initially recognize. Nevertheless, there remains something attractive about a society where crime reduction works, all things considered. But whether crime reduction should be achieved through deterrence or an alternative approach is another consideration.

Should government deter?

Consider the proper role of government. Should government deter? This concern may take many forms, such as whether governments should endorse some alternative justification of punishment. I do not want to address such matters here, but instead focus on a very specific concern that is often overlooked in discussions about deterrence. Surprisingly, this concern arises within the writings of John Stuart Mill, an advocate of deterrence. He offers the following worry: 'the preventive function of government, however, is far more liable to be abused'.[51] Perhaps governments should deter. The problem is this power is most likely to become abused.

Let me address this worry in the following way. It may be argued that a central task of any government is enforcing its laws. The government will have a clear interest in addressing criminality. Deterrence is one way of addressing criminality: governments should address criminality by deterring it, leading to crime reduction. One classic objection to deterrence is that governments fail to treat their citizens with the dignity that they deserve. Deterrence measures may lead governments to treating their citizens as a means to some goal rather than an end in their own right.

We might reply that we use people as a means all the time.[52] For instance, we use taxi drivers to take us to our destinations or we use waitresses to serve us our meals and so on. The question is not whether we use others, but rather whether we use others in a justifiable way.[53] There is a difference between paying another for a consensual service and demanding someone is imprisoned. Nevertheless, this difference does not reflect a problem with the respect of dignity for the imprisoned. Respect can be secured in our ensuring a person is only imprisoned for criminality: no person need be treated merely as a means by deterrence theories of punishment. Thus, deterrence can address people as moral agents and deterrence need not be understood as little better than addressing people like animals.[54]

Mill's worry is not that deterrence denies dignity to others, but that deterrence is more liable to abuse by governments than alternative theories of punishment. Recall that there is a link between the justification of law and the justification of punishment: *there can be no justified punishment for an unjustified law*.[55] If laws are justified, then it becomes possible to justify punishment for criminality. One problem is that governments may use greater threats to deter persons from violating unjustified laws. This might make a bad situation much worse.

Let me explain this point further. Suppose, following Cesare Beccaria, that deterrent punishments should aim to 'make the strongest and most lasting impression on the minds of men, and inflict the least torment on the body of the criminal'.[56] If our aim is to make the biggest impression with the least damage to the criminal, then perhaps our use of punishment should aspire to mislead the public into believing punishments are much worse than they are. This brings us to a famous illustration by Jeremy Bentham: 'If hanging a man *in effigy* would produce the same salutary impression of terror upon the minds of people, it would be a folly or cruelty ever to hang a man *in person*'.[57] The *effect* from punishment is of crucial significance for deterrence proponents. If this effect might be gained without harming anyone through punishment, then such an alternative may prove tempting. Deterrence does not aim to be cruel, but to reduce crime, and such an alternative might fulfil this ambition.

Beccaria argues that 'it is better to prevent crimes than to punish them'.[58] If this is true, then the state may be tempted to broadcast mock punishment in attempts to mislead the public. But this need not be the only result. Instead, governments might attempt to reduce crime without resorting to misleading the public. One reason would be concerns about the likely impact of the public gaining knowledge about any deceit. Mock executions may prove effective where the public are deceived, but backfire catastrophically where the public learn the truth about such matters. Many governments have moved to a greater emphasis on strict liability with the easier convictions this approach brings, albeit for often relatively minor punishments. While governments have many reasons to reduce crime, most do not appear to run afoul of Mill's warning about the likelihood of the abuse of power in the pursuit of prevention strategies. This does not conclusively prove that government should deter, but instead offers some evidence to believe that Mill's warning is not a deciding objection against deterrence.

Conclusion

This chapter has considered the problems and prospects of deterrence approaches. The problems are considerable. First, there is little evidence that deterrence works in any substantive sense. Most studies show limited, if negligible, effects for even severe threats of punishment. Second, there is little evidence that intuitive judgements about deterrence hold much water. These judgements rest upon various assumptions about the knowledge people have about criminal justice that they do not possess. Where we find reduced crime rates, there are often other factors that seem best to explain these changes.

There is also a curious paradox. The public strongly support a 'tough on crime' approach despite a lack of evidence that this approach has any significant beneficial effects. In fact, voters are more likely to vote for candidates who claim a 'tough on crime' policy even where those voters might otherwise favour alternative approaches, such as rehabilitation. Deterrence theories of punishment claim justification because they lead to crime reduction. The problem is that the evidence is inconclusive at best and perhaps even counterintuitive.

There are also clear prospects. The fact that conclusive evidence is lacking does not entail that no evidence can be found, but only that the jury is still out. People may have limited knowledge about criminal justice, but so then we might rely on a more modest understanding of how deterrence might apply. The threat of punishment is clearly one possible factor for potential criminals to desist from engaging in crime. Moreover, crime reduction is desirable: we would prefer a society with less crime to others, all things considered.

The project of deterrence may prove more challenging to offer than its defenders have claimed, but it remains an approach to punishment of real importance.

Notes

1. David Hume, *A Treatise of Human Nature*, 2nd ed., ed. L. A. Selby-Bigge (Oxford: Oxford University Press, 1978): 410.

2. See Mill, *On Liberty*, 10.

3. Plato, 'Gorgias', in *Complete Works*, 525b-c.

4. Ted Honderich, *Punishment: The Supposed Justifications* (Harmondsworth: Penguin, 1969): 59.

5. This important distinction could be further understood as a macro-level approach to deterrence (macro-deterrence) and a micro-level approach to deterrence (microdeterrence). I believe that our understanding of deterrence and deterrent strategies is aided when considering this subject through this distinction.

6. J. S. Mill, 'On Punishment' in *Collected Works of John Stuart Mill*, vol. 21, ed. John M. Robson (Toronto: University of Toronto Press, [1834] 1984): 78.

7. The classic exposition of the incapacitation theory of punishment is William Paley's *Principles of Penal Law* in 1771.

8. The objection includes the qualification of 'virtually' (as in 'virtually everyone') as there would be a need for some persons to administer prisons housing everyone else. Imprisoning everyone is impossible even in a hypothetical case, but this counterexample remains an important argument against incapacitation.

9. Punishment is not always incapacitation. This is because we understand punishment to take more potential forms than imprisonment, but include community sentences, fines, and other possibilities. This is a break from some academic discussions of 'punishment' that have understood 'punishment' as 'imprisonment', especially since Feinberg's distinction between fines and punishment as noted in chapter 1. However, our more inclusive understanding of punishment as a response to crime (and not only responses involving imprisonment) is much closer to how punishment is understood in debates over criminal justice policy by policymakers.

10. This fact about the geography of crime may further problematize the possibility of deterrence. We should not only look to reductions in crime rates amongst the public (e.g. the standard scenario), but also to effects within prison walls. If deterrence is about crime reduction and crime takes place in public and prison, then we must adopt a wider perspective of approaches to crime reduction than often held.

11. Hegel, *Elements of the Philosophy of Right*, §99 Addition.

12. Beccaria, *Of Crimes and Punishments*, 51. Similarly, Green argues that 'will, not force' explains just political obligation although he ultimately rejects deterrence theories. See T. H. Green, *Lectures on the Principles of Political Obligation* (London: Longmans, 1941): sect. 113–36.

13. Plato, 'Gorgias', in *Complete Works*, 472e.

14. J. G. Fichte, *Foundations of Natural Right*, ed. Frederick Neuhouser (Cambridge: Cambridge University Press, 2000): 232.

15. See Bentham, *An Introduction to the Principles of Morals and Legislation*, 93–4.

16. Beccaria, *Of Crimes and Punishments*, 46 (emphasis added).

17. We will examine negative retributivism in further detail in chapter 5.

18. The argument here summarizes Anthony Ellis, 'A Deterrence Theory of Punishment', *Philosophical Quarterly* 53 (2003): 338–51.

19. See Zachary Hoskins, 'Deterrent Punishment and Respect for Persons', *Ohio State Journal of Criminal Law* 8 (2011): 373–4.

20. Ellis, 'A Deterrence Theory of Punishment', 345.

21. See Hegel, *Elements of the Philosophy of Right*, preface.

22. See Anthony Doob and Cheryl Webster, 'Sentence Severity and Crime: Accepting the Null Hypothesis' in Michael Tonry (ed.), *Crime and Justice: A Review of Research*, vol. 30 (Chicago: University of Chicago Press, 2003): 143–95. Some have claimed there is a deterrence effect via incapacitation (or 'incapacitation effect') whereby crime rates have risen in specific cases closely following criminals leaving prison. However, they have not argued that the solution to this problem is to give all criminals life sentences to reduce crime; instead, the argument is that imprisoning most criminally minded persons will reduce crime rates. See Durlauf and Nagin, 'Imprisonment and Crime', 30 and Steven D. Levitt and Stephen J. Dubner, *Freakonomics: A Rogue Economist Explores the Hidden Side of Everything* (New York: Harper Perennial, 2009): 119–29.

23. See Ministry of Justice data at http://open.justice.gov.uk/home/.

24. Patrick A. Langan and David J. Levin, *Recidivism of Prisoners Released in 1994* (Washington, DC: Bureau of Justice Statistics, 2002): 2.

25. For example, see G. Matthew Snodgrass, Arjan A. J. Blokland, Amelia Haviland, Paul Nieubeerta, and Daniel S. Nagin, 'Does the Time Cause the Crime? An Examination of the Relationship between Time Served and Reoffending in the Netherlands', *Criminology* 49 (2011): 1149–94.

26. Patrick Carter, *Managing Offenders, Reducing Crime: A New Approach* (London: Prime Minister's Strategy Unit, 2003): 15.

27. Carter, *Managing Offenders, Reducing Crime*, 10. The situation is no less true in the United States. See ibid. 15 and Editorial, 'The Crime of Punishment', *New York Times* (6 December 2010): A26.

28. See Easton and Piper, *Sentencing and Punishment*, 113.

29. See Durlauf and Nagin, 'Imprisonment and Crime', 28.

30. See *Brown* v. *Plata*, 563 U.S. (2011).

31. See Durlauf and Nagin, 'Imprisonment and Crime', 14, 21–3 and Michael Tonry, 'Less Imprisonment is No Doubt a Good Thing: More Policing is Not', *Criminology & Public Policy* 10 (2011): 138, 140–1.

32. Tonry, 'Less Imprisonment is No Doubt a Good Thing', 143 (quoting Kenneth Clarke).

33. See Ministry of Justice, *2011 Compendium of Re-Offending Statistics and Analysis* (London: Her Majesty's Stationery Office, 2011): 3–4. Reoffending rates do not generally differ between men and women. See Ministry of Justice, *Adult Re-Convictions: Results from the 2009 Cohort (England and Wales)* (London: Her Majesty's Stationery Office, 2011): 14.

34. For example, Levitt and Dubner argue that the US murder rate fell largely as a result of the legalization of abortion: 'the pool of potential criminals had dramatically shrunk'. See Levitt and Dubner, *Freakonomics*, 4. For other factors, see David Lazar (ed.), *DNA and the Criminal Justice System: The Technology of Justice* (Cambridge: MIT Press, 2004) and Barry Sheck, Peter Neufeld, and Jim Dwyer, *Actual Innocence: When Justice Goes Wrong and How to Make It Right* (New York: American Library, 2003).

35. See Cassia C. Spohn, *How Do Judges Decide? The Search for Fairness and Justice in Punishment* (Thousand Oaks: Sage, 2002): 285.

36. Sarah Britto, '"Diffuse Anxiety": The Role of Economic Insecurity in Predicting Fear of Crime', *Journal of Crime and Justice* (2011) (DOI:10.1080/0735648X.2011.631399).

37. Levitt and Dubner, *Freakonomics*, 109.

38. See R. Liedka, A. Piehl, and B. Useem, 'The Crime-Control Effect of Incarceration: Does Scale Matter?', *Criminology and Public Policy* 5 (2006): 245–75 and T. Marvell and C. Moody, 'Prison Population and Crime Reduction', *Journal of Quantitative Criminology* 10 (1994): 109–39.

39. J. G. Fichte, *Foundations of Natural Right*, 228.

40. I am grateful to Brian O'Connor for suggesting this idea to me.

41. Richard L. Lippke, *Rethinking Imprisonment* (Oxford: Oxford University Press, 2007): 41.

42. James Q. Wilson, *Thinking About Crime*, 2nd ed. (New York: Vintage Books, 1985): 121.

43. See Ashworth, 'Ignorance of the Criminal Law', 1–26.

44. For example, see Mandeep K. Dhami and David R. Mandel, 'Crime as Risk Taking', *Psychology, Crime and Law* (2011): 1–15. Thaler and Sunstein argue that only 'Econs', a fictional understanding of people as *homo economicus* and not people like you or me, make such rational choice calculations. Behavioural models must rely upon new models for predicting policy effects. See Richard Thaler and Cass Sunstein, *Nudge: Improving Decisions about Health, Wealth, and Happiness* (London: Penguin, 2008).

45. See Thomas A. Loughran, Raymond Paternoster, Alex R. Piquero, and Greg Pogarsky, 'On Ambiguity in Perception of Risk: Implications for Criminal Decision Making and Deterrence', *Criminology* 49 (2011): 1029–61.

46. Davis, 'How to Make the Punishment Fit the Crime', 735.

47. There is also 'the fallacy of the warden's survey research': the warden observes the many undeterred criminals at his prison and concludes that deterrence does not work. This is a fallacy because the warden reaches this conclusion without any consideration of the possible supermajority outside his prison that were deterred. See Albert Dzur and Alan Wertheimer, 'Forgiveness and Public Deliberation: The Practice of Restorative Justice', *Criminal Justice Ethics* 21 (2002): 15. The problem is not that we cannot know how many people have been deterred, but only how crime rates have changed over time.

48. This is not surprising, in part, because there can be much confusion. Take capital punishment for murder in the United States. The crime of murder is not unitary, but differs: the crime of murder where the victim is a private citizen is separate from the crime of murder where the victim is the US President. Each is criminalized by different jurisdictions and may have different tariffs. For example, murder is normally part of state statutes. While most states have legalized capital punishment, a significant minority have not. Whether or not the murder of another private citizen may warrant the possibility of execution will differ from state to state. Furthermore, the crime of murder of the US President does not fall under any state law, but under federal law and federal law permits the possibility of execution. A person found guilty of the murder of the US President in a state that did not accept capital punishment for murder might still be executed for his crime in that state. This is because he would be guilty of a federal crime even though the act took place in an abolitionist state. This illustration highlights that even the punishment of murder is not straightforwardly clear given the complex relationship between state and federal laws in the United States.

49. The punishment for arson differs across states. For one example, see http://firemarshal.state.md.us/crimes. htm. The punishment of arson in the UK is found in the Criminal Damage Act (1971). I leave it to the reader to discover the sanction for arson in his or her jurisdiction. This exercise further underscores the

difficulty of penal threats having any clear deterrent effect where knowledge about possible sanctions is confusing or difficult to obtain for even the most serious crimes.

50. See Alan Travis, 'Governors Urge Fast Release of 2,500 Prisoners', *The Guardian* (12 October 2010): 8.

51. Mill, *On Liberty*, 95.

52. See Hoskins, 'Deterrent Punishment and Respect for Persons', 374–5.

53. For example, see Martha C. Nussbaum, '"Whether from Reason or Prejudice": Taking Money for Bodily Services', *Journal of Legal Studies* 27 (1998): 693–724.

54. Theorists who argue that deterrence does not address people as moral agents cite a passage from Hegel as supporting evidence. Hegel says (of Paul Johann Anselm Ritter von Feuerbach's theory of deterrence) that '[t]o justify punishment in this way is like raising one's stick at a dog; it means treating a human being like a dog instead of respecting his honour and freedom'. While Hegel did reject deterrence as a primary ground of punishment, he does not oppose deterrence within a unified theory of punishment. See Hegel, *Elements of the Philosophy of Right*, §99 Addition and Thom Brooks, 'Hegel and the Unified Theory of Punishment' in *Hegel's Philosophy of Right* (Oxford: Blackwell, 2012): 103–23.

55. The claim that 'there can be no justified punishment for an unjustified law' does not run afoul of the naturalistic fallacy. This is because what is central is the establishment of justification rather than the establishment of (moral) justice.

56. Beccaria, *Of Crimes and Punishments*, 42.

57. Jeremy Bentham, *The Works of Jeremy Bentham*, vol. 1: *Principles of Penal Law* (New York: Russell & Russell, 1961): 398.

58. Beccaria, *Of Crimes and Punishments*, 74.

Bibliography

Ashworth, Andrew (2010). 'Ignorance of the Criminal Law, and Duties to Avoid It', *Modern Law Review* 74: 1–26.

Beccaria, Cesare (1986). *On Crimes and Punishments*, trans. David Young. Indianapolis: Hackett.

Bentham, Jeremy (1961). *The Works of Jeremy Bentham, vol. 1: Principles of Penal Law*. New York: Russell and Russell.

Britto, Sarah (2011). '"Diffuse Anxiety": The Role of Economic Insecurity in Predicting Fear of Crime', *Journal of Crime and Justice*. DOI: 10.1080/0735648X. 2011.631399.

Brooks, Thom (2012). 'Hegel and the Unified Theory of Punishment' in (ed.), *Hegel's Philosophy of Right: Ethics, Politics, and Law*. Oxford: Blackwell, pp. 103–23.

Carter, Patrick (2003). *Managing Offenders, Reducing Crime: A New Approach*. London: Prime Minister's Strategy Unit.

Davis, Michael (1983). 'How to Make the Punishment Fit the Crime', *Ethics* 93: 726–52.

Dhami, Mandeep K. and David R. Mandel (2011). 'Crime as Risk Taking', *Psychology, Crime and Law* (2011): 1–15.

Doob, Anthony and Cheryl Webster (2003). 'Sentence Severity and Crime: Accepting the Null Hypothesis' in Michael Tonry (ed.), Crime and Justice: A Review of Research, vol. 30. Chicago: University of Chicago Press, pp. 143–95.

Durlauf, Steven N. and Daniel S. Nagin (2011). 'Imprisonment and Crime: Can Both Be Reduced?', *Criminology and Public Policy* 10: 13–54.

Dzur, Albert W. and Alan Wertheimer (2002). 'Forgiveness and Public Deliberation: The Practice of Restorative Justice', *Criminal Justice Ethics* 21: 3–20.

Easton, Susan and Christine Piper (2005). *Sentencing and Punishment: The Quest for Justice*. Oxford: Oxford University Press.

Ellis, Anthony (2003). 'A Deterrence Theory of Punishment', *Philosophical Quarterly* 53: 337–51.

Fichte, J. G. (2000). *Foundations of Natural Right*, ed. Frederick Neuhouser. Cambridge: Cambridge University Press.

Green, Thomas Hill (1941). *Lectures on the Principles of Political Obligation*. London: Longmans.

Hegel, G. W. F. (1991) *Elements of the Philosophy of Right*, ed. A. W. Wood, trans. H. B. Nisbet. Cambridge: Cambridge University Press.

Honderich, Ted (1969). *Punishment: The Supposed Justifications*. Harmondsworth: Penguin.

Hoskins, Zachary (2011). 'Deterrent Punishment and Respect for Persons', *Ohio State Journal of Criminal Law* 8: 369–84.

Hume, David (1978). *A Treatise of Human Nature, 2nd ed.*, ed. L. A. Selby-Bigge. Oxford: Oxford University Press.

Langan, Patrick A. and David J. Levin (2002). *Recidivism of Prisoners Released in 1994*. Washington, DC: Bureau of Justice Statistics.

Lazar, David (ed.) (2004). DNA *and the Criminal Justice System: The Technology of Justice*. Cambridge, Mass.: MIT Press.

Levitt, Steven D. and Stephen J. Dubner (2009). *Freakonomics: A Rogue Economist Explores the Hidden Side of Everything*. New York: HarperPerennial.

Liedka, R. A. Piehl, and B. Useem (2006). 'The Crime-Control Effects of Incarceration: Does Scale Matter?', *Criminology and Public Policy* 5: 245–75.

Lippke, Richard L. (2007). *Rethinking Imprisonment*. Oxford: Oxford University Press.

Loughran, Thomas A., Raymond Paternoster, Alex R. Piquero, and Greg Pogarsky (2011). 'On Ambiguity in Perception of Risk: Implications for Criminal Decision-Making and Deterrence', *Criminology* 49: 1029–61.

Marvell, T. and C. Moody (1994). 'Prison Population and Crime Reduction', *Journal of Quantitative Criminology* 10: 109–39.

Mill, John Stuart (1978). On Liberty, ed. Elizabeth Rapaport. Indianapolis: Hackett.

____(1984). 'On Punishment' in *Collected Works of John Stuart Mill, Vol. XXI*, ed. John M. Robson. Toronto: University of Toronto Press, pp. 77–9.

Ministry of Justice (2011). 2011 *Compendium of Re-Offending Statistics and Analysis*. London: Her Majesty's Stationery Office.

____(2011). *Adult Re-Convictions: Results from the 2009 Cohort (England and Wales)*. London: Her Majesty's Stationery Office.

New York Times (6 December 2010). 'The Crime of Punishment', Editorial, A26.

Nussbaum, Martha C. (1998). '"Whether from Reason or Prejudice": Taking Money for Bodily Services', *Journal of Legal Studies* 27: 693–724.

Paley, William (1771). *Principles of Penal Law*. London.

Plato (1997). *Complete Works*, ed. John M. Cooper. Indianapolis: Hackett.

Sheck, Barry, Peter Neufeld, and Jim Dwyer (2003). *Actual Innocence: When Justice Goes Wrong and How to Make It Right*. New York: American Library.

Snodgrass, G. Matthew, Arjan A. J. Blokland, Amelia Haviland, Paul Nieubeerta, and Daniel S. Nagin (2011). 'Does the Time Cause the Crime? An Examination of the Relationship between Time Served and Reoffending in the Netherlands', *Criminology* 49: 1149–94.

Spohn, Cassia C. (2002). *How Do Judges Decide? The Search for Fairness and Justice in Punishment*. Thousand Oaks: Sage.

Thaler, Richard and Cass Sunstein (2008). *Nudge: Improving Decisions about Health, Wealth, and Happiness*. London: Penguin.

Tonry, Michael (2011). 'Less Imprisonment Is No Doubt a Good Thing: More Policing Is Not', *Criminology and Public Policy* 10: 137–52.

Wilson, James Q. (1985). *Thinking about Crime, 2nd ed*. New York: Vintage Books.

CHAPTER SIX

The Age of Industrialization

Following the development of theories, methods, and policies designed to deter individuals from committing acts of criminal behavior during the preindustrial period, the discussion turns to the issue of criminal justice in the postindustrial age. It would appear that the doctrines arising from the Enlightenment and utilitarian reform movement would also give rise to a system of equality and justice grounded in the principles of modern democracy. What we find, however, is problematic in that the policies and reforms of the utilitarian period somehow morphed into a system designed to manage specific populations of people, most of whom discovered that their very existence was an anathema within modern society. According to research conducted by Barak, Leighton, and Flavin (2010), these people were labeled as *surplus populations*, which are also labeled theoretically as economically marginal persons.[1] In short, they were seen as people who did not work, could not keep a job if they had one, and would rather live off of the state. Furthermore, the creation or social construction of the surplus population led to more extreme policies in the framework of these individuals refusing to conform to their expected role in the U.S. labor market. As a result, they are thought to have issues with conforming to the laws and conventions of modern society.[2] Viewed in this way, these people are naturally criminals, and subject to specific laws, policies, and doctrines designed to not only prevent (deter) them from committing crime, but also participate in the wonders and marvels of the twentieth century.

This chapter provides a framework for examining the intricate mechanisms associated with this historical development by focusing on the preindustrial period following the end

---

1   Gregg Barak, P. Leighton, and J. Flavin, *Class, Race, Gender, Crime: Social Realities of Justice in America* (Lanham, MD: Rowman & Littlefield Publishers, Inc., 2010).
2   Gregg Barak et al. *Class, Race, Gender, Crime.*, 2010.

of the Civil War and policies and practices that gave rise to the evolution of race and class inequality in postindustrial America. Although this historical struggle gave rise to the development of several constitutional reforms leading to the adaptation of criminal justice systems of due process and equal protection under the law, the postindustrial complex inadvertently resulted in the rise of organized crime and backlashes against people of color, which set the stage for the marginalization of a new and theoretically more dangerous class of citizen.[3]

---

3   Gregg Barak, P. Leighton, and J. Flavin. *Class, Race, Gender, Crime: Social Realities of Justice in America*. Lanham, MD: Rowman & Littlefield Publishers, Inc., 2010.

Prohibitions

By Kristofer Allerfeldt

....

I n 1919, the baseball player turned iconic evangelist, Billy Sunday, assured his radio audience of
some 10,000 loyal souls that: "The reign of tears is over. The slums will soon be a memory. We
will turn our prisons into factories and our jails into storehouses and corncribs. Men will soon walk
upright now; women will smile and children will laugh. Hell will be forever rent."[1] This delight was
not caused by the end of the recent war, nor did it mark the end of a deadly influenza epidemic.
Sunday was not talking of some blissed out vision of the Second Coming or even the hyperbolic
campaigning for the election of a new president. It was the result of the passage of the Volstead Act,
by which, as a nation, America—or at least the federal government—repudiated alcohol.

If this seems surprising, it was not as if the Reverend Sunday was alone in the optimism of
his depiction of an alcohol-free utopia. To the members of the Anti-Saloon League and other dry
groups, America was now free to enjoy the benefits of a more sober, healthier, more productive world
free from the curse of booze. Fourteen years later, all except for the most diehard Prohibitionists felt
that the creation of "God's Dry Kingdom" had been a failure. It had led to an increase in reported
drunkenness; it had led to an increase in the prison population and in many urban areas during
Prohibition, there were more bars than there had been before. Statistics showed that booze was
more fashionable in 1930 than it had been in 1910 and the continuation with what was patently
an unenforceable law had made breaking the law a normal part of daily life for a huge number
of Americans.

In spite of this manifest failure, many accounts of the 1920s claim that Prohibition defines
the decade. Nothing illustrates this better than journalist Harry Philips' brilliant summation of
the history of the United States. In 11 immortal words he shows the contempt with which the

public held the dry laws—"Columbus, Washington, Lincoln, Volstead. Two flights up and ask for Gus."[2] In the usual reading of the decade, casual law-breaking went hand in hand with the frenetic partying and reckless speculating—accompanied by the worrying use of credit—followed by even more spending. As if this was not enough, it also had an even darker side. The money to be made from moon-shining, bootlegging and rum running sparked crime on a level never before seen in the US. It spawned characters whose immorality, violence, irreverence and ruthlessness have become legendary in a country already famous for its outlaws and criminals. Considered by many at all levels of American society to be both unenforceable and undesirable, Prohibition has been blamed for blurring even further what was already often a fuzzy distinction between law enforcement and law breaking. Judges and politicians bought booze from known criminals; respectable citizens distilled, bottled and sold "bath tub gin"; police and prohibition agents took huge bribes; small-time hoodlums gained vast criminal empires and through their huge turnover funded an entire network of illegal ancillary industries and laundering operations ranging from transport firms to hitmen.

Yet it should be remembered that Prohibition was itself a crusade, and that however flawed and however unsuccessful that crusade appeared in the 1920s, it had deep roots and an impressive pedigree. It had vocal supporters, in influential areas of US society. Prohibition had been a long time coming and it was by no means the only time that America tried to legislate to preserve the morality of its population. Nor was the "Noble Experiment" the last such experiment. Before the Eighteenth Amendment banned the importing, production, sale or distribution of alcohol, public gambling had come under sustained attack, so much so that by 1914, horse racing was only legal in six states. What was more, the Harrison Act of the same year prohibited the recreational use of most commonly used narcotics. While perhaps less dramatic, these prohibitions outlasted that on alcohol. After the Twenty-First Amendment repealed Prohibition in 1933, Nevada was the only state where most forms of gambling were openly allowed, and the Marijuana Taxation Act of 1937 tried to outlaw cannabis by imposing large fines and lengthy prison sentences on those convicted of possession.

This chapter will investigate three themes associated with these three prohibitions. First, it will examine why these prohibitions were considered necessary. It will look into what drove them; who advocated them, and why the bans were limited to simply alcohol, gambling and narcotics rather than smoking, stock speculation, swearing or other forms of stimulating and seemingly morally questionable behavior. Second, it will investigate how the policing and legislating involved in their being outlawed evolved. It will examine who controlled it, how it was enforced, who it targeted and how effective it really was. Third, and perhaps most significantly, it will look into whether the prevailing view that criminal activity was in fact stimulated rather than controlled by prohibitions, and if so, why they continued—and still continue—for so long.

Turn-of-the-century America was a society in flux. It was an unstable mix of high morals, tradition, and fatalism. This mix was constantly challenged by the self-consciously modern belief in the powers of science, the nation's increasing prosperity, the unstoppable march of "progress," and the potentials contained in the imaginative use of individualism. Poverty, crime, and the social inequalities from which these scourges originated, were viewed as controllable. This, it was argued, could be achieved by two means. It was attainable by strict attention to traditional values of self-reliance, family, thrift, and industry. Alternatively it could be achieved through charity and rational, scientifically based reforms. In America, as in most industrialized societies, it was felt that modernity and its discontents could be managed by a variety of panacea, ranging from improvements in hygiene, diet, and housing to self-restraint, prayer and—in the last resort—by prohibition. Each solution had its advocates, as well as its critics.

The roots of American alcohol prohibition are not particularly difficult to uncover. Alcohol had always played a major part in American life. For many on the early American frontier, whiskey had essentially been a currency. It was a relatively easily manufactured commodity which transformed grain into a product which was as desirable as it was portable, preservable and tradable. At the other end of the alcoholic spectrum, beer, cider and wine had always been seen as safe, staple, thirst quenchers in an age when drinking water supplies might well be contaminated and unpleasant, if not poisonous. In times when life for many was frequently harsh enough to be barely endurable, when communities were scattered and entertainment scarce, booze became the only real, affordable recreation and the saloon, bar or tavern, the only meeting place. There was also a more insidious side to alcohol consumption. In an era when tea and coffee were rare, and consequently expensive, their place was largely taken by intoxicating drinks. It is perhaps indicative that President John Adams would drink hard cider rather than tea or coffee with his breakfast. Alcohol was also connected with the working day. Harvest workers were traditionally entitled to a daily pint of rum throughout much of the first half of the nineteenth century. American workers were in the habit of taking "eleveners" of whiskey in the morning and stopping for a "four o'clock dram" in the afternoon.

All this meant that for one reason or another, by 1830, the average American, over the age of 15, consumed in excess of seven gallons of "absolute" alcohol a year. Nor was this all beer and cider, about two-thirds of the total alcohol drunk was spirits. In our own times, when consumption is on the rise again, the same American consumes less than three gallons.[3] Given this rate of use, it is not coincidence that the main killer of US Army troopers on the frontier during the Plains Wars was alcohol-related illness. Perhaps it should also come as no surprise that it was an American—Benjamin Rush, a signatory to the US Constitution, no less—who was the first physician to diagnose alcoholism as a disease, with a recog-nizable course, and predictable psychological and physical effects. It should also be no surprise that Dr Rush was one of the first modern advocates of temperance.

At the same time as American alcohol consumption peaked at around 1830, the temperance move-ment had recruited over one and a half million members—10 percent of the population—dedicated at this stage to moderating the use of alcohol. While the movement cited moral and health reasons for this moderation, they also began appealing to the rising industrialists by claiming that the sober worker was 25 percent more productive than his inebriated equivalent. These crusaders held rallies—often rowdy and ribald affairs, even without the booze. They organized preachy lectures given to huge and attentive crowds. The campaign had remarkable successes and but also suffered some setbacks. Foremost among their checks was the time that the most celebrated of the movement's speakers was caught dead drunk in a bordello. Nevertheless, over the next 30 years the movement achieved considerable, if short-lived, triumphs.

True prohibition started in 1851 in Maine when the state passed a law forbidding the sale of all alcohol. Similar laws followed the next year in Massachusetts, Vermont, the Minnesota Territory, and Rhode Island. By 1855, Michigan, Connecticut, Ohio, Indiana, New Hampshire, Delaware, Illinois, Iowa and New York as well as the provinces of Nova Scotia and New Brunswick were also dry. However, by 1858, the zeal behind what was at this point a northern crusade was diverted into, and diluted by, the movement for the abolition of slavery with the result that those laws which remained on the statute books were more honored in the breach than in observance.[4]

Not that alcohol alone inspired the reformers, because if alcohol seemed to be *an* American vice, gambling was perhaps *the* American vice. The huge fortunes to be made in extractive industries from trapping, to fishing, to mining, in land speculation and in agriculture excited a speculative streak in nineteenth-century America which was perhaps unmatched in any other culture. Early American society lacked many of the sophistications and diversions of the more densely populated, more established and urban regions of western Europe, but significantly the US did not lack the wealth. Add to this the fact that the real money was not to be made in the relatively sophisticated urban regions of the country, but on the frontier where morals differed from other regions and the proclivity for gambling becomes even more understandable. The legend of the exploitation of the West was knitted in with self-reliance, ingenuity, hard-living, resilience and, perhaps above all, luck.

One of the results of this individualism was that the heroes of this region were less constrained by the niceties of high society. On the frontier, the "greenhorn" was less an innocent to be chaperoned, educated, and pitied, than a "sap" or "sucker"—a moving target to be preyed upon. According to legend, the West was egalitarian and the advantage was with those with wit, daring, and luck, not inherited title, wealth, or polish—although many of the more socially advantaged still did remarkably well as both speculators and gamblers. As one veteran resident of a Death Valley mining camp advised—"If you can whack a sixteen-bull team, hit a drill, engineer a wheelbarrow, deal faro [the most popular card game of the nineteenth century in America] or shoot, come right along. Otherwise stay where you are."[5] This was a dog-eat-dog world where fortunes were made and lost with frightening speed, often by means which—if there had been law—would have been illegal. Moving to America, moving to the frontier was in itself a gamble. Thriving there meant accepting that gambling was a part of the life choice that had already been made.

The nineteenth century generated a variety of stock gambling figures. Playing on the fluctuating fortunes of what was a highly mobile society in an era of massive land speculation, the Mississippi Valley steamship gambler of the 1840s became an iconic figure in dime novels of the 1880s. He was prized for his ingenuity in his often autobiographical accounts of his sharp ruses and mannerly scams. When this Mississippi land boom came to an end this figure evolved to become the card sharp of the Wild West, renowned in mythology for being as quick to draw an ace as a six-shooter. Then there were the Forty-niners in California, and the miners in Virginia City, the Comstock, Deadwood, and Tombstone who panned and dug fortunes from the West's rivers and hills. More often than not, this good luck deserted them. Many swiftly lost their claims, stakes and finds to each other and the ubiquitous, predatory, card sharp of legend.

There was also another uniquely American type of gambler—but while planted firmly in the New World, this group drew more on the Old. The slave-holding Southern plantation owners, as well as their wives and then their children with their leisurely rural lifestyle, consciously imitated the glitterati of the English landed gentry. Seeking both role models and pedigree, this so-called Plantocracy sought to resemble the aristocracy in their studied manners, fine clothing, love of exquisitely expensive bloodstock, lavish entertainments and above all reckless gambling. From the birth of the Colonies through to the advent of the cotton economy in the 1830s and beyond, they had played the world-weary gamblers, running up huge debts and winning and losing family fortunes at the tracks, on the tables and beside the rings.[6]

At the other end of the spectrum came the pauper gamblers whose stakes may have been negligible by comparison with the land speculators, gold-strikers and Plantocracy, but their addiction to gambling was no less apparent in the literature of the day. With little to stake, the planters' slaves gambled among themselves, or against equally poor whites. Perhaps they were motivated by the example of their masters. Perhaps they simply sought enough money to buy their freedom. Whatever their motivation, in a curious example of *noblesse oblige*—or perhaps in recognition of their own vices—planters often allowed slaves to keep their winnings. Alongside these impoverished residents, there was the immigrant on the passage to America. These unfortunates became known as a class who could be duped of their worldly goods at the card or dice game on the floor of the steerage decks during the Atlantic crossing. Their downfall could come at the hands of a fellow passenger or the notorious professional gambler. Whichever it was, the lesson was the same—those who would prosper must first realize that the whole idea of "America" was a gamble.

Among these immigrants were those who brought with them new forms of gambling or improvements on the old ones. Different nationalities were associated with different forms of gambling, in turn creating and conforming to national/ racial stereotypes. The British brought and developed the bloodstock, knowledge, and inspiration for America's thoroughbred racing and the Italians brought faro. Italians were seen as volatile, violent, excitable and superstitious—prone to complex card games, frequently with violent outcomes. The Irish loved their horses—as well as their drink—and would breed and train the horses, make the odds and just as often provide many of the punters for racing. The Russians and Poles with their melancholia would risk all in the suicidal final flutter. The avaricious and immoral Jews would clean up in any game with their inherent ability with money. The unintelligible, clannish and alien Chinese would simply bet on anything.[7]

While many sought to blame the prevalence of gambling on outsiders, perhaps the most widespread and popular form of gambling was the lottery and this had a healthy all-American pedigree. Not only had four separate lotteries been used to raise $10 million to buy supplies for Washington's Continental Army, but also Benjamin Franklin, George Washington and John Hancock all vocally supported lottery financing as a legitimate way of raising revenue for the early Republic. Thomas Jefferson, an inveterate card, backgammon and lottery player, called state lotteries "a painless tax, paid only by the willing."[8] In 1826, he even had plans to improve his personal finances by selling lottery tickets. He died before he could implement them.

By 1832, the nation had some 420 separate lottery draws, which gave revenues totaling over $60 million. An idea of the scale of this figure can be gathered when it is considered that the entire federal budget at the time made up less than 20 percent of that figure and the price of all tickets combined made up around 3 percent of the nation's entire income. What was more, such fundraising was not limited to government activity. Schools, colleges, churches, and private individuals used lotteries to raise funds. In spite of a long-running campaign by religious groups, spearheaded by the Quakers, by 1850, 24 of the Union's 33 states regularly used lotteries to finance capital projects from road construction to government buildings and other major undertakings. The scope for fraud was enormous. A bogus lottery in the 1830s netted over $400,000 and paid nothing in prizes. In Maine, a lottery organizer kept over $10 million for "expenses" although the total ticket sales were $16 million. Given these high profile frauds it is unsurprising that the efforts of the moralists paid off—although only briefly. By the end of the decade, the lottery was banned in all but three border states, although the need to raise wartime funds led to a resurgence of the lottery as a funding option in the South during the years of the Civil War.[9]

With all these nationalities and classes, all over the nation, regularly gambling it was only a question of time before it attracted the attention of those who charged themselves with preserving the public's morals. By the 1820s, gambling houses were technically illegal in all states except Louisiana. There were also periodic controls placed on various sporting events where betting was liable to take place. For example, by the 1820s, most of the more violent blood sports had been banned in most of the states and this was only partially the result of humane considerations. It was more to do with the fact that the brutality, when combined with money changing hands among the lower classes—who made up the majority of those attending the ratting, bull, and bear baiting—was seen as exciting violence and disorder.

More often than not, such bans merely served to drive betting underground, or create a shift in the sports which attracted the punters. For instance, New England and New York banned horse racing between 1792 and 1821. While this ban was in place there was a notable increase in these regions in both bare knuckle boxing and cock fighting which arguably attracted far higher participation and larger stakes. What was more, the period of prohibition did little to diminish the attraction of the sport. When the race tracks were re-opened in New York, the Union race track on Long Island attracted over 60,000 spectators in 1823 to see the northern horse Eclipse race the southern contender Sir Henry for $20,000 prize money.[10]

The final aspect examined in this section is narcotics. The vast majority of laws prohibiting narcotics were instigated after the turn of the twentieth century. That is not to say that there was no recognizable problem, there was. Opiates were the main narcotic of the pre-Civil War era either mixed in with alcohol as laudanum, drunk without alcohol as "black drop" or eaten or smoked as opium resin. However, if a real starting point for America's modern narcotic problem can be found, it must be the invention of the hypodermic syringe in around 1860—a device designed specifically to administer morphine. In the period before this invention, in terms of the recognition of the scale of usage, the inherent dangers and the control of opiates, America lagged behind Britain. In England, the addictions of such notable figures as Samuel Taylor Coleridge and Thomas de Quincy were highlighted and their dependencies seen as having stunted otherwise promising careers. Such high profile cases resulted in an effort within the British medical establishment to understand the mechanisms of addiction while at the same time distancing themselves from irresponsible prescribing; the result was the 1868 Pharmacy Act. Similar regulation would not be introduced in the US until the 1914 Harrison Act.[11]

America's narcotic problem in the pre-Bellum era was to a large extent unrec-ognized and as a result unregulated. The effects of smoking opium were for the most part calming and soporific with relatively mild hallucinogenic effects unless the dosage was beyond the norm. Addicts would frequently go unnoticed. What was more, medicinally it was prescribed for an extraordinarily wide range of disorders—everything from anxiety; to muscle spasm; to cholera or as a wormer—with the result that there was no particular class, nationality or occupation particularly associated with its use, or misuse. In an age when bleeding with leeches was still prevalent, opiates—even if they had little actual physical effect other than pain relief—at least did make patients *feel* better. Opiates were, therefore, little short of miracle drugs in an age when the average physician had a year's training or less and in a time before germ theory when herbalism or non-sterile surgery remained the most effective weapons in the doctor's arsenal. The result was that during the early nineteenth century per capita crude opium imports grew steadily and the drug was incorporated into a variety of patent medicines which were subject to few real controls either in terms of delivery, usage or content until the 1906 Pure Food and Drug Act.

By the turn of the twentieth century the situation was markedly different. The Progressive urge—with its moral tone, investigative commissions and rational solutions—sparked a wave of prohibitions which covered all three of the areas. The campaign to outlaw booze had re-emerged in the 1880s when seven states had declared themselves dry and a further 14 had taken serious steps towards prohibition. In large measure this had been the result of the mobilization of a new force of moral guardians—the women of America. By a mixture of displays of public Christian piety and sheer perseverance, women, first in the Mid-West and then across the nation, managed to close bars and harangue politicians to pass prohibitive legislation.

Although largely excluded from the ballot, women's power lay in a potent mixture of radical militancy and irrefutable logic. It was women who would suffer most from the familial breakdown caused by alcohol abuse. It was women that would be left to bring up the children in the event of the unemployment, illness or bereavement which often followed the workingman's flirtation with the saloon. It was women who could understand the real extent of the self-loathing and degradation associated with other women's moral decline through alcohol and it was women who made up the larger part of the nation's evangelical congregations. The result was that the Women's Christian Temperance Union (WCTU) converted the zeal which had accompanied the abolitionist movement into pressure not only for alcohol moderation but also for a range of causes associated with women, from sexual purity, to day care for children, and most importantly female suffrage. Temperance had become a women's issue which was clearly illustrated by the fact that in 1918 booze was illegal in 12 of the 13 states where women had full suffrage. As the *New York Times* put it: "Liquor is going out as women suffrage is coming in."[12]

While women were the main drivers of temperance in the late nineteenth century, by contrast, they were one of the main groups of narcotic addicts. The use of morphine in the Civil War had left a tragic group of up to 400,000 addicts—largely from the Union, since the Confederacy was too poor to afford morphine in any quantity. While these men no doubt recruited others, unlike the image later associated with opiates, the lion's share of addicts was a large reservoir of white, middle-class, middle-aged, rural women. An 1880 survey of those using opiates in Chicago found that women outnumbered men, 3 to 1 and the average age of user was around 46 years old. Similarly an investigation of users in Michigan in 1878 found that over 60 percent were female.[13] One estimate puts these women as representing between 56 and 71 percent of addicts at a time when the rate of opiate addiction was over twice the estimate for the late 1990s.[14]

Perhaps these figures should not be so surprising. This was an age of prurience and chauvinism, where the feminine world was still governed by the strict mores of propriety and obedience and when morphine, as well as codeine and laudanum, was frequently doled out to silence a wide range of "women's problems." Chief among these was the characteristically Victorian problem—created by the increasing frenetic pace of modern life—neurasthenia, or nervous exhaustion, but they included a range of gynecological and psycho-sexual conditions including post-parturient injuries and post-natal depression, as well as nymphomania and masturbation. In addition, there were a group of women— largely prostitutes—who used large, self-administered, doses of opiates in order to interrupt or stop menstruation as a form of contraception.

It is perhaps because due in part to the medical origins of these habits and the fact that these patriots and middle-class women made up such prominent groups of addicts that even though such behavior was regarded as a "vice," the problem was generally medicalized rather criminalized. Essentially, these users were seen largely as victims rather than criminals. What was more, those addicts of the lower orders who chose to use these drugs would no doubt be picked up for other crimes—perhaps prostitution, robbery or vagrancy—so the necessity, at this point, to create a new level of criminal behavior was largely overlooked. Some would argue that it was only when the class of addict and nature of their drug of choice changed that criminalization became necessary, but in reality the situation was more complex than that. While the class of user is important, the overall legislative drivers were actually more complex, they were also reliant on a combination of who it was that sought reform, why they sought it and who benefited.[15]

The first federal anti-opium law was the 1909 Smoking Opium Exclusion Act. This legislation was aimed at opium processed specifically for smoking, a habit largely associated with a group of unpopular non-Americans—the Chinese. China imported over 95 percent of the world's opium and was home to over 16 million regular opium smokers. Since the onset of Chinese emigration to the Pacific regions of the US in the late 1840s, the opium den had been seen as a hazard. Since this form of opiate was seen as having no form of medicinal value and was purely recreational, it attracted opprobrium from a variety of quarters. Missionaries reported that the lethargic legacy of years of opium smoking had contributed to China's political, military, and moral decline. Temperance advocates saw little difference between the inebriation of the drunkard and the stupor of the opium smoker. Moral crusaders argued that Chinese addicts acted as "pushers" and sought out vulnerable victims—frequently teenage girls—who they turned into addicts, if not worse.

The result was that in 1875, at the height of Denis Kearney's violently anti-Chinese crusade, San Francisco—the city with the largest Chinese population on the West Coast—banned public opium dens. Portland, Seattle and the other main cities of the region swiftly followed suit. However, from 1875 until 1909, the private use of opium remained legal, providing the federal government with a revenue stream averaging a million dollars a year via import duties while contributing to the sinister image of the Chinese in the mind of many Americans.[16] In these years of the "Yellow Peril," even the most liberal-minded of Americans began to see more disturbingly insidious forces at work. Opium was seen as just one more way in which the Mongolian Hordes threatened to overthrow white America, because, as Jacob Riis informed his readers in 1890,

> The Chinaman smokes opium as Caucasians smoke tobacco, and apparently with little worse effect upon himself. But woe betide the white victim upon which this pitiless drug gets its grip. Opium destroys the Chinaman far less surely, quickly and completely than it destroys the Caucasian and Americans in particular.[17]

There were also other racial threats associated with narcotics which tied the various different drugs with similarly prevalent images of a variety of nationalities in America over these years. In line with their image as a more industrious, ruthless, and intelligent race, Japanese immigrants were seen as being involved with the opium trade, but as dealers, pushers, and businessmen, rather than like the Chinese, simply as users and addicts. Mexicans, with their indolence and un-American habits, became indelibly linked with the growing, use, and sale of cannabis. As a Texan Senator bluntly argued "All Mexicans are crazy, and this stuff [referring to marijuana] is what makes them crazy." This link was so strong that even the American term for the drug came from the Mexican slang—Mary Jane or Marijuana—and the drive for banning the drug came from New Mexico and Texas, the two states with the highest proportion of Mexicans in their boundaries.[18]

Nevertheless, unsurprisingly, it was those who constituted the most prevalent and numerous "racial threat" in America who had the greatest impact on US perceptions of crime and race. As the new century opened, cocaine was increasingly seen as fueling the newfound confidence and increasing reports of the aggression of the "Negro." While much of this can be put down to simply white prejudice, there was a genuine proclivity among the Southern black males to use the newly discovered drug. Not only did it provide a pleasant detachment from what was frequently an extremely harsh reality, but it was relatively cheap, easily administered (frequently as a powder), hard to detect and, if necessary, easy to conceal.

Cocaine's popularity among this section of the population probably also drew on its energy-giving properties. It was used by the Mississippi River and New Orleans stevedores in the early 1880s, where it enabled them to work long hours in extremes of both heat and cold. There is also evidence that this practice spread, and employers from planters to mine owners frequently encouraged its use among their manual laborers, some even went as far as replacing the traditional whiskey or rum ration with the energizing powder. The radical unionist, William, "Big Bill," Haywood, saw an even more sinister angle to this, claiming that once addicted, workers would stay with the employer in order to insure their supply of the drug.[19]

Like the opiates before it, from its first synthesis in Germany in 1860 and throughout most of the nineteenth century, cocaine had been regarded as something of a wonder drug. Sigmund Freud famously used the drug himself and recommended it for treating conditions as varied as the ubiquitous neurasthenia and asthma. Other physicians found it valuable as an anesthetic for eye surgery, a treatment for gastric conditions and providing some relief from wasting diseases. Along with Bayer's recently patented opiate derivative, "Heroin" (so-called for its "heroic" properties), cocaine was seen as a very effective tool with which to combat alcohol and morphine abuse and addiction. Given its wide range of applications, like the opiates before it, cocaine was included in a bewildering variety of patent medicines. Through elixirs, tonics to soft drinks, including one with the shockingly honest name of "Dope Cola," it was claimed that the wonder drug could cure sinus trouble and blood disorders and also relieve headaches and toothache. According to one source, in one form or another, Americans consumed almost 11 tons of cocaine in 1906 alone.[20] Most importantly for the criminal implications, cocaine was meant to treat "sexual apathy."

In the minds of the turn-of-the-century white readership of the mass-circulation newspapers, it was felt that the average working-class black male did not suffer from "sexual apathy." Far from it, he was seen as sexually voracious, especially when it came to white women. Supercharging the appetites of these libidinous creatures with drugs and adding the frisson of race was the perfect material for a moral panic and it was the *New York Times* which led the charge. According to the newspaper, here was a terrible national threat. The country was undergoing a "cocaine plague" among the most numerous and most threatening of the underclasses of America. Citing medical "experts" and using sensational language, the public was told how the Southern Negro, usually barbaric, when supplied with cocaine by "every Jew peddler in the South," was made little short of a monster. The *Times* reported "nine men [had been] killed in Mississippi on one occasion by crazed cocaine takers, [and a further] five in North Carolina and three [more] in Tennessee." Since emancipation, the Southern black had been viewed as a threat, and increasingly the root of that threat was sexual. No white woman was safe.

Cocaine was a threat greater than any the nation had so far faced because it formed "a hideous bondage from which [unlike slavery] they [these black cocaine addicts] cannot escape by mere proclamation or Civil War." In the years from 1908 to 1914, the *Times* detailed cases of blacks driven so wild by cocaine that "bullets fired into vital parts that would drop a sane man in his tracks fail to check the fiend[s]." It explained how frustrated Southern sheriffs had been forced to increase the caliber of hand guns from .32 to .38 just to have a chance of stopping berserk "Negro cocaine fiends." The *Times* detailed how as a consequence of this mayhem the sale of cocaine had already been made a felony in many Southern states.[21] This hyperbole was to have huge national and international repercussions. During these years Americans would put their prohibitionist efforts into a campaign which would shape criminality all over the world in which we now live. In order to understand them, it is helpful to look at the influence of one particular activist.

If one single person can be considered the driving force behind this *Times* campaign, it has to be the indomitable Dr Hamilton Wright. Wright was an ambitious Canadian medical researcher specializing in tropical and nervous disorders. However, having married into a wealthy political family, Wright soon realized that he was better suited to the public life and shifted his interests away from medical research and into political lobbying. Through his wife's connections with the upper echelons of the Republican Party, he secured a position on a State Department Opium Commission and quickly rose to become one of the foremost experts on the domestic and international drug control movement. The time was ripe for reform and this commission was to have a major impact. Some historians have argued that this was not because the drug problem in the US was particularly bad, or even that the reformist urge was irresistible—although both hyperbole and the Progressive mood of the times played a part—but, they argue, it more was because the State Department had begun to highlight drug policy as a priority.[22]

While at first glance it may seem curious that the State Department was so interested in narcotics, a closer examination reveals a rational connection. American diplomats realized that opium, morality, and international trade could potentially be beneficially interlinked. The result was that they gave Wright's campaign considerable support. The logic behind the sudden interest was convoluted. It stems back to early twentieth-century diplomacy, where the markets of the decaying empire of China were considered one of the last serious commercial prizes in a world in which all the great colonial gems in Africa and Asia had already been grabbed.

Late to enter the colonization race—at least outside her own continental boundaries—many Americans felt they were not getting their fair share. Having gained Caribbean and Pacific Ocean dependencies in the wake of the Spanish American War, in 1899, the then Secretary of State, John Hay, rather highhandedly demanded what he called an "Open Door" policy on trade with China. Under this agreement the major concessionary powers in China (France, Germany, the United Kingdom, Italy, Russia and, even non-European, Japan) would effectively allow equal access to all Chinese markets for all nations, regardless of the size of the trade concessions the Chinese had already granted. The US was grappling with this effective lock-out from what they saw as potentially limitless markets.

In spite of their public lip service to free trade, rather predictably, the European and Japanese concessionaries ignored the request. As a result, the Americans turned to a strategy of gaining the moral high ground and trying to gain access through gaining popular support in China. Since the trade in opium, led by Britain, was seen as one of the reasons for Chinese decline, American efforts to stamp out the opium trade would, they felt, indicate an unusual degree of sincerity and altruism and hopefully persuade the Chinese that the US was different from the other powers. In essence, the US State Department argued that by advocating the abolition of the opium trade, America would appear more interested in aiding China's battle with narcotics and establishing a true basis of mutually beneficial trade, rather than in feeding off the remains of her decaying empire.

Wright had been one of the American delegates at the 1909 Opium Conference, suitably enough held in Shanghai. At this gathering of all the major powers, the Americans pushed on with their Chinese policy and Wright was in the thick of it. He had personally been instrumental in the Conference's reaching the agreement that all the participating nations would treat the non-medical use of opium via prohibition. On his return he used his considerable influence to make sure that America led, and would continue to lead the way in the pressure for a global criminalization of narcotics use throughout the twentieth century and beyond. Through a mixture of media management, dubious statistics, hyperbole and scare tactics, Wright gained considerable support for the idea that state laws outlawing opium usage or the supply of cocaine were simply not sufficient, what was required was federal legislation. To this end, he sent out questionnaires to law enforcement and prison officers, doctors, and drug companies in order to compile "accurate" statistics on the problem. With this information he lobbied newspapers and congressmen and also put considerable pressure on European governments to control the supplies of opium, cocaine, and Indian hemp coming from their colonial possessions into the United States.

Wright and his colleagues found themselves confronted by a dilemma. When attending a series of narcotics limitation conferences at The Hague between 1912 and 1914, Britain and other colonial powers made it clear that they resented the Americans' moralizing tone. They pointed out that the United States was in no position to preach prohibition to other nations when it had no real, effective, controls at home. The result of this pressure was the relatively unheralded passage of what one of the leading historians of Prohibition memorably referred to as a measure of greater "spiritual malignancy than the Volstead Act"—the 1914 Harrison Act.[23] This Act was highly significant to the development of the crimi-nalization of narcotics in America. Not only did it introduce federal punishments for failure to conform to new requirements for the supply, use, and movement of opiates, cocaine, and marijuana, but as a result of later refinements over the next decade, it effectively criminalized the supply of addicts by doctors. It also set in train the entire framework of modern American drug prohibition.[24]

A previous attempt to introduce similar legislation in 1911, the Foster Bill, had been scuppered by a coalition of drug companies, pharmacists, and doctors resenting the inferences and the interference in their markets by non-experts. By 1914, even their objections were muted and the Act slid through Congress unscathed leaving an admiring Secretary of State, William Jennings Bryan, asking Wright, "How did you manage it?"[25] In keeping with Bryan's incredulity, while most modern texts tend to stress the Harrison Act as being the effective starting point of the US war on drugs, at the time it slipped beneath most of the American public's notice. Some idea of this can be gathered by the fact that although the measure was signed into law by President Woodrow Wilson on December 17, 1914, in spite of the paper's ongoing campaign against narcotics abuse, it was not even reported in the *New York Times* until January 2, 1915. This may seem relatively unimportant given the war being fought in Europe and the holiday nature of the time of year but by contrast the debates surrounding the Volstead Act took up massive amounts of column inches for months before, during, and after it became law. The passage of the Act was the banner headline the day after the Senate overrode Wilson's veto in the same newspaper. As the historian David Musto put it, the question with drugs was one of *how* to outlaw their use, not, as with alcohol, *whether* to ban it.[26]

There were a variety of instructive reasons which each go some way to explain why this fundamental difference existed in the criminalization of the two "vices." In part, it was the result of the seeming anomaly that while a large proportion of Americans condoned moderate drinking, as one expert on opiate addiction put it in 1928, "opium use in any form is regarded by the general public as alone a habit, vice, sign of weak will or dissipation."[27] Once the forces of prohibition had been unleashed on drug taking, the user—however moderate his or her consumption—was regarded as an asocial outcast, a degenerate, and a dangerous criminal. Alcohol had a social function in American society. Some abused it, but it was, and had been, sanctioned by Americans at all levels of society. The Bible even contained references to its manufacture and use. By contrast, opium dens had been seen to be frequented by undesirable Chinese and some weaker members of white society—largely, innocent young girls and weak-willed men. Cocaine was portrayed as a drug for the bestial Negro and the urban poor. The far more numerous mainstream addicts—white, middle-class women; prescription drug and, before the Pure Food and Drug Act of 1906, patent medicine addicts as well as medical practitioners who self-administered their habit—had been more or less invisible until the prohibitionists had highlighted their presence and indicated how, if these Americans could become users, all Americans were at risk.

Once reformers shone their lights into the murky world of narcotics, what they exposed became a warning of the dangers inherent in a whole host of changes taking place in American society at the time. What the public gathered from these highly publicized accounts was that the emerging drug companies, soon to be household names, seemed more than happy to emulate the shocking morals of the Robber Barons, incorporating addictive drugs into their products and resisting legislation which would limit such practices. At the professional and commercial level, these morals were emulated by doctors, pharmacists, and soda-fountain owners who continued the lucrative trade although they knew it to be damaging to their addicted customers and clients. At the lowest end of the social scale, there were the drug dealers who not only fed the vices of their users but used the likes of "janitors, barmen and cabmen ... [as 'pushers'] to help spread the habit."[28]

These were the years of the rapid urbanization of America. The nation had developed from a rural society in 1865, where vastly more Americans lived and worked in the agrarian sectors, to becoming an urban society where, by 1920, the majority of Americans lived in settlements of 2,500 residents or more. This phenomenon was seen as upsetting, if not removing, America's moral compass. To a variety of groups, from the early twentieth-century rural Progressives of the Country Life Movement, to the Ku Klux Klan of the 1920s, the city was seen as a place of squalor, corruption, and temptation. Cities bred the vice and crime associated with booze and narcotics. Popular perceptions dictated that alcoholics were frequently violent, but always wastrels who were incapable of proper work. Narcotics addicts required money to feed their habits. Between them, whether through promiscuity, immorality, robbery or prostitution, the city offered more varied and lucrative possibilities than rural or small town America could offer. The city also attracted the waifs and strays, the hopeful and the gullible, that were more likely to form easy prey for the pushers, pimps, and dealers already living there.

It is an indication of the changing perception of drug use that in the groundbreaking, best-selling, novel *Porgy* of 1925—later immortalized as George Gershwin's *Porgy and Bess*—the heroine, Bess, is seduced by Sportin' Life, a malevolent "city Negro" who uses cocaine in order to break down her resistance.[29] The prevalence of such interpretations grew as temperance propaganda gave way to prohibition, as the user gave way to the addict, but even so, some groups chose to look at the prevalent opinions from another viewpoint. Since it was illegal to sell alcohol, a small sub-group of Americans took the attitude that they may as well use other illegal substances. These was nothing new in this, earlier experiments with prohibition in the South had led to a shift towards the use of cocaine in the poor blacks of the region. In 1914, the *New York Times* had trumpeted that black Southerners, in many of the states where they were a majority, had "taken to 'sniffing' since being deprived of whisky by prohibition."[30] By the 1920s, this attitude had spread across the nation and into different classes.

As the decade progressed, it became increasingly established in the small, decadent, upper-class "fast set" with money and questionable morals. This elite group of society with its image as self-conscious *avant-garde* trendsetters was willing to question the existing norms and mores. While it could be argued that such super-wealthy hedonists always had found—and always will find—their thrills in more dangerous experiments than those available to or desired by the common herd, in these years of excess, prohibition provided another spur. Both male and female "Jazz Age" thrill-seekers smoked opium and marijuana and used cocaine as they mingled with the underworld in night clubs, cabarets, speakeasies and high class private members' clubs where the booze flowed and the police, often handsomely paid to do so, ignored it. Curiously, while this group certainly attracted far more attention, their antics may actually have served to reduce the urban narcotics problem—at least locally. According to one commentator, in the most infamous of these clubs, the Cotton Club and the Plantation Club, in New York's then highly fashionable Harlem district, the money paid by whites for booze, cocaine, opium, and marijuana led to an increase in price which made these commodities way beyond the reach of the far more numerous local residents' pockets.[31]

If illegal drink and drugs spread through all levels of society during this period, gambling was already prevalent at all levels. There was little new in this. It had permeated all levels of American society since colonial days. While the wealthy colonial planters had often frittered away fortunes on the after dinner gambling tables, their indentured servants had been known to use wagers and lotteries as a way to squirrel away enough to terminate their period of indenture. This had continued with the Plantocracy and their slaves. It appears that although these relationships were often riddled with hypocrisy, at least with respect to gambling, a level of, almost, equality sometimes existed. Some planters allowed servants, and even slaves, to keep their winnings. Others enforced strict, if often hypocritical measures, to outlaw any gambling, punishing it with severe floggings.[32] As the twentieth century opened, industrialization had not really changed this, perhaps all it had changed was there were now wealthier gamblers at the top and poorer ones at the bottom. By 1900, betting was still both a mark of conspicuous consumption for the wealthy—a term coined at the turn of the twentieth century by the sociologist Thorstein Veblen—and of desperation for the poor.

Perhaps inevitably just as social reformers no longer relied on purely religious objections to justify their control of drinking and drug taking, the same was true with gambling. As the new century dawned, as the other vices became associated with sexual promiscuity, prostitution and robbery, so gambling was increasingly associated with other criminal and immoral behavior and the lenient attitude taken towards betting was changing. Gambling "dens," "hells," and "dives" increasingly tended to be cordoned off into one area of the town or city, ostensibly facilitating law-keeping and sparing the city's more sensitive residents inconvenience and unnecessary distress. In reality, they simply concentrated many vices into one area. Gambling was frequently carried out in all-male environments—saloons, clubs, tracks, rings or pits—where the only women, and perhaps some of the men, were liable to be prostitutes. It was rare that drink was not a vital element and, given the company and the lubrication, the atmosphere was hardly likely to elicit exemplory behavior.

What was more, gambling was, as the Muckraker of the slums, Jacob Riis, put it "by instinct and by nature brutal, because it is selfishness in its coldest form."[33] As the twentieth century dawned and America underwent one of its periods of reform, the much publicized excesses of the Gilded Age had made such selfishness repugnant. In the decades either side of 1900 the star of the Progressives was very much in the ascendant. A disparate group made up of largely urban, largely Christian and largely white reformers, the Progressives advocated civic responsibility, the Social Gospel and rational, scientific reform. Irrational, unChristian and irresponsible, gambling was one of their targets. In 1894, Louisiana finally outlawed lotteries, making state lotteries illegal across the entire Union. By 1900, only the states of Maryland, Kentucky and New York allowed trackside betting at the races. The process of banning gambling dens was started by California, beginning with specific games, spreading through premises, to house banks and finally all players in 1891. By 1910, casinos and other gambling dens were almost universally illegal in America.

As with drinking or drug taking, there was a strong class influence on attitudes to the legitimacy of gambling establishments. Patrician Americans' use of clubs and salons, where gambling and drinking were frequent and accepted, were not the primary target of the prohibitionists' rhetoric. The bulk of condemnation was aimed at the dingy, dirty saloon, selling rot gut and frequented by working men. As one commentator said:

> The country club people will probably go on boozing until the end of time. The best prohibition can hope to accomplish is to save the poor man. It saves him by making drink too expensive for him.[34]

Similarly, the middle-class, white, woman's laudanum or opium habit, or the physician's self-administered cocaine were not the underlying reason for the prohibitionist Harrison Act. That was motivated by poor blacks' use of cocaine and fear that the Chinese opium fiend would push his wares on poor whites. Similarly, and even more strikingly, the majority of gambling regulations were not aimed at those who like Jay Gould or even Arnold Rothstein, men who would gamble hundreds of thousands or even millions of dollars. Regulation of gambling seemed to be aimed at those who would buy lottery tickets or who would place a bet on a favorite horse. Nothing seemed to illustrate this better than the legislation against the "bucket shop."

Imitating their wealthier fellow citizens, many humble urban Americans took to playing the stock market in the final decades of the nineteenth century. Thousands would use small, illegitimate, unregulated, "boiler rooms" and "bucket shops" to speculate on the movement of the securities and futures in companies listed on the New York Stock Exchange. Arguing that since the bucket shops were unregulated and did not actually sell shares and that no certificates changed hands, such speculation was simply gambling. As the *National Police Gazette* put it:

> The spirit of stock gambling is abroad in the land ... The desire to get rich quick without earning it by the sweat of one's brow is a strong incentive to stock gambling ... Did the Vanderbilts, did the Astors ... did one hundred and one other rich men of this country get rich by stock gambling? Answer this question yourself and if you do this truthfully, it will not be "yes."[35]

Unlike the "speculation of this kind [carried out] by competent men" which Supreme Court Justice Oliver Wendell Holmes claimed was a "means of avoiding or mitigating catastrophes, equalizing prices and providing for periods of want," the customers of the bucket shop simply bet for their own profit and should be outlawed.[36] Since there were no universally recognized professional qualifications for brokers, let alone speculators, quite who constituted a "competent man" must have been open to debate. Nevertheless given this distinction, by the 1920s, in time for the greatest bull market up to that point in US history, most of the major urban centers had effectively outlawed such unregulated brokerages.

However, even without the means of the bucket shop, many foreign observers, as well as Americans, still felt that there was a strong link between gambling and the stock market. The mania that grabbed over three million Americans as the stock boom reached a peak in the late 1920s was difficult to differentiate from the fervor of gambling. It certainly appeared so to the old financial elite. This group grudgingly complained that the times were changing when "bootblacks, household servants, and clerks ... school teachers, seamstresses, barbers, machinists, necktie salesmen, gas fitters, motormen, family cooks, and lexicographers" all had brokerage accounts. They made serious efforts to outlaw such speculation. In February 1928, at the height of the stock bubble, the US Senate Committee on Banking and Currency debated the banning of stock trading. The nation's Senators agreed: "There is no trouble at all in stopping the gambling ... We have a law against poker gambling, and we can have a law against stock gambling."

The debate hinged on the dilemma which had lain behind the banning of bucket shops. How did legislation preserve the "necessary" and "legitimate" being raised on the open market while outlawing that trading which could be viewed as purely speculative and accumulative? The problem was how to recognize what constituted the illegitimate. As US Senator Earle Mayfield of Texas, fresh from the fight to ban alcohol, informed his fellow Senators, "There are millions of stocks and bonds sold every day by people who do not own them and have no idea of owning them. Purely gambling on the market." Such thinking was not limited to the provincial puritans or even the financially naïve. Virginia Senator, Carter Glass, former Secretary of the Treasury under Wilson, one of the devisors of the Federal Reserve System and co-sponsor of the Glass–Seagal Act, illustrated the problem in terms of stock values. He gave the example of a share which he personally owned. It had nearly halved in value in less than a year. The share had done this without reporting any devastatingly poor accounts or any other rational cause. Given this seemingly randomly generated decline, he asked his fellow Senators: "Now what is that but gambling?"[37] Needless to say, given the devastation caused by the 1929 Crash, over a year later, and the turbulence which has occurred so many times since, the concerned Senators failed in these efforts. Many Americans still sought, and still seek, to isolate the gamblers from the speculators: the criminals from the "competent."

If a small group of Senators failed to isolate "stock gamblers" from businessmen, the same failure was not true of another part of the federal government's attempts to ban another vice. The reasons for the success and failure are enlightening. The Federal Bureau of Narcotics (FBN) under its charismatic, ambitious and driven leader, Harry Anslinger, began an active campaign to make the use, transport, and sale of marijuana a federal offense. Since California had banned its use in 1915, marijuana had been outlawed in a growing number of states, until by 1937 it was outlawed in all the states of the Union. Nevertheless, to most Americans who were even aware of its existence, unlike stock speculation, it was not considered to be a serious problem to the morality or wealth of those who indulged in its use.

Unlike the nation's Senators, the FBN saw such legislation falling directly within their remit and there can be little doubt that there was an element of "empire-building" behind Anslinger's enthusiasm. Unlike the Senators, they could produce direct "scientific" data which showed a direct correlation between usage, addiction, and criminal activity. Like the campaign against alcohol, Anslinger mobilized all media. He showed the correlation between the "killer weed" and sexual license, family breakdown, violence, and insanity. As he told the House Ways and Means Committee in 1936:

> Some people will fly into a delirious rage, and they are temporarily irresponsible and may commit violent crimes. Other people will laugh uncontrollably. It is impossible to say what the effect will be on any individual. [Nevertheless] … It is dangerous to the mind and body, and particularly dangerous to the criminal type, because it releases all of the inhibitions.[38]

With this in mind, unlike the Senators, the opponents of marijuana were committed to outlawing what they saw as a minority practice, not one which had devolved down from the respectable classes. This was a drug whose users largely came from Mexico, or were urban blacks. Like the prohibition on cocaine, Anslinger used this segregated usage as an argument to create a moral panic. Here were small, identifiable, alien groups who were attempting to pollute the American nation. It seemed that this was true since, like the revelers who drank, took cocaine and heroin and, indeed, marijuana, in degenerate Harlem, those whites who used the drug tended to be Bohemian, jazz-loving, *demi-monde* types. Unlike the Senators, Anslinger persisted until Congress passed the Marijuana Taxation Act, in 1937.[39]

Deciding which "vices" should be made illegal is only a part of the influence of such prohibitions on criminalization in the history of modern America. Arguably more important than what was outlawed, or why, is the influence that such legislation itself had on crime. Did prohibiting alcohol improve the quality of life for the ex-drinker and his family? Did it do away with the saloons as hubs of criminal activity? Did legislation proscribing more or less free access to narcotics really prevent the creation of addicts, and the resultant criminal activity? Did banning street games, race track betting, casinos, lotteries and other gambling really stop associated criminal behavior? Or were these prohibitions really just responsible for driving such practices underground, increasing the money available to those willing to indulge those addicted to, or simply requiring, alcohol, drugs or other outlawed "kicks"?

America was not the first modern industrialized state to outlaw booze. By the time the Volstead Act came into force in January 1920, alcohol was illegal in the Soviet Union; in Iceland (where beer remained illegal through until 1989); in Norway and in Finland. It had been prohibited, briefly, the year before, in Hungary under Bela Kun's brutally communist regime and Prince Edward Island in Canada would remain dry right through until 1948. With these other examples in mind, why is it that today prohibition is almost uniquely associated with the United States? Certainly, America was the most populous and the wealthiest of these states, but the essence of the answer must most likely lie with the perceived changes it wrought on US society, most importantly conflation of crime with the Noble Experiment. In this regard, America is seen as unique. Unlike the US, the exclusion of booze in Finland over the same period, for example, is not regarded in the historical memory—at least not in America—with shootouts, corruption, bootlegging and gangsterism. In fact, according to one American correspondent in 1929, throughout the period of the ban, which lasted from 1919 until 1932, a large minority of Finns ignored the legislation in much the same way as their American contemporaries. After ten years as a "Dry" state, Finland's figures for alcohol-related illnesses as well as convictions for drunkenness, violent crime and firearms offenses all grew dramatically, as did the prison population. Bootleggers brought in branded liquor, largely from Germany and Poland and the illegally distilled clear spirit, "Ninety-Six"—so-called because of its hideously high alcohol content—was near ubiquitous in all urban and metropolitan cafés and restaurants.[40]

So why is American Prohibition considered unique? It is perhaps the scale of crime it was seen to unleash. According to one survey taken in 30 US cities, there was a 24 percent increase in the crime rate between 1920 and 1931. The rate of arrests on account of drunkenness rose 41 percent, and arrests for drunken driving increased by over 80 percent. Thefts went up by nearly 10 percent, and assault and battery incidents rose some 13 percent. Before Prohibition, there had only been a little over 4000 federal convicts, of whom less than 3000 were housed in federal prisons. By 1932, the number of federal convicts had increased by 561 percent and the federal prison population had grown by over 350 percent. Moreover, it appeared that it was prohibitions which seemed to lie at the root of this increase, since over two-thirds of all prisoners convicted in 1930 were imprisoned on alcohol and drug-related charges.[41]

Prohibition's influences on crime are varied. It is generally held that the 1920s saw an explosion in gangsterism and that this came about as the result of Prohibition. However there is some dispute as to *which* prohibition it was that caused this. The prohibition of alcohol, it is claimed, gave a much needed shot in the arm to flagging professional, organized crime in the 1920s. One perspective sees the Progressive Era as having removed many of the traditional income streams which had fed large-scale criminal activity, after all, during these years the nation was undergoing one of its periodic spells of reform fervor. The cleaning up of metropolitan and urban government had done away with the bread and butter income of many of the strong-arm gangs who had intimidated and cajoled voters and opponents for the machines in local politics. Wartime crusades against prostitution had also done away with another traditional source of the mobsters' income. When the Progressives instigated what was arguably their final reform—banning alcohol—they revived gangsterism and gave gangsters sufficient capital and income to raise professional crime to a new level. Here was an easily produced, relatively valuable, and easily shippable commodity with a huge market. The profits available to those willing to break the law were huge and these massive profits in turn generated economies of scale and entirely new ways of developing criminal businesses.[42]

Another view sees the roots of crime syndication as going way back before this period, and sees gambling as the engine. In this interpretation it is the clampdown on urban gambling houses in the major cities—most notably Chicago, New York, and New Orleans—which provides the impetus for criminal syndication. When New York introduced anti-gaming legislation in 1867, John, "Old Smoke," Morrissey formed an association of professional gamblers, whose aim was to protect themselves from raids by the authorities. By buying off police and other officials, Morrissey's association managed not only to defend itself from disruptive raids, but their mounting wealth also enabled them to become a significant force in the political activity of the city. By the late 1870s, Morrissey's syndicate was challenging and defeating even the mighty Tammany Hall's power in its previously unassailable strongholds in the city's Fourth and Seventh wards.[43] Similar criminal organizations emerged over the next decade in response to other attempted purges on gambling. The most notorious of these was in New Orleans where a formal system of bribing policemen and politicians at all levels ensured that professional gamblers were left in peace. In Chicago, a syndicate used their financial and organizational muscle to replace a particularly troublesome mayor with a more amenable candidate of their own.[44]

As the historian Mark Haller pointed out, the power of these criminal syndications was such that by the end of the nineteenth century in some cities, "it was not so much that gambling syndicates influenced local political organization; rather, gambling syndicates were [the] local political organizations."[45] Syndicated, organized crime depended on the ability of the criminal "underworld" to have connections with, and protection from, a legitimate "upperworld"—police, lawyers, judges, business leaders, and politicians. Without this complicity the syndicate could never really evolve as criminal entrepreneurs. In this respect the outlawing of both gambling and alcohol provided the catalyst for what historian Humbert S. Nelli called crime's "Great Leap Forward." The lack of a genuine consensus supporting the bans, coupled with the huge market and the massive profits available, meant that those willing to take the risks of producing, importing, shipping, and selling alcohol were able to pay previously unheard amounts to those willing to turn a blind eye, or even facilitate their law breaking. Some prescient opponents of the Volstead Act claimed it would re-introduce an "Old Spoils Evil" reminiscent of the worst days of Tammany's graft.[46]

In fact, in many ways, it turned out to be worse. Bribery reached truly epic proportions. The best example of the spoils available to the ambitious is the tale of George Remus. Within two years of the enacting of the Volstead Act, the Cincinnati-based, German-American bootlegger, Remus, had built up a chain of fake drug stores across the Mid-West. The network employed some 3,000 people selling "medicinal whisky" and he was well on the way to having cornered the American whiskey market. Remus' bonded warehouses were selling "industrial" alcohol by the truck or trainload. What was more, it seemed he was living a charmed life, behaving in an ostentatiously generous fashion. He ran a fleet of cars for his own personal use and held huge parties where the most famous and attractive would rub shoulders with the more brutal of Cincinnati's citizens, as the booze flowed, openly. He once gave 50 women who attended one such party of his a new Pontiac car each, as a parting gift.

All this was done without his actually owning a legitimate business to support such extravagance. It later emerged that he was only able to sustain his imperial-scale business and lifestyle by paying out an estimated $20 million a year—probably half of his annual turnover—as bribes and payoffs. Events would prove that even this was not enough. By the end of May 1922, Remus had been sentenced to a two-year jail sentence and fined $10,000 for bootlegging. More or less unconcerned and confident that his powerful connections would prove suffi-ciently motivated to quash the charges, he continued to expand his operation while appealing against his sentence. He was over-confident in their abilities and power. By 1924, with all avenues of appeal finally closed, Remus was imprisoned in Atlanta. He ruefully commented later that—"A few men tried to corner the wheat market only to find there is too much wheat in the world. I tried to corner the graft market only to find there is not enough money in the world to buy up all the public officials."[47]

There were a number of reasons for Remus' downfall, but perhaps the most important was that his over-confidence and extravagance meant he came to the attention of Burt Morgan and Sam Collins, respectively the Prohibition directors of Indiana and Kentucky. These two officials were as committed to keeping their states dry as they were persistent, cunning, and incorruptible. They were also highly unusual. Even if the majority of the nation had been committed to the eradication of alcoholic drinks, the task would have been difficult. With support largely concentrated in the South and rural areas of the Mid-West, the 12,000 miles of US coastline plus the lengthy land borders with Canada and Mexico were nearly impossible to police effectively. The forces charged with prohibition were dreadfully under-resourced. Although they might be able to call on coast-guard and police forces, at their peak in 1930, less than 3,000 Prohibition agents across the nation were pitted against an estimated 50,000 involved in the illegal booze industry in Michigan alone. In New York City, even the diminutive, but feisty, Mayor, Fiorello La Guardia, realized it was a hopeless task. He claimed it would require 250,000 police to stand a chance of making Prohibition work. What was more, as Remus' tale illustrates, the majority of these agents were hardly committed to catching bootleggers or rum runners. LaGuardia was aware of this when he told Franklin Roosevelt that even if he had the required manpower for interception, he would require a further 250,000 to police the police.[48]

Even when the authorities were genuinely dedicated to enforcing the law, they frequently found themselves hamstrung by what appeared to be legal niceties. The necessity to produce a warrant meant that all but those basest of "blind pigs" (low-end drinking dives) would have been forewarned and all but the most inept smugglers and moonshiners would have paid off the relevant agents. One prosecuting attorney in Michigan lamented that the system was weighted against the law when he told the court ruefully that "If the [US] Constitution could speak, it would say 'Thou shalt not traffic in intoxicating liquor, but if you do I shall lend my best efforts to prevent its being proved.'"[49] The result was that the most successful Prohibition agents felt that they could only enforce the Volstead Act by breaking or bending the law themselves. As one confessed, he had entrapped bell boys in hotels through claiming he had the mother of all hangovers and pleading with them to get him a hair of the dog. As he explained, "Then a raid followed, the hotel is pinched and the bell-hop arrested—a most glorious achievement for the officials of the great United States."[50]

Another aspect of the problem was summed up when the Seattle policeman turned bootlegger Roy Olmstead was convicted by the use of illegal wiretaps. The Supreme Court ruled that since force was not used, it could not be unreasonable search and seizure, but two of the Justices dissented. One, Oliver Wendell Holmes, saw the problem clearly and argued that, "We have to choose, and for my part I think it is less evil that some criminals should escape than that the government should play an ignoble part [in their conviction]." The other, Louis Brandeis, warned, "Crime is contagious. If the government becomes a lawbreaker it breeds contempt for the law ... It invites anarchy."[51] Some commentators thought anarchy had already been established. The US homicide rate had quadrupled in the first two decades of the twentieth century, and it reached a peak in the 1920s. Some simply saw the gangsterism unleashed by Prohibition behind this, but it was probably more complex than that. What was more, such violent crime as racketeering engendered tended to be limited to victims from within the bootlegging, gambling or drug communities. For example, when the mobster Hymie Weiss sent a fleet of cars to shoot Capone in the Hawthorne Hotel in 1925, the first car had machine gunners with blanks to disperse "civilians."[52]

It is some measure of how unpopular Prohibition was that figures were frequently cited which "proved" that more were killed in the enforcement of Prohibition, than by bootleggers. By the end of 1920, one Prohibition agent had been killed enforcing the Prohibition laws. By 1930, official figures claimed that 86 Prohibition agents and over two hundred "civilians" had been killed. These figures were disputed by the *Washington Herald* in 1929, which claimed that the figure for civilians should have been 1,360 killed as well as 1,000 wounded. It was not a coincidence that during these years one of the most popular bumper-stickers read, "Don't shoot me, I am not a bootlegger." Nor was this the only way in which the authorities killed the population through their passion to save them from the demon rum. In order to prevent the use of industrial alcohol to manufacture booze, as soon as the Volstead Act was passed it was announced that industrial alcohol would be "denatured"—in other words, deadly toxins were added. While many made fortunes by removing these toxins, others were less effective and skilled and consequently less fortunate. In 1925, the national toll for people poisoned by alcohol was 4,154 as compared to 1,064 in 1920. In 1926, the *New York World* compared the federal government to the Borgias, so great was their skill at poisoning.[53]

Perhaps the most important way in which Prohibition affected crime was by effectively turning a large section of the populace into criminals. In New York City, federal Prohibition agents arrested 11,000 people for violations of the Volstead Act in 1922 alone. By 1933, 40,000 had been imprisoned nationally and in order to contain the massive increase in prisoners, six new federal prisons were needed. The figures for the growth of bars of one form or another in most urban and metropolitan regions show that the legislation did little to halt alcohol consumption. Surveys revealed that the initial acceptance of the laws was replaced by an increasing irritation, a sense that the Volstead Act was at best unnecessary, if not an infringement of civil liberties. To a growing proportion of the population, those who attempted to enforce the legislation were either corrupt, inept or so sanctimonious their piety kept them out of touch with reality. Alcohol proved to be too well entrenched in the social life of America to be removed by legislation. Despite this, the final president of the 1920s, Herbert Hoover, was a teetotaler. His answer to the obvious failures of what he termed the "Noble Experiment" was to increase the penalties for failure to observe the drinking laws. In spite of complaining about the futility of attempting to legislate alcohol out of America, he signed the Jones Act into law, authorizing first offenders under the Volstead Act to be given up to five years in prison or be fined up to $10,000.

The result was that in these final years of Prohibition the punishments seemed little less than Draconian. Perhaps the most infamous was the case in 1929 of Etta May Miller of Lansing, Michigan. Under the state's last ditch four strikes and out policy, this repeat offender, moonshiner, mother of ten children and grandmother to two, was sentenced in Detroit to life in prison for the possession of a single bottle of gin. Sentencing her, the General Secretary of the Board of Temperance gives some idea of the thinking behind such harsh legislation when he told the court, "Our only regret is that the woman was not sentenced to life imprisonment before her ten children were born. When one has violated the Constitution four times, he or she should be segregated from society to prevent the production of subnormal offspring." Nevertheless, reflecting growing public dissatisfaction with Prohibition, and in spite of this attitude, the governor of Michigan freed her in March 1930, after she had served less than a year.[54]

If the decade of alcohol prohibition made criminals of ordinary people, it also created some extraordinary criminals whose glamorous reputations, flamboyant lifestyles and almost unbelievable wealth were far from ordinary and added to the appeal of such criminal behavior. One such figure stands head and shoulders above the other rum runners and bootleggers of his generation. In the Pantheon of American criminals few have achieved the lasting fame to match that of Al Capone, who has become synonymous with Prohibition, Chicago and gangsterism. Unapologetically ruthless in his manner and always surrounded by apelike lackeys, Capone was seen as the archetypal mobster of the 1920s. The exponent of a new and brutal form of urban, hierarchical, organized and integrated crime, he was seen as despicable and bestial by many Americans, but he also had a peculiar draw to a large proportion of others. As Capone himself confessed, he supplied a need, and in so doing broke a law. But as he pointed out, it was a law which as the 1920s progressed and his empire grew, had less and less support among the American public. He neglected to mention, or at least played down, the inconvenient fact that part of his huge turnover was provided by the less acceptable occupations of prostitution, protection, and gambling.

Few people represented this time of brash, new money, and brief celebrity better than Capone. In an era when the president famously claimed that "the business of America is business," Capone saw himself as a businessman, the "Rockefeller of Chicago's bootleggers," and one life history of the master racketeer was sub-titled *The Biography of a Self-Made Man*. It was estimated that Capone made $100 million in 1927 alone and that at his zenith his empire employed over 1,000 people, supplying over 22,000 outlets with booze, with a payroll of $300,000 a week. It was fitting that this businessman was eventually imprisoned, not for murder or racketeering, but for federal income tax evasion.

Few things said more about the new type of gangster than Capone's personal appearance. It was a peculiar mix of ostentation and image management. The gangster was instantly recognizable because of gruesome scars running down the entire side of his face. Those who knew his life history were aware it was the result of three knife slashes on his jaw, neck and face from a drunken customer in his days as a New York bouncer. The image-conscious Capone claimed these wounds had been inflicted while serving his country in the famous "Lost Battalion" in France during the Great War. Either way while he applied talcum powder every day to conceal them, newspapers would often touch up the scars to make them more apparent and Capone's childlike face look more sinister.

Capone was just as fastidious about his clothes. He dressed in flamboyant suits, wore a trademark Fedora hat and ostentatious jewelry studded with diamonds.

What was more, he was as articulate in his underworld patois and trademark drawl, as he was publicity seeking. By the late 1920s, he had become a national media figure and was asked for his opinion on issues ranging from prohibition to the presidency. When he lost weight, reporters pestered him for dieting tips. When he ordered a car, its bullet-proof glass, armor plate, gun loops, v16 engine, 120 mph top speed and $20,000 price tag were almost instantly public knowledge. Not only did Hollywood celebrities—both men and women—vie with each other to be seen with him, but films were made of his life story and stars like James Cagney made their names playing gangsters based on him.

Capone's career clearly demonstrated that the prohibition of alcohol certainly boosted crime. It not only provided a fillip of huge amounts of regular cash for the old-style urban mobs. That income in turn enabled the mobsters to invest in ever faster cars, better weaponry and other benefits of technology. It enabled them to employ more effective lawyers to protect them from prosecution and more effective accountants to bury their profits. It gave them more funds with which to bribe officials and also gave them capital to invest in business diversification—both legal and illegal. Alcohol prohibition fed a sort of symbiosis in the criminal world. Not only could the funds from moon-shining, bootlegging and rum running fund prostitution, labor and protection racketeering as with Capone and his henchmen, but those involved in other prohibited activities, like gambling or narcotics, could use the funds generated by them to enter the booze business.

In the early days of Prohibition, New York's leading criminal fixer, Arnold Rothstein—"the big bankroll," as he was known—used his huge gambling-derived wealth to fund a new style of rum running. He began supplying wholesale high quality, high priced booze directly from European and Canadian producers, rather than moonshine and "naturalized" industrial alcohol. When the market for these goods became too crowded, and not profitable enough, he shifted to supplying narcotics. Perhaps the last word on this symbiosis of crime should go to a law-keeper. Even during the era of alcohol prohibition, it was not solely the finance generated by the ban which fed criminal activity. As Fiorello LaGuardia—never a great fan of Prohibition—told FDR, the concurrent gambling prohibition took up valuable police manpower since, "We have to use a large part of our police force in the supervision, discovery and apprehension of the gentry who run these lotteries ... [which] if legalized would free these officers for other duties." Perhaps he understood better than many others, the real implications of prohibitions. Perhaps it was more that as a proud Italian-American he realized that immigrants—Jews, Irish and most importantly Italians—were, rightly or wrongly, seen as the leading bootleggers, pimps, racketeers, and drug dealers.

In the end, this increase in crime should perhaps be measured against the, sometimes admittedly limited, benefits the prohibitions brought. The narcotics prohibitions did remove at least some addictive drugs from soft drinks, tonics, and patent medicines. They did reduce the number of registered addicts and made people more aware of the dangers of narcotic abuse. However, with this prohibitive approach the United States set in train a war against drugs which arguably can never be won. Through educating the public the Noble Experiment against alcohol reduced the deaths from alcohol-related illnesses—although, significantly as has been described above, not from alcoholic poisoning itself. It also reduced the nation's overall alcohol consumption and it also, arguably, improved the sanitation, safety and standards of many of the nation's saloons, bars and clubs. The final prohibition of this section was less successful. It is difficult to tell what advantages the gambling prohibitions gave the nation. Of all these morally based campaigns, this was arguably the least successful in this period. As LaGuardia succinctly put it, "Men and women will always gamble. If they don't do it one way, they will do it another." Perhaps this was true of all the prohibitions.[55]

Notes

1. Cited in Larry Englemann, *Intemperance* (New York, 1970), p. xi.

2. Cited in Sean Dennis Cashman, *Prohibition: The Lie of the Land* (New York, 1981), p. 18.

3. For details of American drinking habits, see Mark E. Lender and James K. Martin, *Drinking in America: A History* (New York, 1987). For a sophisticated and readable account of the early temperance movement, see James A. Morone, *Hellfire Nation: The Politics of Sin in American History* (New Haven, CT, 2003), pp. 281–317.

4. See John Kobler, *Ardent Spirits: The Rise and Fall of Prohibition* (New York, 1973).

5. Quotation taken from Henry Chafetz, *Play the Devil: A History of Gambling in the United States from 1492 to 1950* (New York, 1960), p. 115.

6. For an example of the Southern aristocratic penchant for gambling, see T. H. Breen, "Horses and Gentlemen: The Cultural Significance of Gambling among the Gentry of Virginia," *The William and Mary Quarterly* 34, 2 (Apr., 1977): 239–257.

7. For an original and comprehensive analysis of gambling in nineteenth-century America, see Ann Fabian, *Card Sharps and Bucket Shops: Gambling in Nineteenth-Century America* (New York, 1999).

8. Jefferson, cited in William N. Thompson, *Legalized Gambling: A Reference Handbook* (Santa Barbara, CA, 1997), pp. 8–9.

9. See Charles T. Clotfelter and Philip J. Cook, *Selling Hope: State Lotteries in America* (Cambridge, MA, 1989), p. 20. For a detailed analysis of lotteries, see John Samuel Ezell, *Fortune's Merry Wheel: The Lottery in America* (Cambridge, MA, 1960).

10. For details of spectator sports in pre-Bellum America, see Elliott Gorn and Warren Goldstein, *A Brief History of American Sports* (Champaign, IL, 2004), pp. 47–152.

11. See Virginia Berridge and Griffith Edwards, *Opium and the People: Opiate Use in Nineteenth-Century England* (London, 1982) and David T. Courtwright, *Dark Paradise: Opiate Addiction in America before 1940* (Cambridge, MA, 1972).

12. *New York Times*, September 29, 1918.

13. Figures taken from Charles Edward Terry and Mildred Pellens, *The Opium Problem* (New York, 1928), p. 13.

14. Figures taken from Humberto Fernandez, *Heroin* (New York, 1998), p. 20.

15. See David T. Courtwright, op. cit., pp. 35–60.

16. See Eric C. Schneider, *Smack: Heroin and the American City* (Philadelphia, PA, 2008), pp. 2–5.

17. Jacob A. Riis, *How the Other Half Lives: Studies Among the Tenements of New York* (New York, 1890), p. 76.

18. Quotation taken from Charles Whitebread, "The History of the Non-Medical Use of Drugs in the United States," a speech to the California Judges Association 1995 annual conference and reproduced in full at http://www.druglibrary.org/schaffer/History/ whiteb1.htm.

19. For details of cocaine in the working population, see Joseph F. Spillane, *Cocaine: From Medical Marvel to Modern Menace in the United States, 1884–1920* (Baltimore, MD, 1999), pp. 90–96.

20. See Jill Jonnes, *Hep-Cats, Narcs and Pipe Dreams: A History of America's Romance with Illegal Drugs* (Baltimore, MD, 1996), pp. 19–21. The consumption figure is taken from Joel L. Phillips and Ronald D. Wynne, *Cocaine: The Mystique and the Reality* (New York, 1980), p. 56.

21. The most important, and most cited article, remains the *New York Times*, "Negro Cocaine Fiends: New Southern Menace," February 11, 1914. For details of the *New York Times* campaign and citation of quotes used, see Doris M. Provine, *Unequal Under Law: Race in the War on Drugs* (Chicago, 2007), pp. 76–82.

22. One of the best analyses of this view can be found in David R. Bewley-Taylor, *The United States and International Drug Control, 1909–1997* (London, 1999), pp. 18–27.

23. Norman H. Clark, *Deliver Us From Evil: An Interpretation of American Prohibition* (New York, 1976), p. 222.

24. For an analysis of the debate over, the structure of and the immediate implications of the Harrison Act, see David F. Musto, *The American Disease: Origins of Narcotic Control* (Oxford, 1999), pp. 54–65.

25. Ibid., pp. 58–63. Quotation on p. 59.

26. Ibid., p. 65.

27. Charles E. Terry and Mildred Pellens, *The Opium Problem* (New York, 1928), pp. 1–2.

28. Quotation taken from interview with a New York prison physician and cited in John C. Burnham, *Bad Habits: Drinking, Smoking, Taking Drugs, Gambling, Sexual Misbehavior and Swearing in American History* (New York, 1993), p. 117.

29. See Duboise Heyward, *Porgy* (New York, 1925).

30. *New York Times*, February 11, 1914.

31. See Kathleen Drowne, *Spirits of Defiance: National Prohibition and Jazz Age Literature, 1920–1933* (Columbus, OH, 2006), especially pp. 144–146.

32. For an idea of the scale of gambling among the slaves of the South, see Jeff Forret, *Race Relations at the Margins: Slaves and Poor Whites in the Antebellum Southern Countryside* (Baton Rouge, LA, 2006), pp. 56–62.

33. Jacob Riis, "Gambling Mania," *Century* 73 (1907): 926.

34. Colonel Patrick H. Callahan, cited in Andrew Sinclair, *Prohibition: The Era of Excess* (Boston, 1962), p. 220.

35. *National Police Gazette*, February 12, 1881.

36. Cited in Ann Fabian, op. cit., p. 199.

37. Quotations taken from Liaquat Ahamed, *Lords of Finance: 1929, the Great Depression, and the Bankers Who Broke the World* (New York, 2009), pp. 214–217.

38. Anslinger, cited in the *Washington Post*, November 23, 1936.

39. For a very brief overview of the issues involved in the campaign, see Erich Goode and Nachman Ben-Yehuda, *Moral Panics: The Social Construction of Deviance* (Oxford, 1994), pp. 16–18. For a very full account of the issues, characters involved in, and progress of, the outlawing processes, see Richard J. Bonnie and Charles H. Whitebread II, *The Marijuana Conviction: A History of Marijuana Prohibition in the United States* (New York, 1999).

40. Rheta Childe Dorr, "The Other Prohibition Country: The Facts about Finland's Noble Experiment," *Harper's Magazine* (September, 1929): 495–504.

41. Statistics taken and extrapolated from Bureau of Investigation, *Uniform Crime Reports* vol. 2: 1 (Washington, DC, 1931), and David E. Kyvig, *Law, Alcohol, and Order: Perspectives on National Prohibition* (Westport, CT, 1985).

42. This view is best espoused in Humbert S. Nelli, *The Business of Crime: Italians and Syndicate Crime in the United States* (Chicago, 1981).

43. See Henry Chafetz, op. cit., pp. 290–293.

44. See Virgil W. Peterson, *Barbarians in Our Midst: A History of Chicago Crime and Politics* (Boston, 1952), pp. 84–91.

45. Mark Haller, "The Changing Structure of American Gambling in the Twentieth Century," *Journal of Social Issues* 35, 3 (Summer, 1979): 88.

46. See *New York Times*, October 16, 1919.

47. Remus, cited in Edward Behr, *Prohibition: Thirteen Years that Changed America* (New York, 1996), p. 102.

48. See Michael A. Lerner, *Dry Manhattan: Prohibition in New York City* (Cambridge, MA, 2007), p. 234.

49. Robert Toms, cited in Larry Engelmann, *Intemperance: The Lost War Against Liquor* (New York, 1979), p. 130.

50. Cited in Michael Woodiwiss, *Crime Crusades and Corruption: Prohibitions in the United States, 1900–1987* (London, 1988), p. 20.

51. Quotations taken from *New York Times*, June 5, 1928. For details of the Olmstead case, see Norman H. Clark, *The Dry Years: Prohibition and Social Change in Washington* (Seattle, 1988), pp. 161–184.

52. This claim was made by Frederick Lewis Allen, *Only Yesterday* (New York, 1929), pp. 185–186.

53. Figures taken from Andrew Sinclair, *Prohibition: The Era of Excess* (London, 1962), p. 10. See also the *New York World*, August 9, 1926.

54. See *New York Times*, January 1, 1929; *Chicago Tribune*, November 24, 1929, and March 12, 1930, and Ernest Sutherland Bates, "From Temperance to Wheelerism," *Commonweal* 11, 24 (April, 1930): 682.

55. LaGuardia quotations taken from Herbert Asbury, *The Great Illusion: An Informal History of Prohibition* (New York, 1950), p. 210.

CHAPTER SEVEN

Extant Nature of Crime in America

The American criminal justice system originated in the European tradition of crime and punishment whereby the abstract concepts of cruel spectacles of punishment gave way to the pressure and necessity of evolving into a more concrete framework of adjudication. Much of this work began with scholars of the Enlightenment who developed philosophical standpoints grounded in the principles of individual autonomy and demonstrative proof. According to the noted philosopher René Descartes, "Accept nothing as truth unless it be demonstrably true, based on the light of reason" (1650). [1]

This thinking serves as the foundation for modern thought, which advanced an age of inquiry leading to major advancements in science and technology. These ideas served to ground the utilitarian reform movement, whereby scholars and political reformers, such as Jeremy Bentham and Cesare Beccaria, questioned the efficacy of the spectacle of punishment as a true deterrence to crime and the need for a moral legislative process designed to institute rehabilitation at the core of punishment and social reform in the criminal mind. This is the body of work that gave way to the modern system of American criminal justice in all of its theoretical and philosophical perfection.

Today, it appears that the criminal justice system is faltering particularly as we devolve into practices reminiscent of inquisition-style policies and practices, which threatens the stability of the American criminal justice system. The following article presents a historical overview of this evolution, thus providing a framework for a critical examination of the extant nature of crime in America.

---

1   Richard Kennington, "Rene Descartes," History of Political Philosophy, ed. Leo Strauss and Joseph Cropsey, pp. 421–439. Copyright © 1987 by University of Chicago Press.

Introduction

Modernity and criminal justice

By Roger Hopkins Burke

··

T his is a book about criminal justice theory. Students of criminal justice and the law–and in reality other disciplines as well–are invariably overwhelmed by the word 'theory' which they seem to subconsciously associate with the esoteric or even the mythical and scary 'rocket science' with the outcome being an inherent resistance to the subject matter. Theory nevertheless in reality means 'explanation' and is simply about how and, most importantly, 'why' we do some things and in the form that we do.

There seems to be no academic consensus as to what exactly constitutes a 'criminal justice theory' but this text approaches the task by explaining from different, often competing, but sometimes complementary, perspectives why the various components of the 'criminal justice system' operate in the way that they do and in whose interest. This book thus considers the theoretical underpinnings of criminal justice and its institutions and in doing so considers the areas of legal philosophy and ethics, explaining criminal behaviour (criminological theory), policing, the court process, punishment or penology and youth justice. The theories discussed are significantly all the products of an era encompassing approximately the past three centuries which has come to be termed the modern age and it is a time period which has its origins in a period of great intellectual ferment and activity known as the European Enlightenment.

The European Enlightenment and the rise of the modern age

The European Enlightenment involved the development of a whole range of thought concerning the nature of human beings, their relationship with each other, institutions, society and the state, and in doing so, provided the guiding ideas of the modern age. This is not to say that all of these ideas have stood the test of time and circumstance, but before the eighteenth century, the human world and the ideas that underpinned it are distinctly less recognisable to modern observers than those which emerged and struggled to gain acceptance in that tumultuous period.

Many of the ideas of the Enlightenment stressed commonalities among people and, in doing so, threatened the social domination of the aristocracy and the established Church. Before this time the common people had been encouraged by the church to simply accept their lot in life but with the rise of Protestantism and the 'Protestant ethic' people came to expect success for hard work in this world and not to have to wait until the 'afterlife'. Consequently, many people could now identify a direct connection between hard work and success, while assumptions about the natural superiority of the powerful aristocracy, and their right to economic wealth and political power, came to be challenged.

Writers of the Enlightenment period were concerned with exploring social conditions and thus, in the late eighteenth century, John Howard wrote *The State of the Prisons in England and Wales*, Immanuel Kant produced his great essay *Fundamental Principles of the Metaphysics of Morals* and Jeremy Bentham presented his *Introduction to the Principles of Morals and Legislation*. Inspired by such ideas and responding to dramatically changing economic and political circumstances, revolutions occurred in the American colonies and in France, giving rise to political systems that would embrace the new conceptions of individual rationality and free will. These revolutions moreover prompted changes in ideas concerning human rights that were championed in many European countries by the merchant, professional and middle classes and these developments introduced significant changes in the nature of systems of government, administration and law.

The eighteenth century was thus a period of enormous and significant change. The authority of the old aristocracies was being seriously questioned, both because of their claims to natural superiority and their corrupt political practices. A new and increasingly powerful middle class was benefiting from the profits of trade, industry, and agricultural rationalisation and in the interests of the latter the enclosure movement dispossessed many of the rural poor from access to common lands and smallholding tenancies. This movement caused great hardship to many of the rural poor yet, at the same time, produced a readily available pool of cheap labour to satisfy the demands of the Industrial Revolution. As a result of these changes, societies were becoming increasingly industrialised and urbanised, with previous standard forms of human relationships based on familiarity, reputation and localism yielding to more fluid, often anonymous interactions which posed significant problems for existing forms of social control.

Traditional conceptions of property and ownership were disrupted by these social changes and the enclosure movement provides a good example. In the interests of maximising the economic viability of agricultural land, many landowners fenced in previously open tracts of common land and this process gradually deprived ordinary people of what had been their customary rights to use common land and its resources such as game, fish, firewood, food plants and fruits. These changes created popular resentment among the poorer sections of the largely rural society and seriously jeopardised the agricultural and rural power base of the traditional aristocracy. The plight of the poor was, moreover, in sharp contrast to the wealth of the newly affluent classes which was displayed in the streets of the growing urban areas, in close proximity to the dispossessed who had migrated to the towns in order to find employment. The rich, even though they tended to reside in separate parts of the new towns and cities from the poor, were nonetheless no longer as geographically isolated in their everyday affairs. Those employed in harsh circumstances in manufacturing or processing, or not employed at all, were at best tempted and at worst provoked. Koestler and Rolph (1961: 34) observe: 'all foreign visitors agreed that never before had the world seen such riches and splendour as displayed in London's residences and shops–nor so many pickpockets, burglars and highwaymen'.

Criminal justice in the pre-modern era

In pre-modern Europe, criminal behaviour had been primarily explained for over a thousand years by notions of spiritualism and demonology–where criminals were said to be possessed by demons who forced them to do things beyond their control–and legal systems during that era were founded on these religious explanations of crime. Little law was written or codified and that which did exist was applied erratically, via judicial discretion and whim, and was targeted predominantly by the powerful aristocracy against the significantly less powerful general population. Those accused of crimes often faced secret accusations, torture and closed trials with arbitrary and harsh sanctions applied to the convicted. The emphasis of punishment was on the physical body of the accused, the bulk of the population possessing little else on which the power to punish could be exercised (Foucault, 1977). Generally there were few written laws and those which did exist were applied mainly to those who were not of the aristocracy.

Punishments inflicted on those found guilty of contravening criminal codes in the pre-modern period were thus extremely severe and brutal. Foucault (1977: 3) provides an account of a form of public execution reserved for the greatest of all crimes under the French *ancien régime*, regicide:

> The flesh will be torn from the breasts, arms, thighs and calves with red-hot pincers, his right hand, holding the knife with which he committed the said parricide, burnt with sulphur, and, on those places where the flesh will be torn away, poured molten lead, boiling oil, burning resin, wax and sulphur melted together and then his body drawn and quartered by four horses and his limbs and body consumed by fire.

Torture was in general use in all of Europe except England, where judicial torture was only available under a special warrant issued by the Crown. In the 100 years from 1540 to 1640 only 89 of these were issued, for offences ranging from treason to horse stealing. In England after 1640, the use of torture appears to have declined. Langbein (1974) argued that general changes in the laws of evidence and proof rendered torture 'unnecessary' in the legal process. It had been previously necessary in order to ensure a secure conviction to have a confession of guilt and/or two eyewitnesses. One eyewitness, or a strong probability of guilt, was insufficient for the courts, thus torture had to be used to secure a confession. Gradually this strict law of proof was relaxed and it was no longer necessary to use torture in order to obtain a conviction. It was thus no longer essential to the successful functioning of the criminal justice system.

Punishment nevertheless frequently involved torture and furthermore the death sentence was very common. In some jurisdictions the possibility of being tortured to death remained a penal option into the nineteenth century but in England penal torture was not used except in exceptional cases for treason. Scotland retained, at least in legal theory, although certainly not in practice, hanging, drawing and quartering for treason until 1948. Punishments such as whipping were, however, common while over 200 offences, such as shooting a rabbit, carried a sentence of death by hanging. Imprisonment was rarely used as a punishment.

Prisons were most commonly places for holding suspects and offenders prior to trial or punishment, except in cases of debt when they were used to hold debtors until their financial affairs could be settled. It would appear that the powerful in society, who framed and administrated the law, enacted and exercised the criminal codes on the premise that it was only the threat of savage and cruel punishments, delivered in public and with theatrical emphasis, that would deter the dangerous, generally materially dispossessed classes who constituted 'the mob' of whom they were mortally afraid.

From the seventeenth to the early nineteenth century the affluent classes, led by the rural English aristocracy, sought to protect their increasing property interests through the exercise of the criminal law. Vast numbers of property crimes were thus made punishable by death, giving this particular sudden increase in legislation the title 'The Bloody Code'. Capital statutes (those which allow for the use of the death penalty) were enacted en masse in the hope that such punishments would strike fear into the hearts of potential malefactors and serve to deter them from offending. In England, the standard form of execution was by hanging in public which was a highly theatrical and symbolic ritual. It was anticipated that such dramatic, public punishment would serve to restore the majesty of the law and those in whose interests it was exercised.

Each eighteenth-century statute permitted a 'branching out' to cover a host of related offences. Radzinowicz (1948) shows how in this way the standard punishment for murder (execution) also became applicable to stealing turnips, writing threatening letters, being found armed or disguised in a forest, stealing from a rabbit warren, poaching, forgery, picking pockets, cutting down a tree, impersonating an outpatient of Greenwich Hospital, damaging a fishpond, or 'consorting with gypsies'. For this last offence 13 people were hanged at one assize (local court sitting).

It is estimated that by 1800 there were more than 250 capital offences and in the early eighteenth century public executions took place every six weeks with five to 15 people hanged on each occasion

(Lofland, 1973). Koestler and Rolph (1961) attribute this flood of savage legislation to three major factors. First, there was England's lead in the Industrial Revolution which meant that there were no precedents for jurists to consider in terms of foreign experience. Indeed, other countries in this period were reducing the rigours of criminal punishment under the influence of the Enlightenment. Second, they identify a traditional British dislike of certain kinds of authority, notably political authority, as illustrated by works such as Burke's *Reflections on the Revolution in France* of 1790 and the Liberal Reform Movements which both vigorously promoted the ultimate sovereignty of the individual.

This British wariness of state interference with individual civil liberties was to a large extent the barrier to the provision of alternative forms of crime control, such as the establishment of a modern, centralised, state directed and controlled police force, as had been developed in France. At this time Britain maintained a highly localised and largely inefficient network of police and watch organisations which were completely breaking down under the chaos of their informality and the new demands for order brought on by the growth of towns and cities. There was nevertheless substantial resistance to efforts to establish a regular professional police force and this came from almost all classes of society, and appears to have been based on a deeply held suspicion and fear that such a force would become state-funded 'spies' on the population. Despite some specialist, local and private provision, the first formal professional police force was not established in England until 1829 and that after considerable resistance and as a result of a carefully brokered political and constitutional compromise.

Third, there was the English state and notably the judiciary. In this period England was ruled by an oligarchy based freely on wealth, preoccupied by the sanctity of the property that comprised that prosperity and with their status-based authority in the nation. The legislators and enforcers of the law were prominent members of this oligarchy and their influence was diffused throughout the country by their local structures of magistrates' benches drawn from the 'squirearchy' of the local gentry.

This observation is well illustrated by the way in which the judges of England dealt with the 'Waltham Black Act'. This was a piece of legislation passed through Parliament, with hardly any debate, in order to introduce new powers and vigour to deal with what was perceived by the aristocracy to be a local crime crisis. The Act was engineered to permit judges to extend the use of the death penalty to punish a whole range of generally minor property offences. Even when faced with protests from reformers, the senior judges, who sat in Parliament, replied firmly in the words of the Chief Justice of the Common Peace, Lord Wynford: Nolemus legus Angliae mutari (We do not wish the laws of England to be changed).

Many judges advocated the extension of capital legislation and their interpretations of existing law established precedents to be followed in subsequent cases. This was a one-way process, making every aggravation of the law irreversible, but this extension of capital legislation and judicial precedent had remarkably little effect on levels of property crime. Many years later, Lord Justice Devlin reflected:

> The judges of England have rarely been original thinkers or great jurists. Many
> have been craftsmen rather than creators. They have needed the stuff of morals

to be supplied to them so that out of it they could fashion law. When they have to make their own stuff their work is inferior.

(Quoted in Koestler and Rolph, 1961: 55)

It was nevertheless the gradual permeation of Enlightenment ideas that was to provide the moral basis to soften the rigour of the draconian Bloody Code.

Despite the vast numbers of offences for which the death penalty could be exercised, and the fact that many thousands were hanged for what might today be regarded as extremely minor offences, the full weight of the law was not always applied. Clemency and leniency, permitted at the discretion of the judge, were used by the rural aristocracy, who also sat as judges and 'Justices of the Peace' (JPs), to demonstrate their power over the 'lower orders'. Evidence of 'respectability' by way of the provision of references from a benevolent landowner, evidence of significant religious observance and piety, or the simple whim of a JP could lead to an offender being handed a lesser sentence. Such discretion allowed transportation to a colony, a non-fatal, if brutal, corporal punishment, or even release, to take the place of hanging (Thompson, 1975; Hay *et al.*, 1975; Hay, 1981).

Social contract theory and utilitarianism

The late seventeenth and eighteenth centuries saw an explosion in writings critical of established religious dictates and interpretations of the nature of the world. Some of these writers were devout, if critical, Christians, some were committed to a distinctly secular view of the world, others deferred to the prevailing religious ideas of the time, often to avoid conflict with established authority. The two major sets of ideas which underpinned this change were *social contract theories* and *utilitarianism.*

Social contract theories

The essence of social contract theories is the idea that legitimate government is the artificial product of the voluntary agreement of free moral agents and that there is no such thing as 'natural' political authority as asserted by the monarchical regimes which preceded and contested the development of the Enlightenment. An influential version of this approach, developed by the philosopher John Locke, could be summarised by his assertion that 'voluntary agreement gives political power to governors' (Locke 1970, originally 1689).

Social contract theories were to undergo something of a revival in the last quarter of the twentieth century, both in the study of politics and economics and as justifications for government policies such as those introduced by Prime Minister Margaret Thatcher in the UK. However, the 'golden age' of social contract theories was the period 1650–1800 and while there are influential precursors of these theories in the works of Ancient Greek philosophy, and later in medieval thought, the 'high points' of the approach are generally considered to begin with Thomas Hobbes and his book *Leviathan* (Hobbes, 1968, originally 1651).

Social contract theories are generally based on the notion that people are able to exercise their *will* freely—or *voluntaristically*—and were probably influenced by parallel developments in Christian theology. From this religious perspective, for a 'good act' to be performed the actor has to knowingly and willingly perform the act and know that it is 'good'. Hence a 'good' form of politics requires the moral assent and volition of individuals. The individual emphasis of this approach was compounded by the growing influence of the individualistically oriented forms of Christianity promoted by the 'Protestantism' that had earlier emerged following the Reformation and which had provided a practical criticism of the established Catholic versions of Christianity, prior to the Enlightenment.

Given the influence of religion on politics, it was predictable that the Protestant view of individual moral autonomy should emerge from theology and moral philosophy into the political arena, providing an intellectual basis for social contract theories. Protestantism thus questioned the automatic 'excellence' of established church institutions and they now required the authorisation and voluntary acquiescence of individuals.

This perspective came to be applied to the authority of states, the basis of whose authority was generally associated with that of churches. Hence, after the seventeenth century the idea of the state as an intrinsically 'good' institution came to be subjected to revisionist arguments that insisted that its power should be *legitimised* by the free assent of its subjects. The influence on contemporary thought of seventeenth-, eighteenth-, and early nineteenth-century writers such as Hobbes, Locke and Rousseau, who raised criticisms of the exercise of arbitrary powers by monarchs, established churches and aristocratic interests, provides the theoretical foundations for specific attacks on previous legal systems and practices. It is to these writers that we now turn our attention.

Thomas Hobbes (1588–1678) emphasised that it is the exercise of human free will that is the fundamental basis of a legitimate social contract. Compliance can be enforced by the fear of punishment, but only if entry into the contract and the promise to comply with it has been freely willed, given and subsequently broken. Hobbes held a rather negative view of humanity and proposed a need for social institutions—the origins of the very idea of modern criminal justice systems—to support social contracts and to enforce laws. He claimed that in a 'state of nature'—or without outside intervention in their lives—people would be engaged in a 'war of all against all' and life would tend to be 'nasty, brutish and short'. He thus proposed that people should freely subject themselves to the power of an absolute ruler or institution—a 'Leviathan'—which, as the result of a political-social contract, would be legitimately empowered to enforce the contracts that subjects make between themselves (Hobbes, 1968).

John Locke (1632–1704) had a more complex conception of what people are like 'in the state of nature' and argued that there is a natural law that constitutes and protects essential rights of life, liberty and property: key assumptions that, subsequently, were to significantly shape the constitutional arrangements of the USA. Locke proposed that the Christian God has presented all people with common access to the 'fruits of the earth', but at the same time individual property rights can be legitimately created when labour is mixed with the produce of the land, for example by cultivating crops or extracting minerals. People nevertheless have a natural duty not to accumulate more land or goods than they can use and if this natural law is observed then a rough equality can be achieved in the distribution of natural resources. Unfortunately, this natural potential towards egalitarianism had been compromised by the development of a money economy that has made it possible for people to obtain control over more goods and land than they can use as individuals.

Locke saw the transition from a state of nature to the development of a political society as a response to desires, conflict and ethical uncertainty brought about by the growth of the use of money and the material inequalities that consequently arose. The expansion of political institutions is thus necessary to create a social contract to alleviate the problems of inequality generated by this distortion of natural law. For Locke, social contracts develop through three stages. First, people must agree unanimously to come together as a community and to pool their natural powers in order to act together to secure and uphold the natural rights of each other. Second, the members of this community must agree, by a majority vote, to set up legislative and other institutions. Third, the owners of property must agree, either personally or through political representatives, to whatever taxes that are imposed on them.

Locke rejected Hobbes' view that people should surrender themselves to the absolute rule of a Leviathan and argued, in contrast, that people gain their natural rights to life and liberty from the Christian God and hold them effectively in trust so they are not, therefore, theirs to transfer to the arbitrary power of another. He moreover argued that government is established in order to protect rights to property and not to undermine them and cannot, therefore, legitimately take or redistribute property without consent. It is not the task of human legislation to replace natural law and rights but to give them the precision, clarity and impartial enforceability that are unattainable in the state of nature.

Although Locke had a relatively optimistic view of human potential in the state of nature, he nevertheless observed the inevitable potential for conflict and corruption that occurs with the increasing complexity of human endeavour and the 'invention' of money. If natural rights are to be preserved, what is required is the consensual development of institutions to clarify, codify and maintain these rights to life, liberty and property. In short, these institutions should constrain all equally in the interests of social harmony (Locke, 1970).

Jean-Jacques Rousseau (1712–1778) was a severe critic of some of the major aspects of the emerging modern world arguing that the spread of scientific and literary activity led to moral corruption. He emphasised that human beings had evolved from an animal-like state of nature in which isolated, somewhat stupid individuals lived peacefully as 'noble savages'. Rousseau (1964, originally 1762) had claimed that humans were naturally free and equal, animated by the principles of self-preservation and pity. It was when they came together into groups and societies, engaging in communal activities that gave rise to rules and regulations, that the 'natural man' evolved into a competitive and selfish 'social man', capable of rational calculation and of intentionally inflicting harm on others. Rousseau thus had a pessimistic view of social change and was unconvinced that the human species was progressing. Civilisation was not a boon to humanity; it was 'unnatural' and would always be accompanied by costs that outweighed the benefits.

With his later work, Rousseau (1978, originally 1775) appeared a little more optimistic about the future of humanity but he still asserted that at the beginning of history people were admirable, fundamentally equal, free individuals and that moral corruption and injustice arose as people came to develop more complex forms of society and become dependent on one another, thus risking exploitation and disappointment. He was, however, now prepared to propose political solutions to the moral corruption of society, arguing the necessity of establishing human laws that consider all individuals equally and give each a free vote on the enactment of legislation.

Rousseau developed the concept of the *general will*, observing that in addition to individual self-interest, citizens have a collective interest in the well-being of the community. Indeed, he traced the foundations of the law and political society to this idea of the 'general will'—a citizen body, acting as a whole, and freely choosing to adopt laws that will apply equally to all citizens.

Rousseau's work presented a radical democratic challenge to the French monarchical *ancien régime* proposing that it was the 'citizen body'—not kings—that were 'sovereign' and government should represent their interests. It was only in this way that individuals could freely vote for, and obey, the law as an expression of the common good, without contradicting their own interests and needs.

Rousseau considered that he had resolved the dilemma of human selfishness and collective interests posed by Hobbes. Moreover, he had done this without denying the potential existence of a positive and active form of civic freedom, based on self-sacrifice for a legitimate political community.

Social contract theories provide an overwhelming critique of pre-modern forms of government and are highly relevant to the development of the rational actor model of crime and criminal behaviour that we will encounter in the following chapter. First, there is the claim that human beings once lived in a state of 'innocence', 'grace' or 'nature'. Second, there is the recognition that the emergence of humanity from its primitive state involved the application of *reason*—an appreciation of the meaning and consequences of actions—by responsible individuals. Third, the human 'will' is recognised as a psychological reality, a faculty of the individual that regulates and controls behaviour, and is generally free. Fourth, society has a 'right' to inflict punishment although this right has been transferred to the political state, and a system of punishments for forbidden acts, or a 'code of criminal law'.

Thus, human beings are viewed as 'rational actors', freely choosing to enter into contracts with others to perform interpersonal or civic duties. Laws can legitimately be used to ensure compliance if they have been properly approved by citizens who are party to the social contract.

Utilitarianism

A further major intellectual contribution to the development of the rational actor model was the philosophical tradition termed *utilitarianism*. Essentially this philosophy assesses the rightness of acts, policies, decisions and choices by their tendency to promote the 'happiness' of those affected by them. The two most closely associated adherents and developers of the approach were the political philosophers Jeremy Bentham and John Stuart Mill.

Jeremy Bentham (1748–1832) proposed that the actions of human beings are acceptable if they promote happiness, and they are unacceptable if they produce the opposite of happiness. This is the basis of morality. His most famous axiom is the call for society to produce 'the greatest happiness of the greatest number'. 'Happiness' is understood to be pleasure and unhappiness is pain, or the absence of pleasure. The moral principle arising from this perspective is that if individuals use their reason to pursue their own pleasure then a state of positive social equilibrium will naturally emerge.

For Bentham, pleasures and pains were to be assessed, or 'weighed', on the basis of their intensity, duration and proximity. Moreover, such a calculus was considered to be person-neutral, that is, capable of being applied to the different pleasures of different people. The extent of the pleasure—or the total number of people experiencing it—was also a part of the calculation of the rightness of the outcome of an act. The overall aim was to provide a calculation whereby the net balance of pleasure over pain could be determined as a measure of the rightness of an act or policy.

John Stuart Mill (1806–1873) generally accepted the position of Bentham including his emphasis on hedonism as the basic human trait that governs and motivates the actions of every individual. Mill nevertheless wanted to distinguish qualities—as well as quantities—of pleasures, and this posed problems. For it is unclear whether a distinction between qualities of pleasures—whether one can be considered more worthwhile than another—can be sustained or measured. Mill emphasised, first, that pure self-interest was an inadequate basis for utilitarianism, and suggested that we should take as the real criterion of good, the social consequences of the act. Second, he proposed that some pleasures rank higher than others, with those of the intellect superior to those of the senses. Importantly, both social factors and the quality of the act were seen as important in seeking an explanation for human behaviour.

Mill has proved to be a formidable and influential philosophical force but it is Bentham who has had the greatest impact on the development of the rational actor model of crime and criminal behaviour. He essentially provided two central additions to social contract theory. First, there is his notion that the principal control over the unfettered exercise of free will is that of fear; especially the fear of pain. Second, there is the axiom that punishment is the main way of creating fear in order to influence the will and thus control behaviour.

Modern societies

The notion of the modern involved a secular rational tradition which can be summarised in the following four origins we observed above. First, there was the emergence of humanist ideas and Protestantism in the sixteenth century. Previously the common people had been encouraged by the established church to unquestioningly accept their position in life and look for salvation in the afterlife. It was with the rise of the 'protestant ethic' that people came to expect immediate material success in return for hard work in this world. At the same time, assumptions about the natural superiority—or the divine right—of the powerful aristocracy came to be questioned. Second, there was the scientific revolution of the seventeenth century where our understanding of the world around us was first explained by reference to natural laws. Third, there was the eighteenth-century philosophical Enlightenment where it was proposed that the social world could similarly be explained and regulated by natural laws. Political systems should be developed that embraced new ideas of individual rationality and free will. Indeed, inspired by such ideas and responding to dramatically changing economic and political circumstances, revolutions occurred in the American colonies and in France. These were widely influential and ideas concerning human rights were championed in many European countries by the merchant, professional and middle classes. Subsequently, there were to be significant changes in the nature of systems of government, administration, law and criminal justice. Fourth, there was the increasingly evident power of industrial society and the prestige afforded to scientific explanation in the nineteenth and twentieth centuries that seemed to confirm the superiority of the modernist intellectual tradition over all others (Harvey, 1989).

The key characteristics that epitomise the idea of modern society can be identified in three main areas. First, in the area of economics there was the development of a market economy which involves the growth of production for profit, rather than immediate local use, the development of industrial technology with a considerable extension of the division of labour and wage labour which became the principal form of employment. Second, in the area of politics there was the growth and consolidation of the centralised nation-state and the extension of bureaucratic forms of administration, systematic forms of surveillance, control and criminal justice, the development of representative democracy and political party systems. Third, in the area of culture there was a challenge to tradition in the name of rationality with the emphasis being on scientific and technical knowledge. The modern world—and the increasingly bureaucratised institutions that came to characterise it—was consequently a very different place from its pre-modern predecessor. Not surprisingly, therefore, modern explanations of crime and criminal behaviour—and the nature of criminal justice interventions that were introduced in order to combat crime—were different from those that had existed in pre-modern times.

Four models of criminal justice development

This book explains from different theoretical perspectives why it is that the various components of the 'criminal justice system' or 'criminal justice process' have come to operate in the way that they do and in whose interests they function in modern societies. Four different models of criminal justice development are thus now outlined, in which the various criminal justice theories that we will encounter in this book can be located and which provide different explanations for how, why and in whose interests the law and the agencies of the criminal justice system have developed during the past 300 years or the modern period. These models of criminal justice development are: (1) the orthodox social progress model; (2) the radical conflict model; (3) the carceral surveillance society model; and (4) the left realist hybrid model.

The orthodox social progress model

The orthodox social progress model is—as its name suggests—the standard noncritical explanation which considers the development of law and the criminal justice system to be predominantly non-contentious. These institutions operate neutrally in the interests of all. The concept of progress in history is the idea of an advance that occurs within the limits of the collective morality and knowledge of humanity and its environment. It is an idea often associated with the Western notion of a straight linear direction as developed by the early Greek philosophers Aristotle and Plato and which was to influence the later Judeo-Christian doctrine. The idea spread during the Renaissance in Europe between the fourteenth and sixteenth centuries and this marked the end of the static view of history and society that had been characteristic of feudalism. By the eighteenth and nineteenth centuries—and during the great Industrial Revolution that was to transform western Europe and instigate the rise of modern society—belief in progress was to become the dominant paradigm non-critically accepted by most people.

Social progress is defined as the changing of society toward the ideal and was a concept introduced in early nineteenth-century social theories especially those of social evolutionists like Auguste Comte (1798–1857) and Herbert Spencer (1820–1903). The former was a philosopher and social visionary and is perhaps best known for giving a name to the discipline of sociology that he nevertheless outlined rather than practised. Central to his thought was his search in chaotic times—exemplified by the major transition from predominantly agrarian to urban societies throughout western Europe—for principles of cultural and political order that were consistent with the apparent forward march of society. Spencer was the major theorist of social evolutionism and held the view that human characteristics are inherited and it was this aspect of his work that was to be a major influence on the development of the predestined actor model of crime and criminal behaviour we will encounter in the next chapter. Spencer went much further than the natural scientist Darwin and explained evolution as the product of the progressive adaptation of the individual character to the 'social state' or society; his major contribution to the development of sociology is his recognition that human beings develop as part of a process of interaction with the social world they inhabit.

The orthodox social progress model of modern criminal justice development in the modern era should thus be seen in this evolutionary context. From this perspective, it proposed that the development of modern societies, their laws and criminal justice systems is the product of enlightenment, benevolence and a consensual society where the whole population shares the same core values and which develops an increasingly progressive humanitarian response to crime and disorder. Cohen (1985) observes that from this liberal perspective the impetus for change is seen to come from developments in ideals, visions, theories, intentions and advances in knowledge. All change is 'reform' and, moreover, this is a term without any negative connotations. All reform is motivated by benevolence, altruism, philanthropy and humanitarianism with the collective outcome of a succession of reforms being progress. Theories of criminal justice—and other associated disciplines such as criminology and psychology—provide the scientific support or knowledge base to inform the particular reform programme, and changes occur when the reform vision becomes more refined and ideas more sophisticated.

Thus, for example, the orthodox social progress perspective on the development of the public police service observes the emergence, expansion and consolidation of a bureaucratic professionalised service to be part of a progressive humanitarian development of institutions considered necessary to respond to crime and disorder in the interests of the whole of society (Reith, 1956). It is observed that the effectiveness of the pre-modern system of policing had been based on stable, homogeneous and largely rural communities where people knew one another by name, sight and/or reputation. During the eighteenth century such communities had begun to break down in the face of the rapid transition to an industrial economy while at the same time the unpaid and frequently reluctant incumbents of posts such as the parish constable and the watch failed to carry out their duties with great diligence. Many employed substitutes who were more often than not ill-paid, ignorant and too old to be effective in their duties. The local watch was also often demoralised, drunk on duty and did little to suppress crime.

The fast-expanding towns and cities were increasingly becoming a haven for the poor and those dispossessed of their land as a result of the land enclosures we encountered above, while the rookeries, slum areas and improvised shelters for the poor grew rapidly in the eighteenth century as the urban areas expanded to serve the labour needs of the growing industrial machine. These areas were extremely overcrowded, lacked elementary sanitation, and were characterised by disease, grinding poverty, excessive drinking and casual violence. Prostitution and thieving were everywhere (Emsley, 1996, 2001). From the orthodox social progress perspective the establishment of the first professional police service in 1829 and its subsequent development occurred in the interest of all groups and classes in society who needed protection from the criminality and disorder in their midst.

Similarly, contemporary notions of childhood and adolescence were formed or socially constructed,[1] to use sociological language, at the outset of the modern era. Children and increasingly their families were disciplined, controlled and placed under surveillance because motivated entrepreneurial philanthropists had genuine humanitarian concerns about poor urban children and young people at risk from the numerous dangers on the streets, including criminality and a failure to find God, and were keen to do something about this problem in the interests of the whole of society and not least of the children and the parents themselves.

Cohen (1985) further observes that, in terms of the orthodox social progress model, criminal justice institutions do not actually 'fail' to achieve their aims and objectives, which might seem to be almost self-evident to the neutral observer. Instead they adapt and modify themselves in the face of changing scientific knowledge and social circumstances. This vision is nevertheless not complacent. The system is recognised to be flawed in practical and even moral terms; bad mistakes are seen to be made and abuses to occur. From the social progress perspective all these problems can be solved, nevertheless, over time, with the provision of more resources (invariably more money), better trained staff and improved facilities. Thus, all can be humanised and improved with the application of scientific principles and reason.[2]

Cohen (1985) observes that the orthodox social progress model is a contemporary variant of Enlightenment beliefs in progress and its supporters and adherents are the genuine heirs to the nineteenth-century reform tradition. It is in many ways the most important model, not least because it represents taken for granted mainstream opinion and is thus the orthodox view held by most. There is, nonetheless, a more recent, radical, cynical, ambivalent, critical variant to this liberal reform story which has emerged from the mid-1960s onwards. Yet, while critical of the purist version of that history it can still be conceptualised in the liberal reform tradition, not least because of its tendency to propose orthodox solutions to even major significant failure. Cohen (1985: 19), in his discussion of the development of the penal system in modern society, observes the extent of that failure:

> The message was that the reform vision itself is potentially suspect. The record is not just one of good intentions going wrong now and then, but of continual and disastrous failure. The gap between rhetoric and reality is so vast that either the rhetoric itself is deeply flawed or social reality resists all such reform attempts.

This revisionist variant of the orthodox social progress model thus tells a less idealist account than the purist history. Ideas and intentions are still important and to be taken seriously, but not as the simple products of humanitarian caprice or even advances in knowledge. They are functional solutions to immediate social changes. Rothman (1971) discusses the establishment and development of the asylum in the USA at the end of the eighteenth century and in doing so provides the original revisionist variant of the social progress model. He observes that in the aftermath of the War of Independence there emerged a new restless, dispossessed, socially mobile and potentially dangerous population while there was a simultaneous widespread sense that the old traditional modes of social control based on small self-policing local communities were now seriously outdated. The asylum was conceived as a microcosm of the perfect social order, a utopian experiment in which criminals and the insane could be isolated from bad influences and would be changed by subjection to a regime of discipline, order and regulation.

This goal of changing the individual was clearly based on a very optimistic worldview on the nature of humanity but there was, however, soon to be a widespread proliferation in these institutions. By the late nineteenth century it was clear that they had failed in their honourable, rehabilitative intentions and had degenerated into mere custodial institutions. Rothman nevertheless observes that regardless of their failure and widespread derogatory criticisms these institutions were retained and sustained because of their functionality and the enduring power of the rhetoric of benevolence. They kept a dangerous population off the streets. Rothman (1980) develops his argument further by observing degeneration in closed institutions in the early decades of the twentieth century which occurred regardless of the introduction of a progressive reform package. The outcome of this disappointment was a search for alternatives, which was to lead to the ideal of individual treatment, the case-by-case method and the introduction of psychiatric doctrines and attempts to humanise all closed institutions. But yet again none of the programmes turned out the way their designers had intended. Cohen (1985: 20) observes that:

> Closed institutions hardly changed and were certainly not humanized; the new programmes became supplements, not alternatives, thus expanding the scope and reach of the system; discretion actually became more arbitrary; individual treatment was barely attempted, let alone successful. Once again, however, failure and persistence went hand in hand: operational needs ensured survival while benevolent rhetoric buttressed a long discredited system, deflected criticism and justified 'more of the same'.

For Rothman the crucial concept is that of 'convenience', which does not, in reality, undermine the original vision or 'conscience' but actually aids in its acceptance. The managers of the system and their staff come to actively embrace the new programmes and use them to their advantage. A useful political alliance is thus developed between the reformers and the managers and this allows the system to survive even though it appears to be a total failure. Rothman (1980) observes that it is essential that we have a critical understanding of the origins of the original reform vision, the political interests behind them, their internal paradoxes and the nature of their appeal, for this creates a story that is far more complicated than terms such as 'reform', 'progress', 'doing good', 'benevolence' and 'humanitarianism' suggest. This revisionist account provides a significantly more critical account than the simplistic purist version of the orthodox social progress model but it nevertheless remains a liberal model that still believes that things can be improved if we learn the correct lessons from history and research. The radical conflict model to which we now turn our attention goes much further and identifies an inherent problematic contradiction in the very nature of capitalist society.

The radical conflict model

Proponents and supporters of the social progress model—whether in its purist or revisionist form— nevertheless fundamentally agree that society is characterised by consensus. Proponents of the radical conflict model, in contrast, argue that society is inherently conflict-ridden. Max Weber (1864–1920) had influentially argued that conflict is intrinsic in society and arises from the inevitable battle within the economic market place—between different interest groups with different levels of power—over the distribution of scarce material resources. The radical conflict model of criminal justice development is heavily influenced by the work of Karl Marx (1818–1883) who—in a simplified account of a complex and highly contested materialist philosophy[3]—goes significantly further than Weber and argues that economic inequality is inherent in society with the outcome being an inevitable conflict between antagonistic irreconcilable social classes. Those who own and control the capitalist mode of production are also in the final analysis in control of the political and civil institutions in society which, in turn, are used to maintain and sustain the capitalist system in the interests of the rich and powerful, to the disadvantage of the poor and powerless or for that matter anyone not owning capital.

From the radical conflict perspective, it is proposed that the story of the development of the criminal justice system during the modern era is neither what it appears to be, nor, for that matter, can it be considered to be in any way a 'failure'. For the new control system served more than adequately the requirements of the emerging capitalist order for the continued repression of recalcitrant members of the working class and, at the same time, continued to persuade everyone (including the reformers themselves) that these changes were fair, humane and progressive.

It is thus argued from this perspective that the professional police were from their very formation at the beginning of the modern period 'domestic missionaries' with an emphasis on the surveillance, discipline and control of the rough and dangerous working-class elements in society in the interests of the capitalist class (Storch, 1975); while contemporary 'hard' strategies such as zero tolerance policing which are ostensibly targeted at socially excluded groups in society are simply a continuation of that tradition (see Crowther, 1998, 2000a, 2000b; Hopkins Burke, 1998a, 2004a). At the same time, children and their families were disciplined and controlled from the early nineteenth century in the interests of an industrial capitalism which required a fit, healthy, increasingly educated, trained, but always obedient workforce (Hopkins Burke, 2008). The motor force of history is thus the political economy and the requirements of the dominant mode of production which in the modern era is capitalism. Ideology is only important in that it succeeds in passing off as fair, natural and just, a system which is basically coercive and unfair. It is only the outside observer, uncontaminated by false consciousness, who can really know what is going on.[4]

Rusche and Kirchheimer (1968, originally 1938) provide the earliest version of the radical conflict model and they begin from the principle that changes in the mode of production correspond with changing dominant forms of punishment in society. Hence, the origins and development of penal systems were determined by and, therefore, must be studied in terms of, primarily economic and fiscal forces. Their central argument is that in societies where workers are scarce and work plentiful, punishment is required to make the unwilling work, and when there is a surplus of labour (or a reserve army) harsh punishments are used to keep the workless under control. The status of the labour market thus determines the form and severity of punishment. The reformed prison renders docile the non-compliant members of the working class, it deters others; it teaches habits of discipline and order; it reproduces the lost hierarchy; it repairs defective humans to compete in the market place and rehabilitation is used in the interests of capitalism. Increasingly, the state takes on a more and more active role in guiding, coordinating and planning a criminal justice system which can achieve a more thorough, rationalised penetration of the subject population.

Melossi and Pavarini (1981) take this argument further and argue that the functional connection between the prison and society can be found in the concept of discipline. The point is to create a socially safe proletarian who has learned to accept being propertyless without threatening the very institution of property. The capitalist organisation of labour shapes the form of the prison as it does other institutions and nothing can change this. The control system continues to replicate and perpetuate the forms necessary to ensure the survival of the capitalist social order.

Ignatieff (1978) produces a rather different 'softer' version of the radical control model and in doing so rejects the rather simplistic straightforward 'economic determinism'[5] and 'left functionalism'[6] of the purist version above and observes the 'complex and autonomous structure and philosophical beliefs' which led reformers to conceive of the penitentiary. It is these beliefs and not the functional necessity of the economic system nor the 'fiction of a ruling class with a strategic conception of its functional requirements' which explains why the penitentiary was adopted to solve the 'crisis in punishment' in the last decades of the eighteenth century. Motives were complex. Driven by a perceived disintegration of the society they valued, the reformers sought a return to what they imagined to be a more stable and orderly society. They may well have acted out of political self-interest but also out of religious belief and a sense of guilt about the condition of the lower orders.

This revisionist version of the radical conflict model is very similar to that presented by Rothman but there are crucial differences. Ignatieff observes organised philanthropy to be a new strategy of class relations and both the property nature of crime and the role of the prison in containing the labour force are essential to his account. He argues that the new disciplinary ideology of the penitentiary—with its attempt to isolate the criminal class from the rest of the working class—was a response to the crisis years of industrialisation. There was thus a specific class problem to be solved and not a vague sense of unease about 'social change'. Cohen (1985: 24) observes that from this perspective:

> The point of the new control system—reforming the individual through punishment, allocating pain in a just way—was to devise a punishment at once so humane and so just that it would convince the offender and the rest of society of the full moral legitimacy of the law.

In this way the system was far from the failure suggested by the orthodox social progress model but, quite the contrary, it was remarkably successful. The carceral surveillance society model takes these arguments further.

The carceral surveillance society model

We have seen that supporters of the orthodox social progress model propose that the development of modern societies, their laws and criminal justice systems is the product of enlightenment, benevolence and a consensual society which develops an increasingly progressive humanitarian response to crime and disorder. Advocates of the radical conflict model essentially reject the consensual view and observe, in contrast, an inherently conflict-ridden society with the development of the criminal justice system as a mode of social control and repression functioning in the interests of the capitalist order. Proponents of the carceral society model do not totally disregard these arguments but consider the situation to be far more complex than that explained by both the social progress and radical conflict models.

It is clear that from the beginning of the modern period many—if not most—philanthropists had genuine humanitarian concerns about those involved—or at risk of involvement—in crime and disorder on the streets. They moreover acted with the best of humanitarian intentions but without fully understanding the full (especially long-term) consequences of their actions. The labelling theorist Howard Becker (1963) helps us to understand further not only the notion of the motivated philanthropist but also the invariably obscure consequences—intentional or unintentional—of their actions. He argues that rules of conduct—including criminal laws—are made by people with power and enforced upon people without power. Thus, rules are made by the old for the young, by men for women, by white people for ethnic minorities, by the middle class for the working class. These rules are invariably imposed upon their recipients against their will and own best interests and are legitimised by an ideology that is transmitted to the less powerful in the course of primary and secondary socialisation. As an outcome of this process, most people internalise and obey the rules without realising—or questioning—the extent to which their behaviour is being decided for them.

Becker observes that some rules may be cynically designed to keep the less powerful in their place but others have simply been introduced as the outcome of a sincere–albeit irrational and mistaken—belief on the part of high-status individuals that the creation of a new rule will be beneficial for its intended subjects. Becker termed the people who create new rules for the 'benefit' of the less fortunate 'moral entrepreneurs'. Hopkins Burke (2008) observes that this account has resonance with the story of how philanthropic entrepreneurs came to define different categories of children and youth as acceptable and non-acceptable to respectable society while, at the same time, developing strategies to ensure their surveillance, control, discipline and tutelage with the intention of reconstructing the non-acceptable in the form of the acceptable. But, yet again, this account is too simplistic. It is clear that not only did many of these philanthropists have little idea of the actual or potential consequences of their actions but they might well have become extremely concerned had they recognised that final reality. Indeed, this predominantly liberal labelling perspective fails to take into account the complexities of power and the outcomes of strategies promoted by agencies at the mezzo level of the institution that often enjoy autonomy from the political centre and implemented by those working at the micro-level of the front-line who often enjoy considerable discretion in the criminal justice field. It is thus the notion of the carceral surveillance society devised by Michel Foucault (1980) and developed notably among others by Jacques Donzelot (1980), Stanley Cohen (1985) and David Garland (2001) that helps us to make sense of this situation and provide the fundamental basis of the carceral surveillance society model.

Foucault observed that the prison is a form of social and political control with significant consequences for the whole of society and is not just an institution which controls crime and criminal behaviour. He observes how the eighteenth century witnessed 'the great confinement' (Foucault, 1971), where whole groups of problematic people were categorised and confined in institutions in order to educate and discipline them for their regeneration as useful citizens. We thus were to see the reform of prisoners (in prisons), the education of children (in schools), the confinement of the insane (in psychiatric hospitals) and the supervision of industrial workers (in factories) as part of an emerging 'carceral society'. Prison, for example, is an institution of power and regulation which is thrust upon a population with a corresponding shift in emphasis from punishment that targets the body (in pre-modernity) to one which focuses on the mind (modernity) with the intention not to take vengeance on the criminal act but to alter the behaviour of the criminal. Thus, the prison was to become concerned with the personality of the offender, seeking to explain why it was that the individual had committed the crime with the purpose of intervention and the ending of any future disobedience. The outcome was to be the proliferation of experts, such as social workers, psychiatrists and criminologists, becoming central components within the criminal justice process.

From this Foucauldian perspective, power is not simply conceptualised as the privilege of an all-powerful state, although that which it does both possess and wield is clearly very significant. Strategies of power are in reality pervasive throughout society with the state only one location of the points of control and resistance. Foucault (1971, 1976) observes that particular areas of the social world—and he uses the examples of, law, medicine, sexuality—are colonised and defined by the norms and control strategies a variety of institutions and experts devise and abide by. He argues that these networks of power and control are governed as much by the knowledge and concepts that define them as by the definite intentions of groups.

Power and knowledge are seen to be inseparable. Humanism, good intentions, professional knowledge and the rhetoric of reform are neither in the idealist sense the producers of change nor in the materialist sense the mere product of changes in the political economy. They are inevitably linked in a power/knowledge spiral. Thus forms of knowledge such as criminology, psychiatry and philanthropy are directly related to the exercise of power, while power itself creates new objects of knowledge and accumulates new bodies of information.

The state, for its part, is implicated in this matrix of power-knowledge, but it is only part of the story, for in this vein it has been argued that within civil society there are numerous 'semi-autonomous' realms and relations—such as communities, occupations, organisations, families—where surveillance and control are present but where the state administration is technically absent. These semi-autonomous arenas within society are often appropriately negotiated and resisted by their participants in ways that, even now, the state has little jurisdiction.

The carceral society model is thus founded on the work of Michel Foucault and, while complementary to the conflict model, recognises that power is both diffuse and pervasive in society. Agents and experts at all levels of the social world have both access to and control of power and although this is invariably exercised in the overall interests of the capitalist class in the long run, those involved in its application at the micro, mezzo and macro levels are not always aware of their contribution to the 'grand design'. Cohen (1985) observes that the 'great incarcerations'—which put thieves into prison, lunatics into asylums, conscripts into barracks, workers into factories, children into school—are to be seen as part of a grand design. Property had to be protected, production had to be standard-ised by regulations, the young segregated and inculcated with the ideology of thrift and success, the deviant subjected to discipline and surveillance. The mode of discipline that was represented by the prison belonged to an economy of power quite different from that of the direct, arbitrary and violent rule of the sovereign in the pre-modern era. Power in capitalist society had to be exercised at the lowest possible cost—economically and politically—and its effects had to be intensive and extended throughout the social apparatus in order to gain control of those populations resistant and previously invisible to the disciplinary control matrix.

The left realist hybrid model

Hopkins Burke (2004a, 2008, 2009) has developed the left realist hybrid model which essentially provides a synthesis of the orthodox social progress, radical conflict and carceral surveillance society models, but with the additional recognition of *our* interest and collusion in the creation of the increasingly pervasive socio-control matrix of the carceral society. It is heavily influenced by left realism—an eclectic and now influential criminological perspective (Hopkins Burke, 2009)—which recognises that crime is a real problem for ordinary and invariably poor people who are targeted by the criminal element living in their own communities and from whom they require a protection that has not always been recognised or forthcoming (Lea and Young, 1984; Matthews and Young, 1986, 1992; Young, 1994, 1997).

Hopkins Burke has subsequently employed the left realist perspective in a historical context to demonstrate that the general public has always had an interest in the development of social progress (orthodox social progress model) but this has invariably conveniently coincided with the requirements of capitalism (radical conflict model) and which has invariably contributed unwittingly to the construction of the disciplinary control matrix that constrains the actions and rights of all. First, in order to explain the development of the public police service from the beginning of the nineteenth century, it is recognised, from this perspective, that crime was as real a problem for ordinary people at the time as it is now, and that the respectable working class has always required protection from the criminal elements in their midst whether these were termed the 'rough working classes' (nineteenth century) or a socially excluded underclass (twenty-first century) (Hopkins Burke, 2004b). Second, this historical variant on the left realist thesis has helped explain the increasing surveillance and control of young people on the streets and elsewhere from the nineteenth century to the present day (Hopkins Burke, 2008). Third, it is observed that in a complex, fragmented, dangerous society it is we the general public—regardless of social class location, gender or ethnic origin—that have a material interest, or an enthusiasm, for the development of the carceral surveillance matrix that restricts the civil liberties or human rights of some individuals or groups (Hopkins Burke, 2004c).

The left realist hybrid perspective readily accepts the carceral society thesis that disciplinary strategies are invariably implemented by philanthropists, moral entrepreneurs, professional agents and practitioners who rarely seem to recognise how their often humble discourse contributes to the grand overall disciplinary control matrix. Thus, the bourgeois child tutelage project of the nineteenth, and early twentieth century we will encounter later in this book can clearly be viewed in that context.

Proponents of the radical conflict model argue that definitions of crime and criminality are class-based with the public police service agents of a capitalist society targeting the activities of the socially excluded, while at the same time ignoring the far more damaging behaviour of corporate capitalism (see Scraton and Chadwick, 1996). Left realists consider the situation to be more ambiguous, crucially recognising that crime is a real problem for ordinary people and that it is therefore appropriate that the criminal justice system—of which the police service is a key institution—should seek to defend the weak and oppressed (see Lea and Young, 1984; Matthews and Young, 1986; Young, 1997; Hopkins Burke, 1998a, 2004a).

Observed from a left realist perspective it is apparent that from soon after the introduction of the new police in the mid-nineteenth century there was a widespread—and admittedly at times tacit and fairly grudging—acceptance and support for this body. The police may well have targeted criminal elements within the working class and they might on occasion have taken the side of capital in trade disputes, but at the same time their moralising mission on the streets coincided conveniently with the increasing enthusiasm for self-betterment among the great majority that has been described from differing sociological perspectives as 'embourgeoisement' (Goldthorpe, 1968–1969) and 'the civilising process' (Elias, 1978, 1982).

The left realist hybrid perspective thus does not dismiss the orthodox social progress, radical conflict or carceral models of criminal justice development but instead produces a synthesis of the three. For it seems self-evident that the police are an essential necessity in order to deal with conflicts, disorders and problems of coordination necessarily generated by any complex and materially advanced society (Reiner, 2000) and hence there is a widespread demand for policing throughout society. Studies have shown that while during the nineteenth century prosecutions for property crime emanated overwhelmingly from the more affluent groups, the poorer sections of society also resorted extensively to the law as victims (see Storch, 1989; Philips and Storch, 1999; Emsley, 1996; Taylor, 1997; Miller, 1999). Indeed, at crucial times these poorer groups had considerable interest in the maintenance of the status quo and the isolation of a growing criminal class. For example, with the end of the Crimean War the prospect of a footloose army of unemployed soldiers returning—at the very time that transportation to the colonies had ended—meant that 'an organised race of criminals' would be roaming the countryside looking for criminal opportunities and from whom all would need protection (Steedman, 1984; Hopkins Burke, 1998c, 1999b).

Thus, while working-class antagonism may have been exacerbated by police intervention in recreational activities and labour disputes, a close reading of the issues suggests a more complex situation than previously supposed (Hart, 1978). There seems to be little doubt that the police were closely linked with the general increase in orderliness on the streets of Victorian society (Gatrell, 1980; Taylor, 1997) and this was again widely welcomed. Indeed, it has been argued that the crucial way in which the police affect law enforcement is not by the apprehension of criminals—for that depends on many factors beyond their control—but by symbolising the existence of a functioning legal order, by having a visible presence on the street and being seen to be doing something (Gatrell, 1980). It is a discourse that coincides neatly with a consistent widespread contemporary public demand for police on the streets frequently expressed in contemporary crime surveys and regardless of the academic policing orthodoxy that has repeatedly stated the service on its own can have little effect on the crime rate (Hopkins Burke, 1998a, 1998b, 2004a, 2004b).

The left realist hybrid variation on the carceral society model proposes that there are further interests involved in the creation of the disciplinary control matrix and those significantly are ours and those of our predecessors. This hybrid model accepts that the orthodox social progress, radical conflict and carceral surveillance society models are to some extent legitimate for there were and are a multitude of motivations for both implementing and accepting the increasing surveillance and control of a potentially dangerous population on the streets and elsewhere. For the moralising mission of the entrepreneurial philanthropists and the reforming zeal of the liberal politician and administrator corresponded conveniently with those of the mill and mine-owners and a government which wanted a fit healthy fighting force, but it also coincides with the ever-increasing enthusiasm for self-betterment among the great majority of the working class. Those who were resistant to that moralising and disciplinary mission—the 'rough working' class of the Victorian era—have subsequently been reinvented in academic and popular discourse as the socially excluded underclass of contemporary society, with the moral panics of today a reflection of those of the past and demands for action remarkably similar. The radical conflict perspective nevertheless demands some prominence in the left realist hybrid model of criminal justice development because significantly everyone in the nineteenth century–and certainly all of us today—are subject to the requirements and demands of the economy. Attempts at self-improvement or embourgeoisement were always constrained and restricted by the opportunities provided by the economy—healthy or otherwise—and this will always be the case as recent events following the virtual collapse of the worldwide banking system have shown. Children and young people were increasingly disciplined and controlled throughout the nineteenth—and first half of the twentieth—century in a form that was functional and appropriate to the needs of mass modern society and an industrial capitalism which required an abundant, healthy and increasingly skilled workforce. With the fragmentation of that modernity and the subsequent retreat from mass industrialism that was to occur in the last quarter of the twentieth century, the requirements for young people were to change accordingly (Hopkins Burke, 1999a, 2008).

Attempts to control the financial services industry, which is a central component of contemporary post-industrial capitalist societies such as the UK and increasingly the USA, have certainly been popular in the past with a general population which has been the victim of financial incompetency/ malpractice/criminality. However, these controls which challenge the practices of market capitalism have not been that successful and only time will tell whether further attempts following the great international banking disaster of 2008–2009 will be any more effective. At the time of the financial scandals at Enron and WorldCom in the USA in 2002 the great economist J.K. Galbraith, then aged 93, observed that large modern corporations—as manipulated by what he terms the 'financial craftsmen' at Enron and elsewhere—have grown so complex that they are almost beyond monitoring and effective control by their owners, the shareholders (Cornwell, 2002). Noting the sheer scale of the inadequacy of the accountancy profession and some of its prominent members in the aforementioned scandals, Galbraith observed the need for the strongest public and legal pressure to get honest competent accounting as part of a greater corporate regulation and public control of the private sector. He argued that steps must be taken so that boards of directors, supine and silent for so long, are competent to exercise their legal responsibility to their shareholders.

Public motivation for the increased policing of the financial services industry, in particular the investment arm of banking, is both apparent and unquestionably understandable in view of the activities of this sector of the economy, particularly but not exclusively in the USA and the UK at the end of the first decade of the twenty-first century, which range from gross incompetence to unequivocal criminality. Other policing, surveillance and control intrusions into various parts of the social world are at first sight equally non-problematic and acceptable both to the general public and informed opinion. Taken individually, they may seem both inoffensive and supportable by most law-abiding right-thinking people; taken collectively they are part of an impressive matrix of social control that restricts our freedom, as the following examples clearly demonstrate.

The freedom of the authorities to access information on our private lives has grown considerably in recent years. Data from a wide range of sources—the Office for National Statistics, the National Health Service, the Inland Revenue, the VAT office, the Benefits Agency, our school reports—can now be collated into a file on a citizen, without a court order showing why this should be the case. Legislative proposals in recent years have included phone and e-mail records to be kept for seven years, the extension of child curfews, keeping DNA of those acquitted of crimes and 'ex-suspects', restrictions on travel of those convicted of drug offences, the extension of compulsory fingerprinting for those cautioned of a recordable offence and public authorities authorised to carry out speculative searches of the DNA database (Wadham and Modhi, 2003). The Social Security Fraud Act 2001 allows for the compilation of a financial inventory from our bank accounts, building societies, insurance companies, telecom companies and the Student Loan Company, while every number on our phone bills may be reverse searched for an address. There may be no evidence that we are involved in fraud for us to be investigated, we may merely belong to a demographic group of people that the authorities feel is 'likely' to be involved in fraud.

The left realist hybrid model of criminal justice development thus proposes that in a complex contemporary society we all have interests in—and indeed a considerable enthusiasm for the introduction of—constraints and restrictions that are placed on particular activities and which restrict the civil liberties or human rights of some individuals or groups in the apparent greater interest. Taken together collectively these many individual restrictions contribute significantly to the ever-expanding and pervasive disciplinary control surveillance matrix that constrains the lives of all in the carceral society.

Four models of criminal justice development summarised

Four models or different ways of theorising the development of criminal justice have been introduced in this chapter. First, the orthodox social progress model proposes that the development of modern societies, their laws and criminal justice systems is the product of enlightenment, benevolence and a consensual society where the whole population share the same core values and which develops an increasingly progressive humanitarian response to crime and disorder. Theories of criminal justice—and other disciplines such as criminology and psychology—provide the scientific support or knowledge base to inform the particular reform programme, and changes occur when the reform vision becomes more refined and ideas more sophisticated. The revisionist variant of the orthodox social progress model tells a less idealist account where the ideas and intentions of the reformers are still seen to be important but where changes occur as functional solutions to immediate social changes. It provides a more critical account than the purist version but nevertheless remains a liberal model which still believes that things can be improved if we learn the correct lessons from history and research and apply them.

Second, the radical conflict model of criminal justice development challenges the notion of a consensual society implicit in the orthodox model and, in contrast, proposes that society is inherently characterised by conflict. From this perspective, the developing criminal justice system has successfully served the requirements of the emerging capitalist order by allowing for the continued repression of non-compliant members of the working class while this oppressive reality is hidden from the general population and the impression given that the changes introduced were fair, humane and progressive. In reality the changes introduced have always been in the interests of the capitalist economy and its maintenance. A revisionist 'soft' variant of the radical conflict model proposes that changes in the development of criminal justice did not simply occur because of the functional requirements of capitalism for the motives of those involved were many and complex. Thus, reformers may well have ultimately acted out of political self-interest but benevolent motives and genuine concerns about the welfare of the target population were also involved.

Third, proponents of the carceral society model of criminal justice development consider both the social progress and radical conflict models to be too simplistic and—while recognising the strengths of each and in particular complementary to the latter—recognise that power is both diffuse and pervasive in society. Agents and experts at all levels of the social world have both access to and control of power and although this is invariably exercised in the overall interests of the capitalist class, those involved in its application at the micro and mezzo levels are not always aware of their contribution to the 'grand design'.

Fourth, the left realist hybrid model of criminal justice development does not completely dismiss the social progress, radical conflict or carceral surveillance society models but recognises at least partial strengths of each and produces a synthesis of the other three while at the same recognising the interest and collusion of the general public—and that means *us*—in the creation of the increasingly pervasive socio-control matrix of the carceral society. It is moreover influenced by left realist criminology which recognises that crime and disorder is a real problem for poor people who are targeted by—and are the principal victims of—a criminal element living in their own communities and from whom they require a protection that has not always been recognised or forthcoming. This model proposes that the general public has since the beginnings of the modern era always had an interest in the development of social progress that has conveniently coincided with the requirements of capitalism and have invariably contributed unwittingly to the construction of the disciplinary control matrix. It is accepted that each of the other perspectives are to some extent legitimate for there were and are a multitude of motivations for both implementing and accepting the increasing surveillance and control of a potentially dangerous population on the streets and elsewhere.

[...]

Notes

1. A social construction or social construct is any institutionalised entity or object in a social system 'invented' or 'constructed' by participants in a particular culture or society that exists because people agree to behave as if it exists or follow certain conventional rules. Social status is an example of a social construct (see Clarke and Cochrane, 1998).

2. This author has conducted interviews with numerous practitioners in different criminal justice –and indeed, other public sector—agencies in very different situations during the course of the past 20 years. Virtually all have considered the solution to the problems of their particular agency to be the almost mythical further resources. Just give us the resources and we will deliver is the message.

3. Materialist philosophy proposes that matter and energy are the only objects existing within the universe, and mental and spiritual phenomena are explainable as functions of the nervous system of people.

4. In Marxist theory, a failure to recognise the instruments of one's oppression or exploitation as one's own creation, as when members of an oppressed class unwittingly adopt views of the oppressor class.

5. The theory of the influence of economics: the belief that the economic organisation of a society determines the nature of all other aspects of its life.

6. Jock Young (1999) has argued that most 'Marxism' is little more than a form of functionalism which replaces the interests of 'society' with those of the 'ruling class'.

References

Becker, H. (1963) *Outsiders: Studies in the Sociology of Deviance*, New York: Free Press.

Bentham, J. (1970, originally 1789) *An Introduction to the Principles of Morals and Legislation*, ed. J.H. Burns and H.L.A. Hart, London: Athlone Press.

Burke, E. (1790) *Reflections on the Revolution in France*, London: J. Dodsley.

Clarke, J. and Cochrane, A. (1998) 'The Social Construction of Social Problems', in E. Saraga (ed.) *Embodying the Social Construction of Difference*, London: Routledge/Open University.

Cohen, S. (1985) *Visions of Social Control*, Cambridge: Polity Press.

Cornwell, R. (2002) 'Shocked and Angry: The Prophet Whose Warnings Over Wall Street Were Ignored', *The Independent*, 1 July.

Crowther, C. (1998) 'Policing the Excluded Society', in R. Hopkins Burke (ed.) *Zero Tolerance Policing*, Leicester: Perpetuity Press.

Crowther, C. (2000a) *Policing Urban Poverty*, Basingstoke: Macmillan.

Crowther, C. (2000b) 'Thinking About the "Underclass": Towards a Political Economy of Policing', *Theoretical Criminology*, 4 (2): 149–167.

Donzelot, J. (1980) *The Policing of Families: Welfare versus the State*, London: Hutchinson.

Elias, N. (1978) *The Civilising Process, Vol. 1: The History of Manners*, Oxford: Blackwell.

Elias, N. (1982) *The Civilising Process, Vol. 2: State-Formation and Civilisation*, Oxford: Blackwell.

Emsley, C. (1996) *The English Police: A Political and Social History*, Harlow: Longman.

Emsley, C. (2001) 'The Origins and Development of the Police', in E. McLaughlin and J. Muncie (eds) *Controlling Crime* London: Sage/Open University.

Foucault, M. (1971) *Madness and Civilisation: A History of Insanity in the Age of Reason*, London: Tavistock.

Foucault, M. (1976) *The History of Sexuality*, London: Allen Lane.

Foucault, M. (1977) *Discipline and Punish—the Birth of the Prison*, London: Allen Lane.

Foucault, M. (1980) *Power/Knowledge: Selected Interviews and Other Writings 1972–77*, ed. C. Gordon, Brighton: Harvester Press.

Garland, D. (2001) *The Culture of Control*, Oxford: Oxford University Press.

Gatrell, V. (1980) 'The Decline of Theft and Violence in Victorian and Edwardian England', in V. Gatrell, B. Lenman and G. Parker (eds) *Crime and the Law: The Social History of Crime in Europe Since 1500*, London: Europa.

Goldthorpe, J.H. (1968–1969) *The Affluent Worker in the Class Structure*, 3 vols, Cambridge: Cambridge University Press.

Hart, J. (1978) 'Police', in W. Cornish (ed.) *Crime and Law*, Dublin: Irish University Press.

Harvey, D. (1989) *The Condition of Postmodernity: An Enquiry into the Origins of Cultural Change*, Oxford: Blackwell.

Hay, D. (1981) 'Property, Authority and the Criminal Law', in M. Fitzgerald, G. McLennan and J. Pawson (eds), *Crime and Society: Readings in History and Theory*, London: Open University Press/Routledge.

Hay, D., Lindebaugh, P. and Thompson, E.P. (1975) *Albion's Fatal Tree*, London: Allen Lane.

Hobbes, T. (1968, originally 1651) *Leviathan*, ed. C.B. Macpherson, Harmondsworth: Penguin.

Hopkins Burke, R.D. (ed.) (1998a) *Zero Tolerance Policing*, Leicester: Perpetuity Press.

Hopkins Burke, R. (1998c) 'Begging, Vagrancy and Disorder', in R. Hopkins Burke (ed.) *Zero Tolerance Policing*, Leicester: Perpetuity Press.

Hopkins Burke, R.D. (1999a) 'Tolerance or Intolerance: The Policing of Begging in Contemporary Society', in H. Dean (ed.) *Begging and Street Level Economic Activity*, Bristol: The Social Policy Press.

Hopkins Burke, R. (1999b) 'The Socio-Political Context of Zero Tolerance Policing Strategies', *Policing: An International Journal of Police Strategies & Management*, 21 (4): 666–682.

Hopkins Burke, R.D. (ed.) (2004a) *'Hard Cop/Soft Cop': Dilemmas and Debates in Contemporary Policing*, Cullompton: Willan Publishing.

Hopkins Burke, R.D. (2004b) 'Policing Contemporary Society', in R.D. Hopkins Burke (ed.) *'Hard Cop/Soft Cop': Dilemmas and Debates in Contemporary Policing*, Cullompton: Willan Publishing.

Hopkins Burke, R.D. (2004c) 'Policing Contemporary Society Revisited', in R.D. Hopkins Burke (ed.) *'Hard Cop/Soft Cop': Dilemmas and Debates in Contemporary Policing*, Cullompton: Willan Publishing.

Hopkins Burke, R.D. (2008) *Young People, Crime and Justice*, Cullompton: Willan Publishing.

Hopkins Burke, R.D. (2009) *An Introduction to Criminological Theory*, 3rd edn, Cullompton: Willan Publishing.

Howard, J. (1777) *The State of the Prisons in England and Wales, with Preliminary Observations, and an Account of some Foreign Prisons*, Warrington: William Eyres.

Ignatieff, M. (1978) *A Just Measure of Pain: The Penitentiary in the Industrial Revolution 1750–1850*, London and Basingstoke: Macmillan.

Kant, I. (1996, originally 1797) *Fundamental Principles of the Metaphysics of Morals*, Cambridge: Cambridge University Press.

Koestler, A. and Rolph, C.H. (1961) *Hanged by the Neck*, Harmondsworth: Penguin.

Langbein, J.H. (1974) *Prosecuting Crime in the Renaissance: England, Germany, France*, Cambridge, MA: Harvard University Press.

Lea, J. and Young, J. (1984) *What is to be Done about Law and Order?* Harmondsworth: Penguin.

Locke, J. (1970, originally 1689) *Two Treatises of Government*, ed. P. Laslett, Cambridge: Cambridge University Press.

Lofland, L.H. (1973) *A World of Strangers: Order and Action in Urban Public Space*, New York: Basic Books.

Matthews, R. and Young, J. (eds) (1986) *Confronting Crime*, London: Sage.

Matthews, R. and Young, J. (eds) (1992) *Issues in Realist Criminology*, London: Sage.

Melossi, D. and Pavarini, M. (1981) *The Prison and the Factory: Origins of the Penitentiary System* trans. G. Cousin, London and Basingstoke: Macmillan.

Miller, W. (1999) *Cops and Bobbies*, 2nd edn, Columbus, OH: Ohio State University Press.

Philips, D. and Storch, R. (1999) *Policing Provincial England, 1829–1856*, Leicester: Leicester University Press.

Radzinowicz, L. (1948–1986) *A History of English Criminal Law and its Administration from 1750*, 5 volumes: i) (1948) *The Movement for Reform*; ii) (1956) *The Clash Between Private Initiative and Public Interest in the Enforcement of the Law*; iii) (1956) *Cross Currents in the Movement of the Reform of the Police*; iv) (1968) *Grappling for Control*; v) (with R. Hood, 1986) *The Emergence of Penal Policy in Victorian and Edwardian England*, London: Stevens & Sons.

Reiner, R. (2000) *The Politics of the Police*, 3rd edn, Oxford: Oxford University Press.

Reith, C. (1956) *A New Study of Police History*, London: Oliver & Boyd.

Rothman, D. (1971) *The Discovery of the Asylum: Social Order and Disorder in the New Republic*, Boston, MA: Routledge & Kegan Paul.

Rothman, D. (1980) *Conscience and Convenience: The Asylum and its Alternatives in Progressive America*, Boston, MA: Little, Brown.

Rousseau, J. (1964) *First and Second Discourses*, ed. R.D. Masters, New York: St Martin's Press.

Rousseau, J.-J. (1978) *The Social Contract*, ed. R.D. Masters, New York: St Martin's Press.

Rusche, G. and Kirchheimer, O. (1968, originally 1938) *Punishment and Social Structure*, New York: Russell & Russell.

Scraton, P. and Chadwick, K. (1996, originally 1992) 'The Theoretical Priorities of Critical Criminology', in J. Muncie, E. McLaughlin, and M. Langan (eds) *Criminological Perspectives: A Reader*, London: Sage.

Steedman, C. (1984) *Policing the Victorian Community*, London: Routledge & Kegan Paul.

Storch, R. (1975) 'The Plague of the Blue Locusts: Police Reform and Popular Resistance in Northern England 1840–57', *International Review of Social History*, 20: 61–90.

Storch, R. (1989) 'Policing Rural Southern England before the Police: Opinion and Practice 1830–1856', in D. Hay and F. Snyder (eds) *Policing and Prosecution*, Oxford: Clarendon Press.

Taylor, D. (1997) *The New Police in Nineteenth-Century England: Crime, Conflict and Control*, Manchester: Manchester University Press.

Thompson, E.P. (1975) *Whigs and Hunters*, London: Allen Lane.

Wadham, J. and Modhi, K. (2003) 'National Security and Open Government in the United Kingdom', in *National Security and Open Government: Striking the Right Balance*, Syracuse University, NY: Campbell Public Affairs Institute.

Young, J. (1994) 'Incessant Chatter: Recent Paradigms in Criminology', in M. Maguire, R. Morgan and R. Reiner (eds) *The Oxford Handbook of Criminology*, Oxford: Clarendon Press.

Young, J. (1997) 'Left Realist Criminology: Radical in its Analysis: Realist in its Policy', in M. Maguire, R. Morgan and R. Reiner (eds) *The Oxford Handbook of Criminology*, 2nd edn, Oxford: Clarendon Press.

Young, J. (1999) *The Exclusive Society: Social Exclusion, Crime and Difference in Late Modernity*, London: Sage.

CHAPTER EIGHT

Morality and the Law

The question central to this chapter relates to whether or not the law should regulate morality. Legal philosophers disagree about the proper approach to the law, as illustrated by the Hart-Devlin debate. The debate refers to an intellectual exchange between *Patrick Devlin* and *H.L.A. Hart,* both British legal scholars who wrote in the mid-twentieth century. Devlin fit the philosophical model of an idealist and Hart fit the philosophical model of the pragmatist.

The debate, which focused on the question of whether the law should attempt to regulate morality, was sparked by the *Wolfenden Report*, which was issued by a British government commission studying laws about prostitution and homosexuality.[1]

The report recommended legalizing private acts of homosexuality between consenting adults in part because the law is not created to govern morality in individuals due to the status of individual autonomy, which is an issue of privacy and choice between people. By contrast, the recommendation regarding prostitution was more complex but essentially drew a distinction between public acts of prostitution, which were to be prohibited, and private acts of prostitution, which were to be tolerated. For example, the report argued that the law, while not attempting to govern individual morality, does have a degree of merit when evaluating the perspective of the public order in which the rights of individuals are threatened by acts of offensive behavior. Furthermore, it is important to draw a distinction between public and private behavior, particularly in the case of prostitution, whereas the report was more concerned about disorder and harm than about the morality of the act.

---

1   *Committee on Homosexual Offences and Prostitution.* Report of the Committee on Homosexual Offences and Prostitution (London: Her Majesty's Stationery Office, 1957).

In this respect, the significance of the discussion to be had, in lieu of the American system of criminal justice, is not to determine the meaning of morality in and of itself, but rather to examine the processes by which individuals decide when or where the definitions are applied. This in turn helps us understand how working criminal justice professionals reach their decisions about strategy, tactics, and discretion, why law enforcement professionals may reach different decisions, and how the process impacts individuals caught up within the system of due process.

The Politics of Prostitution in America

By Ronald Weitzer

Law and Public Policy

Criminalization is the reigning paradigm in the American approach to pros titution, which means that solicitation to engage in an act of prostitution is illegal everywhere, except in certain rural counties in Nevada, where legal brothels exist. Other offenses include pimping, pandering, running a brothel, and transporting a prostitute across state lines.

Approximately 90,000 arrests are made in the United States every year for violation of prostitution laws,[1] in addition to an unknown number of arrests of prostitutes under disorderly conduct or loitering statues. The fiscal costs are substantial. Recent data are lacking, but a 1985 study of the country's sixteen largest cities found that each spent an average of $7.5 million and a total of $120 million per year enforcing prostitution laws.[2] The average cost of arresting, adjudicating, and sanctioning each suspect was $2,000. Nationwide data are lacking on the cost of prostitution control, but since more than 90 percent of prostitution arrests occur in cities,[3] where the cost per arrest may approximate the above figure, 90,000 arrests would cost about $180 million annually. This estimate does not include arrests of prostitutes for loitering or disorderly conduct and it does not include the cost of arresting customers, because the number of such arrests nationwide is not recorded by the government. This means that the total expenditure on prostitution-related arrests, court costs, and incarceration would be significantly higher than the above estimate for prostitute-solicitation arrests.

These expenditures have little noticeable effect on street prostitution. At best, the problem is (1) *contained* within a particular area where prostitutes are occasionally subjected to the revolving door of arrest, fines, brief jail time, and release, or (2) *displaced* into another locale where the same revolving-door dynamic recurs. Containment is the norm throughout the United States;[4] displacement requires sustained police crackdowns, which are rare. Containment may be acceptable to residents of neighborhoods free of street prostitution, but quite aggravating to those living in affected areas (see below).

The United States has not been hospitable to alternatives to criminalization, such as decriminalization or legalization. Total *decriminalization* would remove all criminal penalties and leave prostitution unregulated. Decriminalization could benefit prostitutes insofar as police would shift from arresting to protecting them, and prostitutes would feel less inhibited in reporting victimization to the police. But it would also create new problems. Generally, a laissez-faire approach would give prostitutes advantages unavailable to purveyors of other commercial services. As Skolnick and Dombrink ask, "Why should sexual services be exempted from regulation when other consenting commercial activities are regulated?"[5] Taken to its extreme, decriminalization would allow prostitution in any locale, so long as it did not violate other norms, such as public order or nudity laws.

Proposals for decriminalization run up against a wall of public opposition, and policy makers are almost universally opposed to the idea, making it a non-starter in any serious discussion of policy alternatives. Advocates sometimes manage to get it placed on the public agenda, however. A recent example illustrates the fate of a decriminalization proposal in perhaps the most tolerant of American cities. A Task Force on Prostitution was formed by the San Francisco Board of Supervisors in 1994 to explore alternatives to existing methods of prostitution control. Members included representatives of community and business groups, the National Lawyer's Guild, National Organization for Women, prostitutes' rights groups, the police department, the district attorney's offi ce, and several other groups. From day one the prostitutes' advocates and their sympathiz-ers set the agenda and dominated the proceedings, which led to chronic infighting. Former Supervisor Terence Hallinan was the driving force in establishing the panel but unsatisfied with the result: "I didn't ride herd on this task force. I would have liked a better balance. ... Instead of coming up with good, practical solutions, they spent months fighting about decriminalization and legalization."[6] After a majority of the members voted to recommend a policy of decriminalization in January 1995,[7] the six community and business representatives resigned. One of the community members later told me that the exit of his faction angered the remaining members and shredded the legitimacy of the panel: "Th ey were upset as hell because the task force lost credibility without the citizens' groups participating."[8] While the comment is not made from a disinterested position, the task force report itself expresses regret that consensus was not achieved on its main recommendation.

The panel's endorsement of decriminalization reflected the interests of prostitutes' advocates and their allies and doomed the report's prospect for serious consideration in official circles. The city's Board of Supervisors promptly shelved the report. It is possible, however, that a less radical recommendation would have been received more favorably by city officials; Supervisor Hallinan and even some community leaders had floated the possibility of legalization (zoning in red-light areas) when the task force was first proposed.

Unlike decriminalization, *legalization* implies regulation of some kind: licensing or registration, zoning of street prostitution, legal brothels, mandatory medical exams, special business taxes. Although a segment of the American public favors legalization, this has not crystallized into popular pressure for legal change anywhere in the country, in part because most citizens see it as far removed from their personal interests and because there has been relatively little public debate on prostitution policy.

Advocates of legalization sometimes cite with approval Nevada's legal brothels. Confined to small-scale operations in rural areas of the state (prohibited in Las Vegas and Reno due to opposition from the gaming industry), this model hardly solves the problem of street prostitution in urban areas. Streetwalkers and escort agencies flourish in Las Vegas and Reno, despite the existence of legal brothels in counties adjacent to these cities. What is needed is an urban solution to an essentially urban problem.

Since Nevada legalized brothels in 1971, no other state has seriously considered legalization. Legislators fear being branded as "condoning" prostitution and see no political advantages in any kind of liberalization. On those rare occasions when the idea has been resuscitated, it has had a short life. Bills to permit licensing of prostitutes and brothels were introduced in the California State Assembly in the 1970s, to no avail.[9] In 1992 New York City Council member Julia Harrison offered a resolution for licensing prostitutes, restricting legal brothels to certain parts of the city, and requiring AIDS tests of the workers. Harrison's proposal met with stiff opposition in the city council and quickly died.[10]

Legalization raises several important questions. First, it institutionalizes and seems to condone prostitution, and arguably makes it more difficult for workers to leave the business. Government officials, feminists, and prostitutes' rights advocates alike object to legalization on precisely these grounds. Whether legalization would indeed make it more difficult for workers to leave prostitution than is the case under criminalization would depend in part on whether the workers were officially labeled as prostitutes—via registration, licensing, special commercial taxes, or a registry for mandatory health checks—or whether their identities would remain unknown to the authorities, as might be the case if legalization took the form of zoning.

The second question is whether legalization would lead to a proliferation of prostitution. Would it increase the number of individuals working as prostitutes? The number of prostitutes is partly affected by demand, which might limit the growth of the sex trade, though it is possible that greater supply—especially under conditions of legality—might increase demand. Were legal prostitution limited to one or a few cities, it would undoubtedly attract an influx of prostitutes into that locale. Were it more widespread, each locale would hold less attraction to outside workers, reducing the migration problem.

Third, will prostitutes comply with the law? The decisive factor in the success of any regime of legalization is the willingness of prostitutes to abide by the regulations. Insofar as legalization includes stipulations as to who can and cannot engage in sex work, those ineligible (e.g., underage or HIV-positive prostitutes) would be forced to operate illicitly in the shadows of the regulated system. In addition, every conceivable form of legalization would be rejected by some or many eligible prostitutes, who would see no benefits in abiding by the new restrictions and would resent the infringement on their freedom. It is precisely on these grounds that prostitutes' rights groups denounce licensing/registration, mandatory health checks, and legal brothel systems. A possible exception would be the zoning of street prostitution into a suitable locale: away from residential areas but in places that are safe and unintimidating for prostitutes and customers alike. Some streetwalkers would be satisfied with this kind of arrangement, but others would reject it for personal reasons. Red-light districts in industrial zones have been proposed, for example, but most street-walkers would shun such areas because they typically lack places of refuge and sustenance, such as restaurants, coffee shops, grocery stores, bars, parks, and cheap hotels—amenities required by most streetwalkers.[11] Even if a generally acceptable locale could be found, there is no guarantee that street prostitution could be confined to that area; possible market saturation in the designated zone is only one reason why some workers would be attracted to other locales. Moreover, while zoning presumably would remove street prostitution from residential areas, it would not necessarily remedy other problems associated with street work, such as violence and drug abuse. Indeed, such zones may simply reproduce these problems in a more concentrated manner.

Whatever the possible merits (health, safety, cost-effectiveness, etc.) of any particular model of legalization, is it feasible in a country like the United States? Not very. Advocates face almost impossible odds trying to marshal support from legislators and the public, and proposals for legalization will remain nonstarters in this country for the foreseeable future.

Public Opinion

How does the American public view prostitution? Is there any support for changes in existing laws and public policies?

Most Americans see prostitution as immoral. One survey asked respondents whether they thought "men spending an evening with a prostitute" was morally wrong: fully 61 percent considered it morally wrong; 34 percent did not.[12] An October 2006 poll by the Pew Forum on Religion and Public Life reported that two-thirds of Americans believe that prostitution can "never be justified," while 25 percent considered it "sometimes justified" and 4 percent "always justified." The opinion that prostitution is immoral or not "justified" does *not necessarily* mean, however, that a person supports the current system of criminalization. In fact, citizens' attitudes are mixed regarding current and alternative policies. There is no majority support for relaxation of prostitution laws, but a significant minority does support legalization (unfortunately, most polls leave "legalization" undefined, so it remains unclear what respondents have in mind). Men are more likely than women to favor legalization or toleration, as shown in Table 8.1, questions 1, 2, and 5. Question wording makes a difference. When respondents are provided with a scenario presenting potential benefits of legalization (e.g., reducing

AIDS, question 2), the percentage favoring legalization is higher than when no benefits are mentioned (question 1). Question 3 allows us to track trends in opinion: Between 1978 and 1990 there was a modest increase in approval of legalization ("regulated by law"), declining support for laissez-faire, pure decriminalization ("left to the individual"), and growing approval of criminalization ("forbidden by law"). Increasing support for criminalization is in line with an earlier trend in public opinion, between the 1970s and 1980s.[13] Question 4 again shows little public support for decriminalization: Only 7 percent of the public thought "there should be no laws against prostitution."

In most surveys the term "prostitution" is not broken down into its different types. In fact, the only American poll that disaggregates prostitution was a 1998 survey of residents of Toledo, Ohio (a blue-collar, working-class city). It found that 28 percent supported legal "government-controlled brothels" and 19 percent supported decrimi-nalization of "private call-girl prostitution."[14] (It is unclear why support is lower for the more discreet and invisible call-girl prostitution than for brothels, but it may be related to the general public preference for legalization ["government-controlled"] over decriminalization.) A 1984 Canadian poll found greater support for three types of indoor prostitution. While only 11 percent of Canadians found street prostitution acceptable, there was greater support for designated red-light districts (28 percent), brothels (38 percent), escort and call-girl services (43 percent), and prostitution on private premises (45 percent).[15]

American opinion is put into perspective when compared to public attitudes in other nations. Recent polls suggest that the British, French, and Canadians are more willing to endorse legalization: 61 percent in Britain approved of the idea of legalizing and licensing brothels,[16] while 65 percent of Canadians thought prostitution should be "legal and tightly regulated"; and 6 percent said it should be "completely legal," which appears to mean unregulated.[17] A similar proportion (68 percent) of the French population want legalized brothels: 71 percent thought legal brothels would reduce the spread of sexually transmitted diseases, and similar majorities thought legal brothels would make it easier to control prostitution and that the change would not lead to an increase in the French sex trade.[18] Americans, as we have seen, are less inclined to endorse legalization.

Neighborhood Antiprostitution Campaigns

While there is almost no public debate on prostitution at the national level, citizen activism at the local level has been growing. In the 1980s and 1990s neighborhood antiprostitution groups have flourished in many American cities.

I examined patterns in the grievances and practices of these groups, based on newspaper reports on a dozen cities and interviews in two cities. Analysis of the complaints of these groups shows that they are concerned largely with the tangible *environmental effects* of the sex trade on the streets, more than moral concerns per se; with *overt street behavior*, not the status offense of being a prostitute; with the immediate and long-term *consequences* of prostitution for host communities, not the social and economic causes of prostitution.[19] For community activists, street prostitution is perceived as threatening the quality of life in a neighborhood as well as its image and reputation. It both symbolizes and contributes to neighborhood decay and a sense that law and order is eroding. It also affects residents' own behavior—making them anxious over the future of their neighborhood, wary of venturing outside their homes, and fearful of altercations with marginal people on the street.

Each of the following themes appears frequently in the litany of grievances I uncovered:

Disorderly Conduct. Judging from activists' claims, prostitutes do not ply their trade unobtrusively. Quite the contrary. Th ey often cause commotion, flagging down customers' cars, arguing and fighting with people on the street, partying, and performing sex acts in public (in cars, alleys, bus stops, and on residents' property). Complaints about offensive and disorderly conduct were pronounced in each of the cities studied.

Nasty Paraphernalia. One by-product of street prostitution that is not widely known, but which is a source of frequent complaints in affected neighbor-hoods, is the problem of discarded paraphernalia. Residents often complain that prostitutes leave used condoms and syringes in alleys, sidewalks, and other public places. This paraphernalia is viewed not simply as unsightly trash but also as a public health hazard, vehicles for the possible transmission of AIDS.

Public Health Risks. The spread of AIDS was a concern in its own right. As a San Francisco activist remarked, "Th ese women are very sick, emaciated. I know they are spreading diseases whether or not they're using condoms."[20]

Harm to Children. Residents who live in prostitution zones have complained that it is diffi cult to shield children from the vice in their midst. In several cities activists claimed that prostitutes sell and perform sexual favors in close proximity to schools. Moreover, children are sometimes propositioned. In Manchester, New Hampshire, a resident of one neighborhood reported:

My children go to Catholic school, and there are women working the corner where they wait for the bus. Th ey are always high as a kite. A prostitute approached the son of one of my neighbors while he was on his way to school and asked him if he wanted to turn a trick. … What did she want? His lunch money?[21]

Residents tell horror stories of having observed children playing with used condoms and syringes in the street, fueling fears of AIDS transmission.

Harassment of Women. A common theme in these accounts is that nonprostitute women and teenage girls are often verbally accosted and propositioned by prospective customers. This is not only annoying but has the cumulative effect of impeding women's routine outdoor activities, as illustrated in these remarks: "I can't sit in the park because the gentlemen in the cars slow down and start waving dollar bills at me";[22] "A normal person cannot stand at the bus stop because they think you're a hooker";[23] "My daughter can't even go to the store without being approached by men who are asking her for sex."[24] Customers' remarks can be offensive, vulgar, and degrading. As one person recounted, "You walk down the street, the men say such disgusting things to you; suddenly you feel dirty, like you should go home and take a bath."[25]

Costs to Merchants. In prostitution strolls where local businesses exist, many merchants claim they lose business because of the very presence, noise, and brazen demeanor of prostitutes and pimps on the street. These merchants are likely to reap no benefits from prostitution, as opposed to those owners of cafés, liquor stores, and cheap hotels who profit from it. Owners of higher priced hotels complain that streetwalkers drive away some customers, although at least some hotel owners are not bothered by the prostitutes working in hotel bars, and may even welcome them.[26] A line is drawn between discreet, indoor liaisons and the more obtrusive, outdoor sex trade.

Neighborhood Decline. Coupled with other signs of street disorder and decay, prostitution is seen as contributing to the decline of a locale's quality of life. Property values erode. Prostitution and other street deviance may hinder economic development in a commercial district, deterring entrepreneurs from moving in. This may coincide with a gradual exodus of upstanding residents, further fraying the fabric of public order on the streets. None of this is lost on merchants and residents, who complain about longitudinal deterioration: "Nobody has a right to deteriorate a whole neighborhood. We could see the whole street change";[27] "We're tired of standing around watching our neighborhood decay";[28] "Now we're starting to lose very good parts of San Francisco. There's been a complete breakdown in this area."[29]

The effect of street prostitution on a neighborhood is measured not only by its tangible effects on everyday life, but also by its larger impact on a neighborhood's image. Communities may be stigmatized if a critical mass of disreputable people frequent the street. The former president of the Logan Circle Community

Association in Washington, D.C., lamented, "The image of our neighborhood is one of pimps and prostitutes. We have trick pads and shooting galleries."[30] The current president adds, "It's not a very edifying sight. People don't want to come into the community."[31] (Logan Circle has long been a mecca of street prostitution in Washington.) Neighborhood stigma contributes to a community's decline over time, as more disreputable elements are attracted to the area and "upstanding" residents flee.[32]

Invasion by Outsiders. Community anticrime groups often believe their neighborhoods are under siege by outsiders, a perception shared by anti-prostitution groups. Residents claim that prostitutes, pimps, and johns have invaded the community, which residents seek to "take back." In fact, it does appear that in most cities the majority of customers reside outside these areas, whereas varying numbers of prostitutes are local residents, depending on the locale.[33]

Johns. Several other patterns are found in these accounts, foremost of which is the scorn directed at *customers* as well as prostitutes; in fact, some residents reserve their harshest criticism for the men, who are seen as the root cause of the entire prostitution problem, without whom it would not exist. Customers stand accused of a number of obnoxious behaviors: causing traffi c congestion in their ritual cruising and transactions with steetwalkers, verbally molesting women whom they apparently mistake for prostitutes, and engaging in sex acts in public.

For residents and merchants, therefore, street prostitution is anything but a mere nuisance or "victimless crime." From their perspective, it is a "quality-of-life crime" that victimizes the community by contributing to street disorder and neighborhood decay.

To what extent are the grievances reflections of *moral* concerns? If defined narrowly, it appears that morality is the least of their concerns. Only rarely were complaints made about the degradation of selling one's body, the exploitation of women, or the sinfulness of prostitution. One San Francisco activist remarked, "This is not a moral issue. Prostitutes are spreading disease and disrupting our neighborhood," and another was similarly unequivocal:

Morals don't even come into play when peoples' lives are turned upside down [by street prostitution]. ... The moral issue here is not even in question. I don't care what people do behind closed doors, and I have talked to residents who feel the same way.[34]

This does not mean that moral concerns were completely absent from this discourse. Some activists were alarmed by the performance of sex acts in public, which might be construed as a moral position; others used a discourse that seemed to pit "good" against "evil," such as the need to force "shady" and "low-life" elements out of the community so that it could be restored to its "family-oriented" character; and others said that the sight of prostitutes on the street was an affront to public decency and especially troubling when children were present. In Hartford, Connecticut, for example, a member of a coalition against prostitution stated, "Children are growing up thinking it's okay because it's so open. Th ey see it on a whole row of streets. Our kids are saying, 'Is it O.K.? Is it legal?' Th ey could buy one of these women."[35] While the *conduct* of streetwalkers and customers, more than their mere presence, aroused the strongest condemnation, at least some of this behavior was defined as a threat to conventional *values* as well.

It is possible that many activists harbor strong moral objections but are careful not to express them out of fear of hurting their cause. Moral arguments might seem puritanistic; complaints about tangible social problems are more likely to get a sympathetic reception. Obviously, this question cannot be definitively resolved here, except to reiterate that activists emphasized the specific environmental problems sketched above. It should also be noted that relatively little concern was expressed over off-street, indoor prostitution. Opposition to this variety of prostitution might suggest a broader moral objection to prostitution in general. In both the interview and newspaper data, activists claimed that they did not object to escort agencies, massage parlors, or even isolated brothels. Commercial sex in private appears to be acceptable, so long as it has no spillover effects in the public arena. In San Francisco, a leader of Save Our Streets told me that most residents of his community would not be bothered by indoor prostitution: "My gut feeling is, yes, that would be OK. No one has voiced concern over massage parlors," several of which exist in the neighborhood.[36]

Of course, it is not unheard of for community groups to wage battles against indoor vice establishments. Efforts to shut down adult video stores, massage parlors, and strip clubs have been mounted in various cities, just as there have been broader efforts to "clean up" entire districts, such as Times Square in New York City. But community groups rarely organize specifically against indoor prostitution, especially if it remains discreet. For the reasons cited above, it is street prostitution that arouses the greatest opposition at the local level.

What actions have been taken by these groups to combat street prostitution? Frustrated by the typically haphazard and ineffective responses of the authorities to local prostitution problems, residents of many cities have begun to take direct action. Public humiliation of prostitutes and johns is the favored approach. Common tactics include:

> Citizen patrols—Groups that follow prostitutes and johns along sidewalks for purposes of surveillance and harassment, sometimes videotaping the action or carrying posters declaring, "You're Hooking, We're Looking" or "Prostitution-Free

Zone"; the patrols usually have a temporary effect in scattering sex traders, who reappear once the patrol ends;

Recording customers' license plate numbers, which are then traced to their addresses, to which a warning letter is sent;

Public shaming, such as publishing the names of alleged johns in local newspapers or on television.

Customers have been increasingly targeted, since they are seen as more vulnerable to embarrassment and more easily deterred than prostitutes. As a member of one civic association put it, "These guys are the weak link in this chain. He's the one with the most to lose; that's why he's got to be kept out."[37] The third tactic—public shaming—is all the rage. Kansas City is now experimenting with "John TV"—a weekly cable TV show displaying the names, addresses, and pictures of men arrested for attempting to solicit a prostitute. The city council designed the program to humiliate arrested, rather than convicted, men since so few suspects are ultimately convicted (most plea-bargained down to a lesser offense).[38] Radio and TV stations in some other cities (Aurora, Colorado; Tulsa, Oklahoma) have also stigmatized the johns in this way; some newspapers have also published clients' names, but others have refused on the grounds that it is not newsworthy or that publication might bring lawsuits for defamation. The Pennsylvania state legislature, however, took the unprecedented step of passing legislation (in 1995) requiring courts to publish in the local newspaper the name and sentence of anyone convicted a second time of patronizing a prostitute, in addition to a fine of $300 to $2,500 and a minimum of seventy-five hours of community service.[39]

Other inventive shaming tactics have been used against customers, in addition to those described above. In New Haven, Connecticut, in 1992, posters naming a "John of the Week" were stapled to trees and telephone polls in one prostitution stroll. Included on the poster was the name and address of a man observed soliciting a prostitute, with the warning, "Johns! Stay out of our neighborhood or your name will be here next week."[40] In Miami, freeway billboards have been used to announce the names of convicted johns. In Kansas City, activists created a "hooker hotline" in 1993, a recorded list of the names of persons arrested for soliciting a prostitute. The hotline received several hundred calls per month.

There is considerable public support for shaming johns via the mass media. A 1978 national poll found that 47 percent of the public thought it was not an invasion of privacy for newspapers to publish the names of men who had been accused of soliciting prostitutes,[41] and a 1995 poll found that 50 percent of the public endorsed punishing men convicted of soliciting prostitutes by placing their names and pictures in the news.[42]

A few cities have gone beyond sheer shaming of johns to the creation of programs aimed at consciousness-raising and rehabilitation. One particularly innovative program is the "johns' school" for arrested customers. Since 1995, when San Francisco launched its First Offenders Prostitution Program for customers, several other cities have followed suit, including Buffalo, Las Vegas, Nashville, and several cities in Canada and Britain. The brainchild of community activists, San Francisco's school is a joint effort by the district attorney's office, the police department, the public health department, community leaders, and former prostitutes. The men avoid an arrest record and court appearance by paying a $500 fine, attending the school, and not recidivating for one year after the arrest. Every aspect of the eight-hour course is designed to *shame, educate,* and *deter* the men from future contact with prostitutes. The content and tone of the lectures are designed for maximum shock value. During my observations at the San Francisco school, the men were frequently asked how they would feel if their mothers, wives, or daughters were "prostituted," and why they were "using" and "violating" prostitutes by patronizing them. The audience was also exposed to a graphic slide show on the dangers of sexually transmitted diseases, horror stories about the wretched lives of prostitutes and their oppression by pimps, and information about the harmful effects of street prostitution on the host neighborhoods.

Men buy sex for very different reasons, ranging from a desire for a different kind of sexual experience than what they get from their wife or girlfriend (if they are in a relationship) to a desire for an emotional connection or companionship with a sex worker in addition to sex (the latter are more typical of transactions with escorts and call girls, whereas street prostitutes typically provide only brief sex). Some customers visit prostitutes because they are unable to find a conventional relationship or do not want one. A survey of 169 men enrolled in the Edmonton, Canada, school revealed several additional things. The men like to keep their encounters secret: Only one-quarter had told anyone else that they had seen a prostitute, and only 2 percent had told their spouses or partners. More than half the men were currently in a relationship with a spouse or partner, and 72 percent of these men reported that they had a satisfying sexual relationship with their partner. What is particularly interesting is that 71 percent said they did not enjoy sex with prostitutes, and two-thirds said that patronizing prostitutes had caused problems in their lives.[43] Yet, this did not prevent them from buying sex on the street. Reviews of online message boards and other online forums, where johns discuss their experiences with sex workers, indicate that many of the men who patronize indoor prostitutes—in massage parlors or brothels or those working as escorts or call girls—often enjoy their encounters and become regular customers. Their experiences tend to differ significantly from those of men who buy quick sex on the streets.

My review of responses to open-ended questions on a survey completed by the men at the end of the school in San Francisco found that many seem to experience "consciousness-raising" about the negative aspects of street prostitution and pledge to never again contact a prostitute, but others express cynicism or resentment at getting caught, at having to take the class, at being "talked down to" by the lecturers, and being otherwise demeaned. Some men insist that they were innocent victims of police entrapment.[44]

Unlike other shaming sanctions—such as printing customers' names or photos in local newspapers or cable TV shows—where humiliation or "stigmatizing shaming" of the offender is a goal, shaming in the johns' schools occurs in the context of a day of reeducation about the various harms of prostitution.[45] This is closer to the "reintegra-tive shaming" model which links punishment to rehabilitation, though this ends once the class concludes. A measure of rehabilitation is recidivism: Of the nearly 2,200 graduates of San Francisco's school from March 1995 to February 1999, only eighteen were subsequently rearrested for solicitation. None of the 600 men passing through Toronto's program had been rearrested between the opening of the school in March 1996 and August 1997.[46]

Low recidivism, or "specific deterrence" among the graduates of the johns' schools does not mean that the program is having a larger "general deterrent" effect (on the never-arrested population of prospective johns), since the demand side—the number of johns on the streets—is thus far unabated. Moreover, nonrecidivism may be due to the school experience or to the arrest itself. Offi cial statistics show low recidivism among previously arrested customers generally (including those who had not attended a johns' school), suggesting that the arrest is the decisive deterrent.

Other Antiprostitution Groups

Among the antiprostitution forces active in the United States are local organizations that work to rescue prostitutes from the streets. Notable examples are PRIDE (From Prostitution to Independence, Dignity, and Equality) in Minneapolis,[47] SAGE (Standing Against Global Exploitation) in San Francisco, HIPS (Helping Individual Prostitutes Survive) in Washington, D.C., and the CPA (Council on Prostitution Alternatives) in Portland, Oregon. Some of these groups provide services and do not propound an official ideological position on prostitution, while others (SAGE, CPA) adopt a radical feminist perspective. The CPA, for example, defines prostitutes as oppressed by both individual men (johns, pimps) and by the larger system of patriarchy, and works to empower women to reject such domination and to escape from prostitution. This perspective is influenced both by radical feminism and by the experiences of the street prostitutes with whom they have contact—that is, the population most likely to suffer violence and other abuse, in contrast to the majority of sex workers who work off the streets.

For the most part, antiprostitution campaigns in the United States have been local, not national. A few groups, however, have fought a broader war against prostitution. The most notable group was WHISPER (Women Hurt in Systems of Prostitution Engaged in Revolt, founded in 1985). Articulating a radical feminist perspective, WHISPER denied that women freely choose prostitution, that prostitution is a valid career, and that it can ever be organized humanely. Prostitution is based on male domination, women's commodification, and "enforced sexual access and sexual abuse."[48] Hardly victimless, it is universally an act of violence against women. The violence is not restricted to incidents of physical assault, but includes the sexual interaction itself, which is seen as a sexual and emotional violation by its very nature. Th ose who manage to leave prostitution were referred to as "survivors" who have "escaped." As an abolitionist organization, WHISPER was at loggerheads with the prostitutes' rights movement: It advocated not the rights of prostitutes as workers but the right to escape from prostitution; sought not to normalize but to further stigmatize prostitution; and was committed to universal eradication of the oldest profession. WHISPER ceased operations in 1996.

Antiprostitution groups like CPA and WHISPER can be criticized for their staunch abolitionist political agenda and for a failure to draw distinctions between different types of prostitutes (most of the individuals they work with are street prostitutes, yet most prostitutes in America work in off-street settings). The non-ideological organizations that provide assistance to women who want to leave the streets are involved in a laudable undertaking. Even their opponents in the prostitutes' rights movement endorse such assistance: The World Charter for Prostitutes' Rights proclaims that "shelters and services for working prostitutes and retraining programs for prostitutes wishing to leave the life should be funded."[49]

The Prostitutes' Rights Movement

At the opposite end of the spectrum from antiprostitution groups like WHISPER stand prostitutes' rights groups, which insist that prostitution is not inherently evil and that prostitutes have the *right to engage in sex work*. Such groups advocate the de-criminalization of prostitution because they view it as *a legitimate and valuable service*. Founded in 1973 by former prostitute Margo St. James, COYOTE (Call Off Your Old Tired Ethics) is the premier prostitutes' rights group in the United States, and is affiliated with kindred organizations in the United States and internationally.[50]

Goals

COYOTE's chief goals are (1) public education about the "myths" and "realities" of prostitution, (2) decriminalization, and (3) normalization. Public education takes the form of challenging a number of common misconceptions: that prostitutes are a significant source of AIDS and other sexually transmitted diseases, that organized crime is heavily involved, that most women are forced into prostitution, and that street prostitution is linked to other street crime. Insofar as any harms are associated with prostitution, they are attributed to criminalization, not to prostitution itself: The very illegality of prostitution increases prostitutes' vulnerability to exploitation and victimization. It follows that decriminalization would ameliorate these problems.

COYOTE favors full decriminalization of consensual adult prostitution, that is, the elimination of all legal restrictions on prostitution. It flatly opposes legalization, whether in the form of registration and licensing, special taxes, zoning, compulsory health examinations, or restrictions on brothels.[51] Regulations are rejected because they would allow the state to "regulate what a woman does with her own body."[52] Decriminalization, by contrast, would allow prostitutes maximum control over their bodies.

COYOTE seeks to destigmatize and *normalize* prostitution. It challenges conventional stereotypes of prostitutes by arguing that they have normal needs and aspirations, and that their work is no more degrading than that of other service providers.[53] Although it is a hard sell, COYOTE argues that prostitutes are not involved in immoral behavior. Instead, it is claimed that "the real undermining of morality results from making illegal conduct engaged in between consenting adults and in which no one is victimized"[54] and that it is nonsense "to suggest that society's moral fiber is undermined by 'sex-for-pay' but not by promiscuous sexual behavior without pay."[55] In any event, the state should not be legislating morality anyway.[56] Decriminalization is expected to promote normalization. As one leader told me, "Once they don't go to jail, they can come out of the closet and become normalized."[57]

Leadership and Support Base

COYOTE has been run by a handful of activists. The dynamic and flamboyant founder, Margo St. James, headed the organization for a dozen years, but she was replaced by Priscilla Alexander in 1985, who was followed by Samantha Miller in the early 1990s, after which Margo St. James returned.

Winning popular support poses such an enormous challenge that it has not been prioritized. While COYOTE claimed to have several thousand members in the 1970s, almost all were simply names on a membership list. Support is also measured by the number of adherents, people who endorse movement goals. Public opinion data presented in Table 1 indicate significant support for some form of legalization, but much less for COYOTE's central goal of decriminalization. Attempts to mobilize supporters via specific events (picketing, demonstrations, conventions) have been few and far between. This is a campaign led by entrepreneurs, not a mass movement.

Mobilization of prostitutes has been equally elusive. About 3 percent of COYOTE's members are prostitutes,[58] and most of them have been upscale call girls rather than streetwalkers (it is not clear who makes up the other 97 percent of members). Why such meager involvement of prostitutes? First, COYOTE has not prioritized recruitment: "We don't go looking for constituents," Margo St. James told me, "Th ey come to COYOTE."[59] Given the lack of recruitment efforts, many prostitutes may be unaware of the movement's very existence. Second, open participation in the movement carries risks, such as fear of police harassment, discouragement from pimps, and anticipated repercussions among family and friends.

Surveys have shown that the majority of customers support decriminalization, but this support is virtually impossible to mobilize, given customers' abiding interests in remaining anonymous.

Alliances

Strong alliances with other groups may offset a social movement's lack of internal resources and constituent support. Some influential third parties have formally endorsed decriminalization, but their contribution to the movement has been quite limited. The ACLU is a case in point. It announced its formal support for decriminalization in 1975, and it has occasionally filed suits, lobbied state legislators, and defended individuals prosecuted under prostitution laws. But this is a very low-priority issue for the ACLU. Another example is the National Organization for Women (NOW), which issued a resolution endorsing decriminalization in 1973, a position that remains unchanged today. NOW is in a position to contribute to COYOTE's finances, legitimacy, and membership base, but has offered almost no support of this kind.[60]

Why this lack of third-party support? Prostitution is an unpopular cause, unlikely to yield gains for and more likely to discredit organizations that embrace it in a prominent and sustained fashion. The "contamination" resulting from an individual's association with deviants[61] also may apply to organizations that champion deviant causes. Actively fighting for the decriminalization of prostitution would be a liability for an organization such as NOW, both in terms of its public image and its membership base. Feminists inside and outside NOW are split on prostitution, just as they are on pornography. A libertarian minority sees it as a valid occupational choice, which decriminalization would make safer; an abolitionist majority considers it inherently degrading and advocates the eradication of prostitution. The latter, dominant view prevents most feminists from lending support to COYOTE.

Impact

A social movement's success can be measured by its impact on public opinion, legislation, and the practices of control agents. Trend data presented above show that the movement has had no positive effect on public attitudes regarding prostitution. The vast majority of the public want prostitution laws "strictly enforced," and the percentage who think prostitution should be "forbidden by law" increased between 1978 and 1990.

Nor have local or state policy makers been moved by COYOTE's claims. Since the beginning of the movement in the early 1970s, virtually all state and municipal action on prostitution issues has resulted in passage of increasingly *punitive* measures. Consequently, COYOTE complains that "for most legislators [prostitution] remains a joke except when they think they can gain prominence by attacking prostitutes."[62]

COYOTE has not failed in every area. It has attracted some media coverage, won some minor victories, and given prostitutes a "voice" in the public arena. COYOTE's survival for twenty-five years is also noteworthy, and it has built an international reputation as a vanguard in the campaign for prostitutes' rights. But the movement's arguments and demands have largely fallen on deaf ears among elites and the wider public. An exception that proves the rule is COYOTE's recent involvement in San Francisco's Task Force on Prostitution, mentioned earlier in the article. Even when COYOTE was included in official discussions of the issue, and persuaded the Task Force to endorse decriminalization, the recommendation was dismissed by local officials.

As former COYOTE director Samantha Miller told me in 1993, "For twenty years, nothing has changed" in American public policy; indeed, she considered it time to "move away from the hard-line

COYOTE position on decriminalization" and instead press for the "more realistic" goal of legalization.[63] COYOTE's official position, however, remains the more radical goal of decriminalization, not legalization—which helps to keep it marginalized.

The Netherlands as a Contrasting Case

A brief comparison to the Netherlands will demonstrate that there are alternatives to the American approach to prostitution, and that the failure of prostitutes' rights groups like COYOTE is not preordained everywhere. Prostitution in the Netherlands is not against the law, but third-party involvement in prostitution (such as running a brothel) was legalized in 2000. The owners of brothels, sex clubs, window-prostitution rooms, etc. must now conform to a wide array of government regulations that are intended to improve the health, safety, and working conditions of sex workers in Holland. But even before legalization, the Dutch had long tolerated these types of indoor prostitution. Such tolerance does not seem to have encouraged widespread consumption. One survey found that 22 percent of Dutch men report that they have patronized a prostitute during their lifetime,[64] compared to 16 to 18 percent of American men (according to the General Social Survey).

Dutch views on prostitution differ radically from those of most Americans. A 1997 poll found that 74 percent of the Dutch public regarded prostitution as an acceptable job and 73 percent favored the legalization of brothels.[65] And in 1999, 78 percent said prostitution was a job like any other, so long as there was no coercion involved.[66] As a Dutch woman told me when asked about prostitution in her country, "It doesn't even cross my mind that it should be illegal!"

The American and Dutch scenes also differ strikingly in terms of the role and influence of interest groups. Organizations with a stake in prostitution policy have much more legitimacy and influence over policy makers in Holland than in the United States. Th ey do not have to fight for acceptance and they enjoy more freedom to organize publicly. Unlike the United States, Holland has a state-funded organization that conducts research and develops policy proposals on prostitution, the Mr. A. de Graaf Foundation. This organization takes the view that prostitution is a profession that should be dealt with pragmatically by the government. The foundation neither condemns nor promotes prostitution, but is committed to improving the conditions for workers in the industry as well as building a consensus on policy among all interested parties—all of which meet monthly at the foundation's offices.

Another key player is COYOTE's Dutch counterpart, the Red Th read, a prostitutes' rights organization created in 1985. In a 1997 interview, the then-director, Sietske Altink, was asked to identify the major opponents of the Red Th read. She responded, "Th at doesn't really exist in the Netherlands. It's hard to think of any enemies of Red Th read."[67] There is, of course, some opposition from some church leaders and right-wing politicians, but Red Th read is not locked in conflict with the government or dismissed as irrelevant, as is COYOTE. Instead, says Altink, "We are important for them to correct their policies." In fact, the Dutch government helps *fund* Red Th read, and the group also participates in the training of police offi cers with regard to prostitution issues.

Of course, organizations involved with prostitution experience a degree of stigmati-zation even in Holland. The head of the Brothel Owners Association noted that some people denounce the organization, but people are also curious about its aims:

> You have the possibility to explain, to tell something about the business. If I'm in an ordinary group of people and they've heard what I'm doing, it doesn't take ten minutes and they start talking with me; they want to know everything. And that is my chance to change their minds, but I have to open them.[68]

Unlike brothels, which employ several women and entertain customers in a club atmosphere, "window prostitution" takes place in small rooms rented by independent prostitutes in red-light districts. (Amsterdam has 420 window units and 70 brothels; about 30 percent of Holland's prostitutes work in window units, 40 percent work in brothels, and the remainder work as escorts or on the streets.)[69] A Window Owners Association formed fifteen years ago, and 90 percent of the window owners are members. The goals of the association are more limited than those of the brothel owners' association, since they have much less involvement with the workers, essentially serving as landlords who rent premises and make occasional visits to see that workers are complying with regulations. As the secretary of the organization stated, "The organization exists only to deal with the rules [imposed by the local government, e.g., the prohibition on workers under eighteen, the limit of only one worker per unit], and only when it is necessary to raise our voice with local authorities."[70] The organization is pressing for licensing, in order to increase the legitimacy of window prostitution. The secretary also made the point of insisting that he and his organization were in no way "shamed" by their association with prostitution and that his members were ordinary businesspeople, not really involved in "managing" prostitutes. Th ey shun the "pimp" label and want to be called "entrepreneurs in the relaxation industry."[71]

The Dutch climate is even conducive to the existence of a clients' rights organization, perhaps unique in the world! Created in 1986, the Foundation of Men and Prostitution has the goal of promoting the "legal and moral emancipation of prostitution and all those directly or indirectly involved in the prostitution industry," as stated in the group's brochure. The organization holds meetings for clients during which problems and interests are discussed; it represents clients' interests to the media, government, and other groups interested in prostitution; and it attempts to clarify the rights and obligations of clients. In an interview, the head of the clients' organization elaborated on its raison d'être:

> There is no reason why they shouldn't have a consumer organization. They have rights to good service, not to be maltreated, just like any other consumer. The fact that clients are a big silent group is no reason not to fight for rights, and they

should. We feel there is every reason to enlighten the general population about clients' involvement in prostitution. As I feel prostitution is a valuable asset, I think there's a need for society to be informed of this. The value of prostitution is that men who are in need, or even urgent need, can find relief. ... People are justified to seek outlets for, in many cases, a very burdensome frustration. Of course, a lot of prostitution is fun and entertainment, not just due to man's frustration.

But there is also some vagueness in the organization's goals:

The fact of the matter is we don't know what we want. For the clients, I don't have much hope that they can be reached, and if they can be reached I don't know what to say to them! I'm way out ahead of the rank and file. Th ey couldn't care less about codes of conduct, migrant women, club owners who take advantage of workers, et cetera. ... Some clients we meet find prostitution fascinating and want to learn more or feel a need to unburden themselves from their lonely life or feelings of guilt.[72]

The organization not only works to advance the interests of clients but also exhorts clients to follow a code of conduct in their encounters with prostitutes. The code instructs customers to be polite, clean, sober, and to use condoms. Other commandments include:

"Make clear agreements" with the prostitute.

"Take into account that the prostitute has her own limits" on the services to be provided.

"A contact can be less than successful, often through unfamiliarity with each other. Take this into account and don't be disappointed."

"Remain reasonable in a situation where conflict arises and leave it for what it is. Absolutely do not demand your money back."

"Create as little inconvenience as possible for the surroundings. Neighbors appreciate their sleep and are really not interested in your sexual experiences."

In the Netherlands, in short, there is a vibrant and active network of organizations working on behalf of the interests of different sectors of the sex industry and enjoying a significant measure of success in their efforts. The Dutch government regularly meets with leaders of such organizations and takes their views into account in formulating prostitution-related policies. It seeks to incorporate and balance the views of organizations that have at least somewhat different interests or policy preferences. This state of affairs could not contrast more sharply with the American scene, where prostitutes' advocacy groups are fully marginalized and where criminalization reigns supreme.

Discussion Questions

1. American policy toward prostitution is described as "criminalization," but there are alternative policies as well. (a) What is meant by "legalization" and "decriminalization"? (b) What are the main arguments in favor of each policy, as described by proponents? (c) How likely is it that either policy will be adopted in an American state in the foreseeable future?

2. Anti-prostitution groups have organized in many cities in the United States, with the goal of driving street prostitution out of their neighborhoods. What are these groups' main grievances with regard to street prostitution?

3. There are significant differences between the United States and the Netherlands in the way prostitution is viewed by the public, the influence of prostitutes' rights organizations, and in other ways. Discuss the main differences in the two nation's approaches to prostitution. Do you think that American policy makers should consider adopting at least some of the Dutch approach?

Table 8.1 Attitudes on Prostitution Policies

1."In your opinion, should prostitution involving adults aged 18 years of age and older be legal or illegal?"

	MALES	FEMALES	TOTAL
Legal	32%	21%	26%
Illegal	63%	77%	70%
Don't know/refused	5%	2%	3%
Total	100%	100%	99%
(N)	(497)	(522)	(1,019)

$x^2 = 25.77$, $df = 2$, $p < .001$

Source: Gallup poll, May 28–29, 1996.

2. "Some people feel that in order to help reduce the spread of AIDS, prostitution should be made legal and regulated by the government. Do you agree or disagree?"

	MALES	FEMALES	TOTAL
Agree	46%	34%	40%
Disagree	49%	61%	55%
No opinion	5%	5%	5%
Total	100%	100%	100%
(N)	(604)	(612)	(1,216)

$x^2 = 18.91$, $df = 2$, $p < .001$

Source: Gallup poll, August 29–September 3, 1991.

Table 8.1 Attitudes on Prostitution Policies (Continued)

3. "I will read you some activities that some people feel are matters of private choice or consent that ought to be left to the individual, that other people feel should be regulated by law, and others feel should be forbidden by law altogether. Please tell me how you feel that activity should be treated: Engaging in prostitution."

	1978	1990
Left to individual	35%	22%
Regulated by law	24%	31%
Forbidden by law	37%	46%
Not sure	4%	1%
Total	100%	100%
(N)	(1,513)	(2,254)

$x^2 = 126.65$, df = 3, p <.001

Source: Louis Harris polls, November 30–December 10, 1978; January 11–February 11, 1990.

4. "Which of the following best describes your feelings about prostitution in the U.S.? It should be illegal; it should be legal under certain restrictions; there should be no laws against prostitution?"

Illegal	43%
Legal under restrictions	46%
No laws	7%
No opinion	4%
Total	100%
(N)	(1,200)

Source: Merit Audits and Surveys, Merit report, October 15–20, 1983.

5. "How much do you agree or disagree with the following statement? There is nothing inherently wrong with prostitution, so long as the health risks can be minimized. If consenting adults agree to exchange money for sex, that is their business."

	MALES	FEMALES	TOTAL
Agree strongly	25%	26%	25%
Agree somewhat	25%	16%	20%
Disagree somewhat	22%	16%	19%
Disagree strongly	25%	40%	33%
Don't know/no answer	3%	3%	3%
Total	100%	101%	100%
(N)	(646)	(798)	(1444)

$x^2 = 46.77$, df = 4, p <.001

Source: General Social Survey, NORC, 1996.

Notes

1. Bureau of Justice Statistics. *Sourcebook of Criminal Justice Statistics.* Washington, D.C.: U.S. Government Printing Office, annual.

2. Julie Pearl. 1987. "The Highest Paying Customer: America's Cities and the Costs of Prostitution Control." *Hastings Law Journal* 38: 769–800. San Francisco spent $7.6 million on prostitution control in 1994 (San Francisco Task Force on Prostitution. 1996. *Final Report.* San Francisco Board of Supervisors).

3. Federal Bureau of Investigation. *Uniform Crime Reports.* Washington, D.C.: U.S. Department of Justice, annual.

4. Bernard Cohen. 1980. *Deviant Street Networks: Prostitution in New York City.* Lexington, MA: Lexington Books.

5. Jerome Skolnick and John Dombrink. 1978. "The Legalization of Deviance." *Criminology* 16: 193–208, at p. 201.

6. *San Francisco Examiner,* December 6, 1995. For a discussion of a hybrid, two-track policy toward prostitution, where enforcement would continue against street prostitution but not against indoor prostitution (provided there is no complaint from the public or evidence of harm, such as coercion to work in a brothel), see Ronald Weitzer. 1999. "Prostitution Control in America: Rethinking Public Policy," *Crime, Law, and Social Change* 32: 83–102.

7. "The Task Force therefore recommends that the City stop enforcing and prosecuting prostitution crimes" (San Francisco Task Force, *Final Report,* p. 6).

8. Interview, April 29, 1997.

9. M. Anne Jennings. 1976. "The Victim as Criminal: A Consideration of California's Prostitution Law." *California Law Review* 64: 1235–1284; Raymond Parnas. 1981. "Legislative Reform of Prostitution Laws." *Santa Clara Law Review* 21: 669–696.

10. Interview with Julia Harrison, June 7, 1993.

11. Cohen, *Deviant Street Networks.*

12. *Time/* Yankelovich, Skelly, and White poll. July 26–31, 1977, N=1,044 registered voters.

13. See the poll data in Ronald Weitzer. 1991. "Prostitutes Rights in the United States: The Failure of a Movement." *Sociological Quarterly* 32: 23–41.

14. Charles McCaghy and Stephen Cernkovich. 1991. "Changing Public Opinion toward Prostitution Laws," paper presented at the World Congress of Sexology, Amsterdam.

15. Peat, Marwick, and Partners. 1984. *A National Population Study of Prostitution and Pornography*. Report no. 6. Ottawa, Canada: Department of Justice.

16. ITV poll, reported in *Agence France Presse,* November 16, 1998, N=2,000.

17. Sun Media Newspapers/Compas poll, reported in *Edmonton Sun,* October 31, 1998, N=1,479.

18. "Poll: French Want Brothels Legalized," *Boston Globe,* January 22, 1995.

19. Ronald Weitzer. 1994. "Community Groups vs. Prostitutes," *Gauntlet* no. 7: 121–124.

20. Interview, July 16, 1993.

21. Quoted in Ralph Jimenez. 1993. "Manchester Plans New Push on Johns' ". *Boston Globe,* January 3: NH1.

22. Quoted in Linda Jones. 1989. "Festival Marks Community's Effort to Drive out Drug Dealers, Prostitutes." *Detroit News,* September 15: B1.

23. Quoted in Valarie Busheda and David Grant. 1992. "Prostitution: A Problem That Endures." *Detroit News,* February 19: B4.

24. Quoted in Stephanie Gadlin. 1989. "Hookers Get Out." *Chicago Defender,* September 6: 26.

25. Quoted in Judy MacLean. 1976. "Prostitution and the Community." *In These Times,* December 20: 12–13.

26. Helen Reynolds. 1986. *The Economics of Prostitution*. Springfield, IL: Charles C. Thomas.

27. Quoted in MacLean, "Prostitution and the Community," p. 13.

28. Quoted in Greg Mills. 1992. "Buckeye Neighborhood Coalition Attacks Crime, Grime." *Call and Post* (Cleveland), August 20: A3.

29. Quoted in Scott Winokur. 1993. "Prostitution Crackdown Nets 160," *San Francisco Examiner,* January 20: A3.

30. Quoted in Linda Wheeler. 1987. "Prostitute Disrupts D.C. Hearing," *Washington Post,* May 7: D7.

31. Interview, July 26, 1993.

32. George Kelling and Catherine Coles. 1996. *Fixing Broken Windows*. New York: Free Press.

33. This is certainly the case in the two cities I studied closely, San Francisco and Washington, D.C., based on addresses of arrested customers.

34. Interview, July 9, 1993.

35. Quoted in George Judson. 1992. "Price of a Prostitute: The Client's Car." *New York Times,* December 4: B1.

36. Interview, July 9, 1993.

37. Quoted in Katti Gray. 1991. "Prostitution Opponents Aim to Seize Johns' Cars," *Newsday,* December 5: 25.

38. Art Hubacher. 1998. "Every Picture Tells a Story: Is Kansas City's 'John TV' Constitutional?" *Kansas Law Review* 46: 551–591.

39. Courtney Persons. 1996. "Sex in the Sunlight: The Effectiveness, Efficiency, Constitutionality, and Advisability of Publishing Names and Pictures of Prostitutes' Patrons." *Vanderbilt Law Review* 49: 1525–1575.

40. "Curbing Prostitution on Demand Side," *New York Times,* April 20: B8.

41. Louis Harris poll. November 30-December 10, 1978, N=1,513.

42. *Newsweek* poll. January 26–27, 1995, N=753.

43. *Edmonton Sun,* November 8, 1998.

44. The Portland program, Sexual Exploitation Education Project (SEEP), operated from 1995 to 1997 and, unlike in San Francisco where men who attend the school and do not recidivate avoid an arrest record, men who attended SEEP were convicted of soliciting a prostitute. SEEP was an independent organization, whereas San Francisco's johns' school is under the auspices of the criminal justice system. See Martin Monto. 2000. "Why Men Seek Out Prostitutes," in *Sex for Sale: Prostitution, Pornography, and the Sex Industry,* edited by Ronald Weitzer. New York: Routledge.

45. John Braithwaite. 1989. *Crime, Shame, and Reintegration.* Cambridge, UK: Cambridge University Press.

46. Personal communication from Staff Sgt. Doug Mottram, Metropolitan Toronto Police, August 7, 1997.

47. Molly Greenman. 1990. "Survivors of Prostitution Find PRIDE." *Families in Society* 71: 110–113; Evelina Kane. 1987. "Support for Women Leaving Prostitution: Project Summary and Recommendations," Minneapolis, MN: WHISPER.

48. WHISPER. 1985–1986. *WHISPER Newsletter,* no. 1, p. 1.

49. International Committee for Prostitutes' Rights. 1985. *World Charter for Prostitutes' Rights.* Amsterdam.

50. Part of the following discussion is based on Weitzer, "Prostitutes' Rights in the United States."

51. COYOTE proposes that existing business codes be used to confine prostitution businesses to commercial or mixed residential/commercial areas (Priscilla Alexander. 1979. "National Decriminalization a Must as Hypocritical, Sexist Vigilante Groups Spring into Action across the U.S." *NTFP News* 1: September–October).

52. COYOTE, 1974. "COYOTE Background." *COYOTE Howls* 1 (2).

53. One study found that call girls and brothel and massage parlor workers were well-adjusted: "capable of handling themselves well, manifesting good emotional controls, being well aware of conventionality, and

doing well in the occupation of their choice" (John E. Exner, Joyce Wylie, Antonia Leura, and Tracey Parrill. 1977. "Some Psychological Characteristics of Prostitutes." *Journal of Personality Assessment* 41: 474–485). Studies of escorts, independent call girls, and workers in brothels and massage parlors confirm this (see Ronald Weitzer. 2005. "New Directions in Research on Prostitution," *Crime, Law, and Social Change* 43: 211–235).

54. COYOTE, quoted in Jim Stingley. 1976. "Issues Raised by Decriminalization." *Los Angeles Times,* February 9.

55. Stingley, "Issues Raised."

56. COYOTE. 1974. "Fiction versus Fact." *COYOTE Howls* 1 (2).

57. Interview with Priscilla Alexander, San Francisco, March 16, 1987.

58. Margo St. James. 1989. "Preface." In *A Vindication of the Rights of Whores,* ed. G. Pheterson. Seattle: Seal Press, p. xix.

59. Interview with Margo St. James, September 12, 1980.

60. Some local branches of NOW, such as San Francisco's, have been more actively involved with COYOTE.

61. Erving Goffman. 1963. *Stigma.* Englewood Cliffs, N.J.: Prentice-Hall.

62. National Task Force on Prostitution. 1987. *About the NTFP.* San Francisco, p. 2.

63. Interview with Samantha Miller, June 16, 1993.

64. Ronald de Graaf. 1995. *Prostitutes and Their Clients.* The Hague: Gegenens Koninkijke, p. 15. It should be noted that a significant proportion of customers are foreign tourists and businessmen.

65. October 1997 poll, cited in Chrisje Brants. 1998. "The Fine Art of Pragmatic Tolerance: Prostitution in Amsterdam." Unpublished paper, University of Utrecht.

66. Edgar Danter. 1999. "Green Light at Last for Dutch Red Light Districts," *Deutsche Presse-Agentur,* February 6, N=2,600.

67. Interview with Sietske Altink, Red Th read, Amsterdam, March 24, 1997.

68. Interview with Klein Beekman, chairman of the Brothel Owners Association, Amsterdam, March 24, 1997.

69. Ministry of Justice figures, cited in *AP Worldstream,* January 27, 1999.

70. Interview with secretary of Window Owners Association, Amsterdam, May 28, 1998.

71. Window Owner's Association, quoted in *The Guardian,* January 31, 1999.

72. Interview with the director of the Foundation of Men and Prostitution, The Hague, May 29, 1998.

CHAPTER NINE

Defining Deviance and Social Control

Why do societies need criminal justice systems? There are those who believe that society is so perfect that there is no crime, no disorder, and no need for the agencies of criminal justice. While this is theoretically possible, it is difficult to envision. For example, a truly crime-free society would require unanimous agreement on all aspects of life, which is difficult to imagine given the variety of human opinions, tastes, and preferences.[1]

By contrast, others believe that society without police, courts, and prisons would operate in a state of nature, a free-for-all environment where there is little order, which raises the question: What would life be like without these agencies? In answer, life would be "solitary, poor, nasty, brutish, and short."[2] Individuals would be responsible for enforcing their own self-interest by taking revenge against wrongdoers, while also fearing they would accidentally offend others and then be victims of revenge.

Both have valid points of view. The reality of the situation, however, is that we need the criminal justice system so that we can maintain order in society. Furthermore, we do not live in a crime-free utopia and we do not want to live in a chaotic state without social controls of some type. In this respect, we will examine the concept of the social contract, which is a metaphor that helps us understand the role of government in society and its responsibility to the people.[3]

---

1   Emile Durkheim, *The Division of Labour in Society*, trans. W. D. Halls (New York: Free Press, 1997).

2   Thomas Hobbes, *Leviathan*, ed. Edwin Curley (Indianapolis, IN: Hackett Publishing Company, 1994).

3   Locke, John. *Two Treatises of Government*, ed. Peter Laslett (Cambridge: Cambridge University Press, 1988).

Crime and Deviance

By Jeffrey C. Alexander and Kenneth Thompson

....

W hat leads someone to be labeled a deviant or a criminal? Take the case of John Walker Lindh, a once apparently "normal" Californian young man who suddenly became branded as a deviant and even a criminal because of his association with the Moslem Taliban regime in Afghanistan, which supported the Al-Qaeda terrorist destruction of the World Trade Center in New York on September 11, 2001. At what point did John Walker's harmless eccentricity become deviance and then criminality? And what was the cause?

According to the newspaper article reprinted in the box titled "John Walker's Restless Quest Is Strange Odyssey," Walker seemed a fairly normal American teenager "who had a basketball hoop in his driveway" and a "collection of more than 200 hip-hop and rap CDs." But the article also notes that there was already a hint of eccentricity or deviance, in that he "showed little interest in predictable teenage pastimes." When Walker began to take an interest in the Muslim religion, got rid of his CDs, and started wearing an ankle-length white robe, he was indeed deviating from his peer group of white, middle-class teenagers in Mill Valley, California. He did, however, find acceptance and respect in the Islamic Center of Mill Valley, even though a fellow member admitted that "[n] o one like him had ever come here before." When his devotion to his religion led him to fight for a foreign army that supported terrorists against his own country, it was left to the U.S. courts to judge whether the "deviant" had become a "criminal." Walker was eventually found guilty and sentenced to twenty years' imprisonment.

An Individual or a Social Story?

Whatever else you may think of John Walker's story, it certainly raises many questions about the life journey or "odyssey" in the course of which we develop or are given an identity that may be labeled normal, deviant, or criminal. And it seems that this journey to identity is becoming increasingly influenced by the impressions we gain from the mass media in postmodern culture. A common feature of the stories and explanations we hear in this culture is that they tend to be posed in individualized terms, such as those of individual psychology—Walker was "brainwashed," or a "rebel."

In the postmodern era, newspapers, bookstores, television channels, and cinemas are full of "Gothic horror" stories of violent assault and shocking murders. Fiction and fact vie with each other in representations of dangers that lurk around every corner, whether in the form of the serial murderer in the movie *The Silence of the Lambs,* the killers in the Columbine school massacre, or the destroyers of the World Trade Center. What is striking about many of these stories is that violence and murder are portrayed as occurring in ordinary and "respectable" settings, suggesting that they represent the risks and dangers of everyday life in postmodern society—ranging from the office (the World Trade Center) to the school, park, or home. Such stories have at least one thing in common: They usually present some type of individualistic account—that is, of the *individual criminal.* One version is that of an individual acting under the influence of evil—the evil "Other," an agent of drives or forces outside society as we know it. President Bush repeatedly branded the people responsible for the destruction of the World Trade Center in New York, especially their alleged leader, Osama Bin Laden, as extraordinarily "evil" individuals. (Most Americans agreed with that moral judgment, although they were still left wondering "Why do they hate us and act in this way?") Another version is that of the criminal personality or criminal mind, whereby an individual's biological or psychological abnormalities are said to predispose him or her to commit violent acts.

Postmodern culture (see Chapter 3) presents a confusing mixture of cultural discourses about crime, including religion, science, and various mass media genres. The practices of labeling individuals as "evil" and "born to be bad" have long histories. The former idea dates back to traditional societies, where religious language was dominant. The latter idea—that some people are born to be criminals—came to prominence in the sociobiological evolutionary theories of the nineteenth century, when scientists believed they could find physical differences between criminals and the general population, such as skull shape, showing that criminals were a throwback to a more "primitive" stage in human evolution. More recently, some scientists have sought to link criminal behavior to genetic inheritance or some other biological cause (Samenow and Yochelson 1976; Wilson and Herrnstein 1985). An example of defense lawyers' use of this kind of explanation can be seen in the case of California murder defendant Carl Stayner:

> Carl Stayner is California's most notorious murder defendant, accused of last year's Yosemite slaying. He confessed to slitting the throat of one victim, burning

the bodies of two others and beheading a fourth. But was Stayner destined from birth to commit those gruesome crimes? Was he predisposed—by biology or perhaps some childhood injury—to murder? Stayner's defense team hopes to find answers to such provocative questions with a radioactive brain scan performed at U.C. Irvine that can detect if the motel handyman suffers some sort of cerebral abnormality. (Bailey 2000: A3)

As noted, the common thread among these widely publicized horror stories is that they all focus on the individual and reflect a return to theories about the abnormal, criminal mind, whether possessed by evil or by biological abnormalities. It follows that the most popular solutions are incarceration, medical treatment, and execution, and that the favored prevention policies include not only deterrence through tough sentencing but also increased surveillance measures, medical treatment of potential offenders, and insurance against personal risk. Indeed, such individualistic and "commonsensical" discourses about crime are enjoying renewed prominence in contemporary society. In some respects they represent a reaction against the sociological accounts of crime and deviance in modern society that began to gain currency in the middle of the twentieth century.

Although sociologists have differed in their theories about crime and deviance (see our discussion on theories later in this chapter), they tend to unite in focusing on social and cultural factors rather than on individual factors. In the middle of the twentieth century the focus was on factors such as class inequalities in wealth, housing, education, and family circumstances as well as on the consequent failure to socialize everyone into following the same norms of behavior as those associated with mainstream (white, middle-class) cultural values. Later, in the 1960s, sociological studies of crime and deviance began to focus not so much on crime and its causes as on the processes of social interaction that lead to the constructing or labeling of certain behaviors as crimes, and on the social reactions that such behaviors and crimes provoke (Becker 1963; Lemert 1967). In the twenty-first century, sociologists are still interested in those social factors, but they are also turning their attention to such issues as postindustrialism, consumer society, multiculturalism, and the media-saturated postmodern culture. Not all of these developments are new—many started in the earlier phases of modernity—but, as we will see, they are becoming increasingly significant.

In this chapter we examine five issues:

1. *The nature of deviance and crime.* What forms of behavior constitute deviance and crime, and how have these terms been defined? Are such definitions universal, or do they vary according to time and place?

2. *The extent of crime.* What are the statistics on crime and punishment? Is crime increasing or decreasing?

3. *Responses to crime.* What are the different views about the best ways to deal with crime and criminals?

4. *Explanations of crime.* How do different theories explain crime? How are these explanations related to public opinion and "commonsense" notions about crime in different periods?

5. *Representations of crime.* How do the mass media represent crime? What do people involved with crime have to say about it?

Defining and Describing Deviance and Crime

The terms **deviance** and **crime** seem fairly straightforward at first glance. Deviance refers to behavior that clearly departs from what the majority of a community or society considers to be "normal"—that is, in line with norms. *Norms* are prescribed forms of behavior. *Values* are the more general cultural goals toward which norms are directed (again, see Chapter 3). Whereas a norm prescribes actual behavior, a value justifies that behavior and provides the reason for which some actions garner more approval than others. Crime is any behavior that the law forbids. But what is deviant is not quite so straightforward to determine. It all depends on who is doing the defining in any particular case. For example, what a rich, upper-middle-class white man regards as deviant behavior might not be regarded as such by a poor, lower-class black youth. Even what gets categorized as a criminal act can vary depending on the circumstances. For example, physician-induced suicide and hate crime are two categories of crime about which judgments vary in different jurisdictions.

In the mid-twentieth century, in the midst of the more homogeneous integration that characterized modern society, it seemed reasonable to concentrate on instances of "deviance" from widely observed social norms—such as the ethnic gangs whose conflict is featured in the movie musical from that time, *West Side Story*. But postmodern society is increasingly characterized by cultural diversity and disagreement about what is normal. Alongside values that continue to be shared are the much more loosely integrated networks of subcultures and lifestyles. The latter are particularly evident in the case of youth subcultures, which often vary even within a school or college.

Take the example of Columbine High School. The boys who slew their fellow students were allegedly members of a subcultural group, the Trench-Coat Mafia, who apparently saw themselves as radically different from the more mainstream or "normal" culture of the school, especially that associated with the school's athletes. But some commentators have questioned whether there really was such a clear separation. After all, some of the stylistic elements to which the Trench-Coat Mafia subculture adhered had a wider following within contemporary youth culture. As an expert commentator in *Time* magazine put it:

> The "normal" culture of adolescence today contains elements that are so nasty
> that it becomes hard for parents (and professionals) to distinguish between what
> in a teenager's talk, dress and taste in music, films and video games indicates

psychological trouble and what is simply a sign of the times. Most kids who subscribe to the trench-coated Gothic lifestyle, or have multiple body piercings, or listen to Marilyn Manson, or play the video game Doom are normal kids caught in a toxic culture. (Garbarino 1999: 51)

As noted earlier, *crime* refers to any act explicitly forbidden by legislation (specifically, as interpreted by the courts). This definition seems fairly unproblematic. In practice, however, it is not always so clear-cut. There are variations over time, and even within the criminal justice system, as to what acts are judged to be illegal and worthy of prosecution. For example, the treatment of witches has undergone changes throughout American history. In seventeenth-century Salem, Massachusetts, young girls allegedly indulging in witchcraft were condemned to death (Erikson 1966). But today, witches can practice their rites with impunity, and this postmodern form of *Pagan* or *Wicca* spirituality has close links with New Age religion and some feminist groups (Lewis 1996). Or take the example of racial hate crimes. Until the twentieth century, whites in the South who lynched blacks often suffered no consequences. But in postmodern society, ethnic and cultural differences are more likely to be accorded tolerance and respect—in part, because the criminal justice system now gives more attention to crimes involving discrimination or hate. Since 1990, when President George H.W. Bush signed into law the federal Hate Crime Statistics Act (HCSA), there has been an apparently clear definition of **hate crime:** "crimes that manifest evidence of prejudice based on race, religion, sexual orientation or ethnicity" (quoted in Perry 2001: 7). Implicit in the use of this term is the assumption that there is agreement about what would constitute the commission of a recognized criminal offense and the existence of the motivation of prejudice. But not all states recognize the same categories of prejudice in their hate crime legislation: Some, for instance, exclude the category of sexual orientation, whereas others include that of "whistle blowers" (Perry 2001: 12). Inconsistencies of this sort have implications for the reliability of statistics about hate crimes. Not only do law enforcement agencies vary in their recording of such crimes, but the victims of such crimes may be reluctant to report them. Gay victims as well as sexually abused women, children, and ethnic minorities may fear the consequences of going to the police.

Given the questionable reliability of hate crime statistics, it may be wise to look carefully at the media's claims about trends in crime. As we have seen, some crimes may be underreported by victims or unrecorded by the police. The prosecution of crimes may vary as well. Émile Durkheim's famous work *Suicide* (1897) made generalizations about variations in social solidarity between societies and groups on the basis of official statistics about their suicide rates—for example, there were higher rates of suicide for Protestants than for Catholics. But critics have pointed out that this disparity may reflect the fact that Catholics view suicide more severely than Protestants and are thus more inclined to record death at a person's own hand as "accidental" or due to a "disturbed state of mind" than as a "deliberate" suicidal act. Clearly, statistics for the crime of suicide need to be interpreted with this difference in reporting practices kept in mind.

Although it is important to read crime statistics with some caution, there is no avoiding the conclusion that Americans have the dubious distinction of living in the world's most violent industrial nation (see Table 9.1). Violent crime skyrocketed in the United States starting in the late 1960s, a trend that continued into the early 1990s. In view of this, it is no wonder that crime has consistently been one of the public's major concerns over the past three decades. But since the mid-1990s, most parts of the country have witnessed a sharp drop in violent crime (see Figure 9.1). The FBI's 2000 survey of crimes (see *Public Agenda* 2005), which is reported to the police, showed the overall murder rate at its lowest level since 1967. (Even so, the United States still had higher rates of murder than any other industrial society.) Similarly, the National Crime Victimization Survey, designed to measure both reported and unreported crime, found the lowest overall **crime rate** since the survey began in 1973. The crime rate fell for the ninth straight year in 2000, declining 3.3 percent from 1999, 18.9 percent from 1996, and 30.1 percent from 1991 (Rennison 2001). Criminal justice experts attribute this trend to three possible causes: the decline in cocaine use; the fact that more criminals are in prison, and are serving longer sentences; and the temporary drop in the number of young males, the group most prone to violent crime. (For additional data on the declining crime rate, see Figures 9.2 and 9.3.)

Table 9.1 International Comparison of Selected Crime Statistics, 2000[1]

Country	Crimes Recorded by Police[2]	Violent Crimes Recorded by Police[3]	Homicide Rate per 100,000 Population[4]	Imprisonment Rate per 100,000 Population[5]
England & Wales	5,170,843	733,374	1.50	124
Northern Ireland	119,912	24,323	3.10	60
Scotland	423,172	27,047	2.19	115
Austria	560,306	..	0.90	84
Belgium	848,648	59,791	1.79	83
Bulgaria	127,659	..		..
Cyprus	4,358	113	0.6	43
Czech Republic	391,469	21,996	2.78	208
Denmark	504,231	15,748	1.00	61
Estonia	57,799	1,158	11.43	325
Finland	385,797	34,291	2.60	56
France	3,771,849	243,166	1.68	80
Germany	6,264,723	187,103	1.19	97

Country	Crimes Recorded by Police[2]	Violent Crimes Recorded by Police[3]	Homicide Rate per 100,000 Population[4]	Imprisonment Rate per 100,000 Population[5]
Greece	369,137	9,105	1.55	76
Hungary	450,673	29,144	2.47	157
Ireland (Eire)	73,276	3,312	1.37	76
Italy	2,205,782	74,136	1.50	94
Latvia	50,199	..	6.51	..
Lithuania	82,370	6,176	8.91	257
Luxembourg	22,816	4,280	0.87	92
Malta	17,016	..	1.68	68
Netherlands	1,173,688	90,944	1.40	87
Norway	330,071	20,582	0.93	56
Poland	1,266,910	90,062	2.04	170
Portugal	363,294	19,780	1.35	124
Romania	353,745	20,818	2.36	222
Russia	3,001,748	97,153	20.52	729
Slovakia	88,817	13,549	2.54	132
Slovenia	67,617	1,414	1.14	57
Spain	923,269	119,923	2.77	114
Sweden	1,214,968	74,646	2.06	64
Switzerland	270,733	8,152	1.09	79
Turkey	..	..	2.54	74
Australia	1,431,929	181,999	1.87	113
Canada	2,353,926	301,875	1.79	123
Japan	2,443,470	64,418	1.06	47
New Zealand	427,230	44,887	2.28	149
South Africa	..	..	54.25	385
United States	11,605,751	1,424,289	5.87	685

Source: Adapted from Barclay and Tavares (2003).

Notes:

[1] Definitions of offenses, legal systems, and statistical recording procedures vary between countries and comparisons should be interpreted with caution.

[2] More serious offenses. Excludes misdemeanors.

[3] Includes violence against the person, robbery, and sexual assault.

[4] Intentional killing of a person (murder, manslaughter), excluding attempted murder and death by dangerous driving.

[5] Based on estimates of the national population.

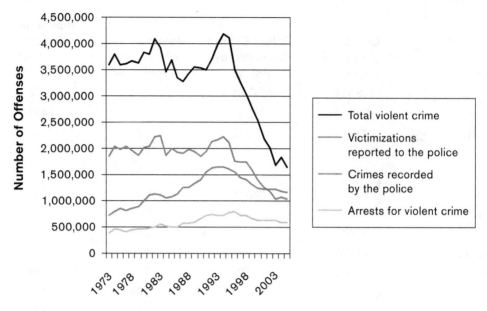

Figure 9.1 Decline in Serious Violent Crime by Four Measures

Note: The category of serious violent crimes referred to in the figure title includes rape, robbery, aggravated assault, and homicide. Two sources of data were used to create the measures. The first source is the National Crime Victimization Survey (NCVS), a household survey started in 1972 that interviews approximately 75,000 people age 12 and above in 42,000 households twice a year about their victimizations from crime. This method tends to report higher rates of crimes because it includes incidents never reported to the police. The second source is the Uniform Crime Reports (UCR), which collect information about crimes and arrests reported to the Federal Bureau of Investigation by law enforcement.

Total violent crime consists of the estimated number of homicides of persons age 12 and older reported to the police plus the number of rapes, robberies, and aggravated assaults from the NCVS, whether or not they were reported to the police.

Victimizations reported to the police consists of the estimated number of homicides of persons age 12 and older recorded by police plus the number of rapes, robberies, and aggravated assaults from the NCVS that victims said were reported to the police.

Crimes recorded by the police consists of the total number of homicides, forcible rapes, robberies, and aggravated assaults recorded in the Uniform Crime Reports, excluding commercial robberies and crimes involving victims under age 12.

Arrests for violent crime consists of the number of persons arrested for homicide, forcible rape, robbery, or aggravated assault as reported by law enforcement agencies to the FBI.

Source: Bureau of Justice Statistics, available online at http://www.ojp.usdoj.gov/bjs/glance/cv2.htm (accessed January 26, 2006).

Despite the falling crime rate, public opinion surveys show that most Americans do not feel much safer (see Tables 9.2 and 9.3). In a 2000 survey, fewer than half of Americans said they felt safe at school or walking in their neighborhood after dark. Their concern may be justified in view of the fact that a majority of Americans, sooner or later, will be victims. Taking into account both violent crime and property crime, the FBI reports that 83 percent of Americans can expect to be a victim of crime at least once in their lifetimes (*Public Agenda* 2000).

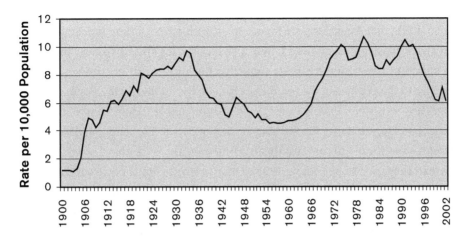

Figure 9.2 Recent Decline in Homicide Rate, 1900–2002

Note: The 2001 rate includes deaths attributed to the terrorism attacks of September 11, 2001.

Source: Bureau of Justice Statistics, available online at http://www.ojp.usdoj.gov/bjs/glance/tables/ hmrttab. htm.

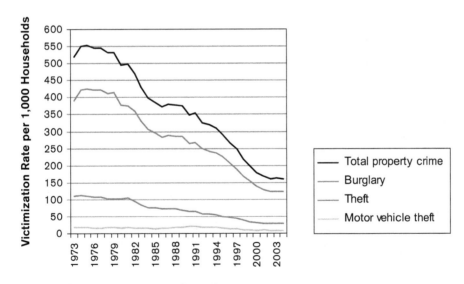

Figure 9.3 Decline in Property Crime Rates

Note: The National Crime Victimization Survey (NCVS) on which this chart is based was redesigned in 1993. The data before 1993 have been adjusted to make them comparable to the data collected since the redesign.

Source: Bureau of Justice Statistics, available online at http://www.ojp.usdoj.gov/bjs/glance/house2.htm (accessed February 2, 2006).

There is no doubt that Americans are preoccupied with crime. Crime is prominent as a subject in television series, news programs, and newspaper reports. It's also listed near the top of citizens' concerns in opinion surveys. Some experts argue that the level of fear of crime in America is a reasonable response to the extraordinary volume of crime in the United States. For example, American homicide rates are consistently many times those of comparable industrial nations (Currie 1985). One researcher has suggested that the fear may be due in part to the changing nature of violence in the United States—specifically, to concerns that it is becoming more "random" and that many offenders are younger than they used to be (Young 1994). Other analysts argue, however, that the high levels of fear and concern besetting Americans are largely caused by media imagery and the rhetoric of enterprising politicians who have an interest in exploiting fears about crime. Indeed, the amount of time devoted to television viewing correlates strongly with fear of crime (Gerbner and Gross 1976; Gerbner et al. 1980). And there is evidence that trends in popular concern about drugs match trends in the amount of prominence given to this issue by politicians (Beckett 1994).

Table 9.2 Percentage of Respondents Reporting Concern about Crime Victimization, by Sex and Race, United States, 2003

SURVEY QUESTION: How often do you, yourself, worry about the following things—frequently, occasionally, rarely or never?	Total	Male	Female	White	Nonwhite	Black
Your home being burglarized when you are not there	48	42	52	47	47	54
Having your car stolen or broken into	45	43	47	44	49	49
Being a victim of terrorism	38	31	44	36	42	41
Having a school-aged child of yours physically harmed while attending school	35	31	38	32	46	51
Your home being burglarized when you are there	30	23	35	28	34	40
Getting mugged	28	21	34	27	32	46
Being attacked while driving your car	26	22	30	26	28	30
Being sexually assaulted	23	5	39	21	26	35
Getting murdered	18	15	21	17	24	35
Being the victim of a hate crime	17	14	18	13	30	35
Being assaulted or killed by a coworker or other employee where you work	9	9	9	7	14	21

Note: "Nonwhite" includes black respondents.

Source: Pastore and Maguire (2003).

Table 9.3 Percentage of Respondents Reporting Whether They Engage in Selected Behaviors Because of Concern over Crime, by Sex and Race, United States, 2003

SURVEY QUESTION: Next, I'm going to read some things people do because of their concern over crime. Please tell me which, if any, you, yourself, do or have done.	Total	Male	Female	White	Nonwhite	Black
Avoid going to certain places or neighborhoods you might otherwise want to go to	49	43	55	47	57	62
Keep a dog for protection	31	28	34	32	27	25
Bought a gun for protection of yourself or your home	27	32	22	26	32	36
Had a burglar alarm installed in your home	25	25	25	22	37	44
Carry mace or pepper spray	19	8	29	17	28	31
Carry a gun for defense	12	17	9	11	16	23

Note: "Nonwhite" includes black respondents.

Source: Pastore and Maguire (2003).

Media portrayals make it difficult to separate the "reality" of crime and the criminal justice system from the ways in which they are perceived. However, we can get a sense of how far the two sorts of information match up by looking more closely at both the relevant statistics and the media portrayals themselves.

Crime and Punishment Statistics

Although the incidence of some types of crime has declined in recent years, the U.S. criminal justice system has been growing rapidly for several decades. Its expansion from the 1970s onward has been dramatic. Between 1972 and 1988, nationwide spending on criminal justice reportedly grew by 150 percent, and between 1969 and 1989, per capita state expenditures on police and correction increased tenfold (Chambliss 1994). This spending financed a doubling in the size of the nation's police force between 1980 and 1990 as well as a massive expansion of the state and federal prison systems. On December 31, 2000, as the United States was entering the twenty-first century, the number of people in prison had reached 1,381,892. Between 1990 and 1999, the average annual growth of crime was 6 percent (Beck and Harrison 2001). And by year's end in 2003, the prison population had increased to 1,470,045, having grown at an annual rate of 3.4 percent (Harrison and Beck 2004). Ethnic and gender differences remain significant. In 2000 there were an estimated 478 prison inmates per 100,000 U.S. residents—up from 292 in 1990. In the same year, the number of women prisoners reached 91,612, compared to 1,290,280 men. And at the end of that year, there were 3,457 sentenced black male inmates per 100,000 black males in the United States, compared to 1,220 sentenced Hispanic male inmates per 100,000 Hispanics and 449 white male inmates per 100,000 white males. Here are some additional statistics to consider:

- If **imprisonment rates** remain the same, one of every fifteen persons in the United States (6.6 percent) will serve time in prison during their lifetime.
- Lifetime chances of going to prison are higher for men (9.3 percent) than for women (1.8 percent) and higher for blacks (18.6 percent) and Hispanics (10 percent) than for whites (3.4 percent).
- Based on current rates of first incarceration, an estimated 32 percent of black males will enter prison during their lifetime, compared to 17 percent of Hispanic males and 5.9 percent of white males. (Adapted from U.S. Department of Justice, Bureau of Justice Statistics 2001)

Surveys show that many Americans want tougher policing and sentencing (see Figures 9.4–9.6). However, statistics reveal that some sections of the population suffer both more crime and more imprisonment than others. Poor blacks and Hispanics are the ones most at risk. It is also the case that they live in inner-city areas, where there is more social breakdown than elsewhere, as indicated by higher male unemployment, more single-parent families, and a higher frequency of failing schools. (For further information on this topic, see Chapter 8, on inequality; Chapter 10, on race and ethnicity;

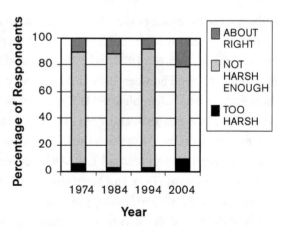

SURVEY QUESTION: Do you favor or oppose the death penalty for persons convicted of murder?

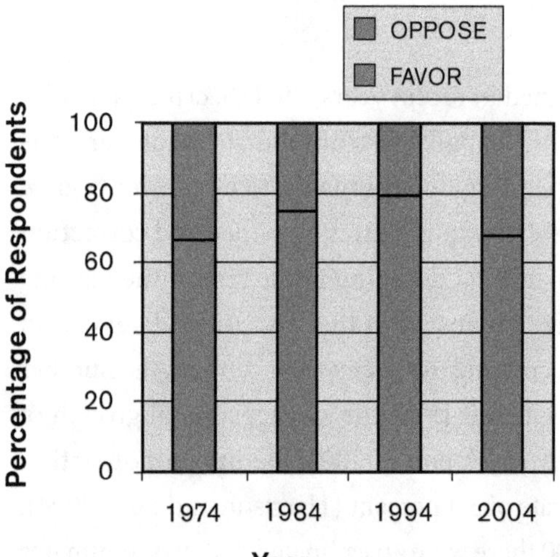

Figure 9.4 Attitudes toward the Death Penalty

Source: Computer-assisted Survey Methods Program (2006).

SURVEY QUESTION: In general, do you think the courts in this area deal too harshly or not harshly enough with criminals?

Figure 9.5 Attitudes toward Court Sentencing of Criminals

Source: Computer-assisted Survey Methods Program (2006).

and Chapter 16, on urbanism and population.) Sentencing policy has hit offenders from these communities hardest—particularly since the introduction of the "three strikes and you're out" policy.

Representations of Crime

The "cultural turn" in sociology has been important for the study of crime and deviance since the 1970s. It played a key part in the development of a "constructionist paradigm" for social problems research. The theoretical perspective known as the social construction of reality or social constructionism is particularly helpful in understanding the impact of the pervasive mass media in defining and interpreting social problems in postmodern society. Constructionist researchers focus on how problems come to be constructed or "framed" in particular ways. For example, Joseph Gusfield (1981) examined the cultural factors that contribute to the framing of "drinking and driving" as a problem stemming

SURVEY QUESTION: We are faced with many problems in this country, none of which can be solved easily or inexpensively. I'm going to name some of these problems, and for each one I'd like you to tell me whether you think we're spending too much money on it, too little money, or about the right amount. Halting the rising crime rate: are we spending too much, too little, or about the right amount on halting the rising crime rate?

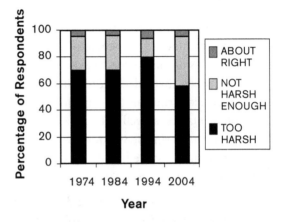

Figure 9.6 Attitudes toward Spending on the National Crime Problem

Source: Computer-assisted Survey Methods Program (2006).

from public transportation policy or the design of automobiles. In the context of fear and concern over crime, the issue's significance for politics and public policy depends on how it is socially constructed and framed (Sasson 1995: 3–4). In other words, the way it is perceived depends on the mental framework that gives it meaning for people—a framework that is based on people's own experiences but also is influenced by the pronouncements of opinion leaders such as politicians and the media. On this score the conventional wisdom is that Americans, in the mass media but also in everyday conversation, construct crime as a threat "from below" (Reiman 1990). The offender is often imagined as black and, even more often, as poor and male. Many people reject the notion that crime is caused by poverty or racial discrimination, instead blaming either individual moral failure or a poorly functioning criminal justice system. They believe that the problem would be solved if the police cracked down on offenders and the courts "got tough." This perspective is referred to as **volitional criminology** (Scheingold 1991), and its advocates are described as having a "law and order" orientation (Dahrendorf 1985; Gordon 1990). It reflects a widespread tendency in America to believe that crimes are the result of individuals' moral failings and their decisions to act illegally—a tendency evidenced by the observation that many

Americans attribute responsibility for a whole range of behaviors to individuals rather than to societal forces (Gans 1988). Although American values tend to stress individual choice and responsibility, there are variations in the ways in which these values are framed, leading to differing interpretations of social problems such as crime. (See box titled "Three Strikes and You're Out.")

A survey by Theodore Sasson (1995) on the kinds of discourses about crime used by opinion leaders in the media, such as politicians and journalists, found that such discourses could be reduced to five basic "frames": *Faulty System, Blocked Opportunities, Social Breakdown, Media Violence,* and *Racist System*. Sasson describes each of these as follows:

1. The *Faulty System* frame is typified by what is referred to as the "law and order" perspective, which maintains that people commit crimes because they know they can get away with it. Advocates of this perspective claim that there are insufficient resources for law enforcement and prisons, that judges are too liberal, and that too many technicalities and loopholes make it possible for criminals to escape justice. It is a view held by many conservative politicians and commentators, as well as by many criminal justice professionals. By failing to take sufficient action, in the ringing words of conservative political scientist James Q. Wilson, "[w]e thereby trifle with the wicked, make sport of the innocent, and encourage the calculating" (Public Agenda Foundation 1993: 15).

2. The *Blocked Opportunities* frame depicts crime as a consequence of inequality and discrimination, especially in the forms of unemployment, poverty, and inadequate educational opportunities. People commit crimes when they discover that legitimate means of attaining goals are blocked. Certain sections of the population have always suffered from these disadvantages, particularly black Americans. The problems of blocked opportunities worsened with deindustrialization from the 1970s onward, as good-paying blue-collar jobs disappeared and were replaced by lower-paid and insecure service jobs. Increasing desperation and frustration promote property crime and violence; "[i]f you're going to create a sink-or-swim society," says criminologist David Bruck, "you have to expect people to thrash before they go down" (quoted in Public Agenda Foundation 1993: 22). This view is put forward by many liberal and Left policy analysts and some liberal Democrat politicians. It is symbolized by references to the only kind of jobs available to inner-city youth—dead-end jobs such as "flipping burgers at McDonald's."

3. The *Social Breakdown* frame depicts crime as a consequence of family and community disintegration. As evidence, supporters of this view cite high rates of divorce and out-of-wedlock births, loss of a sense of community responsibility in the cities, and a general breakdown in the moral and social bonds that previously discouraged crime. This frame is expressed in calls for a return to "family values" and by references to cases such as that of Kitty Genovese, the New York woman who in 1964 was stabbed to death while dozens of her neighbors watched passively from their windows. There are conservative and liberal versions of this frame. Conservative advocates attribute social breakdown to declining "family values," permissiveness and lack of discipline, the protest movements of the 1960s and 1970s (e.g., civil rights, feminism), and

government-sponsored welfare programs, whereas liberal advocates point to unemployment and low wages, de-industrialization, and diminished access to blue-collar careers.

4. The *Media Violence* frame focuses on violent crime and sees it as a consequence of violence on television, in the movies, and in popular music. (For a detailed discussion of this issue, see Chapter 4, on media and communication.) Its supporters argue that, to reduce violent crime, it is necessary to reduce the extent of its portrayal and glamorization by the media. This frame is favored by the antigun lobby and groups concerned with the welfare of children as well as by some members of Congress and officials in the Department of Justice.

5. The *Racist System* frame is a minority view. Focusing on the criminal justice system rather than on the issue of who or what is responsible for crime, it holds that the courts and police are racially biased against nonwhite citizens and, in effect, operate a dual system of justice. Advocates point to the fact that, compared to whites, blacks experience higher rates of arrest and conviction and are more likely to receive the death penalty. This frame is used by many civil rights and civil liberties activists as well as by some Left intellectuals. An incident that gave it credibility was the beating of black motorist Rodney King by white Los Angeles police in 1991, which, caught on video and shown on national television, led to a controversial court case that divided blacks and whites, followed by riots when a mainly white jury found the police not guilty.

For instance, it is possible to think of arguments against each of the "frames." *Faulty System* fails to take account of the fact that imprisonment itself "hardens" offenders and frequently leads to reoffending; it also fails to address the causes of crime. The *Blocked Opportunities* view overlooks the fact that most poor people do not engage in crime. *Social Breakdown* is countered by the criticism that it is triggered by nostalgia for an earlier, idealized community that never existed or, at least, was not very widespread, while references to "family values" may disguise a thinly veiled hostility to feminism. *Media Violence* disregards the hypothesis that aggressive behavior is correlated with—rather than necessarily caused by—media violence. And the *Racist System* frame is limited in its usefulness because it directs attention to only one problematic aspect of the criminal justice system (although an important one).

White-Collar and Corporate Crime

One reason for which crime and prison statistics show a disproportionate number of poor and black people as offenders may be that the crimes they commit—street crimes—are those that are most energetically policed and punished. Americans take for granted that street crime is the worst social problem and that **white-collar crime** is not as dangerous or as costly. Although antitrust violations, false advertising, price fixing, unfair labor practices, embezzlement, and fraud cost society more money and pose greater dangers to public safety than ordinary street crime, the people who commit white-collar crime seldom receive heavy punishment (Reiman 1998). Indeed, white-color offenses tend not to be regarded as "real" crimes; perhaps it is because of their "impersonal" nature that people do not fear them as a threat to themselves. Yet such crimes can have severe effects on individuals, as in the case of the thousands of employees and pensioners who lost their savings as a result of being misled into investing in the energy corporation Enron, which went bankrupt in 2002 after engaging in financial malpractices (see also Chapter 17, on politics, publics, and the state). Although in certain respects Enron was a special case (the seventh-largest corporation in the United States, with ties to politicians in both parties stretching up to Congress and the White House), it was not an isolated one. A considerable number of additional examples of corporate illegal practices could be listed. Below are a just a few from the 1990s that illustrate the scale of the problem and the leniency with which the corporate offenders were treated:

- In 1992, the U.S. Justice Department accused Teledyne, Inc., of systematically falsifying tests on an electrical component used in the construction of sophisticated weapons and spacecraft. The company also sold the government a $6 part for $20 and, over a period of one year, defrauded the U.S. taxpayers of about $250 million (Stevenson 1992, cited in Newman 2000: 207). Although the company was caught committing the same kind of fraud on other occasions, the government has continued to do business with it.
- In 1994, six airlines (American, Delta, Northwest, TWA, Alaska, and Continental) were found to have collaborated illegally to raise airline ticket fares over a four-year period, costing consumers an estimated $4 billion in excess fares. No criminal charges ensued, and the airlines received no formal punishment. They simply agreed not to negotiate ticket-price changes in the future—a settlement that the government was happy to accept.
- In 1997, Florida justice officials discovered that America's largest insurance company, Prudential, had been engaged in a deliberate scheme to cheat its customers for more than a decade. Rather than being subject to criminal prosecution, the company was allowed to settle with a payment of $15 million—a mere fraction of the $2 billion it had gained by defrauding customers (Treaster and Peterson 1997, cited in Newman 2000: 177)

The perpetrators of these white-collar crimes, even repeat offenders, are seldom subject to the massive law-enforcement efforts directed at street crimes such as those committed by prostitutes, beggars, drug dealers, and thieves. Consider, as just one example, the long jail sentences given to low-income individuals who, having already been labeled as criminals, are convicted for stealing small amounts of money. Inequality and harshness also characterize punishment of more violent crimes and the application of the death sentence. In this post-Enron era, efforts have been made by the U.S. Justice Department to combat this patently unjust situation, at least in terms of its most conspicuous representations. We have been treated to scene after scene of the super-rich and powerful being hauled into squad cars with their heads pushed down and their hands handcuffed behind their backs, and judges and juries have sentenced some of these white-collar criminals to heavy jail time. But whether this handful of cases presages a new relationship between the criminal justice system and white-color crime remains to be seen. It will take a lot more than post-Enron attention to balance the scales of justice fairly.

Matters of Life and Death

The ultimate get-tough punishment is the death penalty, which was briefly struck down by the U.S. Supreme Court in the 1970s but has gradually been reinstated by many states and the federal government. At the end of 2003 more than 3,300 people were on death row in the United States, and in the last twenty-five years more than 700 prisoners have been executed. Until the end of the 1990s the numbers being executed rose steeply. After 1999, however, a small reduction occurred, accompanied by numerous reports of mistakes whereby condemned or executed prisoners were found to have been innocent. An overview of crime issues published by *Public Agenda* (2005) cited Columbia University research that found two out of three cap ital convictions were overturned on appeal, often owing to incompetent defense lawyers or because overzealous prosecutors had withheld evidence. The likelihood of being executed also varies among states; Texas leads the field, accounting for 24 of the total of 65 persons (all men) executed in the United States in 2003. Only eleven states carried out executions that year. Of the persons executed in 2003, 20 were black and 41 white; under sentence of death were 1,418 black persons and 1,878 white prisoners (Bonczar and Snell 2004).

Although there is no evidence that capital punishment deters would-be murderers, the majority of Americans continue to support the death penalty (see Tables 9.4–9.6). At times, public opinion in other Western societies has also shown majority support for capital punishment, but many governments in these societies, such as those of Western Europe, have resisted reintroducing it. The fact that European societies have lower rates of murder could be taken as evidence that capital punishment does not act as a deterrent, but it may simply reflect the different cultural attitude toward the ownership and use of firearms. European societies are not necessarily more law-abiding. For example, a comparison carried out for the U.S. Department of Justice showed that in 1996, Brit-ain had higher rates of assault, burglary, and motor vehicle theft than the United States. However, murder rates in the United States were 5.7 times higher. A significant difference was that guns were involved in crime far more often in the United States than in Britain, where there is stricter gun control (Langan and Farrington 1998). The individual's right to bear arms is something that many Americans believe to be a constitutional right and a part of their culture.

Table 9.4 American Attitudes Toward the Death Penalty, 2004

	SURVEY QUESTION: Generally speaking, do you believe the death penalty is applied fairly or unfairly in this country today?			SURVEY QUESTION: Do you feel that the death penalty acts as a deterrent to the commitment of murder, that it lowers the murder rate, or not?		
	Applied fairly	Applied unfairly	Don't know/ refused	Yes, does	No, does not	Don't know/ refused
National	55%	39%	6%	35%	62%	3%
Sex						
Male	59	35	6	41	57	2
Female	51	42	7	31	65	4
Race						
White	59	35	6	37	61	2
Nonwhite	41	51	8	31	64	5
Black	32	58	10	15	80	5
Education						
College postgraduate	43	50	7	31	65	4
College graduate	56	41	3	33	67	0
Some college	59	34	7	28	69	3
High school graduate or less	57	36	7	44	53	3
Community						
Urban area	42	50	8	32	65	3
Suburban area	58	36	6	35	62	3
Rural area	64	31	5	40	58	2
Region						
East	53	40	7	39	58	3
Midwest	52	41	7	36	60	4
South	64	30	6	35	62	3
West	48	46	6	31	67	2
Politics						
Republican	75	20	5	49	49	2
Democrat	42	51	7	25	71	4
Independent	50	44	6	34	64	2

Note: Based on telephone interviews with a randomly selected national sample of 1,000 adults (over the age of 18).

Source: Pastore and Maguire (2003).

Table 9.5 Reported Reasons for Opposing the Death Penalty for Persons Convicted of Murder, United States, 1991 and 2003

Reason for Opposing	**SURVEY QUESTION:** Why do you oppose the death penalty for persons convicted of murder?	
	1991	**2003**
Wrong to take a life	41%	46%
Punishment should be left to God/religious belief	17	13
Person may be wrongly convicted	11	25
Does not deter people from committing murder	7	4
Possibility of rehabilitation	6	5
Unfair application of death penalty	6	4
Need to pay/suffer longer/think about their crime	n/a	5
Depends on the circumstances	n/a	4
Other	16	3
No opinion	6	4

Note: Question asked only to those respondents who answer "no, not in favor" to the question "Are you in favor of the death penalty for persons convicted of murder?" Up to two responses were recorded from each respondent.

Source: Pastore and Maguire (2003).

Theories of Crime and Deviance

Sociologists have long sought to dissociate themselves from what they regard as the errors of individualistic approaches to crime and deviance, whereby the causes of crime are located in the individual's nature—as implied by phrases such as *evil nature* and *born criminal* (those who are born with characteristics that predispose them toward criminal behavior). In this respect, sociological theories differ from theological, psychological, and biological theories:

- Sociological theories characterize deviance and crime as a response to the society in which they occur.
- Psychological theories locate deviance and crime within the psyche or mind of the individual, as the product of inborn "abnormality" or of "faulty cognition processes."
- Biological theories locate deviance and crime within the biological makeup of the individual.
- Theological theories locate deviance and crime within the spiritual or moral makeup of the individual.

Table 9.6 Reported Reasons for Favoring the Death Penalty for Persons Convicted of Murder, United States, 1991 and 2003

Reasons for Favoring	SURVEY QUESTION: Why do you favor the death penalty for persons convicted of murder?	
	1991	2003
An eye for an eye/they took a life/fits the crime	40%	37%
Save taxpayers money/cost associated with prison	12	11
Deterrent for potential crimes/set an example	8	11
Depends on the type of crime they commit	6	4
Fair punishment	6	3
They deserve it	5	13
They will repeat their crime/keep them from repeating it	4	7
Biblical reasons	3	5
Serve justice	2	4
Don't believe they can be rehabilitated	1	2
If there's no doubt the person committed the crime	n/a	3
Would help/benefit families of victims	n/a	2
Support/believe in death penalty	n/a	2
Life sentences don't always mean life in prison	n/a	1
Relieves prison overcrowding	n/a	1
Other	10	4
No opinion	3	2

Note: Question asked only to those respondents who answer "yes, in favor" to the question "Are you in favor of the death penalty for persons convicted of murder?" Up to two responses were recorded from each respondent.

Source: Pastore and Maguire (2003).

The sociological theories we discuss in this chapter are functionalist theory, especially that of Emile Durkheim; labeling theory and the symbolic interactionist perspective; conflict theory, particularly that influenced by Karl Marx; and cultural approaches to crime and deviance, including theories relevant to postmodern society in particular.

Functionalist Theory

Functionalist theory developed in the period from the end of the nineteenth century until the middle of the twentieth. It was based on an analogy between society and the body, with organs or parts that contribute to the smooth functioning of the whole. If any part malfunctioned or became dysfunctional, perhaps as a result of external causes, then the body would react in order to preserve itself—the reaction would be manifested in pathological symptoms, such as sickness and fatigue. According to Durkheim (1893), modern society in his own time was experiencing just such symptoms as a result of the loss of traditional community and the pressures of economic and social change. Whereas traditional society had been bound together by shared group values and norms, people in modern society were becoming less attached to norms (a condition he called "anomie") and thought they could simply pursue their own individual interests. Durkheim recognized that a certain amount of deviation from norms is normal and healthy for any society. It allows for innovation and adaptation to change. Even deviance and crime, in small amounts, could have a reinforcing function in bonding the elements of society together against a common enemy. But too much crime and deviance becomes a problem. He believed this to be the case with excessive individualism in modern society: Too many people thought they could behave as they wanted, ignoring the group and its rules.

The functionalist-based idea of anomie was taken up by Robert Merton (1957), whose interest was in the structural causes of nonconformist (deviant) behavior. He explained crime and deviance as the result of **strain** caused by lack of sufficient legitimate means to achieve socially approved goals. Such goals are symbolized by the American dream, which holds that—provided one works hard—success in the form of a good job, money, a nice house, and an affluent lifestyle can be yours. Americans internalize these values or cultural goals as part of their socialization, but there is a dysfunction or strain resulting from the unequal distribution of the means to achieve such goals. Merton went on to specify five main responses to such strain:

1. *Conformity:* In this scenario, the norms of correct behavior are followed even though the means to achieve them are not available. Conformity is not a deviant response.

2. *Innovation:* Here, the goals are accepted but, because of inadequate means to achieve them, other means are used that have not previously been approved. So-called creative bookkeeping, as practiced by the accountants of large corporations that are not achieving their profit goals, is one kind of innovation that treads a fine line between legality and illegality. (In the Enron crash of 2002, the line was crossed.)

3. *Ritualism:* When people give up hope of achieving goals, even in cases where the means of attaining them are available, they may continue to work within the system but are really only "going through the motions." Ritualism of this sort is common in large bureaucracies, where workers may observe the rules but lose sight of the goals.

4. *Retreatism:* Those who lack the means and have not accepted the goals may drop out or retreat from society—in some instances, by becoming recluses or turning to alcohol or drugs.

5. *Rebellion:* Some people reject the dominant goals and the means to achieve them, but then replace them with their own set of values. This rebellion response could account for acts of politically motivated terrorism or "freedom fighting."

Some critics have maintained that Merton saw deviance too much in terms of individuals and ignored the communal aspects of some forms of deviance. For example, Albert Cohen (1955) and Richard Cloward and Lloyd Ohlin (1960) insisted that deviance, especially youth delinquency, is the result of excluding groups from opportunities to achieve the goals of society based on their position in the social structure. This, the authors noted, is particularly the case for working-class youths. Cohen said that such youths experience "status frustration," because they increasingly became aware that they are denied the means to achieve their goals. Their reaction is to substitute new and deviant goals, which creates a delinquent subculture. Cloward and Ohlin pointed out that some young people lack even the opportunity of joining a gang or making a career of crime. These individuals are "double failures," and many of them retreat into a life of drug abuse and violence.

Labeling Theory and the Symbolic Interactionist Perspective

Labeling theory gradually took over from functionalist approaches to crime and deviance in the 1960s and 1970s. It arose out of the symbolic interactionist perspective that developed out of the work of W. I. Thomas, G. H. Mead, and others at the University of Chicago before World War II. Thomas's "theory of the situation" (the so-called **Thomas Theorem**) states: "If men define those situations as real, they are real in their consequences" (1931 [1966]: 301). Mead's contribution was to show how meanings and identities are constructed through social interaction and to explain that we regulate our behavior by taking account of the way we think others will respond. It was these ideas that labeling theory later applied to deviance and crime to demonstrate the ways in which deviant labels are created, imposed, and resisted through interaction (Mead 1934). Three decades later, Howard Becker made the point that no actions are by nature criminal or deviant, nor are people naturally criminal or deviant. Rather, deviance depends on the norms of the society, and on the reactions of members of society in different situations. In his book, *Outsiders: Studies in the Sociology of Deviance*, Becker stated that groups create deviance by making the rules and then applying those rules to particular people and labeling them as outsiders: "The deviant is one to whom that label has successfully been applied" (Becker 1963: 9).

The effect of this perspective on the sociology of crime and deviance was to shift the focus from why people are criminal or deviant onto the question of why and how people come to be *labeled* as criminal or deviant. Becker also described the **deviant career** in terms of the stages that people undergo in internalizing the label that has been applied to them. This idea is useful for elucidating how young people gradually accept the labels such as "oddball" or "delinquent" that have been applied to them, and even see their identities in those terms. It also helps explain what happens to young prisoners whose criminal identities and criminal careers become hardened as a result of their social interactions in jail.

The two main criticisms of labeling theory are that it can appear to doubt the reality and serious consequences of deviant or criminal acts and that it has nothing to say about the structural causes of crime, such as social conditions of poverty and blocked opportunities.

Conflict Theory

Conflict theory, especially the version influenced by Marx's ideas of class conflict and exploitation (Chambliss 1975; Quinney 1977), points out that inequalities of wealth and power are what lead some people to be branded as deviant or criminal. It is the rich and powerful who make the laws and rules to serve their interests—and anyone offending against these has to be punished and controlled. The state and its agencies—the courts and the police—are simply tools of the ruling class. So it is the system, specifically the capitalist system, that creates criminals. It does this in various ways. First, it punishes any infractions or threats to the functioning of the capitalist economic system itself. Under capitalism the most important value is the right to exploit private property to the fullest so as to make a profit. Crimes against property are severely punished. Second, capitalism is alleged to generate greed and selfishness because it has to create new and bigger markets for its commodities, which entails spending vast sums on advertising and marketing. Third, it stimulates competition for scarce resources, which means that the rich and powerful get and use more than their fair share, to the disadvantage of others. Richard Quinney (1970, 1974), for example, argues that laws in capitalist societies are not about fairness but about forging a tool to control the working class.

The main criticisms of Marxist conflict theory are that it levels blame exclusively against the conflict between the interests of the two classes of capitalists and workers, even though there are laws that protect both capitalists *and* workers. It also ignores other sources of conflict that are not class based.

Not all conflict theorists follow Marx in emphasizing class conflict in discussions of crime and deviance. Indeed, some focus on racial conflict and oppression. They point to the massively disproportionate number of blacks who are stopped by the police and brought to court, and to the more severe sentences they receive compared to whites, including the death penalty. Not just the police and judiciary act on racial stereotypes and prejudices, they argue; even some criminological ideas, such as biological theories, legitimize racism. This was one of the criticisms against Wilson and Herrnstein's best-selling *Crime and Human Nature* (1985), which, along with similar books, was said to have fueled public debates about the supposed links between race and crime (Garland 2001: 136).

Cultural Approaches to Crime and Deviance

In recent years, sociologists have increasingly turned their attention to cultural factors to explain crime and punishment. This endeavor can take several forms, such as undertaking ethnographic research into deviant subcultures and seeking to understand the meanings that criminals attach to their actions, or examining the portrayal of crime in the media. Neither ethnographic studies nor studies of media portrayals of crime are completely new developments in the sociology of crime and deviance. However, both are likely to become more important in the future because of their relevance to the sociological analysis of trends in crime and deviance in postmodern society.

Ethnographic Research

Earlier we looked at some of the "facts" about crime and punishment, as represented by statistics. However, it is important to remember that facts do not speak for themselves—they have to be constructed by those who report and collect the information, as well as by those who interpret it. As we have seen, there are sometimes disagreements over statistics and what they mean. Another way of gaining an understanding about deviance and crime is to undertake firsthand observation of those involved and their cultures. Early examples of this kind of ethnographic field research (*ethno* means "people," *graphic* means "description," and *in the field* refers to "the situation") can be found in the studies performed by University of Chicago sociologists—the Chicago School—such as Frederic Thrasher's *The Gang* (1927), Clifford Shaw's *The Jack Roller* (1930), Nels Anderson's *The Hobo* (1923), and John Landesco's *Organized Crime in Chicago* (1929). These first urban ethnographers were essentially following the advice of the chair of the Chicago sociology department, Robert Park, who instructed students to "go get the seat of your pants dirty in real research" (quoted in McKinney 1966: 71).

This type of research went into partial hibernation during the ascendancy of functionalist sociology around the time of World War II and the period immediately following. A number of professional researchers regarded ethnographic research on deviant groups as "unscientific" and too subjective, believing quantitative (statistical) research to be more objective. (For a more detailed discussion of sociological methods overall, consult Chapter 2.) Some sociologists continued in the Chicago School tradition during the postwar era, especially those pursuing the study of juvenile delinquency. Others focused on individuals who sought to maintain social control by rousing public opinion on moral issues, termed "moral entrepreneurs" (Becker 1963). An example of such a moral crusade—or "moral enterprise" (Becker 1963)—is the Temperance movement against alcohol, described in Joseph Gusfield's *Symbolic Crusade* (1963).

In the 1960s, the main center of ethnographic research moved to California, where the study of deviant, alternative, countercultural, and illegal groups flourished. Researchers studied these groups at close proximity in order to find out what constituted their realities. Readers were treated to in-depth accounts of the underworld of horse racing (Scott 1968), religious cults (Lofland 1966), skid row (Wiseman 1970), and nude beaches (Douglas and Rasmussen 1977).

One work in the Chicago tradition, though carried out largely in New York (with some historical research in England), was Ned Polsky's *Hustlers, Beats, and Others* (1967)—an ethnographic study of poolroom hustlers that demonstrates the advantages of this kind of research in understanding the motivation of those who pursue a risky career (involving deception and illegal gambling) within a deviant subculture. Polsky explains that "hustlers are social deviants, in the sense that they gamble for a living and, in the process, violate societal norms of 'respectable' work and of fair dealing." Yet within their working-class subculture, they are not regarded as particularly deviant and so are not stigmatized as "poolroom bums" by their own subculture's norms. Furthermore, "once embarked in the hustling life, hustlers prefer to stay in it: it's exciting, it has a tradition and ideology that can make them feel heroic, it's fun (the game is enjoyable as such), it's not routine, and so on" (Pol-sky 1967: 85–86, 90).

During the 1960s it could be said, the hustling career shared deeply, often passionately, in every one of the orientations that sociologists have described as "focal concerns" of American lower-class subcultures—"trouble (with the law), smartness (in the sense of being able to con and of being no one's dupe), excitement, fate, toughness ('heart'), and autonomy" (Miller 1958, quoted in Polsky 1967: 90). But it's important to realize that this was a time when a large, inner-city, blue-collar working class was employed in manufacturing and laboring jobs, and that such jobs were mainly masculine in ethos. This working-class subculture has declined with the rise of the postindustrial economy. There is now a proliferation of consumer lifestyles rather than class-based subcultures, although inner-city ethnic groups may still be said to have distinctive subcultures (containing some of the "focal concerns" earlier attributed to the working class) and to be more tolerant of behavior that the larger society labels as deviant or criminal.

Ethnographic studies of deviant and criminal groups were discouraged by many universities in the 1980s and 1990s on the grounds that they could be judged unethical, especially if they involved a covert role for the observer, lacked parental consent (in cases where deviant youth were being studied), or did not have signed consent forms from those being observed. Government agencies and other organizations have also been unsympathetic to such research, especially when researchers have tried to protect the privacy and confidentiality of their sources. One graduate student researcher, Rik Scarce, at Washington State University, was jailed for six months for contempt of court because he would not divulge information about the members of the radical environmental movement he was studying. Scarce's later request to conduct field research with inmates was denied by his university (Ferrell and Hamm 1998: xv).

Despite the difficulties encountered in doing ethnographic field research on deviants and criminals, there has been a resurgence of such studies in recent years. In *Ethnography at the Edge: Crime, Deviance, and Field Research* (1998), sociologists Jeff Ferrell and Mark Hamm describe the horrors, perils, and joys of their deep involvement with such diverse groups as skinheads, phone-sex workers, drug dealers, graffiti artists, and homeless people. They recount how doing this kind of research involved such episodes as illegal drug use, drunk driving, weapons violations, assault at gunpoint, obstruction of justice, and arrest. Clearly, ethnographic field research is not for the fainthearted. But it does add a valuable source of data that are not available from more "orthodox" or quantitative research. Indeed, it not only provides an understanding of the meanings and emotions of those under scrutiny in a particular situation—the moments of pleasure and pain, the emergent logic and excitement—but also allows researchers, through attentiveness and participation, to appreciate the specific roles and experiences of criminals, crime victims, crime control agents, and others caught up in the day-to-day reality of crime and deviance.

Among the important results of this kind of research are findings that concern the emotions and the situated logics (what "makes sense" in particular situations) of those involved in specific criminal or deviant cultures. Such an understanding cannot be attained from "outside," solely on the basis of statistical data. In addition, whereas the adrenaline-rush experiences often studied by ethnographic researchers, such as joyriding, drug taking, shoplifting, and gangbanging, might appear to be isolated, individual, or impulsive experiences, ethnographic study shows that they reflect a shared vocabulary of motive—a repertoire of meanings common to those involved in them (Mills 1940). In short, the emotions and the meanings of deviants and criminals are constructed collectively out of the common experiences of subcultural participants and the shared cultural codes of their groups. They cannot be understood solely on the basis of individual psychology or statistics, even though these are the types of explanation favored by media reports and many criminal justice professionals.

Ethnographic studies show that strong emotions, such as the thrill of danger, pleasure, excitement, anger, and frustration—as experienced in instances of shoplifting (Katz 1988), graffiti writing, neo-Nazi skinheads "going berserk" (Hamm 1993), or Latino gang members "going crazy" against rival gangs (Vigil 1988)—are important elements in some deviant and criminal subcultures. As reported by Kenneth Tunnell (1992), even adult property criminals, though operating on the basis of rational calculation about how much they could make, report that stealing gave them a feeling of exhilaration. Another study reveals that many adult burglars are "committed to a lifestyle characterized by the quest for excitement and an openness to 'illicit action'" and that some go so far as to burglarize occupied homes in order to make "the offence more exciting" (Wright and Decker 1994: 117).

As we will see in the next section, the same two themes—pleasure and risk—are prominent in mass-media portrayals of crime and deviance in postmodern society.

Media Portrayals of Crime and Deviance

Early sociologists viewed modern society in terms of theories of the progressive development of a rational society based on scientific principles, while still allowing for occasional setbacks and persisting pockets of irrational thought and antisocial behavior. Functionalist sociologists conceded, with Durkheim, that a limited amount of crime and deviance could be healthy for society, but they expected that better organization and scientific endeavor could limit the pathological effects. For example, it was thought that better socialization of youth through education would minimize juvenile delinquency or rebellion. Conflict theorists looked to reform or revolution of the social system to cure structural problems of which crime and deviance were symptoms. Labeling theorists' ideas were taken on board by teachers and other professionals, who got the message that sticking a label on someone—for example, "the troublemaker"—could have the result of causing that person to live up (or down) to that label. Hence, careful calculation of the effects of labeling was needed.

As we have discussed throughout *A Contemporary Introduction to Sociology*, by the second half of the twentieth century the idea of linear social progress had begun to look less convincing, not just in light of horrific events such as the Holocaust and the development of atomic weapons but also because some of the means to progress, including science and the mass media, seemed to be among the causes rather than the cures of these events.

Great faith was placed in the potential of modern communications media to promote social progress. The earliest forms of mass media, such as newspapers, had something of the character of informational and educational channels, with dense columns of sober print communicating information to the literate public. (Note, however, that the first American papers were extremely partisan and short-lived.) Subsequently, with the rise of the popular "penny" press catering to a mass readership (see Chapter 4, on media and communication), the content became more sensational and entertaining, with crime stories predominating. The advent of television carried this development much further. It has been estimated that, from the 1960s to the 1990s, crime and justice programming amounted to one-fourth of all prime-time shows, making it the largest single subject matter on television (Surette 1998: 35–36). In addition to the many fictional crime series now available on TV, crime news has become the mainstay of hybrid news-entertainment (infotainment) shows. One paradoxical result of this extensive crime coverage is that the media are simultaneously perceived as both a major cause of crime and violence and an untapped but powerful potential solution to crime. On the one hand, the media are accused of spreading glamorous images of crime, which can lead to copycat behavior; but on the other hand, the media are expected to aid in reducing crime, assisting in manhunts, and bolstering the criminal justice system. Another paradoxical effect is that the criminal justice system is often not shown positively, yet the solution rate on television exceeds 90 percent (Surette 1998: 21). This results in an unrealistic picture of crime and justice that can only lead to dissatisfaction when real-life crimes are not cleared up or reduced in number.

There are many indications that crime rates have dropped over the past decade, but this fact has hardly caused a decline in crime reporting. If you watch the local news tonight, chances are you will see at least one crime story. Figures 9.7 and 9.8 show some of the findings from an extensive survey of local television news stations across the United States. Crime is by far the most common topic of news stories, by a margin of 2:1 over any other category. Correspondingly, over a quarter of the people you will see on the news are people involved in crime, such as victims, criminals, law enforcement officials, and judges.

A consequence of the all-pervasive nature of mass media in postmodern society is that a large amount of attention is being focused on a few criminal events, producing a kind of spiral effect. The public is led to believe that a certain kind of deviant behavior is spreading rapidly and is a symptom of an underlying moral decline in society, or among certain groups (such as youth). Sociologists have referred to this sequence as **moral panic** (Cohen 1972; Thompson 1998). The term was first used by sociologist Stanley Cohen to characterize the outraged reactions of the media, the public, and agents of social control to the youth disturbances—fights on the beach between "Mods" and "Rockers"—that were occurring during holiday weekends in 1960s Britain:

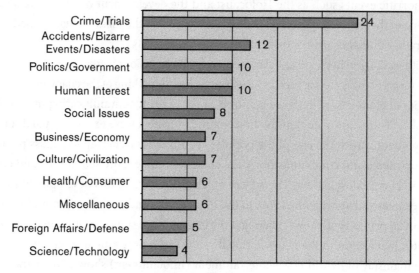

Figure 9.7 Top Coverage of Local TV News Stories, 1998–2002

Note: These data are based on content analysis of local news from 154 stations from 15 to 20 markets that were randomly selected with controls for station size and geographic diversity. Weather and sports coverage were not included. Totals may not equal 100 due to rounding.

Source: PEJ (2004).

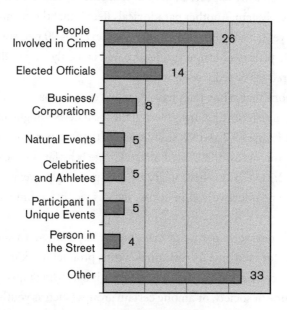

Figure 9.8 Main Subjects of Local TV News Stories (percentage of stories)

Note: These data are based on content analysis of local news from 154 stations from 15 to 20 markets that were randomly selected with controls for station size and geographic diversity. Weather and sports coverage were not included. Totals may not equal 100 due to rounding.

Source: PEJ (2004).

Societies appear to be subject, every now and then, to periods of moral panic. A condition, episode, person or group of persons emerges to become defined as a threat to societal values and interests; its nature is presented in a stylized and stereotypical fashion by the mass media; the moral barricades are manned by editors, bishops, politicians and other right-thinking people; socially accredited experts pronounce their diagnoses and solutions; ways of coping are evolved or (more often) resorted to; the condition then disappears, submerges or deteriorates and becomes more visible. (Cohen 1972: 9)

Employment of the phrase *moral panic* to describe such events has been criticized on the grounds that *panic* implies an irrational reaction. However, the usefulness of the concept depends not on the meaning of *panic* but, rather, on the fact that the concept draws attention to the processes by which the media can set in motion a spiral effect that amplifies a threat and plays on people's fears and their sense of being at risk (even if, statistically, they are not). A similar phenomenon is invoked in Philip Jenkins's (1994) description of the social construction of serial murder in the 1980s, in which a few cases were made to appear as an exploding, pervasive social problem.

Indeed, as the mass media have become more pervasive and intrusive in postmodern society, their role in the construction of crime and deviance has become increasingly significant. As noted above, the result is an increased sense of being at risk, even if the objective possibility of risk has not actually increased. Sociologist Ulrich Beck (1992) writes about the new "Risk Society" as if increased danger were literally a fact (see also Adam, Beck, and van Loon 1992). Such a noncultural understanding can hardly do justice to the mass media's role in constructing such dangers as crime. It is the media's construction or representation of crime that produces the kind of gothic fascination and emotional involvement that characterize the postmodern imagination and give rise to unrealistic demands for the elimination of crime and other risks.

The Future of Crime and Deviance in Postmodern Society

The emphasis, in recent ethnographic and media studies, on the importance of emotions such as the excitement associated with acts of crime echoes the ideas of one of the leading postmodern thinkers, Michel Foucault. His writings about pleasure (1985), the body (1978), and the changing regimes of discipline and control in different historical periods (1977) led him to pronounce that "power is in our bodies, not in our heads" (quoted in Fraser 1994: 11). By that, Foucault meant that **social regulation** of people's bodies, including their emotions, is of paramount concern. Each major historical epoch, he argued, is distinguished by a predominant form of regulation or control. In traditional feudal society, physical punishments, including the most ferocious forms of torture and execution, were common. This phase was succeeded in the early-modern, industrializing societies of the late eighteenth and early nineteenth centuries by incarceration of offenders in what Erving Goffman, in *Asylums* (1961), called "total institutions," characterized by "barrier(s) to social intercourse with the outside and to departure that is often built right into the physical plant, such as locked doors, high walls, barbed wire, cliffs, water, forest or moors" (Goffman 1961: 4). These institutions used surveillance, discipline, and rituals to strip occupants of their deviant personality features and then to remake them in a common mold.

Foucault described the modern correctional regime as one based on techniques and "scientific" discourses, aimed at disciplining the mind-body of the prisoner. The story that Foucault presented in *Discipline and Punish* (1977) is a history not just of the modern prison but also of the emergence of a more generalized regime of discipline and control in modern society, involving other disciplinary occupations (e.g., doctors, psychologists, and teachers). Foucault's focus was on the emergence of what he termed *power-knowledge*—the complex range of practices and schemes of professional knowledge and everyday "common sense" increasingly put to use in the control of unruly, difficult, or simply disturbingly different (deviant) populations. For Foucault, and those influenced by him, modern society is to be understood through "discourse analysis"—focusing on the specific sets of practices and ideas that provide meaning in specific spheres of social life. Specifically, Foucault's idea was that, instead of permitting the state increasingly centralized control in modern society, social regulation would be decentralized and exercised through institutions such as medicine and education. And not only deviants and criminals would be corrected and reformed through these various disciplines. Rather, in Foucault's account, the whole of modern society would become a disciplinary or "carceral" society. Ironically, Foucault's proposals led many liberals to become extremely critical of community-based policies aimed at reforming and reintegrating offenders, rule breakers, and deviants. When this criticism from the left side of the political spectrum combined with criticisms from the right, it became easier for politicians, from the 1970s onward, to bow to pressure to concentrate on punishment rather than reform of offenders.

Postmodern society is characterized by diversity and contradiction. If Foucault had been right, imprisonment would have given way to the more subtle techniques of disciplinary control. What we find instead, however, is a parallel growth of the prison population and the reintroduction of capital punishment, alongside other disciplinary techniques such as psychiatry, drug treatments, electronic tagging, private security measures (including armed guards in some schools), and gated communities. Powerful platforms for these new techniques have been provided in the new patterns of consumerism. Today's malls are privatized versions of the old public spaces of inner-city shopping streets and squares, but with their own security forces and electronic surveillance measures. Many residential communities, too, are not only gated and walled off from the surrounding public spaces but equipped with surveillance systems that identify deviant-looking intruders. The result is one of the fastest-growing dimensions of social control in market-driven, consumer society: "the management of risk." Risk management and risk assessment are indeed central to the new strategies and tactics of policing. Large numbers of key operational decisions about the deployment of police resources are now made by local police forces by reference to data on patterns of criminal offending, produced through software computer programs that deliver such information to the level of individual streets. But this kind of "objective" data doesn't necessarily correspond to people's own "subjective" sense of being at risk, which is affected not only by their personal experiences but also by media representations and the cultural climate more generally. The cultural climate of postmodern society is increasingly fluid and fragmented, a kaleidoscope that is constantly in motion. It gives rise to a pervasive sense of insecurity and risk that no amount of policing can allay.

Conclusion

The case of John Walker Lindh and the publicity given to it, as described at the beginning of this chapter, illustrate some of the main points that have been made about sociological explanations of crime and deviance. Sociology is interested in social trends, and in discovering general social and cultural factors that can be used to explain them. It asks questions such as "Is this case a typical example of a social and cultural trend?" and "What are the social and cultural factors that might account for its occurrence and the ways in which it is perceived?" Indeed, individual cases, such as that of John Walker Lindh, can be examined in this light. If we considered just the bare facts of this case, there would appear to be little to justify the public fascination with it, nor would it seem sufficiently socially typical to be of interest to sociologists. After all, Walker was simply a single young American abroad, who was found fighting on the wrong side in a distant war in Afghanistan. In normal times, people might have accepted the psychological explanation that he was just a mixed-up individual. What made his capture a sensational event, however, was the cultural context that gave it meaning. This context was the heightened sense of insecurity and risk that resulted from searing images of the destruction of the World Trade Center, followed by a campaign on behalf of patriotism and national solidarity. The image of this highly deviant-looking American Muslim fighter, with his filthy robes and straggling beard, symbolized the threats to national security and solidarity.

The John Walker Lindh case and, indeed, September 11 itself were exceptional events; but it was the cultural construction of them, via the media, that tapped into the underlying feelings of horror and fascination that pervade postmodern society. In this respect such events parallel other examples of the social construction of deviance and crime. For instance, Joel Best (1991) describes the media's role in constructing the new "crime problem" of highway violence, news coverage of which is dominated by an emphasis on the random, senseless quality of such incidents, employing terms like *Mad Max*, *Road Warrior*, and *Freeway Rambo*. And in Philip Jenkins's (1994) account of the social construction of serial murders, the author observed that the media immediately linked these shocking homicides to other publicly hyped phenomena—missing children, pedophilia, sexism, racism, and homosexuality—so as to raise the sense of threat. These symbolic linkages fanned public anxieties about the structural stresses and strains in a changing society, such as pressures on the family unit, the changing roles of women, high unemployment in some minority groups, and the greater freedom granted to homosexuals.

Although the media may provide sensationalized accounts of individual criminal acts and help to create "moral panics" about the threats facing society, there are real causes of anxiety that they plug into. People are concerned about the stresses and strains to which the social fabric is being subjected as a result of global and local social changes. And politicians and judges are responding to those perceived anxieties when they introduce or impose the penal sanctions that account for why America has the largest prison population in the developed world. However, although rapid social changes create real strains in the social structures of postmodern societies, comparisons of America with similar developed societies suggest that we have to look to cultural factors in order to explain its higher rates of imprisonment and more severe sentencing policies. Not only is America unique in maintaining capital punishment, it is the only developed country with a large and growing number of prisoners serving life sentences without parole. A survey by the *New York Times* (Liptak 2005a: A1) found that the number of lifers almost doubled between 1995 and 2005 and that the number of prisoners serving life sentences without the possibility of parole had risen and amounted to 28 percent of all lifers in 2005. In 2005 alone, about 9,700 were serving life sentences for crimes committed before they were 18, and more than a fifth had no chance of parole (Liptak 2005b: A1). The cultural reasons underlying America's distinctiveness in this dubious regard are hard to pinpoint, but they merit thinking about. In the *New York Times* article noted earlier, two experts are quoted as attributing it to America's Calvinist religious tradition. Said one commentator: "It's the same reason we're not a socialist welfare state. ... You deserve what you get, both good and bad" (Liptak 2005a: A1).

This argument is probably too simplistic, if only because there are other developed societies with a Calvinist religious tradition that have different attitudes toward crime and its punishment. Furthermore, Calvinist Protestantism is not the only brand of religion that is prominent in America—the Catholic population, for example, is long established and has increased dramatically with Latino immigration. Granted, America is unusually religious for an economically developed society, but a valid explanation will have to account for the full range of other factors that are distinctive to America, such as its particular racial history and its political system and culture. In the final analysis, it is the complex interplay of all these social and cultural factors that will be found to explain the trends in American crime and deviance and society's perception of them.

Study Questions

1. What trend in the rate of violent crime has been dominant in the United States over the last ten years? Has the American public's fear of crime mirrored this trend?

2. What trend in the imprisonment rate has been dominant in the United States since 1990? Which demographic groups have the highest chance of going to prison?

3. What is volitional criminology? In what ways does this orientation reflect American values?

4. Which is more costly to society: street crime or white-collar crime? Why does the public perceive street crime as the more serious social problem?

5. What is the difference between sociological and individualist approaches to crime and deviance? Describe where each of the individualist approaches locates the causes of crime and deviance.

6. According to Émile Durkheim, how could deviance have a positive function in society? When did it become a problem? What did he mean by the term *anomie*, and what was the cause of this condition?

7. According to labeling theory, how is deviance created? What is meant by the term *deviant career*?

8. According to conflict theory, how does capitalism create criminals?

9. What is ethnographic field research? What are the risks and limitations of this methodology in researching crime? What are the benefits?

10. What is a moral panic? What role do the media play in it?

11. Describe the forms of social regulation that were dominant in traditional, early-modern, and modern epochs. According to Foucault, what important development in discipline and control emerged during the modern era? In this new regime, which institutions exercised social regulation, and over whom?

Further Reading

Anderson, Elijah. 1978. *A Place on the Corner,* 2nd ed. Chicago: University of Chicago Press. Reprinted in 2001.

Chancer, Lynn S. 2005. *High-Profile Crimes: When Legal Cases Become Social Causes.* Chicago: University of Chicago Press.

Dotter, Daniel L. 2005. *Creating Deviance: An Interactionist Approach.* Walnut Creek, CA: AltaMira Press.

Garland, David. 2001. *The Culture of Control.* Chicago: University of Chicago Press.

Heimer, Karen, and Candace Kruttschnitt, eds. 2005. *Gender and Crime: Patterns of Victimization and Offending.* New York: New York University Press.

Moore, Mark H., Carol V. Petrie, Anthony A. Braga, and Brenda L. McLaughlin. 2003. *Deadly Lessons: Understanding Lethal School Violence.* Washington, DC: National Academies Press.

Pattillo, Mary, David Weiman, and Bruce Westera, eds. 2004. *Imprisoning America: The Social Effects of Mass Incarceration.* New York: Russell Sage Foundation.

Bibliography

Adam, Barbara, Ulrich Beck, and Joost van Loon, eds. 1992. *Risk Society and Beyond: Critical Issues for Social Theory*. Thousand Oaks, CA: Sage.

Andersen, Nels. 1923. *The Hobo: The Sociology of the Homeless Man*. Chicago: University of Chicago Press.

Bailey, Eric. 2000. "Defense Probing Brain to Explain Yosemite Killings." *Los Angeles Times*, June 15, 3.

Barclay, Gordon C., and Cynthia Tavares. 2003. "International Comparisons of Criminal Justice Statistics, 2000." *Home Office Statistical Bulletin*.

Beck, Allen J., and Paige M. Harrison. 2001. "Prisoners in 2000." Washington, DC: U.S. Department of Justice, Office of Justice Programs, Bureau of Justice Statistics.

Beck, Ulrich. 1992. *Risk Society: Towards a New Modernity*. London: Sage.

Becker, Howard Saul. 1963. *Outsiders: Studies in the Sociology of Deviance*. New York: Free Press.

Beckett, Katherine. 1994. "Setting the Public Agenda: 'Street Crime' and Drug Use in American Politics." *Social Problems* 41, no. 3: 425–447.

Best, Joel. 1991. "'Road Warriors' on 'Hair-Trigger Highways': Cultural Resources and the Media's Construction of the 1987 Freeway Shooting Problem." *Sociological Inquiry* 61: 327–345.

Bonczar, Thomas P., and Tracy L. Snell. 2004. "Capital Punishment, 2003." U.S. Department of Justice, Office of Justice Programs.

Chambliss, William J. 1975. "Toward a Political Economy of Crime." *Theory and Society* 2, no. 3: 149–170.

_____. 1994. "Policing the Ghetto Underclass: The Politics of Law and Law Enforcement." *Social Problems* 41, no. 3: 177–194.

Cloward, Richard A., and Lloyd E. Ohlin. 1960. *Delinquency and Opportunity: A Theory of Delinquent Gangs*. New York: Free Press.

Cohen, Albert Kircidel. 1955. *Delinquent Boys: The Culture of the Gang*. Glencoe, IL: Free Press.

Cohen, Stanley. 1972. *Folk Devils and Moral Panics: The Creation of the Mods and Rockers*. London: MacGibbon and Kee.

Currie, Elliott. 1985. *Confronting Crime: An American Challenge*. New York: Pantheon.

Dahrendorf, Ralf. 1985. *Law and Order*. Boulder, CO: Westview.

Douglas, Jack D., and Paul K. Rasmussen. 1977. *Nude Beach*. Beverly Hills, CA: Sage.

Durkheim, Emile. 1893. *The Division of Labor in Society*. Glencoe, IL: Free Press. Reprinted in 1964.

_____. 1897. *Suicide, a Study in Sociology*. Glencoe, IL: Free Press. Reprinted in 1951.

Erikson, Kai. 1966. *Wayward Puritans: A Study in the Sociology of Deviance*. New York: Wiley.

Ferrell, Jeff, and Mark S. Hamm. 1998. *Ethnography at the Edge: Crime, Deviance, and Field Research*. Boston: Northeastern University Press.

Foucalt, Michel. 1977. *Discipline and Punish: The Birth of the Prison*. New York: Pantheon.

_____. 1978. "Introduction." In *The History of Sexuality,* by Michel Foucault. New York: Pantheon.

_____. 1985. "The Use of Pleasure." In *The History of Sexuality,* by Michel Foucault. New York: Pantheon.

Fraser, Nancy. 1994. "Foucault on Modern Power." In *Social Control: Aspects of Non-State Justice*, 3–20. Aldershot, UK: Dartmouth.

Gans, Herbert. 1988. *Middle American Individualism: The Future of Liberal Democracy*. New York: Free Press.

Garbarino, James. 1999. "Some Kids Are Orchids." *Time*: 51.

Garland, David. 2001. *Culture of Control: Crime and Social Order in Contemporary Society*. Chicago: University of Chicago Press.

Gerbner, George, and Larry Gross. 1976. "Living with Television: The Violence Profile." *Journal for Communication* 26, no. 2: 172–199.

Gerbner, George, Larry Gross, Nancy Signorielli, and Michael Morgan. 1980. "Growing Older: Perceptions and Representations; Aging with Television: Images on Television Drama and Conceptions of Social Reality." *Journal for Communication* 30, no. 1: 37–48.

Goffman, Erving. 1961. *Asylums: Essays on the Social Situation of Mental Patients and Other Inmates*. Garden City, NY: Anchor.

Gordon, Diana R. 1990. *The Justice Juggernaut: Fighting Street Crime, Controlling Citizens*. New Brunswick, NJ: Rutgers University Press.

GSS. 2006. "General Social Surveys, 1972–2004 [Cumulative File]." Computer-Assisted Survey Methods Program.

Gusfield, Joseph R. 1963. *Symbolic Crusade: Status Politics and the American Temperance Movement*. Urbana: University of Illinois Press.

———. 1981. *The Culture of Public Problems: Drinking-Driving and the Symbolic Order*. Chicago: University of Chicago Press.

Hamm, Mark S. 1993. *American Skinheads: The Criminology and Control of Hate Crime*. Westport, CT: Praeger.

Harrison, Paige M., and Allen J. Beck. 2004. "Prisoners in 2003." U.S. Department of Justice, Office of Justice Programs, Bureau of Justice Statistics.

Jenkins, Philip. 1994. *Using Murder: The Social Construction of Serial Homicide*. New York: de Gruyter.

Katz, Jack. 1988. "Seductions of Crime: Moral and Sensual Attractions in Doing Evil." New York: Basic Books.

Landesco, John. 1929. *Organized Crime in Chicago*. Chicago: University of Chicago Press.

Langan, Patrick A., and David P. Farrington. 1998. "Crime and Justice in the United States and in England and Wales, 1981–1996." U.S. Department of Justice, Office of Justice Programs, Bureau of Justice Statistics.

Lemert, Edwin McCarthy. 1967. *Human Deviance, Social Problems, and Social Control*. Englewood Cliffs, NJ: Prentice-Hall.

Lewis, James R. 1996. "Introduction." In *Magical Religion and Modern Witchcraft*, edited by James R. Lewis, 1–5. Albany: State University of New York Press.

Liptak, Adam. 2005a. "To More Inmates, Life Term Means Dying Behind Bars." *New York Times*, 1.

———. 2005b. "Locked Away Forever After Crimes as Teenagers." *New York Times*, October 3, 1.

Lofland, John. 1966. *Doomsday Cult: A Study of Conversion, Proselytization, and Maintenance of Faith.* Englewood Cliffs, NJ: Prentice-Hall.

McKinney, John C. 1966. *Constructive Typology and Social Theory.* New York: Appleton-Century-Crofts.

Mead, George Herbert. 1934. *Mind, Self, and Society from the Standpoint of a Social Behaviorist.* Chicago: University of Chicago Press.

Merton, Robert K. 1957. *Social Theory and Social Structure.* Glencoe, IL: Free Press.

Miller, Walter. 1958. "Lower-Class Culture as a Generating Milieu of Gang Delinquency." *Journal of Social Issues* 14: 5–19.

Mills, C. Wright. 1940. "Situated Actions and Vocabularies of Motive." *American Sociological Review* 5, no. 6: 904–913.

Newman, David M. 2000. *Sociology: Exploring the Architecture of Everyday Life,* 3rd ed. Thousand Oaks, CA: Pine Forge.

Pastore, Ann L., and Kathleen Maguire, eds. 1994. *Source-book of Criminal Justice Statistics.* Washington, DC: U.S. Government Printing Office.

PEJ (Project for Excellence in Journalism). 2004. "State of the News Media 2004: An Annual Report on American Journalism."

Perry, Barbara. 2001. *In the Name of Hate: Understanding Hate Crimes.* New York: Routledge.

Polsky, Ned. 1967. *Hustlers, Beats, and Others.* Chicago: Al-dine.

Public Agenda Foundation. 1993. *Criminal Violence: What Direction Now for the War on Crime?* New York: McGraw-Hill.

———. 2000. "Clarifying Issues 2000." Available online at http://www.publicagenda.org.

———. 2005. "Crime Overview." Review of reviewed item. Available online at http://www.publicagenda.org.

Quinney, Richard. 1970. *Social Reality of Crime.* Boston: Little, Brown.

———. 1974. *Critique of Legal Order: Crime Control in Capitalist Society.* Boston: Little, Brown.

———. 1977. *Class, State, and Crime: On the Theory and Practice of Criminal Justice.* New York: Longman.

Reiman, Jeffrey H. 1990. *Justice and Modern Moral Philosophy.* New Haven, CT: Yale University Press.

Rennison, Callie Marie. 2001. "Criminal Victimization, 2000: Changes 1999–2000 with Trends 1993–2000." Washing-ton, DC: U.S. Department of Justice.

Samenow, Samuel, and Stanton E. Yochelson. 1976. *The Criminal.* New York: Aronson.

Sasson, Theodore. 1995. *Crime Talk: How Citizens Construct a Social Problem.* New York: de Gruyter.

Scheingold, Stuart. 1991. *The Politics of Street Crime: Criminal Process and Cultural Obsession.* Philadelphia, PA: Temple University Press.

Scott, Malvin B. 1968. *Racing Game.* Chicago: Aldine.

Shaw, Clifford Robe. 1930. *The Jack Roller: A Delinquent Boy's Own Story.* Chicago: University of Chicago Press.

Stevenson, Richard W. 1992. "Maker Is Accused of Faulty Tests on Parts for Missiles and Aircrafts." *New York Times,* April 23.

Surette, Ray. 1998. *Media, Crime, and Criminal Justice: Images and Realities.* Belmont, CA: Wadsworth.

Thomas, William Isaac. 1931. *On Social Organization and Social Personality; Selected Papers.* Chicago: University of Chicago Press. Reprinted in 1966.

Thompson, Kenneth. 1998. *Moral Panics.* New York: Routledge.

Thrasher, Frederic. 1927. *The Gang: A Study of 1,313 Gangs in Chicago.* Chicago: University of Chicago Press. Reprinted in 1936.

Treaster, Joseph B., and Melody Peterson. 2000. "Florida Study Claims That Prudential Cheated Customers." *New York Times,* December 22, 20.

Tunnell, Kenneth D. 1992. *Choosing Crime: The Criminal Calculus of Property Offenders.* Chicago: Nelson-Hall.

U.S. Department of Justice, Bureau of Justice Statistics. 2001a. "Criminal Offenders Statistics, 2001." Washing-ton, DC: Bureau of Justice Statistics.

_____. 2001b. "Property Crime Rates Continue to Decline." Bureau of Justice Statistics.

Vigil, James Diego. 1988. *Barrio Gangs: Street Life and Identity in Southern California.* Austin: University of Texas Press.

Wilson, James Q., and Richard J. Herrnstein. 1985. *Crime and Human Nature.* New York: Simon and Schuster.

Wiseman, Jacqueline P. 1970. *Stations of the Lost: The Treatment of Skid Row Alcoholics.* Englewood Cliffs, NJ: Prentice-Hall.

Wright, Richard T., and Scott H. Decker. 1994. *Burglars on the Job: Streetlife and Residential Break-Ins.* Boston: Northeastern University Press.

CHAPTER TEN

Criminology Theory

For a large part of modern history, we have engaged in the search for cause and effect. What causes people to commit crimes, and what methods can be used to prevent crimes form happening? In the beginning, and as seen in our discussions on the Inquisition, the answers lay in abstract frameworks related to simple phenomena. Herein the causes of crime are answerable in spiritualist explanations grounded in theories of demonology, ancient animism, and various forms of mysticism. Today, while we think of ourselves as having moved beyond such laughable concepts, the tendency to revert to similar forms of theoretical revelation have brought us no closer to a more concrete understanding of crime.

For example, there are those who blame elements of modern society such as rap music and violent films and video games as the causes of crime. It is seen, however, that exercises of this type have no merit and are usually used to obfuscate the truth for political purposes. The reality of this situation is that crime and criminal behavior is serious and simplistic answers are not useful tools in the search to prevent the types of predatory behavior practiced by a hard-core criminal class. Concrete answers are obviously related to more complex phenomena, which means that the study of criminology must set a much higher standard. The study of criminology theory opens the door to this endeavor.

Understanding Crime and Criminology

By Tim Newburn

What Is Criminology?

This is a question that is deceptively simple in appearance, but really quite tricky to answer with great certainty. It is tricky partly because, as we will see, criminology is a mixture of different disciplines, differing objects of study and some dispute over where, precisely, its boundaries actually lie and should lie. Importantly, however, the fact that we begin with this question assumes that you are new to this subject. Indeed, that is the underlying assumption. This book is designed as an introduction for students who are studying criminology. I have endeavoured not to make too many assumptions about pre-existing knowledge of the subject and, wherever possible, I will hope to begin from basics and work progressively toward more complex ideas or arguments.

Criminology is a strange beast. With origins in applied medico-legal science, psychiatry, a scientifically oriented psychology and in nineteenth-century social reform movements, for much of the second half of the twentieth century British criminology has been dominated by sociology or at least a predominantly sociological approach to criminology. Times are changing again, however, and a new strand of technical and highly policy-oriented 'scientific' criminology is now emerging. During the course of this book you will meet all these variants and should learn how to assess their competing claims.

In a masterly analysis of the emergence and development of criminology in Britain, David Garland (2002: 8) introduces the subject in the following way:

> I take criminology to be a specific genre of discourse and inquiry about crime –a genre that has developed in the modern period and that can be distinguished from other ways of talking and thinking about criminal conduct. Thus, for example, criminology's claim to be an empirically grounded, scientific undertaking sets it apart from moral and legal discourses, while its focus upon crime differentiates it from other social scientific genres, such as the sociology of deviance and control, whose objects of study are broader and not defined by the criminal law. Since the middle years of the twentieth century, criminology has also been increasingly marked off from other discourses by the trappings of a distinctive identity, with its own journals, professional associations, professorships, and institutes.

In this history, Garland argues that modern criminology is the product of two initially separate streams of work:

- *The 'governmental project'* –empirical studies of the administration of justice; the working of prisons, police and the measurement of crime.
- *The 'Lombrosian project'* –studies which sought to examine the characteristics of 'criminals' and 'non-criminals' with a view to being able to distinguish the groups, thereby developing an understanding of the causes of crime.

During the twentieth century, he suggests, these gradually merged and changed to form the basis for what we recognise these days as criminology. The term *criminology* seems first to have been used by Paul Topinard, a Frenchman studying the body types of criminals, though the invention of the term itself is generally credited to an Italian academic lawyer, Raffaele Garofalo. Both are associated with the second stream of work identified above –that Garland names after the Italian scholar, Cesare Lombroso. This work, in various forms, was concerned with attempts to identify physical and other characteristics that set criminals apart. Such work varied from the measurement of physical characteristics such as head shape and the shape and size of the jaw and cheekbones, through to work which focused more upon the environmental conditions that produced criminality. Though, by and large, crude attempts to identify and measure characteristics that distinguish criminals from others have largely disappeared, Garland's argument is that one very significant stream of criminology has continued to be concerned with identifying the individual, social and environmental factors that are associated with offending.

An Interdisciplinary Subject

Thortsen Sellin, an American criminologist writing in the 1930s, once observed that the 'criminologist does not exist who is an expert in all the disciplines which converge in the study of crime' (Sellin, 1970: 6). As a criminology student you will quickly discover just how many disciplinary approaches are utilised in studying crime and criminal justice. In this book you will come across work by psychologists, sociologists, political scientists, lawyers, historians, geographers and others, all working within the subject of criminology. Indeed, this is one of criminology's great strengths.

Different disciplines have been dominant at different points in the history of criminology, and there are differing orientations to be found within criminology in different countries. Nevertheless, as you will see as this book progresses, criminology is influenced by, and draws upon, psychology, sociology, legal theory, history and other subjects besides. This raises a number of issues. It means that not only will you find a number of different approaches being taken to the subject matter, but that sometimes these approaches will appear rather at odds with each other. This is one of the great challenges within criminology and, though it can occasionally seem daunting, it is one of the characteristics which I think makes the discipline attractive. Linked with this is the question of whether it is appropriate to use the word *discipline* at all. Criminology, as I have suggested, draws from disciplines such as psychology and sociology, and there has been quite some debate about whether criminology can lay claim to such status itself (I tend to think not).

This is not an argument we can resolve here. The British criminologist David Downes once described criminology as a 'rendezvous subject'. He did so precisely to capture the fact that it is an area of study that brings together scholars from a variety of disciplinary origins, who meet in the territory called crime, and this seems to me a more than satisfactory way of thinking about it. Indeed, we do not need to spend a lot of time discussing the various positions that have been taken in relation to it. It is enough for current purposes that we are alerted to this issue and bear it in mind as we cover some of the terrain that comes under the heading *criminology*.

There is a further distinction that we must briefly consider, and it concerns *criminology* on the one hand and *criminal justice* on the other. Although the study of the administrative responses to crime is generally seen as being a central part of the criminological enterprise, sometimes the two are separated, particularly in the United States. In America there is something of a divide between those who think of themselves as doing criminology and those who study criminal justice. In fact, the distinction is anything but clear. Criminological work tends to be more theoretically informed than criminal justice studies and also more concerned with crime and its causes. Both, however, have clear concerns with the criminal justice and penal systems. In discussing this distinction, Lacey (2002: 265) suggests that criminology 'concerns itself with social and individual antecedents of crime and with the nature of crime as a social phenomenon', whereas criminal justice studies 'deal with the specifically institutional aspects of the social construction of crime' such as policing, prosecution, punishment and so on. We will consider what is meant by the social construction of crime in more detail below. Before we do so, let us look once more at the parameters of criminology.

Defining Criminology

Even the very short discussion so far should have alerted you to the fact that criminology is a complex subject, which has a number of historical roots and, as we will see, a number of quite different approaches in its contemporary guise. On this basis, coming up with a definition of our subject matter is almost certainly not only a difficult task but, quite probably, an impossible one. However, in order to bring a tiny bit more certainty to this rather uncertain terrain, I will borrow an approach to our subject matter first offered by one of the towering figures of twentieth-century criminology.

Edwin Sutherland—someone who you will get to meet regularly throughout this book—defined criminology as the study of the making of laws, the breaking of laws, and of society's reaction to the breaking of laws. Whilst this is by no means a comprehensive definition of criminology—criminologists may be interested, for example, in various forms of behaviour that do not involve the breaking of laws but, nevertheless, bring forth some form of social sanction –it does help point us in the direction of what are arguably the three great tributaries that make up the subject:

- The study of crime.
- The study of those who commit crime.
- The study of the criminal justice and penal systems.

Sutherland (1937) went on to argue that the 'objective of criminology is the development of a body of general and verified principles and of other types of knowledge regarding the process of law, crime, and treatment or prevention'. Now, having indicated that this is the general approach that informs much of what follows in this book, I want to pause and look briefly at work that is critical of the very enterprise that is criminology. I do so, not because I think the criticisms that are made are sufficient to make us abandon this project (as you can tell because there are another 1,000-odd pages to go before the end of the book), but because they should make us think very carefully about the assumptions that underpin criminology and should make us question the limitations of this particular enterprise.

The critique is associated with what we will come to think of as 'critical criminology' and can be found in various forms since at least the 1970s. Hillyard and Tombs (2004), for example, argue for a change of focus away from 'crime' and toward 'social harm' (see also Dorling *et al.*, 2005). They do so on the basis of four major lines of criticism:

- *Crime has no ontological reality*—The category 'crime' has no reality beyond the application of the term to particular acts. The acts themselves are not intrinsically criminal. Thus, to kill someone during peacetime may well be treated as murder; to do so on a battlefield will most likely not. We return to this below.

- *Criminology perpetuates the myth of crime*—Despite the criticism above, criminology tends to talk of 'crime' as if the category were relatively unproblematic. The continued attempts to explain the causes of crime are illustrative of this.
- *Crime consists of many petty events*—A great many 'criminal acts' create little physical or financial harm and often involve no victim.
- *Crime excludes many serious harms*—Many things which result in fairly sizeable harm are not dealt with via the criminal law—i.e. are not treated as 'criminal'. One of these might be large-scale tax fraud which is rarely prosecuted.

What is clear from this critique is that criminology's organising focus—*crime*—is potentially a highly contestable and problematic term. In studying criminology this is something we must try not to lose sight of. It was this, in part, that the well-known criminologist Stanley Cohen (1988: 46) undoubtedly had in mind, when he said:

> [Criminologists] like leeches, live off a very large body on which they are wholly parasitic. In the same way that our courts, prisons, probation officers and police 'need' crime, so does the criminologist. The gap, though, between the real world of crime and the artificial world of criminology is enormous. One reason for this is that the mere existence of something called criminology perpetuates the illusion that one can have a general theory of crime causation.

Understanding Crime

Crime, like so many things in our social world, has a certain taken-for-granted or common-sense nature. When we use the term, we assume the category is meaningful; that is, we assume that those to whom we are talking will understand what we're talking about and will tend to use the term in the same way as we do. This, of course, is the basis upon which the social world operates –on assumptions about the taken-for-granted meaningfulness of the vocabulary we use and the behaviours we enact. Yet, as scores of sociologists have illustrated, this shared meaningfulness has to be achieved; it is not *given*.

The apparent orderliness of our world can fairly easily be disturbed. This becomes clear when those with whom we are interacting do not share our assumptions or, alternatively, when they react to what we say or do in ways that we didn't predict, expect or perhaps understand. The word *crime* is used regularly in everyday conversation. That it is used in this manner implies that there is a sufficient level of common understanding. On one level this is undoubtedly the case. However, this masks a number of complexities. As we will see, identifying the boundary between acts that are crimes, and acts that are not crimes is often far from straightforward.

To illustrate this let's consider a couple of examples involving things that might be thought of as *crimes,* both of which involve assault. The first occurs at night time. It is dark and a person is walking alone and it is late. They are confronted by a total stranger who asks for money. When refused, the stranger becomes violent. The stranger robs the pedestrian and leaves them needing hospital treatment. There is little doubt that most people, on having this situation described to them, would call what happened 'a crime'. Indeed, in many ways this example represents one of the most common fears that many of us have (Stanko, 1990).

Box 10.1   The Spanner Case

During a raid in 1987 the police seized a videotape which showed a number of identifiable men engaging in heavy sado-masochistic (SM) activities including beatings, genital abrasions and lacerations. The police claim that they immediately started a murder investigation because they were convinced that the men were being killed. This investigation is rumoured to have cost £4 million. Dozens of gay men were interviewed. The police learned that none of the men in the video had been murdered, or even suffered injuries which required medical attention.

The Verdicts

In December 1990, 16 of the men pleaded guilty on legal advice to a number of offences and were sent to jail, given suspended jail sentences or fined. The men's defence was based on the fact that they had all consented to the activities. But Judge Rant, in a complex legal argument, decided that the activities in which they engaged fell outside the exceptions to the law of assault.

A number of the defendants appealed against their convictions and sentences. Their convictions were upheld though the sentences were reduced as it was felt they might well have been unaware that their activities were illegal. However the Appeal Court noted that this would not apply to similar cases in the future. The case then went to the House of Lords. The Law Lords heard the case in 1992 and delivered their judgment in January 1993. They upheld the convictions by a majority of three to two.

The Evidence

The evidence against the men comprised the videotape and their own statements. When they were questioned by the police, the men were so confident that their activities were lawful (because they had consented to them) that they freely admitted to taking part in the activities on the video. Without these statements and the videotape, the police would have had no evidence to present against the men and would have found it impossible to bring any prosecutions.

The Law of Assault

In law, you cannot, as a rule, consent to an assault. There are exceptions. For example, you can consent to a medical practitioner touching and possibly injuring your body; you can consent to an opponent hitting or injuring you in sports such as rugby or boxing; you can consent to tattoos or piercings if they are for ornamental purposes. You can also use consent as a defence against a charge of what is called Common Assault, where there is no significant injury involved.

The Judgment

The Law Lords ruled that SM activity provides no exception to the rule that consent is no defence to charges of assault occasioning actual bodily harm or causing grievous bodily harm. These are defined as activities which cause injuries of a lasting nature. Bruises or cuts could be considered lasting injuries by a court, even if they heal up completely and that takes a short period of time. Grievous bodily harm covers more serious injury and maiming. Judge Rant introduced some new terms to define what he considered to be lawful and unlawful bodily harm. Judge Rant decreed that bodily harm applied or received during sexual activities was lawful if the pain it caused was 'just momentary' and 'so slight that it can be discounted'. His judgment applies also to bodily marks such as those produced by beatings or bondage. These too, according to him, must not be of a lasting nature. In essence, Judge Rant decided that any injury, pain or mark that was more than trifling and momentary was illegal and would be considered an assault under the law.

Source: http://www.spannertrust.org/documents/spannerhistory.asp

(If you want to follow up more recent case law in this area, you could start by looking at: http://www.publications. parliament.uk/pa/cm200607/ cmpublic/criminal/memos/ucm40702.htm)

The second example is more unusual. It arises out of the seizure of videotapes during a police raid. One of these videos shows a number of men engaging in fairly extreme sado-masochistic activities, including beatings and genital abrasions. The police launch an investigation (the men in the tape are clearly identifiable) which ends in prosecution despite the fact that the men involved all argued that they consented to the activities. Indeed, all freely gave statements to the police believing themselves not to have done anything *criminal*. Were they right? This, in fact, is a real case. In what subsequently became known as the 'Spanner case', 16 men pleaded guilty on legal advice to assault. Some were jailed, some received suspended prison sentences and others were fined. The judgment was upheld by the Court of Appeal, the House of Lords and the European Court of Human Rights.

So, how are we to approach the subject matter of criminology? What are the different ways in which we understand crime? An apparently straightforward way is simply to view crimes as being offences against the criminal law. However, even a brief analysis shows that such offences vary enormously historically and culturally, and that the formal application of the criminal law only occurs in relation to a small minority of behaviours that could, in principle, be treated as criminal.

Crime and the Criminal Law

In some senses the most obvious, and most commonly used, definition of crime is simply to view it as an infraction of the criminal law. Within the criminal law, a crime is conduct (or an act of omission) which, when it results in certain consequences, may lead to prosecution and punishment in a criminal court. Straightforward as this seems there are a number of problems with it. As Zedner (2004) observes, 'crime' may be both a criminal and a civil wrong simultaneously. The legal classification doesn't help tell us why certain conduct is defined as criminal, it merely helps identify it.

She continues: 'To think about crime, as some criminal law textbooks still do, as comprising discrete, autonomous legal categories remote from the social world, is to engage in an absorbing but esoteric intellectual activity' (2004: 61). At its most extreme, a crude legalistic approach to crime implies that if there were no criminal law, then there would be no crime. In its more extreme version it also suggests that no matter what acts someone may have committed, if they are not subject to criminal sanction, then they cannot be considered criminal.

Much of criminology, though aware of some of the problems inherent in legal definitions, nevertheless proceeds on the basis of precisely such an approach to defining crime. Much of what criminologists do uses categories derived from the criminal law and, moreover, uses statistics taken from the operation of criminal justice agencies enforcing or administering the criminal law. This led the American sociologist Tappan (1947: 100) to argue that:

> Crime is an intentional act in violation of the criminal law ... committed without defence or excuse, and penalized by the state as a felony or misdemeanour [more or less serious criminal acts]. In studying the offender there can be no presumption that ... persons are criminals unless they also be held guilty beyond a reasonable doubt of a particular offence.

Does this mean that there is nothing common to all those things that are the object of our study as criminologists other than they happen currently to be defined as 'criminal'? Can we limit our attention solely to those things that might lead to a conviction in a criminal court? Edwin Sutherland (1949: 31), one of whose major concerns was 'white-collar crime', thought not:

> The essential characteristic of crime is that it is behaviour which is prohibited by the state as an injury to the state and against which the state may react, at least as a last resort, by punishment. The two abstract criteria generally regarded by

legal scholars as necessary elements in a definition of crime are legal description of an act as socially harmful and legal provision of a penalty for the act.

However, as we will see in relation to white-collar crime, he felt that our attention as criminologists should not be limited to those acts that would be punished by the criminal law. There are other forms of punishment and regulation and it is the fact that acts are 'punishable' that makes them fall within our view.

Crime as a Social Construct

Writers starting from this position see 'crime' as a label applied, under particular circumstances, to certain acts (or omissions), suggesting that crime is something that is the product of culturally bounded social interaction. As Edwin Schur (1969: 10) once noted: 'Once we recognise that crime is defined by the criminal law and is therefore variable in content, we see quite clearly that no explanation of crime that limits itself to the motivation and behaviour of individuals can ever be a complete one.'

Put a different way, Schur was simply observing that if we take the criminal law to be the thing that defines what is criminal, then the very fact that the criminal law varies—often very significantly— from country to country, makes it immediately clear that there is nothing *given* about crime.

Particularly influential in this regard has been labelling theory. Associated with a number of influential American sociologists such as Howard Becker, labelling theory, as its own label implies, places primary emphasis on the definitional power of the application of labels—in our case here, the label 'criminal'. Labelling theory distances itself from the view that defining someone as criminal somehow represents some natural order of events and, rather, analyses such processes as illustrations of the use of power by the state, and others, to define people in particular ways.

In recent times, theorists within criminology have tended not to refer to symbolic interactionism and phenomenology—the roots of labelling theory and related ideas—and it has become fashionable in this general area to talk of 'social

Signs limiting or banning alcohol consumption in public have become increasingly common.

constructionism': the idea that crime like other social phenomena is the outcome or product of interaction and negotiation between people living in complex social groups. Central to such an approach is the observation that the power to label certain acts, and certain people, as criminal is one which is restricted and, indeed, keenly contested. Because it involves the exercise of power, the process of labelling acts and people as criminal—generally known as *criminalisation*—tends to reflect power differentials, or particular interests, within society. As we will see in later chapters, there is a radical tradition in criminology, influenced by such insights, which views the criminal law and the operation of the criminal justice and penal systems as clear illustrations of elite or class interests. Put perhaps rather too crudely, it is one means by which the wealthy and powerful discipline and control the poor.

A radical version of social constructionism has recently been offered by the Norwegian criminologist, Nils Christie. In his book, *A Suitable Amount of Crime,* he argues:

> Crime does not exist. Only acts exist, acts often given different meanings within various social frameworks. Acts and the meanings given to them are our data. Our challenge is to follow the destiny of acts through the universe of meanings. Particularly, what are the social conditions that encourage or prevent giving the acts the meaning of being crime?

> (Christie, 2004: 3)

Historical Variation

Similarly, we can gain considerable insight into the socially constructed nature of crime by looking at how our treatment of certain behaviours varies, often considerably, over time. The 1960s in Britain are often referred to as the 'permissive age'. This was intended to convey what was perceived to be a general loosening of moral codes in the period. It was also a time when a series of liberalising laws were passed. The Abortion Act 1967 made it possible for women, under specific circumstances, to have a pregnancy terminated. Prior to 1967 abortion was illegal. Similarly, prior to the passage of the Sexual Offences Act 1967, it was illegal in Britain for men of any age to have consensual sex together. On the other hand, it was perfectly legal to take heroin and cocaine up until the time of the First World War. After that, the use of opiates was restricted, but they could still be prescribed by a doctor. Those of you that have read Conan Doyle's Sherlock Holmes stories will know that the great detective was an opium user—though even by Victorian times it was quite closely associated with criminality. Nevertheless, its consumption wasn't a criminal act.

One of the best examples of historical variation in criminal law is the period of American prohibition. An amendment to the Constitution of the United States—the National Prohibition Act (or Volstead Act)—was passed in 1919 and remained in force until 1933, banning the production and sale of alcohol. Now, as is well known, the Act neither prevented the manufacture nor the sale of alcohol. Indeed, it provided the basis of an extraordinary period in the history of American organised crime.

However, what is important for our purposes here is the fact that for a period of 13 years the making and selling of alcohol was illegal, criminal.

Let's consider one final example, again related to substance use, this time illustrating the way in which laws change over time, and vary geographically. Until very recently it was perfectly possible in the United Kingdom to smoke in pubs. However, the law has changed and since March 2004 it has not been possible to smoke in pubs in the Irish republic, similarly in Scotland since March 2006, in Wales since April 2007 and since 1 July 2007 in England, too.

The examples of cultural and historical variation given above all share an implicit assumption: that is that the power to determine what is or is not a crime resides in the nation state. However, we have clearly entered a period of history in which the boundaries between nation states are now rather more porous than they were, say, a century ago. The processes generally understood by the term 'globalisation' mean that the countries and peoples of the world are now increasingly interdependent. What happens in one part of the world has greater and more immediate significance for other parts of the world.

Since the Second World War, and the realities of the Holocaust became visible, one question that has repeatedly been asked is under what circumstances is it appropriate or necessary for one or more states to intervene in the affairs of other states? And, linked with this, to what extent is it possible to conceive of a moral order that spans an international community? The last decade or so has seen the emergence of international human rights law, the establishment of an international criminal court and, latterly, the prosecution of war criminals using these international treaties and institutions. The processes involved in bringing cases to justice, however, are highly complex and problematic and, in their own way, illustrate some of the problems involved in seeking answers to the deceptively simple question, 'what is crime?'. These include:

- There is no international consensus as to what constitutes 'crimes' in the international arena. Thus, for example, nations such the United States, India and China, among others, are not even signatories to the International Criminal Court.
- Securing international cooperation against particular states is often very difficult to achieve.
- Bringing to trial alleged 'war criminals'—often people who occupy, or who have previously occupied, powerful positions—has proved very difficult (see, for example, the cases of General Pinochet, Slobodan Milošević [Robertson, 1999] and, more recently, Ratko Mladic.
- The machinery of justice—in this case the International Criminal Court or other *ad hoc* tribunals—only has a limited capacity. In cases where genocide is alleged there are often hundreds, if not thousands, of perpetrators.
- Where private corporations are involved in alleged war crimes—such as the torture of prisoners in Abu Ghraib prison in Iraq—enforcing the criminal law is often even more difficult.

Slobodan Milošević, at one time President of Serbia, and later President of Yugoslavia, was eventually indicted for war crimes at the International Criminal Court in the Hague.

Indeed, one of the problems with international criminal law is—in some respects like domestic criminal law—that there is not necessarily any consensus as to what constitutes 'rights' on the one hand, or 'crimes' on the other. One of the criticisms sometimes levelled at international endeavour in this area is that rather than reflecting *universal* values it is actually another instance of the West seeking to impose its values and priorities on the world. In such circumstances, we are asked to acknowledge that politics lies behind much of this activity. Discussions of crime, the operation of criminal justice processes, the application of labels—such as '(war) criminal'—are not neutral activities, but are, in important respects, linked with institutions of power and authority—be those domestic or international.

Crime and Politics

Never forget that crime, and the study of crime, occurs within a social and political context. What we think about crime, and what we think we know about crime, reflects the times in which we live. As we will see—continually—the ways in which we respond to crime are also very much a reflection of the nature of the contemporary world. Indeed, the work of a number of very distinguished criminologists has focused on using crime and responses to it as a means of understanding the nature of our social order.

End of the Bipartisan Consensus

Crime and criminal justice policy is now accepted as being a major political issue. That is, not only do we expect politicians to spend a lot of their time talking about crime and criminal justice, but we expect them to disagree. This has not always been the case, and the fact that crime is now highly *politicised* is a very important factor in many of the issues that we will discuss in other parts of this book. As many commentators have noted (for example Brake and Hale, 1992; Rawlings, 1992; Downes and Morgan, 1994, 2007), for many years there existed something approximating a *bipartisan consensus* on issues to do with policing, crime and punishment. By this is meant that there once existed little difference in the general approach to law and order by the two main national political parties.

Box 10.2   The 1979 Conservative Party manifesto

THE MOST DISTURBING THREAT to our freedom and security is the growing disrespect for the rule of law. In government as in opposition, Labour have undermined it. Yet respect for the rule of law is the basis of a free and civilised life. We will restore it, re-establishing the supremacy of Parliament and giving the right priority to the fight against crime.

The Fight against Crime

The number of crimes in England and Wales is nearly half as much again as it was in 1973. The next Conservative government will spend more on fighting crime even while we economise elsewhere.

Britain needs strong, efficient police forces with high morale. Improved pay and conditions will help Chief Constables to recruit up to necessary establishment levels. We will therefore implement in full the recommendations of the Edmund Davies Committee. The police need more time to detect crime. So we will ease the weight of traffic supervision duties and review cumbersome court procedures which waste police time. We will also review the traffic laws, including the totting-up procedure.

Deterring the Criminal

Surer detection means surer deterrence. We also need better crime prevention measures and more flexible, more effective sentencing. For violent criminals and thugs really tough sentences are essential. But in other cases long prison terms are not always the best deterrent. So we want to see a wider variety of sentences available to the courts. We will therefore amend the 1961 Criminal Justice Act which limits prison sentences on young adult offenders, and revise the Children and Young Persons Act 1969 to give magistrates the power to make residential and secure care orders on juveniles.

We need more compulsory attendance centres for hooligans at junior and senior levels. In certain detention centres we will experiment with a tougher regime as a short, sharp shock for young criminals. For certain types of offenders, we also support the greater use of community service orders, intermediate treatment and attendance centres. Unpaid fines and compensation orders are ineffective. Fines should be assessed to punish the offender within his means and then be backed by effective sanctions for non-payment.

Many people advocate capital punishment for murder. This must remain a matter of conscience for Members of Parliament. But we will give the new House of Commons an early opportunity for a free vote on this issue.

Source: www.conservative-party.net/manifestos/1979/1979-conservative-manifesto.shtml

Now, it is sometimes assumed that 1979—the election of the first Thatcher government—marked the point at which all this ended. And, whilst the 1979 general election was indeed the first time that a party had successfully used law and order as one of the major elements in its electoral strategy, nevertheless the trend had been toward greater politicisation of crime and justice issues since about 1970 (Downes and Morgan, 1994; Hall *et al.*, 1978). From that point onwards, the major political parties began to blame each other for what was happening in relation to crime, and began to look to make political capital out of their criminal justice and penal policies.

The end of the bipartisan consensus coincided in very rough terms with declining faith in the idea of rehabilitation. Where for much of the twentieth century it had been assumed that one, and perhaps the most important goal, of punishment was to reform the offender, there was by this stage declining faith that this could be achieved very effectively, and there were growing demands for greater emphasis upon punishment. The Conservative Party was elected in 1979 on a ticket that suggested that the Labour Party was responsible for the increases in crime that had occurred in the latter half of the 1970s and could not be trusted to provide sufficient resources and support for the police. 'Never, ever, have you heard me say that we will economise on law and order' said Margaret Thatcher in 1985 (quoted in Nash and Savage, 1994: 142–3). However, although expenditure on the police in particular was increased markedly in the early 1980s it did not lead to the hoped-for reductions in crime. Far from it: crime rates continued to rise and to do so at a dramatic rate.

Managerialism

Partly as a consequence of the dismay politicians felt at the perceived ineffectiveness of criminal justice agencies in bringing down crime, especially given the sums of money being spent, government policy came increasingly to be dominated by what has come to be called *managerialism*. From the mid-1980s onwards a policy of 'tight-resourcing' was applied not only to the police, but also to the probation service and to the courts system (Raine and Willson, 1993). Through the application of the Conservative government's Financial Management Initiative (FMI), the construction of performance indicators, the use of management information systems and, from later in the 1980s, scrutiny by the Audit Commission and the National Audit Office, radical changes in the management of criminal justice agencies were encouraged.

One of the solutions successive governments have pursued in relation to the problems they have faced in crime and criminal justice has been to seek to make criminal justice agencies more business-like. 'The perceived attributes of the well-run private sector company (of high efficiency, of explicit accountabilities, of clear objectives, and of measured performance)' have increasingly been applied to management in the police, prison and probation services and other agencies (Raine and Willson, 1993: 23). Such changes are often identified using the term New Public Management (NPM). The term is interpreted in a range of ways, though it is generally held to involve an increased emphasis on performance measurement, together with the use of things like league tables, and an increased likelihood of competition with the private sector and other providers (McLaughlin *et al.*, 2001). Much of the literature, and many speeches made by politicians, also tend to emphasise the idea of devolution of responsibility from the top of organisations down to middle managers and below. Although there has been much talk of devolution of responsibility in relation, say, to the police service, arguably the dominant tendency over the past decade has been toward the progressive centralisation of control.

Centralisation

The gradual accretion of power to the centre can be seen across the criminal justice system (indeed the public sector generally, including universities) and is visible, as we will see in later chapters, for example, in relation to police, probation, prisons and youth justice. For present purposes, a couple of examples will suffice. In relation to probation, what originally emerged from the voluntary sector to become a locally based service has been radically changed, first to create a *national* probation service and, subsequently, to merge probation with the prison service to create NOMS: the National Offender Management Service. The last 30 years have seen the Home Office seek to extend its control over probation (though this responsibility has now passed to the Ministry of Justice). It initially sought to do so via national standards. When this proved insufficient, the service was turned into a national one and any emphasis on local control was reduced.

In relation to the police, a similar process has been taking place. Indeed, the entire history of the police service can, in part, be read as a continual process of centralisation of control. Despite what was intended by the Police Act 1964—which put in place the building blocks for the governance of police which have existed ever since—local police authorities have always occupied a relatively powerless position when compared with chief constables and the Home Office. Since the early 1990s, several reformist and interventionist Home Secretaries have sought to impose their own vision on policing and to ensure that messages emanating from the Home Office are unquestionably the ones that chief constables should pay greatest attention to. Again, through national standards, national inspection systems, shared objectives and the threat of the Home Office taking control of forces if they are deemed to be 'failing', government has progressively extended its reach of what police forces do, and how they do it.

Penal Populism

We noted earlier that the 1979 general election was the first in modern times in which 'law and order' was a central plank. It was also the last in which a government pinned faith in the apparently simple equation that spending more on criminal justice would help reduce crime. From the early 1980s onward, criminal justice agencies were encouraged to form partnerships and inter-agency groupings and, more importantly, the wider 'community' was itself encouraged to take responsibility for the fight against crime (Garland, 2001). Prison numbers rose quite substantially as the decade wore on and new legislation concerning sentencing passed in 1991 sought to reorient practices in such a way as to reduce prison numbers and encourage greater use of community penalties.

For a while prison numbers did fall and there was a sense of optimism, fuelled also by the Woolf Report on prisons, that the problems of overcrowding and poor conditions that had bedevilled the prison system for decades might be alleviated. However, penal politics were about to change and to do so dramatically. In early 1993 a young Tony Blair had become Labour Party Shadow Home Secretary and had set about reshaping and repositioning the Party's stance on crime and criminal justice. In particular, having seen how Bill Clinton's Democratic Party had repositioned itself in American politics—in order to shed its previously liberal reputation and become much more hard-line in relation to law and order—Blair wished to achieve something similar in the UK. Initially as Shadow Home Secretary, and then as leader of the Labour Party after John Smith's death in 1995, he was unshakeable in his belief that such changes were necessary if the Labour Party was to have any hope of making itself electable. His most famous soundbite—'tough on crime, tough on the causes of crime'—expertly captured the shifting stance of the Labour Party.

A few months after Blair became Shadow, Michael Howard was appointed Home Secretary. In his first Party conference speech, Howard announced a new 'law and order' package—one which took a rather different approach from that adopted by previous Home Secretaries, particularly in relation to punishment. The fact that they were under increasing pressure from the Labour opposition was undoubtedly important in this process. The package of measures that Howard announced were punitive in character and involved a reassertion of prison in a range of sanctions he interpreted as having deterrence as their primary aim. The outcome would almost certainly mean a rise in prison numbers. Howard recognised this and welcomed it:

> I do not flinch from that. We shall no longer judge the success of our system of justice by a fall in our prison population ... Let us be clear. *Prison works.* It ensures that we are protected from murderers, muggers and rapists –and it makes many who are tempted to commit crime think twice.
>
> (quoted in Newburn, 2003; *emphasis added*)

The speech was a pivotal moment in a recent British law and order politics, ushering in nearly three years of almost uninterrupted bidding wars by the two main parties in which each sought to present itself as 'tougher' than the other. Much of this new presentation of law and order politics has been played out in and been stimulated by the popular media. Crime has become staple tabloid newspaper fodder. The stance taken by the two parties has generally come to be characterised as 'penal populism' (Pratt, 2007) or 'populist punitiveness' (Bottoms, 1995). This is an approach to crime and penal policy in which particular policy positions are normally adopted in the clear belief that they will be popular with the public (and usually with an awareness that, in general and abstract opinion polls, punitive policies are favoured by a majority of the public ...). Hence, the term 'populist punitiveness' is intended to convey the notion of politicians tapping into, and using for their own purposes, what they believe to be the public's generally punitive stance.

(Bottoms, 1995: 40)

The year 1993 represented an important turning point in British penal politics, therefore. Since that time government and opposition have been locked into a new bipartisan consensus: one that stresses the importance of punishment and deterrence, and that views punitiveness not only as chiming with public views but, crucially, as being critical to electoral success. Being 'tough on crime' is now the political bottom-line for those seeking political office in Westminster and similar trends are visible in many other jurisdictions. Best known of all—no doubt because it represents the most extreme example in the West—is what has occurred in America over the last four decades or so.

In the USA, during a period in which 'tough on crime' politics became embedded in national culture, the number of people in prison has expanded from around a quarter of a million in the early 1970s to well over two million today. The USA has the highest incarceration rate (i.e. the highest number of citizens sent to prison per head of population) in the world. And, since you must surely be wondering, this cannot be explained as a result of its crime rate. First, for a significant part of the period concerned, crime in most American cities was declining—and quite dramatically at that. Second, the crime rate in America, with the very notable exception of homicide—is really not that different from the crime rate in Britain. Yes, there are some differences—in relation to some crimes the rates are higher in Britain—but in the main crime rates in the big cities in the USA and the UK are on a similar scale. Even though Britain is the highest incarcerator in Western Europe, its incarceration rate is only one-fifth (or less) of that in America.

At least two important and related points emerge from this necessarily brief discussion. First, in thinking about crime and crime policy it is always important to

Tony Blair shortly after becoming Shadow Home Secretary in 1993. Would it be fair to say he was tougher on crime than the causes of crime during his subsequent premiership?

bear in mind the cultural and political context in which things take place. Crime is socially constructed, politically influenced and historically variable. Second, there is no direct link between crime rates and types and levels of punishment. Punishment, like crime, is historically and culturally contingent. We no longer think it appropriate in Britain to hang people. Less than half a century ago we still did so. Many nations still execute citizens. What type of punishment we inflict, how much of it we inflict, and whether or not we inflict it, also depends very much on the political circumstances of the time. We will return to such observations regularly throughout this book. I want to conclude this chapter, however, by making a similar point about criminology. I want to look briefly at the recent history of criminology in Britain, partly to sketch out one or two of its contours simply so that you will know about them, but also to illustrate the point that criminology—like the things it studies—is a product of its particular historical moment.

Criminology in Britain

The first lectures under the banner of 'criminology' in Britain were delivered in 1921–22 in Birmingham to postgraduate medical students. At that time 'criminology' in the UK primarily involved psychiatrists. It was quite unlike the much more sociologically influenced subject that it became by the 1970s and, to a significant extent, remains today. The journal, *Sociological Review,* was established in 1908 and carried nothing that was obviously criminological until the late 1930s.

The first professional organisation in the area was established in 1931. Initially called the 'Association for the Scientific Treatment of Criminals' it became the 'Institute for the Study and Treatment of Delinquency' (ISTD) later in the decade (a name it retained until relatively recently). In 1933 it founded the Portman Clinic as the base for the practice of psychoanalytic and psychiatric treatment. Criminology was still not a widespread subject of academic study. By 1948 only three people held jobs in British universities teaching what might be thought of as criminology: Leon Radzinowicz at Cambridge, Max Grünhut at Oxford and Hermann Mannheim at the LSE.

The *British Journal of Delinquency* was established by ISTD in 1950. It had three joint editors, two psychiatrists and Hermann Mannheim. The journal was renamed the *British Journal of Criminology* in 1960, though it had the subtitle 'Delinquency and Deviant Behaviour'. According to its editors this was 'to indicate that criminology must be based on the broadest studies of the individual and social determinants of character and conscience'.

It was some considerable time before British criminology took its sociological turn. Terry Morris's *The Criminal Area* was published in 1957 but, arguably, it was not until the publication of David Downes's *The Delinquent Solution* in 1966 followed by a number of other important works that criminology influenced by American sociological theory really began to flourish. There were also a number of important institutional developments around this period that contributed to the further development of British criminology. In the late 1950s the Institute of Criminology at Cambridge

'First Minister' . . . Paisley

Unionists' 'cabinet' majority

UNIONISTS will make up the majority of the next Northern Ireland Executive if power-sharing returns later this month, it emerged last night.

Democratic Unionist Party leader the Rev Ian Paisley is due to be First Minister and Sinn Fein's Martin McGuinness his Deputy after all 108 seats were filled in the Assembly election.

However, it was unclear if power-sharing would be in place by PM Tony Blair and Irish Taoiseach Bertie Ahern's March 26 devolution deadline.

Northern Ireland Secretary Peter Hain warned the Assembly would close if parties failed to form a government by the deadline.

The final tally of seats saw the DUP the largest party with 36 – up four – followed by Sinn Fein with 28, also up four.

The DUP insisted any decision they made on power-sharing depends on republicans showing support for the police.

The Sun Says – Page Six

'Inspiration' . . . Mick

Face of Brit hero

A BRITISH commando gunner blown up in a Taliban grenade attack was named yesterday as Sgt Major Mick Smith.

The 39-year-old from Liverpool died after the attack on the UK base at Sangin in Afghanistan's Helmand Province.

He joined the Army in 1985 and 29 Commando Regiment Royal Artillery two years later.

His commanding officer Lt Col Neil Wilson described him as an "inspiration". He said: "His loss is an enormous blow to every one of us."

PM TROOPS SNUB

Premier Tony Blair was thwarted in Brussels yesterday in his bid to recruit more EU troops to fight the Taliban.

TOP JUDGE'S SHOCKING OUTBURST

Let killers out

..THEY'RE CLOGGING UP JAILS

By GEORGE PASCOE-WATSON
Political Editor

KILLERS should be let out of jail early to ease the prisons crisis, Britain's top judge said yesterday.

Lord Chief Justice Lord Phillips warned that jails would be stuffed with "geriatric" inmates if no action was taken.

He suggested the country would look back in shame in 100 years time at the length of sentences for killers and rapists.

His comments caused a storm last night – as he in charge of sentencing guidelines in England and Wales.

Prime Minister Tony Blair and Home Secretary John Reid both dismissed the Law Lord's outburst.

A Home Office spokesman said: "The Lord Chief Justice is entitled to his view and has expressed it.

"The Home Secretary believes that murderers and other dangerous offenders should be kept in prison as long as is necessary to protect the public."

And the PM's official spokesman said: "We do not agree."

Crime victims were up in arms at Lord Phillips' remarks.

Norman Brennan, director of the Victims of Crime Trust, said: "Lord Phillips has taken leave of his senses if he believes that releasing murderers early will help alleviate the prison

'I'm not in favour of mandatory jail terms...in 30 yrs prisons will be full of geriatric lifers'

population. He also makes the comment that prisons risk becoming full of geriatric lifers but that has to be the case if necessary. At least they still have their lives.

"There was a time in the not too distant past where some people or some murderers were hanged for their crimes, then it became life imprisonment.

"So when some murderers serve as little as eight years for such a grave and devastating crime it makes a mockery of the lives of those who have been murdered.

"A life without a loved one will never change so it is only right and proper that the prison sentence remains in place for those who commit these grave crimes."

Lord Phillips sparked outrage when he called for an end to automatic life sentences for killers.

He said: "I'm not i n

favour of mandatory sentences, full stop. If sentences are to be just, then the effect of mitigating and aggravating factors should be very significant, so that sentences fill the spectrum between these two starting points.

"I am not sure that in practice they do and I believe that the starting points are having the effect of ratcheting up sentences in a manner that will be regretted many years hence."

Lord Phillips said the effect of the sentencing guidelines in the Criminal Justice Act 2003 had been to double sentences.

He added: "In 30 years time, the prisons will be full of geriatric lifers.

"That is not to say that I do not recognise that there are certain crimes which require a sentence of that length or longer to protect the public.

"But I detect an incitement to the public to exact vengeance from offenders that is not dissimilar to the emotions of those who thronged to witness public executions in the 18th century.

"I sometimes wonder whether, in 100 years time people will be as shocked by the length of the sentences we are imposing as we are by some of the punishments of the 18th century."

Lord Phillips has argued before that jail overcrowding can only be eased by keeping convicts OUT of jail.

Mr Blair's spokesman said: "The Government recognises that the Lord Chief Justice has this view, but we disagree. We believe that people should be kept in prison as long as

'I wonder in the future if people will be shocked by the length of our sentences'

they are judged to be a danger to society." Former prisons minister Ann Widdecombe attacked the judge's call last night.

She said: "To have to release a dangerous person seems to me a very peculiar position.

"If you remove the life sentence and you give a tariff, you have no control at that point.

"If the authorities have severe reason to doubt that this person is ready for release, they have no control.

"And we are talking about murderers, not people who pinched 3p off the bus fare. I am certainly not convinced."

Lord Phillips' controversial views were last night expected to boost support for The Sun's campaign to get rid of soft judges.

The Sun Says – Page Six

GET CASH FOR YOUR STORIES

63000

TEXT OR CALL **63000** *from your mobile*

EMAIL **63000@** *thesun.co.uk*

DIAL **084508 63000** *from a landline*

Calls from landlines charged at local rate, mobiles charged at normal rates.

BINGO: PAGE 36

GIVE the No1 Sun your EXCLUSIVE stories with our brilliant 63000 service. Just call or text 63000 from your mobile – or email 63000@thesun.co.uk

You can still ring 020 7782 4100, text 07917 576539 – or email our news desk at exclusive@the-sun.co.uk

Readers with queries about Sun promotions should ring 020 7860 1129.

SKY NEWS

DRY with sunny spells across most of the country with the best of the sunshine in the South and East. Cloudy and windy with some rain in the far North. Top temp: 14°C (57°F)

Latest forecast at www.thesun.co.uk/news for UK & world weather call 09067 524449 (75p per min)

TV: PAGE 38

'Penal populism' in practice. 'Soft' judges (in this case the ex-Lord Chief Justice, Lord Phillips) have been a particular target for the *Sun* and several other newspapers. Lord Phillips also incurred criticism in the popular press when he sought to popularise community sentences as an alternative to custody.

was established. In 1957 with both Mannheim and Grünhut about to retire, the Home Secretary, R.A. Butler, approached London and Cambridge universities in order to explore the possibility of establishing a new institute. London University turned him down, but in 1959 the new Institute of Criminology opened in Cambridge under the direction of Radzinowicz. In addition, Butler also helped the university secure independent financial support for the creation of the first chair in criminology. Thus was established the Wolfson Chair in Criminology, held for many years by Radzinowicz and, after his retirement, by Tony Bottoms.

The second major institutional development was the creation of a research unit within the Home Office. The Criminal Justice Act 1948 had given the Home Secretary the power to spend money on research. The sum initially allocated was £2,000. The first external grants were made to the three eminent émigrés: £250 each to Radzinowicz and Grünhut, and £1,500 to Mannheim to begin his famous borstal study. By 1956 the external expenditure on research had risen to £2,500. In 1957 the Home Office Research Unit was established, later becoming known as the Research and Planning Unit—and now the Home Office Science, Research and Statistics Directorate (with other researchers working in research directorates in the new Ministry of Justice). There are now hundreds of research staff and a budget of millions.

Sir Leon Radzinowicz (1906–1999), appointed first director of the Institute of Criminology at the University of Cambridge in 1959. A commanding figure in the history of British criminology, he was also the author of a five-volume *History of English Criminal Law and its Administration from 1750.*

The third of the developments—though they all occurred at roughly the same time—was the establishment of the British Society of Criminology (BSC). ISTD had established a 'Scientific Group for the Discussion of Delinquent Problems' in 1953. However, not everyone was happy with its activities and discussions, in particular with the continued dominance of psychiatric and other clinical perspectives. A number of members broke away in the late 1950s and established the BSC. Though this was intended to herald a shift in perspective, it would not do to exaggerate it. In a paper to the 1971 British Sociology conference, Stan Cohen observed that the BSC was multidisciplinary 'with a heavy bias in a clinical direction'.

No doubt it was this which, in part, led a group of British sociologists to establish the 'National Deviancy Symposium', later the National Deviancy Conference (NDC). It held its first conference in autumn 1968 and then for a period of years provided a location in which a more radical British criminology could thrive. David Downes said of the NDC that its great appeal 'was not only to sociologists of crime in search of a congenial forum, but also to younger sociologists who saw in deviance an escape route from the positivist methods and functionalist orthodoxy of much British sociology'. A large number of people were recruited into criminology in the 1960s and 1970s—what Rock (1994) called the 'fortunate generation'—and thereafter recruitment declined substantially.

Since that time, British criminology has expanded massively and also changed in character and focus. Whereas much early, and classic, British criminology took offenders as its focus, there has been a profound shift over the past 25 years or so towards a preoccupation with the operation of the criminal justice system—the rise of what Jock Young called 'administrative criminology'. Arguably, there has also been something of a shift away from theory and theorising.

It is increasingly difficult to characterise British criminology, however; the sheer scale of the expansion now means that it is all the more difficult to grasp, capture and summarise its character. The BSC held its first conference in 1987—and there were concerns at the time about how much interest there would be. It now hosts an annual conference at which there are usually around 400–500 delegates. The Society has close on 1,000 members. There are upwards of 70 higher educational institutions offering degrees (half or full) in criminology and a further 40 or more running Masters degree programmes. By any standards this is remarkable growth. In the chapters that follow I will endeavour to take you through many of the major issues and debates in contemporary criminology, and to explore with you many of the most important questions that people working within this discipline have grappled with. It is—I hope you will find—an exciting journey. We move next to looking at crime and justice in history.

Further Reading

If you want to learn more about the emergence and development of criminology then David Garland's (2002) essay, 'Of crime and criminals' in the 3rd edition of *The Oxford Handbook of Criminology* is undoubtedly the place to start. The essay is available online at: http://www.oup.com/uk/orc/ bin/9780199205431/01student/ chapters/. There is also a wonderful essay by Roger Hood, entitled 'Hermann Mannheim and Max Grünhut' (2004) *British Journal of Criminology,* 44, 469–95.

On more recent developments in British criminology you should look at the range of essays in: Rock, P. (1988) *A History of British Criminology,* Oxford: Oxford University Press; I would also suggest consulting: Downes, D. (1978) 'Promise and performance in British criminology', *British Journal of Sociology,* 29, 4, 483–502; and Rock P. (1994) 'The social organisation of British criminology', in Maguire, M. *et al.* (eds) *The Oxford Handbook of Criminology,* 1st edn, Oxford: Oxford University Press.

On understanding what is meant by crime, a very fine introduction and overview can be found in the first section of: Muncie, J. (2001) 'The construction and deconstruction of crime', in Muncie, J. and McLaughlin, E. (eds) *The Problem of Crime,* London: Sage.

A more focused and developed treatment of the relationship between crime and law is: Lacey, N. and Zedner, L. (2012) 'Legal constructions of crime', in Maguire, M. *et al.* (eds) *The Oxford Handbook of Criminology*, 5th edn, Oxford: Oxford University Press.

Lucia Zedner's (2004) *Criminal Justice*, Oxford: Oxford University Press, provides a thorough grounding in the major philosophical debates (and is probably especially valuable for those studying law).

On politics and crime the best overviews and analyses are available in the chapters written by David Downes and Rod Morgan in *The Oxford Handbook of Criminology*. In the most recent (5th) edition, it is called: 'Overtaking on the left? The politics of law and order in the Big Society'. Anyone interested in this subject, however, should also consult the essays by these authors in the first four editions.

Finally, the really keen might like to follow up some of the essays in Bosworth, M. and Hoyle, C. (eds) (2011) *What is Criminology?*, Oxford: Oxford University Press.

Bibliography

Bottoms, A.E. (1995) 'The philosophy and politics of punishment and sentencing', in Clarkson, C. and Morgan, R. (eds) *The Politics of Sentencing Reform*, Oxford: Oxford University Press.

Brake, M. and Hale, C. (1992) *Public Order and Private Lives: The politics of law and order*, London: Routledge.

Christie, N. (2004) *A Suitable Amount of Crime*, London: Routledge.

Cohen, S. (1988) *Against Criminology*, New Brunswick, NJ: Transaction.

Dorling, D., Gordon, D., Hillyard, P., Pantazis, C., Pemberton, S. and Tombs, S. (2005) *Criminal Obsessions: Why harm matters more than crime*, London: Centre for Crime and Justice Studies.

Downes, D. (1966) *The Delinquent Solution: A study in subcultural theory*, London: Routledge and Kegan Paul.

Downes, D. and Morgan, R. (1994) 'Hostages to Fortune? The politics of law and order in post-war Britain', in Maguire, M., Morgan, R. and Reiner, R. (eds) *The Oxford Handbook of Criminology*, 1st edn, Oxford: Oxford University Press.

Downes, D. and Morgan, R. (2007) 'No turning back: The politics of law and order into the millennium', in Maguire, M., Morgan, R. and Reiner, R. (eds) *The Oxford Handbook of Criminology*, 4th edn, Oxford: Oxford University Press.

Garland, D. (2001a) *The Culture of Control: Crime and social order in contemporary society*, Oxford: Clarendon.

Garland, D. (2001b) *Mass Imprisonment: Social causes and consequences*, London: Sage.

Garland, D. (2002) 'Of crime and criminals: The development of criminology in Britain', in Maguire, M., Morgan, R. and Reiner, R. (eds) *The Oxford Handbook of Criminology*, 3rd edn, Oxford: Clarendon Press.

Hall, S., Critcher, C., Jefferson, T., Clarke, J. and Roberts, B. (1978) *Policing the Crisis: Mugging, the state and law and order*, Basingstoke: Macmillan.

Hillyard, P. and Tombs, S. (2004) 'Beyond criminology?', in Hillyard, P., Pantazis, C., Tombs, S. and Gordon, D. (eds) *Beyond Criminology: Taking harm seriously*, London: Pluto Press.

Lacey, N. (2002) 'Legal constructions of crime', in Maguire, M., Morgan, R., Reiner, R. (eds) *The Oxford Handbook of Criminology,* 3rd edn, Oxford: Oxford University Press.

McLaughlin, E., Muncie, J. and Hughes, G. (2001) 'The permanent revolution', *Criminology and Criminal Justice,* 1, 3, 301–318.

Nash, M. and Savage, S. (1994) 'A criminal record? Law, order and Conservative policy', in Savage, S., Atkinson, R. and Robins, L. (eds) *Public Policy in Britain,* Basingstoke: Macmillan.

Newburn, T. (2003) *Handbook of Policing,* Cullompton: Willan.

Pratt, J. (2007) *Penal Populism,* London: Routledge.

Raine, J.W. and Willson, M.J. (1993) *Managing Criminal Justice,* New York, London: Harvester Wheatsheaf.

Rawlings, P. (1992) 'Creeping privatization? The police, the Conservative government and policing in the late 1980s', in Reiner, R. and Cross, M. (eds) *Beyond Law and Order: Criminal justice policy and politics into the 1990s,* Basingstoke: Macmillan.

Robertson, G. (1999) *Crimes Against Humanity: The struggle for global justice,* London: Penguin.

Rock, P. (1994) *A History of British Criminology,* Oxford: Clarendon Press.

Schur, E. (1969) *Our Criminal Society,* Englewood Cliffs, NJ: Prentice Hall.

Sellin, T. (1970) 'A sociological approach', in Wolfgang, M.E. *et al.* (eds) *The Sociology of Crime and Delinquency,* New York: Wiley.

Stanko, E. (1990) *Everyday Violence: How women and men experience sexual and physical danger,* London: Pandora.

Sutherland, E.H. (1937) *The Professional Thief: By a professional thief,* Chicago: University of Chicago Press.

Sutherland, E. H. (1949) *White Collar Crime,* New York: Dryden.

Tappan, P.W. (1947) 'Who is the criminal?', *American Sociological Review,* 12, 96–102.

Zedner, L. (2004) *Criminal Justice,* Oxford: Oxford University Press.

CHAPTER ELEVEN

Law Enforcement and Policing

One of the most significant aspects of the criminal justice system is the institution shaping the field of law enforcement in the U.S. Therefore, it is thought to be the part of the system familiar to most U. S. citizens. For example, from childhood we can identify a police officer and an officer's cruiser and understand the basic functions of the police, which are to protect and serve the community and inevitably arrest individuals who commit criminal acts. However, the role of law enforcement is more complicated than that. In reality, police officers are dispatched to deal with a host of matters ranging from the mundane (checking on the security of a home while the owner is traveling), to the bizarre (finding ghosts in a home), to the most serious (homicide), and nearly every imaginable crime that can be conceived.[1]

It is also interesting to note that law enforcement officers are expected to resolve many of society's problems and are entrusted to use force only when necessary. Ideally, they make decisions quickly, use discretion, show courage and sacrifice in the face of danger, and treat individuals with dignity and respect even when threatened, harassed, abused, or assaulted. In recent years, police responsibilities have moved into the educational setting as school resource officers and educators raise awareness about crime, drugs, and prevention. Community-based initiatives have tried to foster a more collaborative relationship between police and citizens to address crime control and prevention.[2] The issue of concern here relates to the possibility that some of the original ideals shaping the philosophy of law enforcement in America are going by the wayside and raises questions pertaining to the efficacy of policing in the postmodern world.

---

1   R. E. Masters, L. B. Way, P. B. Gerstenfeld, B. T. Muscat, M. Hooper, J. P. J. Dussich, L. Pincu, and C.A. Skrapec, *CJ: Realities and Challenges* (McGraw-Hill Companies, Inc., 2011).
2   R. E. Masters etl al., *CJ: Realities and Challenges*, 2011.

Three Eras of Policing

By James J. Chriss

H uman societies have always attempted to control the behavior of their members. Even among the most primitive tribes, there exist customs and beliefs which everyone accepts and which typically are adhered to, primarily out of fear of punishment for violating them. These systems of control are more or less informal, embodied in the stocks of knowledge members have about their world and how to act within it. Many of the beliefs and practices of early human beings would appall modern sensibilities, but it must be understood that such primitive practices did not emerge out of thin air. Rather, whatever has been reported or discovered about early human behavior is typically reflective of the environments within which these human groups lived. Virtually all acts taking place within human groups are collective attempts to survive given the limitations of environmental resources and the threats to life and limb, whether real or perceived.

For example, as William Graham Sumner (1906) summarizes in his book *Folkways*, in particular times and places in the human past cannibalism was an acceptable practice. Wherever cannibalism was found to be practiced, it was almost always a result of a defect in the food supply. In short, where food supplies are meager—especially when there is a shortage of meat—cannibalism may be practiced. Yet, even if a particular primitive group practices cannibalism, there are rules regarding who can and cannot be eaten, and under what conditions. For example, members of the same tribe rarely eat their own. Instead, they may eat the flesh of enemies or strangers. Under the harshest conditions, however, the males of the tribe may eat other members who are deemed sickly or weak, but almost never will they eat a woman (Sumner 1906, p. 330).

In the condition of the primitive tribe (or the even more remote "primal horde"; see, e.g., Giddings 1896), members of the group police themselves to the extent that the folkways—the norms and customs of the group—are known to all and are expected to be enforced by all. Only when disputes arise over some important event will higher authorities be called to judge the believability of one side or the other in the dispute. Overwhelmingly in primitive human societies, these esteemed authorities are the elders, and they gain their authority and prestige on the basis of tradition and the fact that they have survived to a relatively old age even in a harsh physical environment where average life expectancies are short. In short, even in the most primitive of societies there are typically patterns of association among members dedicated in certain crucial instances or social situations to the regulation of norms and to the sanctioning of members who violate these folkways, customs, or norms.

Good examples of this are various types of association among Native American tribes which serve explicitly political functions. Among the Plains Indians (including the Hidatsa, Crow, Mandan, Blackfoot, Dakota, and Pawnee), the work of government was carried out by associations of male members of the tribe. For example, an important event among these Plains Indians was the communal buffalo hunt, and the association in charge of the hunt was vested with the power to confiscate the kill of any hunter who did not abide by the ground rules (for example, starting the hunt too soon or taking more than his fair share). In extreme cases of malfeasance the offending parties could even be put to death. Buffalo hunt police could not act outside of their narrow jurisdiction associated with the activities of the hunt, and each year typically new members were named to the association (Krader 1968, p. 34).

In the long march out of human savagery, human beings slowly changed the way they controlled and coordinated the activities of fellow human beings. Rather than relying on informal control, whereby clans, families, or associations regulate the behavior of their own members and defend themselves against persons outside of the group, more advanced societies started relying on specialized agents to carry out control functions for the wider society. When societies move to more advanced stages, their populations grow larger and the informal systems of control based upon blood ties and familiarity between all members are rendered less effective. Some of the earliest systems of control in Britain and Colonial America that moved beyond pure informal control, such as "hue and cry," frankpledge groups, and "watch and ward," utilized aspects of law enforcement or policing, although the persons taking on these roles were not professionals nor were they trained in the specific tasks necessary to do the job.

Early Policing in London

In Britain, for example, even as late as the late 1600s residents of city wards were expected to act as night watchmen if selected, and they were instructed to cry out and send an alarm if they observed anything suspicious. They were expected to provide this service free of charge, and anyone who shirked his or her duty faced heavy fines or other penalties in the Lord Mayor's Court (Fletcher 1850, p. 222). Over time, however, persons started resisting volunteering for watch and ward duty, and this necessitated developing special categories of watch persons, some of which received pay. By the early 1700s Britain passed the Watch Acts, whereby pay was given to night watchmen as supervised and regulated within each ward. This system of night policing stayed relatively intact until the 1830s, at which time, due to various changes in London specifically and Western society more generally—urbanization and industrialization being the two most important factors—the night watch was replaced by a more systematic and professional system of policing.

The early impetus toward modern municipal policing was embodied in Robert Peel's Metropolitan Police Act, which was passed by British parliament in 1829. Concomitant to the establishment of the new police force of metropolitan London, there was also a description of the expansion of police powers. Some of the new regulations specified as enforceable by the new police were as follows:

- The regulation of routes and conduct of persons driving stage-carriages and cattle during the hours of divine services;
- Public houses to remain shut on Sundays, Christmas day, and Good Friday;
- Liquor shall not be supplied to persons under sixteen years of age;
- Power is given to the police to enter unlicensed theatres, and to regulate the activities taking place in coffee houses and cook shops;
- Pawnbrokers who receive pledges from persons under the age of sixteen are subjected to penalties;
- Drunkards guilty of indecent behavior may be imprisoned (Fletcher 1850, pp. 235–236).

Also included was the specification of a vast array of "street offences" for which police could take persons into custody for their violation, including illegal posting of bills or other papers on public buildings, walls, or fences; prostitution, night-walking, or loitering; distribution or exhibition of profane, indecent, or obscene books or papers; and regulation of threatening, abusive, or insulting words or behavior which threaten to or actually "provoke a breach of the peace" (Fletcher 1850, p. 237).

The establishment of a sworn, paid police force in London was symbolic of the new levels of political control and oversight which the city of London was eager to establish, even in the face of opposition among many of its residents who felt, from the very beginning, that the police were either corrupt, inefficient, or simply inattentive to some of their sworn duties, particularly in the areas of "protecting" and "serving." This theme, namely, the ambivalence of the citizenry toward sworn police officers, has resonated and continues to resonate across most societies. In his massive study of poverty in turn-of-the-century London, Charles Booth (1970 [1902–1904]) commented frequently on the role of police in the lives of Londoners and the generally negative views of them shared especially among the poor. Booth quoted one resident of Bethnal Green as saying "[The police] won't interfere to stop the most hideous disorder in the streets." Another Bethnal Green resident complained of the police that there are not "half enough of them, and [they] see as little as possible," and that they are "afraid to assert themselves in a district like this" (Booth 1970 [1902–1904], p. 132).

Even with these negative sentiments, in some rough areas the police are seen by the residents as effective in maintaining at least a modicum of order on the streets, primarily by making a point of knowing "by name and sight" who the "rough" characters are. The police will generally not intervene in activities taking place within homes or other private areas, but if it spills out into the streets, such as a drunken brawl, the police will make a show of corralling the primary aggressors and giving them a good "going over" (Booth 1970 [1902–1904], p. 137). This order-maintenance strategy is still practiced by modern police, as confirmed in Bittner's (1967) study of policing in skid row where police apply a standard of "rough informality" to keep the regulars in line, thereby often avoiding the need to invoke their formal powers of arrest.

The American Situation

By the late 1830s American cities began establishing police forces modeled on the London Metropolitan police. The negative effects of urbanization and industrialization that had earlier prodded the development of policing in London were now starting to affect larger American cities in the East. In America, in fact, urbanization and industrialization combined with other factors to produce a unique set of social circumstances that shaped early American policing and made it somewhat distinct from the British model even as it was based upon it. As David Johnson (1981, pp. 22–25) points out, these other factors in America were nativism, racism, social reform, and politics.

Nativism refers to negative treatment or attitudes toward persons on the basis of their being perceived as outsiders, especially those of foreign birth. The influx of Catholics, especially after the 1840s with the arrival of large numbers of Irish Catholics, led to high levels of social and economic discrimination against them. Many riots that occurred—in Boston in 1834, Philadelphia in 1844, and Louisville in 1855—can be traced to these and other forms of nativism.

Racism, against Blacks but also against Hispanics and American In-dians (or Native Americans), was a staple of American life not only in the South, where slavery was legal until 1865, but also in parts of the country where Blacks were presumably "free" but nevertheless often mistreated. As Johnson (1981, p. 23) notes, between 1829 and 1850 five major race riots erupted in Philadelphia alone, all of which required military intervention.

Social reform also sparked violence, instigated primarily among those who looked unfavorably on the proposed reforms. The two major reforms leading to social unrest were the abolition of slavery and the temperance movement. The temperance movement caused class antagonisms between social reformers as "do-gooders" who tended to come from the higher strata of society, and middle–to lower-class Americans who viewed the attempt to restrict their drinking as an unacceptable infringement on their freedom. Slavery and the question of its abolition was a source of antagonism in America since its founding, culminating of course in the Civil War and continuing into the era of Reconstruction as freed African-Americans sought better opportunities wherever they could find them, including on the Western frontier.

Finally, these and other issues led to protracted *political battles*, as urban political leaders staked out positions on divisive issues, while opponents became entrenched on the opposite side. This was the beginning of American partisan politics, and by the time of their establishment in each local community, police departments were inexorably shaped by these varied political entanglements.

Political Spoils[1]

Following Kelling and Moore (1988) with modifications developed by Chriss (2007b), there have been three eras of American policing, described as political spoils; reform and early professionalization; and community policing (1970s to present).[2]

The first phase of modern policing, running from the 1830s to the 1920s, is referred to as the *political spoils era*. In this earliest stage of development police departments were controlled by city government as well as ward bosses who wielded considerable influence not only on how police were to be used, but also who would be chosen as police officers. There was no pretense of choosing officers on the basis of objective criteria of competence or ability. Rather, officers during the first era were chosen on the basis of political loyalty and ascribed characteristics such as family connections, race or ethnicity, or friendship. Such close relations between city government and police officers produced an entitlement mentality among ward leaders and the administrative staff of the police organization, and because police were poorly paid, all parties tended to look the other way when officers engaged in questionable activities. As a result, patronage abuses abounded and police engaged in many under-the-table or quid pro quo arrangements with various constituents in the community.

As Kelling and Moore (1988) note, policing of the political spoils era was scrabbled together haphazardly and willy-nilly, as there were no organizational mandates yet established for proper police procedures or defining the role of police officers in the community. As a result, the political class within each local community determined goals and activities for the police, thus contributing to the fragmentation of policing and the great variability in police organization from community to community. Police were simply an appendage of the political machine, beholden to those in power at the moment. When a new administration came in, it was not uncommon to see a complete housecleaning take place as the new mayor or city hall put into position "their" men (and women) in policing roles.

During the political spoils era police provided a wide array of services, including crime control, order maintenance, and various social services such as running soup lines, providing temporary lodging for new arrivals to the city, and working with ward leaders to help find work, especially for newly arriving immigrants. Additionally, early police were not as centralized as later more professional departments organized along quasi-military design. This is because cities were divided into wards, and police departments into precincts. Precinct-level police managers worked closely with city ward leaders in hiring, firing, and assigning personnel. This meant that there were lots of quid pro quo arrangements.

Police had tremendous discretion out in the field since all they had to tie them back to the precinct house was the call box.[3] Fire call boxes started appearing in American cities as early as the 1860s (a glass front that any citizen could break to alarm the fire department), but police call boxes appeared about two decades later. Police call boxes were sealed boxes which a patrol officer could access with a key. The patrol officer would enter the call box and flip a switch to notify a central command center that his patrol was proceeding as normal and that no assistance was necessary. Police officers pulled a different box switch on their patrol route every thirty minutes. It also featured a telephone that officers could use to communicate problems to the central command. These earliest patrol routes were called Carney Blocks, named after an officer that devised the system. The police call box was painted blue, and illumination of the light at night provided an officer the location of the box in case of emergency if or when they needed to call for backup. Each box had a number affixed, and policemen quickly identified problem areas in neighborhoods by the unique call box number. All early police boxes were on party lines, so the beat cop would have to pull the box lever to identify which box he was at on the circuit. There was also a pointer in the early boxes for ambulance, paddy wagon, riot, fire, and other safety or order-related issues. The front door had a citizen's key, and any passerby could insert the key and call a wagon for any manner of accident or emergency.

The decentralization of early policing fit in well with foot patrol (walking a beat), and as they were directly visible and available citizen demands focused on them, while ward politicians focused on the organization more generally. Demand for police services appeared at street level, with respect to average citizen calls and encounters, and also at the precinct level, with regard to the local requirements for use of police personnel by ward bosses, city hall, and as directed by police administration.

Aside from the early call box, the primary program or technology for police during this era was foot patrol. A system of "rough informality" (Bittner 1967) was the rule of the day, and much "off the books" activities occurred, including the third degree, widespread use of police informants, and police being at the beck and whim of ward bosses and the political machine for whatever purposes they deemed appropriate. It was not uncommon, for example, for politicians to use detectives to get dirt on people. In this sense, the earliest policing tended to be more person-centered than offense-centered.

Finally, the expected outcomes of police work were crime and crowd control, order maintenance, and urban relief (where police dealt with such issues as poverty, homelessness, and "poor relief" more generally). This sounds much like the basic goals or expected outcomes of more modern policing, and in many ways it is. However, the major difference between policing in this first era and policing in later eras is the level of professionalization: in the earliest political spoils era there were no pretenses that police officers should be trained or that a certain class of individual was necessary to fill these roles. Although relatively well paid because of the real or potential danger of the work, nineteenth-century police were poorly trained, and virtually anyone with the right political connections and an inclination to violence could be lured into police work. With no real training, police had to learn "on the fly" and fashioned their own personal strategies for dealing with whatever or whomever they encountered in their day-today rounds (Lane 1992, p. 13).

Even so, police attempted to maintain a precarious balancing act between assuring citizen satisfaction (at the street level) and political satisfaction (at the precinct level). Since there were few if any rules in place to regulate the behavior of police or to recruit new members into the department, police had almost no checks on their personal behavior. Of course, the department could censure or punish members, including suspending or firing officers, but since there was no meaningful reporting of the department's activities, public accountability of the police was nonexistent. Attempts to change this set of conditions would occur in the next policing era.

Reform and Early Professionalization

The second policing era ran from approximately the 1920s through the 1960s. This second era of policing, referred to as *reform and early professionalization*, was dedicated to correcting some of the problems associated with first-era policing, especially the patronage abuses, graft and corruption, and brutality which characterized early policing. In order to keep officers in line, more attention was given over to organizing departments along military lines, and the new forms of bureaucracy emerging under Taylorism was also useful in setting up a system of overt checks and balances to ensure that the actions of police met the expectations of the department as well as the wider community. Police were also concerned with gaining more autonomy, and they did this by placing greater distance between themselves and local political influence. And to address the graft and corruption, police moved away from an emphasis on foot patrol to more impersonal relations with citizens.

The impulse toward (early) professionalization resulted in a strategy whereby police felt they should no longer engage in the various activities that marked their work in the earlier era. Instead of running soup kitchens or dealing with runaway children, the police opted to professionalization through specialization, and the special role they chose was that of the crime fighter. With the mass production of the automobile beginning in the 1930s, police departments were able to kill two birds with one stone, in terms of both reform and early professionalization, by shifting the mode of patrol from foot to automobile. This created an instantaneous expansion of coverage for calls arriving through dispatch, but also quicker response times, hence further meeting the goals of professionalism and efficiency.

The other advantage of automobile patrol was that the police placed greater physical distance between themselves and citizens, and in so doing mitigated to some extent the graft and corruption of the previous era. But this professionalism was early, incipient, and provisional because there was not yet consideration given to systematically increasing the amount or content of training for police officers, as up to this time there was still the widespread sentiment that policing was a blue-collar job—a craft, not a profession—which could be filled by virtually any able-bodied person with an inclination to that sort of work. The move toward full professionalization, complete with attention to the educational background of police candidates and implementation of ongoing training, would not be realized until the community-policing era (to be discussed below).

Vollmer, Wilson, and Beyond

Attention to some of the background elements of this second era of police reform and professionalization should be noted. Berkeley, CA police chief August Vollmer was one of the first to push for police reforms during the 1920s and early 1930s. Vollmer saw the police as guardians of societal morality, and the goodness of officers would be judged on the quality and integrity of their work. As chief of the Los Angeles Police Department, Vollmer wrote an annual summary of conditions in the department for the year 1924. Many of the themes of modern policing, including emphases on education, training, specialization, and efficiency were evident in Vollmer's 1924 report. One key passage is worth noting:

> If [police] were thoroughly trained for the service before being appointed, they would soon be able to teach, preach and write concerning the obligation that rests upon every individual in the community to cooperate in creating reverence for law. Accordingly a tentative outline of courses for policemen has been prepared and is on file at police headquarters. It has been found that specialization is necessary in modern police organizations. The duties are too varied and control of the multiplicity of details must be done through a staff of competent experts. Police departments cannot continue to operate as in the past and efficiency will be impossible until highly specialized functions are placed in the hands of persons who have been trained for their profession (Vollmer 1974 [1924], p. 11).

O.W. Wilson, Vollmer's protégé, wrote explicit texts on municipal police administration, following what J. Edgar Hoover had done at the federal level with the FBI. Hoover professionalized the investigative function of the bureau and pushed for more stringent educational and training requirements for FBI recruits. Although Hoover's FBI was the model of professionalization for state, county, and local policing after the 1930s, Hoover himself engaged in a range of improper behaviors—such as domestic spying on particular Americans for overtly political purposes—which required further reforms of the FBI beginning in the 1960s (Johnson et al. 2008).

Wilson's *Police Planning* stood as the "bible" for police management and organizational training for many decades after it was first published in 1952. Wilson also crafted the Law Enforcement Code of Ethics, adopted in 1956 by the Peace Officers' Association of California. Even today, this code of ethics (see Figure 11.1) is recited by a majority of police recruits newly graduating from their respective programs, albeit with some modifications of language to comport with today's sensibilities (e.g., dropping "God" at the end of the oath).

Law Enforcement Code of Ethics

As a Law Enforcement Officer, my fundamental duty is to serve mankind; to safeguard lives and property; to protect the innocent against deception, the weak against oppression or intimidation, and the peaceful against violence or disorder; and to respect the Constitutional rights of all men to liberty, equality and justice.

I will keep my private life unsullied as an example to all; maintain courageous calm in the face of danger, scorn, or ridicule; develop self-restraint; and be constantly mindful of the welfare of others. Honest in thought and deed in both my personal and official life, I will be exemplary in obeying the laws of the land and the regulations of my department. Whatever I see or hear of a confidential nature or that is confided to me in my official capacity will be kept ever secret unless revelation is necessary in the performance of my duty.

I will never act officiously or permit personal feelings, prejudices, animosities, or friendships to influence my decisions. With no compromise for crime and with relentless prosecution of criminals, I will enforce the law courteously and appropriately without fear of favor, malice or ill will, never employing unnecessary force or violence and never accepting gratuities.

I recognize the badge of my office as a symbol of public faith, and I accept it as a public trust to be held so long as I am true to the ethics of police service. I will constantly strive to achieve these objectives and ideals, dedicating myself before God to my chosen profession...law enforcement.

Figure 11.1. O.W. Wilson's Code of Ethics (circa 1956)

The reform aspects of this second era of policing are tied to several high-profile failures of the political spoils system which eventuated in the passage of the federal Pendleton Act in 1883. In 1865 President Abraham Lincoln was assassinated, largely because his handpicked bodyguard, a federal police officer by the name of John Parker, decided to go off drinking in a saloon while leaving Lincoln unattended next door at Ford's Theater. This gave John Wilkes Booth unfettered access to the president, who took the opportunity to shoot Lincoln in cold blood (Oates 1984). Sixteen years later, in the summer of 1881, a disgruntled office seeker, Charles Guiteau, shot President James A. Garfield, who died in September, 1881 from his wounds (Theriault 2003).

By this time, the political patronage system, whereby persons were given positions of authority and trust without explicit guidelines in place to determine their fitness for the position, was in deep disarray, and the call for meaningful civil service reform was being taken seriously. The resulting Pendle-ton Act passed by Congress required that those seeking positions in federal government be selected by competitive testing. It was referred to as the merit system, the forerunner to the now well-established civil service examination (Hogenboom 1959). Although originally designed to screen applicants for federal positions, somewhat later state and local governments began following suit, including of course the screening of applicants for municipal policing positions.

By the time of the Progressive Era beginning in the 1890s, then, reformers rejected politics as the basis of local governance in general and police legitimacy in particular. New civil service regulations for hiring, firing, and promotion of public personnel were favored by progressives, thereby presumably eliminating informal "good old boys" networks while championing achievement over ascription. This also served to move police further away from the citizens they served as well as the influence of local politics. This also coincided with a new claim of special police knowledge and expertise, based on knowledge of law and professional responsibilities. As a result of such specialization and professionalization, police were seen as more autonomous and not beholden to city hall, ward bosses, or others seeking to use the police for personal or political purposes.

Additionally, this focus on the law meant that the police started narrowing their agenda to crime control and criminal apprehension. They became law enforcement agencies, rather than safety organizations or peace forces. From the perspective of the organization, there was no need for police to entangle themselves in the political, social, cultural, or economic conditions presumably contributing to disorder and crime. In other words, police should not try to solve root causes of crime because they are neither social workers nor behavioral scientists. They should merely use their technical legal expertise to combat crime. Specialization of this sort also meant that medical and emergency services were shifted to private providers and/or firefighting organizations. In sum, in the second-era police were no longer an agency of urban government, but now part of the criminal justice system.

Further, the organizational design for policing beginning in the early 1900s was influenced by Frederick Taylor's ideas regarding control and efficiency within large, formal organizations (Bendix 1947). Within this formal organizational or bureaucratic model, the assumption is that workers are not all that interested in work, so economic incentives are the key. Conceptualizing police organization in this way implies that worker productivity is linked to employees' rewards. To achieve control of this process a specialized, well-regulated division of labor is required. The military command-and-control model of hierarchical, top-down, supervision of lower-level personnel was useful for these purposes, where emphasis is placed on a chain of command and explicit rules are designed for each officeholder. There is also an attempt to reduce officer discretion by holding up the universality of the criminal code applied to all persons equally (rather than specificity). This further implies a legalistic rather than a service orientation. Further refinements in the police division of labor give rise to specialized units such as vice, juvenile bureaus, drugs, tactical/SWAT, gangs, and the like.

And just as J. Edgar Hoover used propaganda methods to sell the public on the growing problem of urban crime and the need to invest more resources and trust in law enforcement at all levels of government, so too did police reformers discover that public relations and increased use of media could be effective in publicizing police activities and related public concerns, whether good or bad.

The second era of policing established public relations as an integral aspect of police practice, and it grew in importance into the third, community-policing era. The group image that was presented was that police are first and foremost crime fighters. Foot patrol was deemed outmoded and inefficient, which also served to keep officers at arm's length from citizens. This also led to the increased reliance on the use of the squad car for routine police patrols. Additionally, centralization is an organizing element in second-era policing, insofar as citizens are expected to contact police headquarters rather than individual cops on a beat.

As mentioned above, during the reform and early professionalization era police claimed to be specialists in crime control, and it was also upon this basis that police professionalization was assured (Kelling and Moore 1988). August Vollmer initiated the development of a uniform system of crime classification, which was later codified by the International Association of Chiefs of Police (IACP) in 1930. This early attempt by the IACP to codify crime statistics was seen as so promising that the FBI took over the collection and reporting of crime statistics a year later, eventually becoming the Uniform Crime Reports (Mosher et al. 2002). Since then all police departments have measured their effectiveness against this standard, especially in terms of such key measures as the crime rate, clearance rate, response time in patrol and other field operations, and so forth. This was an effective reform strategy during the relatively stable 1940s and 1950s, but was somewhat rigid and inflexible in the face of rapid social changes occurring during the 1960s, especially with regard to rising crime rates during the decade, fueled largely by the baby boom (1946–1963; see Cohen and Land 1987). As defenders of the status quo, police could not adjust rapidly enough to the sweeping cultural and social changes occurring during the 1960s.

Community Policing

As mentioned above, the third era of policing, running from the 1970s to the present, is known as community-oriented or problem-oriented policing. Community-oriented policing (COP) or simply *community policing*, along with the closely-related problem-oriented policing (POP), emerged out of the social transitions of the 1960s. With new challenges to the status quo in the form of social movements such as feminism, civil rights, gay rights, as well as war and campus protests, the police were forced into high-profile and sometimes violent clashes with these and other groups, and as defenders of a status quo under siege they were easy targets for protests and demands for reform beyond those of the second era. It seemed that the professionalism upon which the police staked their claim in the previous era was badly out of touch with the realities of a new and rapidly changing urban landscape. Out of this came the impetus towards real reform, such as developing explicit guidelines for improved training and education of police, as well as attempts to recruit police candidates who matched more closely the sociodemographic characteristics of the populations they served, especially in the areas of gender and race.

Coming out of a tumultuous period of sometimes violent clashes with social movement actors, the police were certainly eager to retool their image and show themselves to be committed to solving problems besetting communities with a spirit of collaboration and mutual respect. This also meant that police would relinquish the claim of specialists in crime control and start taking on a variety of roles in the community, being especially keen to bolster their positive presence in the community through order maintenance, service, and a more scientific approach to studying and solving community problems. To pull off this new ability to take on multiple roles, urban policing became committed to improving educational requirements of their officers, not only in the area of "hard" skills (the newest police technologies) but also with regard to "soft skills" (training in human relations where police act like counselors, psychologists, social workers, and sociologists if need be).

To reiterate, in the third era of community policing police departments made a concerted effort to be more "user friendly," including the downplaying of automobile patrol in favor of foot patrols, bike patrols, and other "slower" forms of police response and presence. Police endeavored to get more information to citizens about the nature of police operations and of crime and disorder in their community. Police started taking an overt interest in fear of crime, studying ways to reduce or eliminate it. This led to a thriving "fear of crime" industry, in effect launching a partnership with higher education to conduct studies/surveys about citizen fears and wants. In sum, there was a push to work more closely with citizens to address issues of the community (Renauer 2007). Indeed, this problem-solving or problem-oriented focus of community policing is embodied in the SARA acronym, which represents the elements or stages of police work aimed at identifying and resolving problems in the community. SARA stands for:

- **Scanning**—Initial identification of community problems to be addressed;
- **Analysis**—Collecting information and analyzing the data;
- **Response**—Developing a strategy to address the underlying condition;
- **Assessment**—Evaluating the effectiveness of the intervention or response (White 2007, pp. 96–98).

This problem-solving methodology assumes that citizens are prepared to work alongside police in a collaborative effort to solve community problems. A recent meta-analysis of a number of published evaluations of problem-oriented policing initiatives found that, for the most part, the SARA method is effective in helping police respond to and alleviate the various problems they and citizens of the jurisdiction identify (Weisburd et al. 2010). Nevertheless, it is important to examine more closely not only this but other assumptions which underlie community policing. Riechers and Roberg (1990) have summarized this bundle of assumptions, which include:

- **Fear of crime**—Beyond the obvious problem of crime, police should also be concerned with citizen fear of crime and set up monitoring systems (such as citizen surveys) to measure it;
- **Active shaping of community norms**—In collaboration with citizens, police can and should actively shape community norms and standards;

- **Demand for police services**—The public demands that police be more involved in the issues of interest to them, and that these citizen demands can be measured and defined;
- **Initiation not domination**—Although police spearhead and initiate community services and programs that citizens want, police neither dominate nor dictate community standards (although they *do* shape and guide them based upon feedback from the citizenry);
- **Value-neutrality**—Police can act in a value-neutral way, consistent with the professional orientation of the previous (reform and early pro-fessionalization) policing era;
- **Organizational change**—The old top-down, command-and-control, quasi-military organizational structure can be transformed into a flatter, more organic, more user-friendly form, including increased use of citizens within the organization (or so-called "civilianization");
- **Higher-quality personnel**—With increased educational requirements and more stringent screening systems, a better class of people can be recruited into policing who are more attentive to community needs and demands;
- **Police as community leaders**—Although a complex and difficult undertaking, the project of community restoration and safety is one that the police are in the best position to fulfill (see also Reed 1999).

For the most part these are assumptions generated from the perspective of law enforcement practitioners themselves, and as such at least some of them may play more of a rhetorical function than reflecting the perspectives of actual citizens. For example, one of the assumptions above is that citizens "demand" community-policing programs and services, but the reality is that many citizens are at best apathetic about these services and at worst don't trust the police or simply want to be left alone (see Buerger 1994; Herbert 2006a).

Themes in Community Policing

Whether merely rhetorical or grounded in the actual operational realities of policing citizens in a community, and acknowledging the great diversity of community-policing programs taking place in particular communities (Skogan 1994), it is nevertheless possible to produce an even more narrowly focused view of the essential elements of community policing. Mastrofski (1998, pp. 162–166) argues that community policing can be distilled down to four fundamental themes: debureaucratization, professionalization, democratization, and service integration. Early in its history municipal policing adopted a quasi-military, bureaucratic model of organization which emphasized political control (especially in the first, political-spoils era), rules, strict adherence to proper communications and a chain of command, centralization (such as command-and-control imperatives emanating from police headquarters), and specialization (especially beginning in the second era of policing). By the 1970s and the emergence of the community-oriented policing era, there was a feeling that the legal and technical requirements of the old bureaucratic model of policing should give way to a more humanistic and *debureaucratized* organizational model. Rather than being distant from citizens and coldly efficient "snappy bureaucrats" (Klockars 1980) specializing in crime control, police are now expected to work side by side with citizens and other stakeholders in the community to solve community problems collectively.

The second theme, *professionalization*, actually began in the second policing era of reform and early professionalization (as summarized above). Yet, professionalization of the third era does not come by way of organizational rules or centralization of command, but by increasing educational requirements for police recruits and training officers in the newest technologists as well as in the vagaries of human behavior. Under this model, police are given even more autonomy to act, since their training is grounded not only in the technical aspects of police work but also in the scientific knowledge base of sociology, psychology, and other pertinent disciplines teaching human or "soft" skills. Indeed, under problem-oriented policing the police are rewarded more for taking initiative to formulate and solve problems in the community rather than the traditionally valued outcomes, namely the "good pinch" (i.e., arrests).

The third theme according to Mastrofski is *democratization*. Community-oriented policing could be described as a sort of democratic policing to the extent that there is an explicit attempt to get citizens more involved in the day-to-day operations of the police department. This appears not only with regard to the emergence of a number of community-policing programs which invite higher levels of citizen participation, but also citizen review boards as a crucial source of external accountability for police departments. Additionally, community policing coincides with the trend of civilianization, namely, the continuing increase in the number of civilians employed in police departments (Crank 1989). These civilian employees are said to act as important bridges or intermediaries between citizens of the community on the one hand and sworn police officers on the other.

A fourth theme of community policing is *service integration*. If police are now taking the approach of solving problems via collaboration with stakeholders in the community, they must do so under the condition that all key community resources should be brought to bear on these problems and that they should be integrated into a seamless whole (this is a concept borrowed from therapeutic practices such as drug-addiction counseling, child services, or clinical social work, namely, helping the client in need with the provision of all-encompassing "wraparound services"; see, e.g., Toffalo 2000). Hence, more than ever before police have developed organizational linkages not only with other city safety forces, but also with schools, social service agencies, housing services (especially in the case of housing authority police), businesses, and colleges and universities in the local area. In addition, police service provision is being made in increasingly intimate settings, as police are now spending more time in people's homes, whether for domestic violence or calls for assistant for family issues such as runaways, delinquency, abandonment, child support and custody cases, or missing persons.[4]

All of these ideal aspects of community policing—debureaucratization, professionalization, democratization, and service integration—are evident in one of the biggest and most ambitious experiments in community-policing implementation, namely, Chicago Alternative Policing Strategy (CAPS). As described by Skogan (2006a, p. 3), who has studied the program extensively, CAPS "features extensive resident involvement, a problem-solving approach toward tackling chronic crime and disorder problems, and coordination between police and a wide range of partner agencies." There are always operational realities impinging on the implementation of community policing, in that under certain conditions some aspects of the program are muted or less apparent than under other conditions. For example, like other large urban areas, Chicago has distinct areas of town that are predominantly White, Black, or Hispanic. Skogan (2006a) found that community-policing implementation and effectiveness varied along sociodemographic characteristics of the community, and race was one of those significant sociodemographic variables. Indeed, Skogan's (2006a) study of community-policing implementation in Chicago is subtitled "A Tale of Three Cities."

The short story is that, although community policing-implementation and involvement of the citizenry went well in White and Black communities, there were significant barriers to CAPS implementation in Latino communities. Why was this? First, Latinos were the youngest of the three groups, and as a rule young people do not participate in community-policing programs. Second, home ownership and length of time at residence was one of the strongest predictors of involvement in community-policing programs. But out of the three groups, Latinos had the lowest level of home ownership, and were more likely to move and hence possessed lower stakes in the program. Third, Spanish-speaking Latinos especially, even more so than their English-speaking counterparts, tended to retreat from involvement with the police because of immigration concerns. What this illustrates is that more needs to be understood about the conditions and factors which reduce or enhance citizen involvement in and commitment to community-oriented policing programs. We will return to this topic shortly.

Beyond Community Policing?

Notice that there has been a shortening of the length of policing eras over time. Political spoils ran a full century (1830s to 1920s). Reform and early professionalization ran about fifty years (1920s to 1960s). The third, community-oriented policing, has had about a forty year run, from the 1970s to the present. And there is talk of the emergence of yet another era of policing, so-called post 9/11 policing (to be discussed in Chapter 5). These collapsing eras may simply be a function of the pressures to remain new and fresh, both from the perspective of police practitioners out in the field as well as scientists observing the police. It may indeed reflect the sort of modernist myopia which Lester F. Ward (1903) referred to long ago as the "illusion of the near." We "modern folk" are fond of talking about how, due to advances in technology as well as other factors, the pace of life is quickening. In policing as well as in many other areas of life, there is the idea that a newfangled "next big thing" is just around the corner, nurtured along by continuous improvement, best practices, and the sheer growth of knowledge. This reflects the idea that innovations and improvements in both technology and everyday life are happening so rapidly that things that used to be considered the "cutting edge" rapidly become obsolete.

There does seem to be some truth to the notion that modern societies continue to place an overweening premium on quickness, speed, and efficiency. Just the other day I plunked down an extra five dollars a month for a quicker DSL connection for my home Internet. In fact, French cultural theorist Paul Virilio made a nice career for himself placing this emphasis on speed and efficiency front and center in his writings. Virilio (1986) refers to his own study of speed as dromology (the science of the journey; see Haggerty 2006). One point Virilio makes in his dromological studies worth briefly noting is that high social status also brings with it the ability to have things literally at your fingertips. Those with money, power, and the right connections can speed up access to goods and services that the average person either could never access or would have to wait in line for for a very long time. And just as is the case for many other things, the wealthy and powerful are looked up to by those further down the status ladder, and they covet those things that they do not have. In effect, the middle and lower classes have a tendency of adopting and striving for the objects, resources, signs, and symbols that characterize the well-to-do.

Savvy entrepreneurs pick up on this, and set up marketing campaigns promising to give speedy access to things persons covet even if they can't afford them. The credit system functions as much as anything to allow mere commoners to keep up with the Joneses, and to maintain the outward appearance of a middle-class lifestyle. Lester Ward (1893) made note of this phenomenon in a general sense, which he called "the principle of deception." Influenced by Ward, a few years later and more famously economist Thorstein Veblen called it "conspicuous consumption." This emphasis on speed and quickness, which operates on both the consumption and production sides with regard to goods and services, is now a generalized phenomenon across society. This means that the police, too, are judged on how well they are keeping up with current trends, and how quickly and efficiently they make available to the public their various goods and services.

Rather than a passing fad (although granted it has been around for some forty years now), Wesley Skogan (2006c) believes community policing is pretty much here to stay. In fact, in many ways the argument made by proponents of community policing is that local governments, city leaders, and police administrators should resist temptations to give in to new fads, because presumably the major elements of community policing (described above) represent the way policing in a modern, industrial, and culturally diverse society ought to be done. This temptation is made even more palpable when tight budgets challenge the delivery of services and programs community-policing departments think they should be providing (Skogan 2006c).

Stephen Mastrofksi (2006) wonders how community policing, as a process or programmatic orientation, should be measured. Perhaps much of what passes for community policing is more rhetoric than reality. If indeed local communities decide for themselves which kinds of services and programs community-oriented policing departments should provide, how do we make sense of this massive diversity? There are ways of indirectly measuring such things as the level of citizen participation in community-policing programs, the extent to which local police departments are moving toward decentralization, and whether or not problem solving by the police, in collaboration with the citizenry, is really going on. Presumably research teams could go to local communities and survey residents about their needs and their view of the effectiveness of police services, as well as conducting on-site observations of the police in action (Mastrofski 2006, p. 49). Of course, the limitation of such approaches is the limitation of the case method in general, in that it is difficult to produce generalized knowledge about community policing from individual cases. Local communities have their own unique histories, needs, and resources, so implementation of community policing in any of these locations will likewise be limited by such realities.

Measuring the Implementation of Community Policing

Yet even in the face of these difficulties, research continues to move forward regarding how to understand and conceptualize what community policing is doing, and to what extent it is being implemented community by community (Roberg 1994). Jeremy Wilson (2006), for example, has undertaken an ambitious effort to develop an empirical model for actually measuring the level of community-policing implementation in American cities. Wilson's (2006) review of the existing literature (e.g., King 1998; Maguire 2003; Maguire and Mastrofski 2000) led him to posit three broad factors that could explain the level of community-policing implementation (as measured in 1999):

- Organizational context, including such factors as size of the police department, the department's task or goal orientation (e.g., legalistic, service, or watchmen-oriented), demographic characteristics of the community being served, levels of funding for COP programs, and region;
- Organizational structure, including two main subvariables: *structural complexity* (e.g., number of stations or precincts, level of specialization within the department) and *structural control* (e.g., degree of centralization, degree of formalization, and administrative weight, or the proportion of total employees within the police organization assigned to administrative and technical support tasks; Wilson 2006, p. 64);
- Level of community-oriented policing (COP) implementation as measured in 1997.

After running appropriate statistical tests, Wilson (2006) found that some of these factors were significant in predicting community-policing implementation, while others were not. For example, with regard to organizational context, neither size of the department nor task scope affected COP implementation. Additionally, police chief turnover negatively affected COP implementation (that is, as police chief turnover increased COP implementation decreased). This seems to indicate that continuity of leadership of the police organization is important in creating a commitment to community policing over the long term.

One community characteristic affected COP implementation, and that was population mobility. Specifically, as population mobility increased COP implementation increased. Presumably high levels of population turnover creates more uncertainty within the police organization, as its planners and leaders may be uncertain about which services or orientations are appropriate for the community. In such a condition of uncertainty, police organizations may be more open to COP implementation. The funding variable was also significant: police departments which receive greater funding for specifically community-oriented programs and orientations are more likely to implement community policing. Region was also significant: police departments located in the western United States were more likely than departments in other regions to move toward COP implementation. Perhaps given the uneven and peculiar history of policing in the West (to be covered next chapter), western police departments are more progressive, innovative, and aligned with the philosophical orientation underlying COP implementation.

What about the organizational structure variables? First of all, structural complexity was insignificant: the number of stations or the degree of task specialization was not related to the level of COP implementation. The findings regarding structural control were mixed. On the one hand, neither centralization nor administrative weight affected the level of COP implementation. However, formalization did influence COP implementation: formal directives regarding COP implementation had a positive effect on actual COP implementation.

Finally, and no big surprise at all, the level of COP implementation in 1997 significantly predicted the level of COP implementation in 1999 as measured in the Law Enforcement Management and Administrative Statistics (LEMAS) survey. However, although statistically significant, the strength of the relationship was weaker than expected. This may have to do with the fact that police departments are not consistent, or that procedures vary from department to department, with regard to identifying community-policing programs, services, and orientations and reporting these in the LEMAS survey.

Informally Embedded Formality

It would seem that the positive relation between formality and the level of community-policing implementation is a somewhat counterintuitive or unexpected finding. Standard professional policing is driven by a top-down bureaucratic model shot through with formalized rules and operating procedures concerning how police are to act and which goals are to be pursued. Indeed, the highly formalized nature of policing of the second era viewed the police as "snappy bureaucrats" who pursued the goal of crime control and who, as highly-trained professionals, did not need "mere" citizens to help carry out their duties. Indeed, under traditional professionalization everyday citizens were barely tolerated, as they were described as "know-nothings" according to Van Maanen's (1978) famous typology. The third era of community policing was supposed to cut into this heavy formality, by the creation of flatter organizational hierarchies and the sincere effort to incorporate citizens of the police district into police planning, organization, and provision of services. This seemed to indicate that informality would be favored over stiff or mechanical formality, and therefore the number of rules in place guiding police activities would be minimized in favor of the human element and a more organic organizational structure, which would thereby also be open to negotiation, dynamism, and flux as conditions on the ground dictated.

But finding both higher formality *and* higher levels of community-policing implementation—as Wilson's (2006) research indicates—can be explained if we take into consideration the work of Arthur Stinchcombe (2001), who wrote a book on when and how formality works. Stinchcombe is correct to note that, traditionally, formality has been viewed negatively because of the perception that it somehow distorts and unduly restricts the agency and creativity of real flesh-and-blood human beings. The idea is that if an extra set of guidelines has to be developed to steer certain types of activity—as in the case of the myriad laws, ordinances, policy initiatives, and governmental regulations characteristic of modern living—then this is an *ipso facto* admission that the mere informal norms and rules of everyday life have somehow broken down and are no longer effective in generating social order or the "good life" more generally. From this perspective, the formalizations of law or bureaucratic regulation are seen at best as "necessary evils" but, if left unchecked, can eventually lead to an "iron cage" of stultifying routine and harsh rules which are enforced as ends in themselves (Weber 1978).

Although an important starting point, the Weberian tradition of bureaucracy, rationalization, and formalization has typically not been concerned with a fine-grained analysis of what these terms actually mean beyond common-sense understandings, or what the analytical connections are between formality and informality. Formalization is an abstraction which dictates a set of rules or procedures for carrying out some type of work in some human social setting. But all formalizations have some unstated or tacit elements which allow human beings who are carrying out the directives to use their professional judgment—otherwise known as discretion—to complete the task at hand. For example, Stinchcombe notes that the highly formalized procedures embodied in the blueprints for constructing a building leave certain bits of information out. Blueprints tend to be very precise about planning and construction, and graphical representations are provided concerning configuration of space and materials to be used. The size and location of the foundation, the load points, the nature of the subsoil upon which the building is to be erected, and the amount and type of concrete needed by building contractors are some of the many points formally designated and enumerated within blueprints. But much of the smaller details are left to the craft workers—plumbers, carpenters, stone masons, etc.—and these are not part of the blueprint. Stinchcombe (2001, p. 59) describes the types of informality that creep into the discretionary work of construction craftpersons as follows:

> The actual floor [as constructed] may be easily an eighth of an inch off; a plumbing connection between a toilet and a waste line that is an eighth of an inch off can put a lot of sewage on the floor. Neither the exact location of the plumbing in the walls nor the exact location of the fixtures is described in the blueprints, and both are designed with adjustable connectors...so that they can be adapted to the building as built.

Likewise, drawing on the work of Llewellyn (2008), Stinchcombe notes that although the great majority of appellate decisions are based upon the technical aspects of law embedded in the procedures taking place in the lower court as well as general principles of precedent—indicating of course that judges maintain a high level of fidelity with the formalizations of law—about 9% of cases are decided on the basis of *obiter dicta* or "other reasons." This means that in about 10% of the cases, rather than relying on the formalizations of legal procedures and precedents, judges go "off the books" and use their professional discretion to decide these cases based upon hunch, instinct, a sense of fairness or social justice, mitigating circumstances, their training, or a whole host of additional possibilities. This is a condition Stinchcombe (2001) refers to as "informally embedded formality."

Returning to the case of Wilson's finding of the correlation between formality and the implementation of community policing, if we take the concept of informally embedded formality seriously, then what we see is that the rather abstract and elusive configuration of activities described as "community policing" are made better sense of by real flesh-and-blood human beings when a set of guidelines—a "connect-the-dots" for community policing if you will—are put into place, and clear paths are illuminated with regard to "how to do" community policing and recognizing it as such. Where such guidelines are lacking, all that is left for police practitioners to do is to rely on their standard understandings of traditional policing—which is done according to the formal dictates developed for such policing—while any attempts at community policing likely "slip through the cracks" because they are not anchored effectively within the abstractions of the formalities necessary to pull off this type of work.

Conclusion

In considering the work of Wilson (2006), it is clear that the project of identifying community-policing components and measuring to what extent they are being implemented in communities is an exceedingly complex undertaking. As thorough as Wilson's model is, it explains only about 28% of the variance in the relationship between the various variables he considered (organizational context, organizational structure, and level of prior COP implementation) and the outcome to be explained, namely later implementation of community policing. This is not the fault of Wilson, for there are a host of other variables which were not measured or which could not be brought into the model, and these missing or unmeasurable variables surely play a large part in reducing the robustness of the model's explanation. As is the case for research in most other areas of sociology and criminology, the issue of community-oriented policing and the factors associated with its level of implementation will require further analytical refinement and research out in the field.

Notes

1. This section and later sections discussing the three eras of policing draw in part from Chriss (2007b, pp. 96–98).

2. There are several anomalies not adequately addressed in the Kelling and Moore (1988) three-era model of the history of American policing. First, there were slave patrols in the American south, stretching as far back as the 1740s, which took place well before the alleged first era of municipal policing beginning in the 1840s. These police forces acted to maintain the racial and social status quo of the southern slave system (see Hadden 2001; Williams and Murphy 2006). The second anomaly is the uneven development of municipal policing that took place west of the Mississippi, in what is known as the western frontier, beginning in 1857 in San Francisco, presumably the first western police department, as defined by the date of adoption of police uniforms (Monkkonen 1981). Although the story of policing in the Wild West is just now beginning to be told, there are several scholarly studies (see, e.g., Dykstra 1968; Gard 1949; Prassel 1972) of the more individualistic lawman versus gunslinger model which has, of course, been so widely depicted in movies and other popular accounts. Chapter 3 is devoted to studying the transition from the solitary lawman to the establishment of police departments across the western frontier. Nevertheless, even given these caveats and blind spots, as far as the three eras of policing are concerned, the Kelling and Moore (1988) typology is a useful approximation of how policing emerged over these periods.

3. For the history of the call box in particular and early police patrols in general, I draw upon Thale (2004). Another source of information on this topic was gleaned from Kelsey and Associates, an organization dedicated to the architectural history of Washington, DC. Part of this project involves a careful documentation of the history of fire and police call boxes in DC. This information can be found at http://www.washingtonhistory.com/Projects/CallBox/index. html.

4. Interestingly enough, the recent case of Anthony Sowell in Cleveland has brought the issue of police response to missing persons into the critical spotlight. Upwards of eleven bodies were discovered in and around Sowell's house, all African-American women living in poverty and who were either drug addicts or prostitutes. Some had gone missing for months or years, and although missing persons cases had been filed on most of them, police investigations came to a dead end. The implication here is that Cleveland police did not take these missing cases seriously because of the race of the missing persons. Hence, we also have another example of the ease with which criminal justice officials in general, and the police in particular, can be accused of biased or even racist actions.

Bibliography

Bendix, Reinhard. 1947. "Bureaucracy: The Problem and Its Setting." *American Sociological Review* 12 (5):493–507.

Bittner, Egon. 1967. "The Police on Skid-Row: A Study of Police Keeping." *American Sociological Review* 32 (5):699–715.

Booth, Charles. 1970 [1902–1904]. *Life and Labour of the People in London*, final volume. New York: AMS Press.

Buerger, Michael E. 1994. "The Limits of Community." pp. 270–273 in *The Challenge of Community Policing*, edited by D.P. Rosenbaum. Thousand Oaks, CA: Sage.

Chriss, James J. 2007b. *Social Control: An Introduction*. Cambridge, UK: Polity Press.

Cohen, Lawrence E. and Kenneth C. Land. 1987. "Age Structure and Crime: Symmetry versus Asymmetry and the Projection of Crime Rates through the 1990s." *American Sociological Review* 52 (2):170–183.

Crank, John P. 1989. "Civilianization in Small and Medium Police Departments in Illinois, 1973–1986." *Journal of Criminal Justice* 17 (3):167–177.

Dykstra, Robert R. 1968. *The Cattle Towns*. New York: Alfred A. Knopf.

Fletcher, Joseph. 1850. "Statistical Account of the Police of the Metropolis." *Journal of the Statistical Society of London* 13 (3):221–267.

Gard, Wayne. 1949. *Frontier Justice*. Norman: University of Oklahoma Press.

Giddings, Franklin H. 1896. *Principles of Sociology*. New York: Macmillan.

Hadden, Sally E. 2001. *Slave Patrols*. Cambridge, MA: Harvard University Press.

Haggerty, Kevin D. 2006. "Visible War: Surveillance, Speed, and Information War." Pp. 250–268 in *The New Politics of Surveillance and Visibility*, edited by R.V. Ericson and K.D. Haggerty. Toronto: University of Toronto Press.

Herbert, Steve. 2006a. *Citizens, Cops, and Power: Recognizing the Limits of Community*. Chicago: University of Chicago Press.

Hogenboom, Ari. 1959. "The Pendleton Act and the Civil Service." *American Historical Review* 64 (2):301–318.

Johnson, David R. 1981. *American Law Enforcement: A History*. St. Louis, MO: Forum Press.

Johnson, Herbert A., Nancy Travis Wolfe, and Mark Jones. 2008. *History of Criminal Justice*, 4th ed. Newark, NJ: LexisNexis.

Kelling, George L. and Mark H. Moore. 1988. "The Evolving Strategy of Policing." In *Perspectives on Policing*, No. 4. Washington, DC: National Institute of Justice.

King, W.R. 1998. *Innovations in American Municipal Police Organizations*. Ph.D. diss., University of Cincinnati.

Klockars, Carl B. 1980. "The Dirty Harry Problem." *Annals of the American Academy of Political and Social Science* 452:33–47.

Krader, Lawrence. 1968. *Formation of the State*. Englewood Cliffs, NJ: Prentice-Hall.

Lane, Roger. 1992. "Urban Police and Crime in Nineteenth-Century America." pp. 1–50 in *Modern Policing*, edited by M. Tonry and N. Morris. Vol. 15 of *Crime and Justice*, edited by M. Tonry. Chicago: University of Chicago Press.

Llewellyn, Karl N. 2008. *Jurisprudence: Realism in Theory and Practice*. New Brunswick: Transaction Publishers.

Maguire, E.R. 2003. *Organizational Structure in American Police Agencies: Context, Complexity, and Control*. Albany, NY: SUNY Press.

Mastrofski, Stephen. 1998. "Community Policing and Police Organization Structure." pp. 161–189 in *How to Recognize Good Policing*, edited by J. Brodeur. Thousand Oaks, CA: Sage.

_____. 2006. "Community Policing: A Skeptical View." pp. 44–73 in *Police Innovation: Contrasting Perspectives*, edited by D. Weisburd and A.A. Braga. Cambridge, UK: Cambridge University Press.

Monkkonen, Eric H. 1981. *Police in Urban America, 1860–1920*. Cambridge, UK: Cambridge University Press.

Mosher, Clayton J., Terance D. Miethe, and Dretha M. Phillips. 2002. *The Mis-measure of Crime*. Thousand Oaks, CA: Sage.

Oates, Stephen B. 1984. *Abraham Lincoln, the Man behind the Myths*. New York: Harper and Row.

Prassel, Frank Richard. 1972. *The Western Peace Officer: A Legacy of Law and Order*. Norman: University of Oklahoma Press.

Reed, Wilson E. 1999. *The Politics of Community Policing: The Case of Seattle*. New York: Garland Publishing.

Renauer, Brian C. 2007. "Reducing Fear of Crime: Citizen, Police, or Government Responsibility?" *Police Quarterly* 10 (1):41–62.

Riechers, L.M. and R.R. Roberg. 1990. "Community Policing: A Critical Review of Underlying Assumptions." *Journal of Police Science and Administration* 17:105–114.

Roberg, Roy R. 1994. "Can Today's Police Organizations Effectively Implement Community Policing?" pp. 249–257 in *The Challenge of Community Policing*, edited by D.P. Rosenbaum. Thousand Oaks, CA: Sage.

Skogan, Wesley G. 1994. "The Impact of Community Policing on Neighbor-hood Residents: A Cross-Site Analysis." Pp. 167–181 in *The Challenge of Community Policing*, edited by D.P. Rosenbaum. Thousand Oaks, CA: Sage.

_____. 2006a. *Police and Community in Chicago: A Tale of Three Cities*. Oxford, UK: Oxford University Press.

_____. 2006c. "The Promise of Community Policing." pp. 27–43 in *Police Innovation: Contrasting Perspectives*, edited by D. Weisburd and A.A. Braga. Cambridge: Cambridge University Press.

Stinchcombe, Arthur L. 2001. *When Formality Works*. Chicago: University of Chicago Press.

Sumner, William G. 1906. *Folkways*. Boston: Ginn & Company.

Thale, Christopher. 2004. Assigned to Patrol: Neighborhoods, Police, and Changing Deployment Practices in New York City before 1930. *Journal of Social History* 37 (4):1037–1064.

Theriault, Sean M. 2003. "Patronage, the Pendleton Act, and the Power of the People." *Journal of Politics* 65 (1):50–68.

Toffalo, Douglas A. Della. 2000. "An Investigation of Treatment and Outcomes in Wraparound Services." *Journal of Child and Family Studies* 9 (3):351–361.

Van Maanen, John. 1978. "The Asshole." Pp. 221–238 in *Policing: A View from the Street*, edited by P.K. Manning and J. Van Maanen. Santa Monica, CA: Good-year.

Virilio, Paul. 1986. *Speed and Politics*, translated by M. Polizotti. New York: Semiotext(e).

Vollmer, August. 1974 [1924]. *Law Enforcement in Los Angeles*. New York: Arno Press.

Ward. Lester F. 1893. *Psychic Factors of Civilization*. Boston: Ginn & Company.

———. 1903. *Pure Sociology: A Treatise on the Origin and Spontaneous Development of Society.* New York: Macmillan.

Weber, Max. 1978. *Economy and Society*, vol. 2, edited by G. Roth and C. Wit-tich. Berkeley: University of California Press.

Weisburd, David, Cody W. Telep, Joshua C. Hinkle, and John E. Eck. 2010. "Is Problem-Oriented Policing Effective in Reducing Crime and Disorder? Findings from a Campbell Systematic Review." *Criminology and Public Policy* 9 (1):139–172.

White, Michael D. 2007. *Current Issues and Controversies in Policing.* Boston: Allyn and Bacon.

Williams, Hubert and Patrick V. Murphy. 2006. "The Evolving Strategy of Police: A Minority View." Pp. 27–50 in *The Police and Society*, 3rd ed., edited by V.E. Kappeler. Long Grove, IL: Waveland.

Wilson, Jeremy W. 2006. *Community Policing in America.* London: Routledge. Wilson, O.W. 1958. *Police Planning*, 2nd ed. Springfield, IL: Charles C. Thomas.

CHAPTER TWELVE

Criminal Court System

As suggested in the previous chapter, most people have little or no idea how the court systems are constructed in the U.S. Of course, unless part of the system, most of us will never see the inside of a courtroom, particularly a criminal courtroom. Therefore, it is impossible for anyone to know the reality of the courts outside of what they get from media representations. The old *Perry Mason* television series, and recent courtroom dramas like *Law and Order*, *Suits*, and *Boston Legal*, are prime examples of this kind of representation. All are very entertaining to be sure, and some are better than others; however, they very seldom provide an accurate representation of the criminal court system and how it fits within the function of justice in America.

The United States, in reality, is very unique mainly because we have a dual court system made up of state courts and federal courts.[1] Crimes against state laws are prosecuted in state courts and crimes violating federal statutes are adjudicated in the federal court systems. State courts differ from state to state, but all have trial courts and appellate courts, where cases can be appealed. By contrast, the federal system consists of district courts (comparable to the state trial courts), appellate courts or circuit courts (where appeals are heard), and the Supreme Court (the court of last resort). What is significant to this system, and oftentimes different to the systems found in other countries, is that a prosecutor is the principle authority who decides whether to prosecute a case. If a decision is made to do so, he or she presents the case against the individual charged with a crime

---

1   R. E. Masters, L. B. Way, P. B. Gerstenfeld, B. T. Muscat, M. Hooper, J. P. J. Dussich, L. Pincu, and C.A. Skrapec, *CJ: Realities and Challenges* (McGraw-Hill Companies, Inc., 2011).

(defendant) on behalf of the state or federal government. A grand jury then decides whether a case should go to trial. The prosecutor is then responsible for arguing that case at trial.[2]

As suggested in the previous chapter, there is an issue of great concern here relating to the possibility that the original ideals shaping the philosophy of justice in America are failing. This raises questions pertaining to the efficacy of the criminal justice system in the postmodern world and the potential for individuals to receive justice from a standpoint of equality. As argued in chapter two, research indicates that variables such as race and social class impact the way we define criminal behavior, and subsequent punishments, as well as the manner in which certain individual's circumvent any form of real punishment due to the unequal distribution of law, selective prosecutorial discretion, questionable adjudication processes, and uneven sentencing practices in relation to racial and social ascriptions.[3]

---

2   R. E. Masters, L. B. Way, P. B. Gerstenfeld, B. T. Muscat, M. Hooper, J. P. J. Dussich, L. Pincu, and C. A. Skrapec, *CJ: Realities and Challenges* (McGraw-Hill Companies, Inc., 2011).

3   T. F. Tolbert, "From the Case Files of Cain and Abel: A Case/Content Analysis of the First Homicide and Historical Impact on the Definitions of Crime and Punishment in the Postmodern World of Criminal Justice," Presented at the 45th Annual Western Society of Criminology Conference, February 3, 2018.

"Putting Cruelty First"

Liberal Penal Reform and the Rise of the Carceral State

By Jason Vick[*]

···

W hy are so many people in prison today? What accounts for the fact that about 2.2 million Americans are behind bars, and approximately one in 35 adults are subjected to prison, jail, probation, parole, and other forms of surveillance?[1] How do we make sense, more generally, of the fact that all the world's liberal democracies rely on incarceration as an essential tool of punishment?[2] Specifically, why do the discourses and practices surrounding punishment in today's liberal democracies consider torture and other forms of physical abuse to be unacceptably cruel, while long-term incarceration is considered unproblematic?[3] To approach this problem, I consider the liberal reformism of Cesare Beccaria and Jeremy Bentham, which helped to pave the way for a transition from irregular, and usually corporal, punishment to the regular, systematic liberal justice system that eschews corporal punishment but relies heavily on incarceration.

In developing this argument, I engage with the literature that focuses on the role of cruelty within liberalism, in particular the work of Judith Shklar (her phrase, "putting cruelty first," appears in the article title). Shklar argues, as does Richard Rorty (1998), that liberalism's defining feature is its opposition to cruelty. In other words, before it is concerned with individual rights or limited government, liberalism is fundamentally against cruelty. This sensitivity is found in a number of early liberal thinkers, from Montaigne to Montesquieu (Shklar 1984).[4] By drawing on Shklar's distinction between physical cruelty (which liberals abhor) and moral-psychological cruelty (about which

---

[*] JASON VICK (email: jvick@uci.edu) is a PhD candidate in Political Science at UC Irvine. He specializes in political theory, with a focus on contemporary democratic theory, in particular participatory and radical-agonistic theories of democracy. His research updates and revitalizes the participatory democratic theory of the 1960s and 1970s for the challenges of the twenty-first century. He has also written on liberal penal reform and philosophies of punishment, Foucault, and mass incarceration.

Jason Vick, "'Putting Cruelty First': Liberal Penal Reform and the Rise of the Carceral State," *Social Justice*, vol. 42, no. 1, pp. 35-52, 146. Copyright © 2016 by Social Justice. Reprinted with permission. Provided by ProQuest LLC. All rights reserved.

liberals are ambivalent), I am able to better illuminate how such humane reformists as Beccaria and Bentham could be opposed to corporal punishment while favoring incarceration as a satisfactory liberal solution to the issue of punishment that minimizes (physical) cruelty.

Most of this article focuses on Cesare Beccaria and Jeremy Bentham, two European thinkers whose work in the eighteenth and nineteenth centuries established their place as standard bearers of liberal penal reform. I argue that they attempt to justify the shift toward what we would recognize as a liberal justice system, which includes the prohibition of torture, the reduction or elimination of capital punishment, equal protection before fixed, public law, proportional (and generally mild) punishments, deterrence as the sole justification for punishment, and an attempt to render the justice system regular, systematic, and universal. In making these arguments, Beccaria and Bentham helped to establish the justifications for a penal system in which the authorities imposing the penalties are in principle as accountable to the law (and the public) as are the suspects being tried and potentially punished.

Both thinkers are motivated by a strong concern with cruelty and the desire to reduce or even eliminate its role in the penal system. However, their sensitivity to physical pain and torture does not translate into an equivalent sensitivity toward incarceration and the psychological harm it produces. Jeremy Bentham's Panopticon, in particular, is an example of a system of carceral punishment that avoids physical abuse, but it would likely result in troubling psychological consequences for those detained within. These thinkers worked to discredit the physical, arbitrary sovereign forms of punishment diagnosed by Foucault while also defending, often explicitly, the shift to universal, regular, disciplinary punishment by way of incarceration, which should be just as problematic for a society defined by (or aspiring to) democratic self-government, the reduction of cruelty, and individual rights.

This is not to suggest that either Beccaria or Bentham intended, or could have envisioned, the creation of the carceral state in the United States, or its lesser siblings in England and Western Europe. They did, however, provide the rationale, by means of philosophical argument and public activism, for the shift from a system based on direct corporal punishment to one based on (often long-term) detention. Thus, they are central figures in the heritage that has produced the punishment imaginary of today, where physical torture, if discovered and reported, generates outrage, while sentences of 20, 30, or even 50 years in prison fail to merit much attention. In diagnosing this feature of the liberal justice system, I am arguing that Beccaria and Bentham, and reformers like them, helped to demolish a harsh, cruel, and unfair penal apparatus, but also helped to replace it with an entirely new regime of cruelty, one equally antithetical to a society that values strong democratic governance,[5] the reduction of (all forms of) cruelty and pain, and the protection of the individual.

Liberalism's blindness to moral-psychological forms of suffering renders it unable to fully understand and diagnose the cruelty and injustice in the US system of mass incarceration. This blindness, which is a profound moral failing on the part of liberalism, in turn makes it inadequate to the task of undoing mass incarceration. Indeed, some of the most effective recent challenges to prison expansion have come from conservatives concerned with cutting costs, not liberal reformers motivated by the prospect of human suffering. And neither conservative budgetary concerns nor liberal reformism seem likely to challenge the bases of the carceral state, which include, among other things, the War on Drugs.

At stake here are the institutions, practices, and discourses that together comprise the carceral state and the liberal justice system. Only through a better understanding of how we arrived at this moment, with the institutions and practices of the carceral state and its attendant discourses and philosophical justifications, can we hope to challenge it. My focus is not on specific policy choices, or on macroeconomic trends that may have driven these changes, but rather on examining the philosophical justifications and discourses that accompanied the transition to a liberal justice system (and with it, the rise of the carceral state). These are so entrenched that we struggle to go beyond them. To find creative solutions that are sensitive to physical and moral forms of cruelty and that may ignite and inspire future popular movements to challenge our reliance on mass incarceration, we must understand the philosophy of liberal reformism that justifies the carceral state.

The body of this article consists of three sections. The first discusses and assesses the reformist agenda of Cesare Beccaria and Jeremy Bentham, primarily by examining two key texts, Beccaria's *On Crimes and Punishments* and Bentham's *The Rationale of Punishment*. I show that Beccaria and Bentham argue for the main features of a liberal justice system. The second discusses in greater detail the role of cruelty in the reformism of Beccaria and Bentham, focusing on Judith Shklar's definition of liberalism as a political philosophy that puts cruelty among its chief concerns. I then discuss some of the new moral and psychological cruelties associated with incarceration, and liberalism's insensitivity to the possibility that imprisonment might constitute a new system of penal cruelty, one distinct from but filled with as many cruelties as the system it replaced. This is particularly evident in Bentham's presentation of the Panopticon, a proposed institution of inspection built around solitary confinement and perpetual surveillance, which Bentham depicts as a model for prison life shorn of all cruelty. In the conclusion, I turn to Friedrich Nietzsche and Angela Davis to suggest possible lines of thought that move beyond the liberal philosophy that justifies the cruelties of the carceral state. Finally, I suggest some basic steps for going forward in terms of policy, activism, and political thought.

The Liberal Reformism of Bentham and Beccaria

I. Here I discuss the basic elements of liberal penal reform found in the work of Jeremy Bentham and Cesare Beccaria. In particular, I explore their opposition to torture and capital punishment, the insistence on the importance of public, impartial laws, the codification of punishments that are proportional to the severity of the crime, and a shift in the justification for punishment from retribution to social protection. After presenting the reformist agenda of each thinker, I turn to the question of cruelty in traditional corporal punishment and in its replacement, incarceration.

In 1764, Cesare Beccaria published his famous reformist text, *On Crimes and Punishments*. This work remains his most enduring text and is a classic statement of the principles of the liberal justice system. Beccaria presents, in embryonic form, many of the essential features of a liberal justice system that we recognize and defend as desirable today. Beccaria stresses the importance of impartial, fixed law, which is publicly known and applied with equal intensity to all. "The greater the number of people who understand the [law] and who have it in their hands, the less frequent crimes will be," for ignorance of the law is the enemy of lawful obedience (Beccaria 1764/1986, 9–10). Fixed, public laws serve the cause of obedience, while protecting the individual from the capricious whims of the sovereign. "Fixed and immutable laws" provide "personal security" for the individual because they leave "the judge no other task than to examine a citizen's actions and to determine whether or not they conform to the written law" (ibid., 12). In this case, fixed, public laws serve the cause of obedience and social cohesion, but they also protect the individual from government abuse. The legal expectations of the citizen are as public and predictable as the government response. This, of course, is recognizable as an early articulation of the liberal justice principle of equality before the law, with the concomitant elimination of feudal privileges and titles.

The next crucial element in Beccaria's approach concerns the need for proportionality in the distribution of punishments. The need to prevent crimes, or actions contrary to the public good, increases with the severity of the crime. In other words, mild crimes merit mild punishments, for they cause little harm and do not merit a harsh response. More serious crimes—those that do great harm to the public good—must be punished accordingly so as to prevent (or at least minimize) their occurrence in the future. As Beccaria puts it, "obstacles that restrain men from committing crimes should be stronger according to the degree that such misdeeds are contrary to the public good." In establishing this standard, Beccaria provides for the use of harsher penalties, but also establishes a realm of protection for the individual. If the crimes are mild, they do not merit harsh penalties, regardless of how such crimes were previously handled.

One of the most interesting elements in Beccaria's case for reform is his opposition to torture. As he notes, torture of the defendant during trial is "sanctioned by the usage of most nations," generally for the purpose of extracting a confession (ibid., 29). The problem with this use of torture is that it does not respect the rights of the accused, who are innocent until proven guilty. Along with this, the evidence obtained through torture is of no value, for speaking "amid convulsions and torments is no more a free act than staving off the effects of fire and boiling water," which leaves the victim "no liberty but to choose the shortest route to ending the pain" (ibid., 31). Torture is thus problematic on two levels: it treats the accused as one who is guilty and deserving of punishment, though this has not yet been established, and it extracts confessions of guilt that are not reliable. Moreover, a person convicted of a crime should face the publicly established, lawful penalty, not the arbitrary inclinations of a torturer. Here Beccaria justifies the basic liberal protections that are integral to the liberal justice system, including the presumption of innocence and the (at least formal) protection against bodily abuse. Similarly, Beccaria provides a series of arguments against the use of capital punishment, though space is lacking here to deal with them adequately. Suffice it to say, he characterizes capital punishment as a "cruel example" offered to the citizenry, made all the worse because it "is carried out methodically and formally" (ibid., 48–51).

The next feature of Beccaria's penal reform is a shift in the ends for which punishment is carried out. Beccaria, much like Bentham after him, seeks to eliminate the vengeful, retributive element in public punishment and to replace it with a milder, non-vindictive deterrent justification. The point of punishment is no longer to hurt the criminal but to deter the commission of future crimes. Prevention, not retribution, is the watchword of the liberal reform movement. In other words, the "purpose of punishments is not to torment and afflict a sentient being or to undo a crime which has already been committed"; indeed, the latter goal is not possible. As a sort of necessary evil, punishment can and should "dissuade the criminal from doing fresh harm to his compatriots and to keep other people from doing the same" (ibid., 23). Physical *cruelty is thus removed from the world of punishment*. More generally, political systems should be built around eliminating the causes of punishment, rather than punishing crimes after the fact. As Beccaria himself says, "it is better to prevent crimes than to punish them. This is the chief purpose of every good system of legislation," which is achieved through the creation and promulgation of clear, simple laws, easy to understand and obey (ibid., 70–71). With the focus on prevention of crime through smart legislation, the necessity and justification for harsh, physical punishments has largely eroded.

The final element of Beccaria's liberal reform agenda concerns the need to render punishment as systematic and regular as possible. This includes the establishment of a justice system that provides for swift, public charge and trial as soon as possible after the crime has been committed. Preventive custody, in which the suspect is held before trial, must "last as short a time as possible and be as lenient as possible." Similarly, the "trial itself must be completed in the shortest time possible," so as to protect the individual from the caprice of a cruel judge and to ensure she receives her fair chance in the justice system (ibid., 36). Making punishment systematic and regular also includes the elimination of "every distinction, whether it be in honor or wealth," that would privilege certain citizens and degrade others before the law (ibid., 39). Beyond abolishing feudal privileges of status and rank, punishment must be regular to the point of inescapability. If punishment is moderate, humane, and derived from simple public laws, there is no need for pardons or asylum. Says Beccaria, "let the laws, therefore, be inexorable … but let the lawgiver be gentle, indulgent, and humane." In summary, the necessary penal reforms will render punishment "public, prompt, necessary, the minimum possible under the given circumstances, proportionate to the crimes, and established by law" (ibid., 80–81).

Beccaria's remarkable work sets forth an agenda that is striking in its familiarity and resonance with our approach to punishment today, even though it was published before the American Revolution and two of the most radically transformative centuries in human history. Beccaria's reform agenda sets up a powerful series of protections for the individual, all designed to replace the arbitrary power of the sovereign with a set of clear, fixed laws and penalties, which apply equally to all and are subject to public scrutiny. Most of these protections are still regarded as essential today, including the right to a speedy trial, humane treatment while in prison, and equal protection before the law. However, there are certain less appealing elements to this agenda. The liberal hope of minimizing and humanizing punishment blurs into the bureaucratic hope of making punishment everywhere, always, and strong.[6] Similarly, despite Beccaria's remarkable sensitivity to the brutal torture and capricious executions that often defined the punishment of his day, he displays little concern for the potential brutality of detention, other than to assure that prison conditions are not too harsh. We have here, in embryonic form, the main features of the modern liberal justice system.

II. Jeremy Bentham's reformist agenda overlaps heavily with that of Beccaria, but the two are not indistinct. Apart from the reformist elements mentioned above, several elements of Bentham's reformism are noteworthy. Bentham justifies his reformist agenda for punishment in more explicitly utilitarian terms than does Beccaria. His primary work in this area, *The Rationale of Punishment,* was written between 1774 and 1776, only a decade after Beccaria's *On Crimes and Punishments* (Bentham 2009, 13). Bentham's utilitarian approach seeks to minimize the amount of pain and maximize the amount of happiness experienced by the greatest majority in a given society. Given that Bentham's utilitarian philosophy eschews all appeals to natural rights, it may seem unfair to place his work in the liberal tradition. This, however, would be a mistaken judgment. Although Bentham's concern for "scientific legislation" includes a utilitarian emphasis on social engineering to produce the greatest outcome for the greatest number, he is ultimately concerned with liberation "in the direction of democratic individualism" (Fuller 1987, 717). Furthermore, Bentham's reformist agenda with regard to punishment shares many remarkable similarities with that of Beccaria and has helped to provide the philosophical justifications for the liberal justice system.

Bentham's utilitarianism, much like Beccaria's, allows him to recognize that the infliction of punishment is an evil, since it directly produces harm to the individual being punished. Thus, punishment is a first-order evil, which consists of harming the offender, in the service of a second-order good, that of preventing future crime and protecting those in society. Along these lines, Bentham constructs an economy of punishment in which the penalty must be proportional to the severity of the crime, and the social impact of the punishment is ultimately of more importance than the actual harm inflicted on the offender. Since the infliction of suffering through punishment is harmful to the general utilitarian goal of maximizing happiness, punishments should be economically performed, where the "desired effect is produced by the employment of the least possible suffering" (Bentham 2009, 66). Since the primary utilitarian goal is to reduce and prevent crime, the social impact of the punishment is more important than its personal impact on the criminal who directly suffers the punishment. In other words, "the real punishment ought to be as small, and the apparent punishment as great as possible" (ibid., 67). Bentham, much like Beccaria, is sensitive to the unnecessary and harmful effects of overly harsh punishment and seeks to establish a system in which these can be minimized.

Also strikingly similar to Beccaria is Bentham's insistence that prevention is the only possible purpose of punishment. Prevention comes in two varieties: "*particular prevention,* which applies to the delinquent himself; and *general prevention,* which is applicable to all the members of the community without exception" (ibid., 61). This is justified in utilitarian terms, whereby punishment establishes a painful consequence for criminal activity, thus making those inclined to criminal activity less likely to do so. Particular prevention works in the sense that it removes the offending criminal, who now cannot recommit his crime. Once released, this criminal no longer desires to commit the crime for fear of experiencing that punishment again. General prevention takes precedence, however, since the real purpose of penal law is to teach through example those who have not committed a crime that they will profit by continuing to be law-abiding and suffer undesired consequences if they choose to violate the law. In the most general sense, then, punishment is a necessary evil done for the sake of the social good, justified only as a deterrent against future crime and not as an act of vengeance.

The Death and Rebirth of Cruelty

A key element in the liberal reformism of Bentham and Beccaria is the desire to reduce cruelty. In this section, I consider the relation between cruelty and liberal thought, the efforts by these two thinkers to reduce the amount of cruelty in the penal system, and their inability to consider the alternative forms of cruelty that emerge with long-term incarceration.

What is the role of cruelty in liberal political thought? Judith Shklar, in a provocative set of essays, contends that the desire to put cruelty first is one of the distinguishing characteristics of liberalism. She defines cruelty as "the willful inflicting of physical pain on a weaker being in order to cause anguish and fear." The liberal focus on cruelty, and the desire to reduce its role in human affairs, puts liberalism "at odds not only with religion but with normal politics as well." This is because, by focusing on a "vice that disfigures human character," one is making "a purely human verdict upon human conduct" and is reducing the concern for violations of divine commands or normal human rules (Shklar 1984, 8–9), This can be seen in certain early liberal thinkers, such as Montaigne, who are more concerned with the horrors of cruelty than with the crimes of dishonesty or adultery, which tend to be less cruel.

Beyond the liberal focus on physical cruelty, Shklar also introduces the concept of moral cruelty, which is the infliction of "deliberate and persistent humiliation, so that the victim can eventually trust neither himself nor anyone else" (ibid., 37). One finds in Nietzsche a deep concern with moral cruelty, hypocrisy, and dishonesty, and thus an impassioned critique of Christianity due to "the self-torment of its internalized morality" (ibid.). Nietzsche is not, however, a traditional liberal thinker, a point I discuss later. As Shklar reminds us, when these early liberal thinkers turned their attention to cruelty, as did Montaigne, Montesquieu, and later Beccaria and Bentham, they primarily had physical cruelty in mind.[7] Hypocrisy and betrayal, though objectionable, did not arouse the concern of these liberal thinkers in the same manner that physical cruelty did.

What role did cruelty (and the desire for its elimination) have in the work of Beccaria and Bentham? Beccaria was raised in a wealthy family in Milan and earned a doctor's degree in law in 1758. He soon became active in literary clubs and published several works. In this context, his attention turned to penal reform. The most common methods for dealing with criminals then were capital punishment and "bodily mutilations." Petty offenses were often punished by flogging or mutilations, such as "slitting or piercing the tongue, and cutting or burning off the hand" (Maestro 1973, 13). Without a doubt, the eighteenth century penal system in Italy and much of Europe was defined through its considerable physical cruelty. Aside from mutilations, capital punishment was common and torture was routinely practiced to elicit confessions. The desire to eliminate such brutal, unnecessary cruelties guided much of Beccaria's writing and political activism.

A similar hatred of physical cruelty motivated Bentham's reformism and was a key feature of his utilitarian philosophy, which sought to maximize the greatest happiness for the greatest number. As Judith Shklar (1984, 35) notes, "a moral theory that begins by identifying evil with pain will obviously take cruelty seriously; and indeed, Bentham did hate it." With this hatred of cruelty in mind, we turn to Bentham's model prison, the Panopticon.

Bentham first introduced the idea of the Panopticon in various letters written in 1787. He developed the idea further in a series of postscripts in the following years. Bentham's letters introduce an ideal for any and all houses of inspection, including hospitals, schools, mental asylums, detention houses, and sites of longterm imprisonment. He focuses on how the ideal can be used with regard to crime and punishment. The central principle behind the Panopticon is that "the more constantly the persons to be inspected are under the eyes of the persons who should inspect them, the more perfectly will the purpose of the establishment have been attained" (Bentham 1995, 33–34). If maintaining constant inspection of those housed in the Panopticon is not feasible, they should at least believe themselves to be under constant inspection. The Panopticon is simply an inspection house, in this case a place of imprisonment, architecturally designed and guarded so that the inmates are under near-constant inspection from a central watchtower. They are thus forced to regulate their own behavior, even though (and precisely because) they cannot see the guards who watch over them.

The Panopticon perfectly illustrates Bentham's liberal reformism. Inspection replaces cruelty and torture; reform of the individual replaces vengeance and harsh punishment. This happens through the *"apparent omnipresence* of the inspector ... combined with the extreme facility of his *real presence"* (Bentham 1995, 45). A similar regime of inspection will be established over the Panopticon guards as well, such that "servants and subordinates of every kind will be under the same irresistible controul with respect to the head keeper or inspector, as the prisoners or other persons to be governed are with respect to them" (ibid.). The architecture of the Panopticon facilitates the surveillance of the inmates and the "publicity of official actions," affecting the behavior of inspector and inspected (Schofield 2006, 257). The Panopticon is a perfect reformist prison house in that it eliminates the need for physical cruelty. With "every motion of the limbs, and every muscle of the face exposed to view," there is no room for misbehavior, since all such instances will be instantly spotted and stopped (ibid., 49). Furthermore, since each prisoner is isolated in his individual cell, and prevented from communicating with fellow inmates, the prospects for plotting, fighting, and other forms of misbehavior are eliminated.[8] Through constant inspection, and absent the fear of violent torture, the Panopticon moves "the emphasis from punishment for doing wrong to enhancing incentives for doing right" (Fuller 1987, 717).

The system will further guard against abuse by the public nature of detention. The principle of inspection, which through the guards keeps the prisoners in line, and through the head inspector keeps the guards in line, will be extended to public citizens, who may visit the detention center at any time. Therefore, through publicity and constant inspection, the proper functioning of the institution is ensured, along with the proper treatment of the individuals housed within.

Thus, for Beccaria and Bentham (and Shklar as well), punishment can be done with as little cruelty as possible, through the elimination of corporal punishment and the shift toward humane detention. Shklar even suggests, much like Bentham, that since the criminal "did injure, terrify, and abuse a human being," a liberal regime of punishment actually reduces social cruelty through its limited individual application in particular instances of punishment (Shklar 1989, 37). Beccaria felt similarly, for "society must protect itself ... and this can involve cruelty, for the hatred and the fear of the crime are sufficient motives to apply cruel measures of prevention and/ or correction," provided they are done rationally and without unnecessary cruelty (Baruchello 2004, 307). The liberal approach to punishment thus demands that the infliction of physical cruelty be reduced to the bare minimum necessary for the social goal of deterrence.

The transition to the liberal justice system did not, however, eliminate unnecessary cruelty as its proponents wished. First, there is the telling insensitivity to moral cruelty, or cruelty that harms through psychological and emotional abuse. Bentham and Beccaria, as well as liberal thinkers today, are so focused on physical harm that they are blind to the different regime of cruelty that defines the modern carceral system of punishment. To illustrate this, I turn to the account of an ordinary day in prison, written by an inmate held in a maximum-security facility in Illinois.

The first and defining feature of prison life is its unending boredom. "The dull sameness of prison life, its idleness and boredom." grind prisoners down. "Everything is inconsequential other than when you will be free and how to make the time pass until then. But boredom, time-slowing boredom, interrupted by occasional bursts of fear and anger, is the governing reality of life in prison" (Morris and Rothman 1995, 228). The fear of gang violence is ever-present and life is characterized, in addition to boredom, by a sense of "impending danger." Most maximum-security prisoners are illiterate, many have not even graduated from high school, and, cramped together in cells, fights are not uncommon. Even after offering this description, the author concedes that "it fails to capture the constant unhappiness of prison life and the constant sense of danger ... the relentless, slow-moving routine ... the tension mixed with occasional flashes of fear and rage; it misses the consuming stupidity of living this way" (ibid., 235–36).[9]

Regarding solitary confinement, particularly in maximum-security and supermax prison facilities, prisoners have even stronger characterizations. Says one," It's pretty much like not living. You're locked in a cell twenty-three hours a day .... That's it ... No outside air ... you can't see out the windows" (Rhodes 2004, 29). Another inmate described his first 30 days in solitary confinement with the following words:

> Your lights are on all day ... it really kind of dulls your senses .... It makes you numb. You get easily mad .... It's terrible in here. It think they go out of their way to turn this into hell. (Ibid., 30)

These accounts present a compelling, if necessarily limited, picture of the moral cruelty that characterizes prison life. Obviously, conditions and security in minimum-security facilities are less harsh and less strict than those in medium-security facilities. The "persistent anguish" and humiliation that Shklar used to characterize moral cruelty fittingly describes the dread and monotony of prison life. Beccaria and Bentham did not anticipate or advocate such a system of punishment, but as liberals focused on reducing physical cruelty, they were unable to consider the new set of cruelties that could emerge in a system of incarceration.

Bentham's Panopticon, as a model prison, is a horrifying example of moral cruelty run rampant. It is undoubtedly emblematic of "that modern sensibility which abhors the infliction of pain" and treats punishment as a necessary social evil, to be reduced and humanized as much as possible (Fuller 1987, 717). Yet neither solitary confinement nor long-term detention seem problematic to Bentham's sensibility. For him, if the individuals being detained are held in isolation, this provides unique opportunities for reform. This serves the purpose of prevention, and if the stigma attached to the man who has served his time is not too great, it allows for effective integration back into society. Along with these advantages, imprisonment holds the dual advantages of simplicity and infinite divisibility, such that it can be modified as needed to fit the nature of the crime. Though Bentham is attentive to some of the negative aspects of prison life, including the common "school of vice" charge, he is shockingly insensitive to the potential horrors of long-term solitary confinement, or even the possibility that such punishment might exceed any brutality inflicted through physical torture. For Bentham, such a thought is inconceivable.

In his Panopticon letters, Bentham addresses this concern and dismisses the possibility that solitary confinement might be harmful to the detainee. The fact that the Panopticon, through a feat of architectural design, changes the psychology of its detainees, forcing them to self-police and thus behave properly, does not strike Bentham as in any way cruel. This constant inspection would be expected to produce unending fear, terror, resentment, humiliation, and a twisted, totalitarian form of self-control among the inmates.[10] The features that made liberal reformism such an effective tool in challenging the monarchical forms of corporal punishment render it unable to effectively engage with the new cruelties that emerge in a system of incarceration.[11]

Given how deeply liberal reformers like Bentham and Beccaria abhorred physical cruelty, and how concerned contemporary liberals are with cruelty, why were they so oblivious to the new regime of cruelty that emerges in the system of incarceration? The primary reason is that liberalism is inadequately sensitive to what Shklar terms moral cruelty. The psychological cruelties associated with incarceration were invisible to these liberal reformers, even when, as in the case of Bentham, they had themselves designed an almost unimaginably cruel model prison.[12] Similarly, Beccaria favored imprisonment because he saw in it a "civilized method" of punishment (Maestro 1973, 26). In this sense, Beccaria and Bentham's reformism is a far cry from Nietzsche's ideal of the strong society, which attains "such a *consciousness of power* that it could allow itself the noblest luxury possible to it—letting those who harm it go *unpunished*," and in which physical and moral cruelty could be reduced or eliminated.[13] Punishment, though transformed from a regime of physical cruelty to one of moral cruelty, is still essential for these two thinkers.

Conclusion: Moving Beyond Incarceration

This article has sought to better understand the shift to incarceration as the punishment of choice for liberal democracies in the nineteenth and twentieth centuries. Of particular concern is the growing carceral state in the United States, which with more than two million inmates is unprecedented in US (and human) history. Millions more are on probation, parole, or other forms of community surveillance, and former felons, "barred from public housing by law, discriminated against by private landlords, ineligible for food stamps ... and denied licenses for a wide range of professions ... find themselves locked out of the mainstream society and economy—permanently."[14] I approached this problem by considering the influential reformist works of Cesare Beccaria and Jeremy Bentham, which provide a philosophical and polemical justification for the move toward a liberal justice system, along with the concomitant move toward incarceration as the primary mode of punishment.

In examining the works of these liberal reformers, we can see how the attempt to eliminate physical cruelty in punishment produced a new, troubling form of moral cruelty that characterizes incarceration and the liberal justice system more broadly. Both Beccaria and Bentham campaign for mild, proportional punishments, equality before the law, and the elimination of torture and capital punishment, motivated by a concern for the protection of individual rights and the elimination of (physical) cruelty. At the same time, their campaign includes a demand for a system of punishment that is regular, universal, inescapable, defined through surveillance, and is utterly insensitive to the cruelties of this new economy of punishment. These reformers thus helped to enact a system of punishment that is often quite cruel, albeit in a different manner than before. My hope is that by gaining a better understanding of how we got here, we will be better equipped to critique and challenge the carceral state, first by targeting its remarkable expansion in the past few decades, and then by rethinking the carceral approach to punishment more broadly.

In Peter Moskos's provocative op-ed, "In Lieu of Prison, Bring Back the Lash," he asks, "Is there a third way, something better than both flogging and prison?" I will conclude by exploring the possibility of a "third way," such that we might begin to slowly unravel the practices, institutions, and discourses that comprise the carceral state. What concrete steps might we take? As Marie Gottschalk (2006, 255–257) argues, criminologists, lawyers, and other "experts" will not undo the carceral state themselves. "The public has to be mobilized and organized to undo the carceral state." One way this can happen is for scholars, journalists, and activists to continue to make "prisons, jails, and the lives they mark more visible to the wider society." Many of the works cited here are important interventions in rethinking the carceral state. In terms of specific policy mobilizations, undoing the criminalization of nonviolent drug activity and rethinking the harsh and costly "three strikes" laws are areas of intervention at the state and national levels. One concern for all reformist efforts is to avoid "striking compromises that leave the carceral state slightly leaner and less mean but more entrenched" (ibid., 257).

What philosophical basis is there for a new, post-carceral approach to punishment? An important resource is the work of Friedrich Nietzsche.[15] Judith Shklar (1984, 37) articulated the distinction between moral and physical cruelty, and we can see in Nietzsche a lifelong attention to the "deliberate and persistent humiliation" found in moral cruelty. For Nietzsche, the Christian era produced feelings of pity and guilt on the part of the individual, which, when internalized, "transform physical cruelty into the moral tormenting of other people" (ibid., 41). Nietzsche found the impulse of moral judgment and condemnation to be terribly cruel, to the point that physical cruelty would even be preferable. It is not sensible to return to physical cruelty, but Nietzsche provides helpful tools for exploring a turn to a post-carceral, less punitive approach to punishment.

Of course, we should retain the liberal reformist abhorrence of physical cruelty. This impulse was and remains a crucial tool in combating torture and physical abuse, whether de facto or de jure, within the penal system. We should also keep Bentham's utilitarian impulse regarding punishment. Since punishment involves hurting the one who is punished, it ought to be eliminated or reduced to a minimum in all circumstances. As Bentham (2009, 52) notes, punishment is an evil inflicted out of "the direct intention of another." Consistent with a large body of literature, I argue that the moral and psychological cruelty of incarceration is distinct from, but just as objectionable as, the physical cruelty of flogging and other forms of corporal punishment.

What can Nietzsche offer to inspire future research? He articulates the dangerous connections between moral condemnation and moral cruelty. As long as the project of punishment is harsh and built around the moral guilt of those being punished, it will involve insensitivity to the moral cruelties that necessarily come with locking a human in a cage. "Punishment is supposed to possess the value of awakening the *feeling of guilt* in the guilty one." This, however, rarely works, for generally speaking, punishment makes men hard and cold; it concentrates, it sharpens the feeling of alienation; it strengthens the power of resistance. If punishment destroys the vital energy and brings about a miserable prostration and self-abasement, such a result is certainly even less pleasant than the usual effects of punishment. (Nietzsche 1968, 517)

Nietzsche is not simply speaking in generalities. Many inmates say very similar things. As one prisoner told Lorna Rhodes (2004, 35), "I'm walking around here like a caged animal—it makes you feel so inadequate, so inferior, so *less than*." Most inmates convey a palpable sense of feeling *trapped*—cold, dull, and cut off from the outside world. Another prisoner described solitary confinement as "an environment where you can't talk to anybody else, you can't have any contact ... unless you yell or scream." Prison officers have admitted that "there's probably few more negative places in this world" than the Panoptic supermax or control prison (ibid., 31).

Attentive to the moral cruelties of modern punishment, Nietzsche predicts the resistance they engender. His insight into Panoptic forms of punishment is that rather than reform and feelings of guilt, they provoke rage, alienation, and torment. This is because "the sight of the judicial and executive procedures prevents the criminal from considering his deed ... reprehensible: for he sees exactly the same kind of actions practiced in the service of justice and ... with a good conscience." Nietzsche summarizes this as "the whole cunning and underhand art of police and prosecution, plus robbery, violence, defamation, imprisonment, torture, murder," all of which are useful to the law and the administration of justice, but are prohibited and punished when utilized by the criminal (Nietzsche 1968, 518). He overstates the case, but the important element of truth here is that the criminal may very well regret his act, particularly if it was a violent one. Yet he is very unlikely (and it is usually a "he") to come to believe, after his time in prison, that it is a good institution, that it serves a social good to keep people in such a place for months and years on end. The prisoner is more likely to come to believe, with the officer, that there are probably few worse places on earth.

What about incarceration and practical alternatives to detention? Angela Davis suggests that the carceral state is so difficult to dislodge because it is composed of a "set of symbiotic relationships among correctional communities, transnational corporations, media conglomerates, guards' unions, and legislative and court agendas." To move in a post-carceral direction, we must get beyond "prisonlike substitutes for the prison," such as house arrest (Davis 2003, 107; 2005). Instead, we need a strategy that works at multiple levels, reducing the need for incarceration and responding to crime in a different manner. This would include several positive steps, such as "demilitarization of schools, revitalization of education at all levels, a health system that provides free physical and mental care to all, and a justice system based on reparation and reconciliation rather than retribution and vengeance" (Davis 2003, 107). Responses to criminal behavior would include drug treatment programs, for the affluent and poor alike, and the decriminalization and de-policing of drug and other nonviolent activity that does not merit detention as a response. In addition, restorative justice and reparation have the potential to break the seemingly untouchable link between crime and harsh punishment.[16]

Challenging the carceral state has two key aspects. The first is reformist, policy focused, and defined through the need to undo the destructive effects of nearly a half-century of the "war on crime" and the "war on drugs." These two "wars," with their attendant policies and discourses, have largely defined the way we think and act regarding crime and punishment. In a material sense, the policies defining these two "wars" are largely responsible for the massive boom in incarceration since the 1970s and 1980s. Reversing these destructive policies is the first step in challenging the US carceral state. The second aspect is distinct from the activism and legislative campaigns called for in the first step. It entails a rethinking of the discourses that prop up and are interwoven with the carceral state. The goal, as Marie Gottschalk has noted, is not to construct a slightly nicer carceral state, with shorter sentences, but to fundamentally rethink and rebuild our sociopolitical approach to crime and punishment.

In my view, it would be a terrible mistake to entirely dispense with the liberal justice system. The reforms enacted by Beccaria, Bentham, and others played a critical role in challenging and ultimately overthrowing the penal systems of feudal monarchy. They remain an essential resource that reminds us of the horrors of a system of punishment that is unaccountable, brutal, arbitrary, defined by public spectacle and terror, and able to crush the individual without recourse. Liberal reformers are correct when they reject the cruel and (always) unnecessary infliction of torture and capital punishment. They are right to insist on protections for the individual. The next move is to push toward a more participatory, democratic, and community-based system of dealing with crime and punishment, one that foregoes the cruelties of torture and mass incarceration, and that replaces these forms of punishment, whenever possible, with drug treatment, reparation, restoration, and rehabilitation, as Davis suggests. Such an approach offers two strengths: it allows us to retain the key insights of the liberal justice tradition (abolition of physical cruelty, protection of the individual from arbitrary state power) while transcending its more troubling features and insisting that the system of mass incarceration inscribes new cruelties into the penal system, which may be just as harmful to the individuals involved as the system of sovereign monarchical power they replaced. Going beyond detention and deterrence, we can move toward community solutions built on reconciliation between parties, reparation for the harmed, and rehabilitation for the criminals.

Acknowledgments: I would like to thank Daniel Brunstetter and Kevin Olson for their insightful comments and criticisms throughout the writing process and Keith Topper for his invaluable mentoring. An earlier version of this article was presented at the Western Political Science Association Annual Conference (2013) and I am very grateful for the helpful suggestions and conversations with fellow panelists and audience members. Final thanks go to Professors Etienne Balibar, Shawn Rosenberg, Annette Schlichter, and Cecelia Lynch, and of course to Carole Pateman for keeping the dream of participatory democracy alive and well in the academy.

Notes

1. For official government figures, see the Bureau of Justice Statistics report, at *www.bjs.gov/content/pub/pdf/cpus12.pdf.* The year 2012 marked the fourth straight year in which the national prison population declined. It is nevertheless alarming that roughly 3.2 percent of US adults are either incarcerated or under other forms of surveillance, "a rate of state supervision that is unprecedented in U.S. History" (Gottschalk 2006, 1–2). Moreover, the corollary of the carceral state is that "once a person is labeled a felon, he or she is ushered into a parallel universe in which discrimination, stigma, and exclusion are perfectly legal, and privileges of citizenship such as voting and jury service are off-limits" (Alexander 2010, 92). Although I do not specifically address the racialized element of the US criminal justice system, it is central to understanding how it functions. A substantial and growing body of literature exists that demonstrates the particularly destructive effects of the carceral state on urban African Americans and other minorities. See also Tonry (1995). For general reference, see Currie (1998) and Wright (1973). Gerstle (2001) offers a thoughtful history of the role of racial thinking in the American civic identity.

2. For instance, the penal code of 1810 in France prescribed prison as the primary form of punishment, which was more severe than fines but less so than death. During most of the seventeenth and eighteenth centuries, however, "imprisonment—and on this point many countries were in the same situation as France—had only a limited and marginal position in the system of penalties" (Foucault 1995, 114–118, and, more generally, Part Two, Chapter 2).

3. Michael Ignatieff (1978) explores this question in A *Just Measure of Pain,* which focuses primarily on English prison reformers and the contestation over implementing the reformer's strict vision of a disciplined, well-run prison built around solitary confinement and moral reform of the prisoner. The history and argument presented by Ignatieff relates to, but is distinct from, my argument.

4. For a broad perspective on the development of modern sensibilities, see Elias (1939/1994). For more on how our modern sensibility to cruelty and punishment evolved and affected institutions of punishment, see Spierenburg (1984).

5. See Benjamin Barber's (1984, 151) rough definition of strong democracy, in which "active citizens govern themselves directly … not necessarily at every level and in every instance, but frequently enough and in particular when basic policies are being decided and when significant power is deployed." For an argument that mass incarceration is inconsistent with core American values, see Albert W. Dzur (2012).

6. There are obvious resonances between this claim and Foucault's ideas. In particular, his diagnosis of the rise of disciplinary power as a form of power that produces docile subjects through surveillance and their internalized self-policing is relevant to my focus on liberal penal reform. The emergence of disciplinary power in the late eighteenth and early nineteenth century coincides with the birth of the prison as a disciplinary institution. I cannot deal directly with Foucault in this article, but his spirit animates it throughout. See, for instance, Michel Foucault (1980, 1995, 1999). For a Foucauldian look at the history of the US penal system, see also Thomas Dumm's excellent *Democracy and Punishment* (1987). For alternative perspectives, see Pieter Spierenburg (1984) and Georg Rusche and Otto Kirchheimer (2003).

7. Indeed, Shklar contends that if one "puts moral cruelty first … one can readily adopt every one of Machiavelli's cruel maxims." I explore the distinctions between physical and moral cruelty below, but cannot critique Shklar's (1984, 42) unfair reading of Machiavelli. See also Rorty (1998).

8. Writing before the era of the modern prison, Bentham did not have a sense of the ingenuity that would emerge in the effort to communicate with fellow inmates.

9. For an account that describes in detail those brief moments of violence, rage, and abuse, both among prisoners and at the hands of prison guards, see Santos (2006).

10. It could be argued that the supermax prison, which involves solitary confinement for 23 hours a day and uninterrupted surveillance, is the modern incarnation of Bentham's Panopticon. See Rhodes (2004). With regard to supermax incarceration, a corrections officer told Rhodes, "There's probably very few more negative places in this world. If nothing happened it was a great day." See, in particular, Chapter 1 for further connections between maximum-security prisons and Bentham's Panopticon.

11. The moral cruelties of the prison system engender a wide range of practices of resistance on the part of inmates, from violence directed at guards to illicit drug trafficking. An innovative form of resistance involves the use of urine and feces as a projectile directed at corrections officers. See Rhodes, Chapter 1. Such resistance may intensify as prisons increasingly become spaces for housing dangerous populations and abandon any pretense of rehabilitation. See Feeley and Simon (1992).

12. Shklar (1984, 36) notes that Bentham's separate project for the design of a poorhouse was "a model of moral cruelty," in which physical abuse would be eliminated, but the life of the poor within would be "prescribe[d] in the most minute detail."

13. One concern with Nietzsche, which Shklar recognizes, is that he is sensitive to moral cruelty to the point that he often dismisses concern for physical cruelty altogether. See Nietzsche (1968, 508). For additional thoughts on judgment, moral responsibility, and retribution, see several chapters in Connolly (1999).

14. See Alexander (2010, 92). who estimates that there are currently 5.1 million Americans on probation and parole.

15. Future work would do well to return to Montaigne. His sensitivity to different forms of cruelty and his willingness to see "barbarity" in our own domestic practices could help to provide a foundation for a post-carceral and post-corporal approach to punishment.

16. Davis (2003, 112) insists on recognizing that "punishment does not follow from crime in the neat and logical sequence offered by discourses that insist on the justice of punishment." Indeed, there is no reason why we cannot respond to crime, even when violent, in a radically different manner. Thus, Davis insists upon prying apart the snug connection between crime and punishment advocated by Beccaria, Bentham, and later, Hegel.

References

Alexander, Michelle 2010. *The New Jim Crow*. New York: The New Press.

Barber, Benjamin 1984. *Strong Democracy*. Berkeley: University of California Press.

Baruchello, Giorgio 2004. "Cesare Beccaria and the Cruelty of Liberalism: An Essay on Liberalism of Fear and Its Limits." *Philosophy & Social Criticism* 30(3): 303–13.

Beccaria, Cesare 1764/1986. *On Crimes and Punishments*. Indianapolis: Hackett Publishing Company.

Bentham, Jeremy. 1995. *The Panopticon Writings*. New York: Verso.

———. 2009. *The Rationale of Punishment*. Amherst, NY: Prometheus Books.

Connolly, William E. 1999. *Why I Am Not a Secularist*. Minneapolis: University of Minnesota Press.

Currie, Elliott 1998. *Crime and Punishment in America*. New York: Metropolitan Books.

Davis, Angela Y. 2003. *Are Prisons Obsolete?* New York: Seven Stories Press.

———. 2005. *Abolition Democracy*. New York: Seven Stories Press.

Dumm, Thomas L. 1987. *Democracy and Punishment*. Madison: University of Wisconsin Press.

Dzur, Albert 2012. *Punishment, Participatory Democracy, and the Jury*. New York: Oxford University Press.

Elias, Norbert 1939/1994. *The Civilizing Process*. Malden, MA: Blackwell.

Feeley, Malcolm M. and Jonathan Simon 1992. "The New Penology: Notes on the Emerging Strategy of Corrections and Its Implications." *Criminology* 30(4): 449–74.

Foucault, Michel 1980. *Power/Knowledge*. New York: Pantheon Books.

———. 1995. *Discipline and Punish*. New York: Vintage Books.

———. 1999. *Abnormal*. New York: Picador.

Fuller, Timothy 1987. "Jeremy Bentham and James Mill." In *History of Political Philosophy,* edited by Leo Strauss and Joseph Cropsey, 732–60. Chicago: The University of Chicago Press.

Gerstle, Gary 2001. *American Crucible: Race and Nation in the Twentieth Century*. Princeton: Princeton University Press.

Glaze, Lauren E. and Erinn J. Herberman 2013. "Correctional Populations in the United States, 2012." *Bureau of Justice Statistics*.

Gottschalk, Marie 2006. *The Prison and the Gallows*. New York: Cambridge University Press.

Ignatieff, Michael 1978. *A Just Measure of Pain*. New York: Pantheon Books.

Maestro, Marcello 1973. *Cesare Beccaria and the Origins of Penal Reform*. Philadelphia: Temple University Press.

Morris, Norval and David J. Rothman (eds.) 1995. *The Oxford History of the Prison*. New York: Oxford University Press.

Moskos, Peter 2011. "In Lieu of Prison, Bring Back the Lash." *Washington Post,* June 10.

Nietzsche, Friedrich 1968. *Basic Writings of Nietzsche*. New York: The Modern Library.

Rhodes, Lorna A. 2004. *Total Confinement*. Los Angeles: University of California Press.

Rorty, Richard 1998. *Achieving Our Country*. Cambridge, MA: Harvard University Press.

Rusche, Georg and Otto Kirchheimer 2003. *Punishment and Social Structure*. New Brunswick: Transaction Publishers.

Santos, Michael 2006. *Inside: Life Behind Bars in America*. New York: St. Martin's Griffin.

Schofield, Philip 2006. *Utility and Democracy: The Political Thought of Jeremy Bentham*. New York: Oxford University Press.

Shklar, Judith N. 1984. *Ordinary Vices*. Cambridge, MA: The Belknap Press of Harvard University Press.

————. 1989. "The Liberalism of Fear." In *Liberalism and the Moral Life,* edited by Nancy Rosenbaum, 21–38. Cambridge, MA: Harvard University Press.

Spierenburg, Pieter 1984. *The Spectacle of Suffering*. New York: Cambridge University Press.

Tonry, Michael 1995. *Malign Neglect*. New York: Oxford University Press.

Wright, Erik Olin 1973. *The Politics of Punishment*. New York: Harper Colophon Books.

"Putting Cruelty First": Liberal Penal Reform and the Rise of the Carceral State Jason Vick

Why are so many people in prison today? How do we make sense, more generally, of the fact that all the world's liberal democracies rely on incarceration as an essential tool of punishment? Specifically, why is it that the discourses and practices surrounding punishment in today's liberal democracies consider torture and other forms of physical abuse to be unacceptably cruel, while long-term incarceration is considered unproblematic? Vick approaches this problem through a consideration of the liberal reformism of Cesare Beccaria and Jeremy Bentham, which helped to pave the way for a transition from irregular, and usually corporal, punishment to the regular, systematic liberal justice system that eschews corporal punishment but relies heavily on incarceration. To develop this argument, the author engages with the literature that focuses on the role of cruelty within liberalism, in particular the work of Judith Shklar. By drawing on Shklar's distinction between physical cruelty (which liberals abhor) and moral-psychological cruelty (about which liberals are ambivalent), the author is able to better illuminate how humane reformists such as Beccaria and Bentham could both oppose corporal punishment and favor incarceration as a satisfactory liberal solution to the issue of punishment that minimizes (physical) cruelty.

Keywords: Beccaria, Bentham, penal reform, liberalism, cruelty, incarceration, Shklar, Nietzsche

CHAPTER THIRTEEN

Prison Systems and Corrections

Once an individual is charged, adjudicated, and convicted of a crime, the issue of what to do with them emerges as an issue of paramount concern. As discussed in previous chapters, the U.S. has struggled to develop a system of punishment consistent with the ideals of democracy, equality, and humaneness, particularly with respect to the care and safety of the individual once the system of due process has run its course. The key to this evolutionary process pertains to the question of how to develop a system designed to rehabilitate the individual while providing a framework also for punishment for crimes committed against society, particularly in cases of extreme violent crime.

According to Owen et.al. (2015), corrections in the U.S. is defined as the systematic organized effort by society to punish offenders, protect the public, and change an offender's behavior.[1] These efforts, they argue, are realized through programs, services, and facilities that deal with the offender before and after conviction. The philosophy grounding this initiative is to achieve specific goals of punishment including but not exclusive to retribution, deterrence, incapacitation, rehabilitation, (re)integration, and restitution.[2] For the most part, the U.S. has reached some of these goals by establishing, at least philosophically, the framework for a system based on the tenets promised in the utilitarian mandate. This is to rehabilitate individuals under the belief that most offenders are individuals who lost their way. These individuals, therefore, can be changed and motivated to become contributing members of society once the punishment for the crime is complete. The issue here, as discussed in chapter one, is that the criminal justice system works as a system in theory, but the reality is oftentimes something quite different.

---

1   S. S. Owen, H. F. Fradella, T. W. Burke, and J. W. Joplin, *Foundations of Criminal Justice*, 2nd edition (New York, NY: Oxford University Press, 2015).

2   S. S. Owen et al., *Foundations of Criminal Justice*, 2nd edition, 2015.

For example, the U.S. has evolved from the mandate of rehabilitation as the theoretical basis shaping the system of corrections in America, to a system of punitive justice. To be clear, much of the argument presented here is purely antidotal in nature. However, when examining the reality of life in a variety of state and federal prisons in the U.S., it is clear that the extent to which inmates are left to their own devices, and where predatory criminal behavior and gang activity exists, is the extent to which a general gladiatorial atmosphere is pervasive to modern prison culture. In this respect, incarceration today is more punitive than rehabilitative in nature.

Statistics also indicate that the number of inmates in relationship to race and social class has increased significantly, particularly for individuals charged with drug-related offenses since the 1980s.[3] This evolutionary process has created a system of overcrowding, which gives rise to greater competition between inmates, as well as an atmosphere of violence and predatory behavior. At issue then is the question of how the move from rehabilitation to punitive justice in America serves as a deterrence to crime, and at what point in time do we see the reemergence of Inquisition-style polices and the spectacle of punishment as the hallmark of a system that appears to have lost its way.

---

3   U.S. Bureau of Justice Statistics, *Office of Justice Programs*, 2016, https://www.bjs.gov/index.cfm?ty=tp&tid=11.

A Social History of Punishment and Prisons

By Michael Welch

Chapter Outline

- Introduction
- Emergence of formal and legal punishment
- Ancient Greece
- Ancient Rome
- The Middle Ages
- The sixteenth and seventeenth centuries
- The Enlightenment and its enduring impact on corrections
- Conclusion
- Summary
- Review questions
- Recommended readings

> *Those who do not remember the past, are condemned to repeat it.*
>
> (George Santayana)

Learning Objectives

After studying this chapter, you should be able to answer the following questions:

1. What were the early developments in punishment and corrections?

2. What were the popular forms of punishment in ancient Greece, ancient Rome, the Middle Ages, the sixteenth and seventeenth centuries, and the Enlightenment?

3. How did politics, economics, religion, and technology shape punishment throughout history?

4. How did Cesare Beccaria, Jeremy Bentham, and John Howard contribute to penal reform?

> On 2 March 1757 Damiens the regicide was condemned to 'make the *amende honorable* before the main door of the Church of Paris', where he was able to be 'taken and conveyed in a cart, wearing nothing but a shirt, holding a torch of burning wax weighing two pounds'; then, 'in the said cart, to the palace de Greve, where, on a scaffold that will be erected there, the flesh will be torn from his breasts, arms, thighs and calves with red-hot pincers, his right hand, holding the knife with which he committed the said parricide, burnt with sulphur, and, on those places where the flesh will be torn away, poured molten lead, boiling oil, burning resin, wax and sulphur melted together and then his body drawn and quartered by four horses and his limbs and body consumed by fire, reduced to ashes and his ashes thrown to the winds.'
>
> (*Pièces Originales*, 1757: 372–4)

> 'Finally, he was quartered', recounts the *Gazette d'Amsterdam* of 1 April 1757. 'This last operation was very long, because the horses used were not accustomed to drawing; consequently, instead of four, six were needed; and when that did not suffice, they were forced, in order to cut off the wretch's thighs, to sever the sinews and hack the joints.'
>
> (Foucault, 1977: 3)

Introduction

Exploring the social evolution of punishment enhances our understanding of contemporary corrections. Because punishment—in many forms, not just imprisonment –has remained an integral part of the social order throughout time, much of contemporary corrections cannot be understood apart from its history. This chapter traces the history of punishment and corrections from the emergence of formal and legal punishment, through ancient Greece and Rome, the Middle Ages, the sixteenth and seventeenth centuries, and the Enlightenment. This chapter also describes with considerable detail various forms of punishment and corrections in their historical contexts. However, because of the importance of surpassing mere description, the primary emphasis is on the analysis of penalties and prisons, especially in light of the social forces that shape them—politics, economics, religion, and technology.

Historically, political structures have determined how different social classes are treated by the criminal justice system. Economics also has played a vital role in punishment and corrections, as evidenced by the practices of monetary fines and confiscation of property, as well as the economic tendency to exploit cheap labor (through penal slavery, indentured servitude, prison industries, etc.). Religion, as a social force, has also had considerable impact on the rationale and justification for punishment and corrections, particularly in light of the belief that offenders ought to be morally reformed or corrected. Finally, technology has remained an important social influence. Throughout history, various methods of punishment have emerged from the application of science –the guillotine, the electric chair, and sundry other torture devices. Although these social forces may seem to be distinct, they overlap considerably. Correctional programs emphasizing *both* work and prayer, for instance, demonstrate the interplay between religious and economic forces. Similarly, technology commonly merges with political forces, producing mechanisms designed to exert power and control over citizens through state-of-the-art surveillance technology.

Emergence of Formal and Legal Punishment

Exploring the various social forces that shape punishment and corrections requires understanding the ideas, rationales, and circumstances from which those forces derive. Punishment is as old as civilization itself. From the time people began living together as a society, there existed some form of social control intended to curb undesirable conduct. The rationale behind such control, or punishment, reveals the prevailing social forces.

> Doctrines about the desirability and objectives of punishment have been closely related to theories of crime and criminal responsibility. In primitive times with their theory of diabolical possession, the conventional notion of punishment was either to exorcise the devil or to exile or execute the wrongdoer. In part, this was to protect the community against further outrages by the dangerous offender, but the major purpose was to *placate the gods*.
>
> In the next stage of the doctrine of punishment more stress was laid upon *social revenge*. Crime was now considered the willful act of a free moral agent. Society, outraged at this act of voluntary perversity, indignantly retaliated. Many forms of crime were later identified with sin and were believed to offer a challenge to God and orthodox religion.
>
> (Barnes and Teeters, 1946: 391)

Our historical discussion of punishment begins at the point when legal codes were first established. The development of language and writing skills led to the formalization of legal codes, which subsequently

Figure 13.1 Castle window —indoor shot of a trellised historic window at Wertheim Castle in Southern Germany where light is falling.

© iStockphoto.com

served as the official guidelines of society. The Code of Hammurabi, most popularly known by the phrase 'an eye for an eye, and a tooth for a tooth,' was among the first written legal codes, dating back to 1750 BC in Babylon. The basis for punishment, according to the Code of Hammurabi, was the concept *lex talionis*, meaning 'the law of retaliation,' which refers to vengeance. In most cases, the penalties were harsh, usually in the form of whipping, mutilation, and forced labor. Moreover, the injured parties themselves sometimes carried out the punishment. Hence, from the beginning, the rationale for legally sanctioned punishment was retribution, or getting even. The principle of *lex talionis* remained popular throughout early civilization. It is found in the ancient Sumerian codes *Manama Dharma Astra* of India, the *Hermes Trismegitus* of Egypt, as well as the Mosaic Code.

Beheading, as a form of retribution, is traced to pre-Christian times and symbolizes the individual urge to avenge a crime. However, the precise rationale underlying beheading is subject to debate. One theory suggests that beheading was a sacrificial act to placate the gods, whereas other explanations suggest that beheading was an *apotropaic act*, that is, one that served to ward off evil. Furthermore, under some circumstances, beheading was considered an honorable death.

> Both the sword and the axe are significant sacred symbols. The axe and hammer especially were used by the Greek gods, and the sword was the symbol of valor in battle at a time when fighting was the most important social occupation that

a young Greek or Roman could engage in. Thus to die in battle, usually by the sword or axe, was a most honorable death: in fact, the best way to go. The use of the tool of beheading is thus explained, as is the consistently high social status of those beheaded, since these people were the champions of battle and war throughout the ages.

(Newman, 1978: 32–3)

Although vengeance stems primarily from an individual urge to avenge a crime, it is also rooted in a strong social pressure to fulfill a tradition. When those individual and societal forces merge, a brutal type of retribution is formed—collective punishment, such as lynching, the firing squad, and the Halifax gibbet: an ancient contraption similar to the guillotine that was operated by citizens. An interesting feature of collective punishment is that it permits individuals to participate in the execution while avoiding direct responsibility for the death.

Among the oldest forms of collective punishment is stoning to death, a form of retribution in which members of the community enthusiastically contribute to the execution. The stone itself, like the sword and axe, had sacred meaning since it was probably humankind's first weapon. Moreover, in early societies, meteoric stones were believed to be sent to Earth from the gods (Newman, 1978). Some scholars have suggested that stoning also had a sacrificial function; others have noted that stoning had a cleansing effect on the community. The Greeks, for instance, preferred stoning offenders because it removed criminal 'pollution' from their society (Strom, 1942).

The fundamental notion of *lex talionis* stood as the principle behind various forms of retribution. That law of revenge served as the legal rationale for mutilation whereby the penalty set out to duplicate the injury inflicted. Accordingly, the blinding of a victim was punishable by blinding the perpetrator. Compounding matters, there was a preventive rationale for the practice of mutilation. While cutting off the hand of a thief certainly imposed a type of stigma (i.e. mark of social disgrace), it also was intended to prevent the offender from stealing again. Likewise, spies had their eyes gouged out, perjurers had their tongues torn out, and in ancient Assyria and Egypt, rapists were punished by castration (Barnes and Teeters, 1946: 408).

Throughout history, various forms of corporal punishment, torture, and execution were combined—as was the case with Damiens (described at the beginning of the chapter). In his book *The Lords of the Scaffold*, Geoffrey Abbott presents a brutal display of punishment taking place in 1746 in London:

After he had hung six minutes, he was cut down and, having life in him, as he lay on the block to be quartered, the executioner gave him several blows to the breast, which not having the effect designed, he immediately cut his throat; after which he took off his head, then ripped him open and took out his bowels and heart and threw them in a fire which consumed them. Then he slashed his four quarters and put them with the head into a coffin, and they were carried to the new gaol at Southwark, and on 2 August the head was put on Temple Bar and his body and limbs suffered to be buried.

(Abbott, 1991: 51–2)

Box 13.1   Comparative Corrections

Controversy over Amputation in Saudi Arabia

The 1987 United Nations Convention Against Torture prohibits various forms of corporal punishment, including torture and the amputation of limbs. That international treaty has 129 signatory countries that have agreed to report periodically on the measures they have taken to comply with the Convention's requirements. In 2002, diplomats from Saudi Arabia clashed with the United Nations Committee Against Torture over whether the amputation of limbs and flogging violate the international treaty. The UN committee ordered the Saudis to cease such forms of corporal punishment but Saudi delegates angrily defied the order, arguing that the committee had no jurisdiction over Shariah, the Islamic legal code derived from the Koran. Sharia law allows amputations for theft, and floggings for certain sexual offenses and drinking alcohol. Although those forms of punishment are banned by the committee mandate, other provisions of Sharia do not apply to the international treaty, such as executing murderers, drug dealers, and rapists. Taking exception to the UN committee, Turki alMadi, a Saudi diplomat, said: 'This law has existed for 1,400 years. And the committee wants to change it. I am sorry, you cannot' (Olson, 2002: A5). On behalf of the committee, Peter Thomas Burns, a Canadian law professor, stated: 'The committee itself had no doubt that flogging in almost any case constitutes torture. And amputation of limbs, in every case, would constitute torture under our definitions' (Olson, 2002: A5). Still, Saudi Arabia maintains that floggings, amputations, and other corporal punishments are not torture. A Saudi delegate reasoned: 'You can't say cutting off a hand is so severe. It harms only the criminal who harms society. Sharia protects society, not the criminal' (Olson, 2002: A5).

Ancient Greece

Greek philosophers, reacting against the rationale of retribution as a basis of punishment, proposed instead that the offender be reformed. Plato believed that following imprisonment, the offender should emerge 'a better man, or failing that, less of a wretch,' thus affirming the notion of reform

(Johnson, 1987: 3, 1984). In many ways the rationale of reform was considered rather progressive. However, due to what critics would call a 'class bias' in punishment, it was not considered progressive enough. In ancient Greece, offenders who were citizens of the Greek city-states would customarily face only monetary fines. Slaves who were convicted of crimes, on the other hand, were severely punished –often by whipping.

Other notable punishments passed on to ancient Greeks from earlier days included stoning, burning alive, strangling, banishing, branding, and penal slavery. Crucifying, gibbeting (exposing to public scorn), and garroting (strangling with an iron collar), however, originated in ancient Greece, along with breaking on the wheel. The wheel not only is a symbol of the sun in both Greek and Roman mythology, but along with the circle was believed to ward off evil. Hence, breaking on the wheel, like most other ancient punishments, possessed sacred meaning. Sometimes the execution took place without a wheel. 'The culprit was laid out on a flat board, or sometimes a crosspiece, and pegged to it with irons. The executioner then systematically broke all the major bones of the wretched criminal with sharp blows from an iron bar' (Newman, 1978: 37).

Class bias, with different punishments employed for different classes of people, was evident in the use of poisoning, which emerged as an elitist form of capital punishment. Socrates remains one of the most famous figures to be executed in that manner. Banishment (or ostracism), usually for a period of ten years, also was considered an elitist type of punishment. It is interesting to note that the decision to banish an offender derived from a vote of the citizens (Wines, 1971 [1895]). In some ways, banishment served as a symbolic death since the offender was out of sight and out of mind. Imprisonment was used by the ancient Greeks only to detain those awaiting trial or execution and to confine those who failed to pay their fines (Sellin, 1976).

Ancient Rome

Unlike the ancient Greeks, the ancient Romans used imprisonment for purposes beyond detention— incarceration itself was intended to punish lawbreakers. Yet the structures used for incarceration were essentially makeshift: heavy cages, basements of public buildings, and stone quarries. Although such structures were not originally intended for the purpose of imprisonment, the security they offered made them suitable for close confinement (Mattick, 1974; Johnston, 1973).

One of the most notable structures was the Mamertime prison, established about 64 BC by Ancus Maritus. Located under the Cloaca Maxima, the Mamertime prison was a primitive sewer of Rome best known for its vast system of dungeons (Johnston, 1973; American Correctional Association (ACA), 1983; Peck, 1922). Prisoners were confined to cages within dark and stench-ridden sewers. By using the sewer as a makeshift prison, Romans symbolically equated human waste, contamination, and infection with crime and deviance. 'It is as if the Fathers of Rome saw the threats of public health posed by human waste and by human deviance as equivalent, and opted to expel both from the sight and consciousness of the Roman citizenry' (Johnson, 1987: 7). To be discussed in Chapter 3, the rise of the penitentiary in America was inspired by similar environmental theories of crime, assuming that some features of social life were morally corrupting (Rothman, 1971). Because of the 'out of sight, out of mind' quality of imprisonment, it is often viewed as another version of banishment.

Economic and labor motifs of punishment also were evident in Roman times. Forced labor on public works is among the more readily documented practices; other economically driven punishments included the payment of fines and the forfeiture of property and possessions. Slaves, viewed as property as well as sources of forced labor, suffered various forms of punishment. A primary purpose of punishing slaves was to discipline them. Whipping, mutilation, branding, and confinement to stocks and furcas (V-shaped yokes designed to be worn around the neck, forcing the arms to remain stretched out) were common penal practices (Newman, 1978). Furthermore, some slaves were confined to ergastulums, primitive types of prisons designed to discipline offenders by subjecting them to hard labor while being chained to workbenches (Sellin, 1976).

Occasionally, citizens were punished by being formally pronounced slaves, thereby losing their liberty and being forced to spend their lives in penal servitude. Because such punishment was regarded as 'civil death,' the offenders' property was confiscated and their wives declared widows, eligible to remarry (Sutherland *et al.*, 1992). Disobedient or cowardly soldiers were publicly humiliated, whipped, demoted, and fined. For severe infractions, soldiers were subject to stoning and beheading. 'In the case of mass conduct, such as may occur in battle, decimation was used: i.e., every tenth man was executed. There was one occasion, however, when 370 deserters from Hannibal were recaptured. They were all flogged and thrown from the Tarpenian Rock, the usual punishment for traitors' (Newman, 1978; 70). Like the ancient Greeks before them, ancient Romans relied on numerous forms of torture and execution—breaking on the wheel, burying alive, drowning, burning, as well as branding criminals on their foreheads (Barnes and Teeters, 1946; Newman, 1978).

The most notable documents of legal punishment during this period were the Bergundian Code and the Justinian Code. The Bergundian Code (c. AD 500) categorized types of punishment according to social class (e.g. nobles, middle classes, and lower classes). The Justinian Code, written by Emperor Justinian I of Rome in AD 529, evolved from the Law of the Twelve Tables, the earliest code of Roman Law, which had been in existence for a thousand years. The Justinian Code formalized punishment with an unusual degree of precision and uniformity insofar as crimes were listed beside their assigned penalty. In many ways, the Justinian Code reflected an attempt to make the punishment fit the crime. But it was not without its administrative headaches; because of the ambitious and lengthy inventory of crimes, enforcement was difficult. Even after the fall of the Roman Empire (AD 476), remnants of the Justinian Code continued to serve as a foundation for most of the legal codes that developed later in the Western world.

The Middle Ages

The Middle Ages refers to the period of Western European history beginning with the fall of the Roman Empire in the fifth century and ending with the emergence of the Renaissance in the fifteenth century. With the dissolution of the Roman Empire, commerce declined and the social order consequently underwent serious problems. During that era, the Roman Catholic Church prevailed as a dominant social force exerting influence over all the major institutions. Similarly, feudalism emerged as the prevailing political economy whereby service was exchanged for land, protection, and justice. The social arrangement was hierarchical. At the top of the hierarchy was the Holy Roman Emperor: below him were kings and princes, then warriors and knights, with peasants occupying the bottom strata of the vast social structure.

Crime, Punishment, and the Church

The first several centuries of the Middle Ages—the fifth through the eleventh—are known as the Dark Ages. This era was characterized by excessive and brutal measures of social control imposed mainly by the Church. As a result of the prevailing religious forces, certain acts were criminalized, most notably heresy and witchcraft. Some sexual offenses were regarded as unnatural acts, including homosexuality and bestiality.

Under the rule of Charlemagne (c.742–814), church officials set out to 'prohibit all superstitious observances and remnants of paganism' (Newman, 1978: 80). During that era, bishops were granted authority to act as secular judges, allowing them to rule on secular matters. That development was consistent with the early religious theme of punishment since it targeted the 'sinful' nature of some crimes. Consequently, offenders had to pay their debt both to God and to society, thereby blurring the boundaries between church law and state law.

Due to the significant role of the Church in structuring and maintaining the social order, enormous emphasis was placed on monitoring religious beliefs. In its efforts to stamp out heresy, the Church replaced trials with ordeals, in which guilt or innocence was determined by the suspect's ability to avoid injury while engaging in dangerous and painful tests of faith.

> Medieval punishments included trials of fire, water, the rod, and the stake. In the trial of cold water, the accused had to jump into a lake that had been blessed with offerings. He was considered guilty if he floated and innocent if he sank, in which case he would be pulled out by ropes. Servants were commonly subjected to the trial of boiling water, in which the accused was forced to grab something from the bottom of a pan of water on fire. He was found innocent if his arm came out unharmed, something that occurred very rarely.
>
> (Lombroso, 2006b: 180)

The rationale underlying ordeals was divine intervention—meaning that if the accused were truly innocent, God would intervene to prove their innocence. Needless to say, those who were subjected to these tests of faith were rarely found innocent of their charges, producing high rates of conviction (Ives, 1970 [1914]; Newman, 1978).

Confronting the threat of heresy became a central theme of formal social control, and the Holy Inquisition was established as an official law enforcement campaign in 1231. In a widespread effort to combat heresy, the Inquisition set out to save the souls of the accused. Those who refused to repent or confess were punished by having their land confiscated or by being fined, imprisoned, condemned to wear crosses, tortured, or burned alive. The Inquisition continued for several centuries throughout Europe (and Latin America) during which time thousands of people accused of heresy were brutally tortured and executed (Lea, 1969 [1887]).

That religious movement was not without its political agendas. In 1542, for instance, the Inquisition was used in Italy to counter the Protestant movement. The execution of Joan of Arc probably best illustrates the religious and political elements of social control. After being accused of heresy and witchcraft, Joan of Arc was burned at the stake in 1431. Yet her religious offenses were complicated by her political activism. Joan of Arc claimed to have had visions from God to lead French citizens away from the British occupation. Incidentally, her conviction of heresy was overturned in 1456, and she was canonized in 1920.

Other overlapping themes of crime and sin also shaped the practice of imprisonment. Early versions of prisons reflected a concern for order and discipline, thereby facilitating the task of reform by way of penance. Incarceration took place in makeshift arrangements, at times even inside monasteries. Conveniently, the monastery itself served as a model of future institutions in which criminals were isolated from the secular world so that they might privately repent and reflect (ACA, 1983). To be clear, the term *penitentiary* derives from the Latin words meaning 'penitence' and 'repentance,' yet also shares the same root with the words *punishment, pain,* and *revenge* (Norris, 1985).

Feudalism and Social Control

Feudalism eventually became the prevailing social, economic, and political system in which obedience and service stood as its primary cornerstones. Between the eighth and thirteenth centuries in Europe, feudalism emerged as a strict aristocratic, militaristic, and theological social order. Such a hierarchy, however, depended greatly on a high degree of societal legitimacy. That is, those in power went to great lengths to appear morally justified to be at the top of the hierarchy, especially in the eyes of the subordinate. In more complex terms, the legitimacy afforded to feudalism rested on the theological notion that the power structure was divinely ordained. In other words, feudal society was arranged according to the will of God, and of course it was in the best interest of those in power to perpetuate that belief.

It has been proposed that the objective of punishment is to protect society, an idea that became known as the 'social defense' thesis. With greater conceptual refinement, however, perhaps punishment should be viewed instead as a means of protecting a particular form of society (Michalowski, 1985). In the case of feudalism, punishment was often designed and implemented with the explicit purpose of maintaining the social order. Furthermore, forms of punishment contained in a particular social order are shaped by economic forces. Therefore punishment is aimed at preserving not only the social order but the economic order as well. As Michalowski postulates:

> The nature of the basic productive activities of a given society will determine the forms of punishment appropriate to that society. During the feudal era the basic productive activity was agricultural in nature, and the relations of production were such that serfs –the basic laboring class –were tied to a form of involuntary servitude by the feudal bond.
>
> (1985: 225)

The structure of punishment under feudalism, Michalowski asserts, was patterned by economic forces in several ways. First, the population distribution in agrarian society was widely scattered, which meant that there could be no high concentration of offenders. Hence, the use of penal institutions that would centralize the criminal population would be inconsistent with the decentralized nature of the agricultural society. Second, the laboring class was already attached to the land—indeed, their work was a form of involuntary servitude. Therefore punishment by way of forced labor, such as slavery, indenture, or imprisonment would be redundant. Compounding matters, the authorities 'would place the offender in a situation generally not much worse than that he or she was in prior to the crime both with respect to the conditions of life and the exploitation of his or her labor power' (Michalowski, 1985: 225). Eventually, fines and corporal punishment emerged as the primary methods of punishment because execution and banishment would result in the loss of the labor the offender had to offer (Rusche and Kirchheimer, 1968 [1939]; see O'Malley, 2009).

Early Imprisonment and Makeshift Prisons

During the Middle Ages, incarceration practices resembled those of ancient Rome, insofar as makeshift structures were used for confinement. Due to their secure features, fortresses, castles, abutments of bridges, town gates, cellars of municipal buildings, and even private dwellings were convenient places to hold prisoners. Dungeons became synonymous with harsh imprisonment, but chambers specifically designed to house prisoners within castles did not appear until after the twelfth century. Eventually, castles were used almost exclusively as prisons and jails. That development had much to do with the advent of gunpowder, thereby altering military strategies. Consequently, the need for fortified dwellings became obsolete (Johnston, 1973). Throughout history, and even today, makeshift arrangements remain an important method of expanding jail and prison capacities given their availability and convenience (Welch, 1991c).

Galley Slavery

As discussed throughout, economic forces have shaped the course of punishment throughout history. Still, as governments became more sophisticated, they recognized the significant value of labor that offenders had to offer. In fact, Thomas More proclaimed that 'it is unwise to execute offenders because their labor is more profitable than their death' (Rusche and Kirchheimer, 1968 [1939]). In light of that realization, galley slavery emerged as a routine method of punishment explicitly designed to exploit physical labor in the form of oarsmen for vessels. Although galley slavery existed in ancient Greece and Rome, it was not institutionalized as a penal practice until 1348: then it flourished during periods of global expansion, imperialism, and colonization, enduring to the year 1803. Given their enormous size, each vessel required hundreds of galley slaves. Toward the end of the fifteenth century, naval wars in the Mediterranean prompted military powers to recruit oarsmen from among prisoners. The large vessels needed as many as 350 galley slaves while smaller ships used 180. At the height of his authority, Don Juan d'Austria commanded some 5,600 galley slaves (Rusche and Kirchheimer, 1968 [1939]).

As the need for oarsmen multiplied, criminal justice officials widened their net by sentencing not only serious offenders but also thieves, beggars, and vagabonds to galley slavery. Although convict labor was greatly valued by private contractors, the slaves' ability to propel the vessels was drastically impaired by mistreatment. Before being confined to the galley, criminals were forced to march across the countryside. Whatever strength they had following the journey was further debilitated by being chained to an oar, confined in proximity to their own excrement, and infected with diseases caused by the vermin-infested conditions of the ships. The following passage captures the lives of galley slaves:

> The prisoners reached the sea-port on foot, traversing a large part of France in scanty clothing and chained by the neck in large gangs. Once drafted on board ship and posted to his bench, he remained there always unless taken to the hospital or the grave. Six slaves, chained to the same beach, tugged at each oar, which was some fifty feet in length: they were compelled to keep time with the others before or behind, or they would have been knocked senseless by the return stroke. They rowed naked to the waist, partly to save clothing, still more to offer their backs to the thongs of the *souscomites* or quarter-master who flogged freely, and backed up every order with each stroke. When not rowing they sat at their benches at night, and slept where they sat. In all naval engagements of those days the oars were shot at first, hence the galley-slaves suffered first and most, and were often decimated while the garrison and crew escaped untouched.
> (Marteilhes, 1894: 164–5; reprinted in Barnes and Teeters, 1948: 437)

LE MONDE ILLUSTRÉ

JOURNAL HEBDOMADAIRE

Figure 13.2 Galley slavery, January 10, 1863. The French artillerymen distribute biscuits among the galley slaves in Veracruz during the war between France and Mexico. In the picture above, cherubs decorate a montage of Parisian landmarks. (From *Le Monde Illustré —Expédition du Mexique*, published 1963, from an engraving by C. Maurand of a sketch by M Brunet.)

Photo by Hulton Archive/ Getty Images.

Galley slavery was often a life sentence. Often while the ships were at port during the winter, many galley slaves were branded (for the purposes of identification and stigma) and forced to labor in workhouses, known as bagnes, located in the dockyards (Newman, 1978). The practice of galley slavery diminished during the eighteenth century. Among the reasons for its decline were technological forces, such as advanced sailing methods that rendered galley servitude obsolete. With a surplus of galley slaves, many prisoners were later assigned to work in mines while others were transported to work in colonial lands. "What is significant in the development of the galley as a method of punishment is the fact that economic considerations alone were involved, not penal. The introduction and regulation of galley servitude were determined solely by the desire to obtain necessary labor on the cheapest possible basis" (Rusche and Kirchheimer. 1968 [1939]: 55).

The Sixteenth and Seventeenth Centuries

Although the 1500s are characterized as a period when earlier forms of penal sanctions remained routine (e.g. execution, corporal punishment), other innovations appeared to reflect a reconceptualization of punishment. The sixteenth and seventeenth centuries mark a pivotal point in the history of punishment as workhouses and houses of correction emerged along with the practice of transportation and the use of hulks as prison 'warehouses' (see Spierenburg, 1984),

Workhouses and Houses of Correction

The breakdown of feudalism led to the development of early mercantile capitalism as the primary mode of production, thereby causing changes to the prevailing forms of punishment. During the transition from an agrarian economy to one that combined agriculture with guild-based production of mercantile goods, there was a shift of population from rural areas into villages, towns, and eventually cities (Michalowski, 1985). Soon serfs and laborers were stripped of their land and forced to live as scavengers. As they drifted into urban areas, they were met with hostility by well-to-do townspeople. Soon perceptions of a growing 'social disorder' became the source of alarm, prompting the state to take action against a rising underclass (see Chapter 4 on radicalism).

In London, King Henry VIII dealt with the underclass and the growing number of unemployed vagabonds by way of corporal punishment and penal slavery. Those measures of social control, however, could not keep pace with economic forces that contributed heavily to the massive influx of the homeless and jobless into urban centers. Soon workhouses or houses of correction emerged as part of the enclosure movement: that is, the practice of confining offenders and undesirables to institutions featuring punishment, work, and religious instruction. In 1556, the Bridewell was converted from an old royal palace (known as Saint Bridget's Well) to an institution in which the poor as well as the lewd and idle were confined with rogues, vagabonds, prostitutes, and an array of less serious offenders (Sutherland *et al.*, 1992). Under strict discipline, they were assigned such tasks as spinning wool, baking, and making furniture, clothing, shoes and even tennis balls for members of the elite class. Foreshadowing the contemporary form of privatization in corrections, the Bridewell was operated by businessmen under a contractual agreement with local government (Van der Slice, 1936–7; Rusche and Kirchheimer, 1968 [1939]).

Operating under the assumption that pauperism was rooted in basic laziness, those institutions relied on a rehabilitative rationale. Workhouses were aimed at instilling a work ethic and the habits of industry as well as providing skill training for their inmates. Nevertheless, prison reformers criticized officials for exploiting slave labor to produce marketable goods cheaply for private profit (Dobash, 1983). As is the case with many correctional innovations, it is sometimes difficult to distinguish genuine humanitarianism from the calculating motives of profit (Johnston, 2009).

As a unique form of social control, the workhouse movement can be interpreted as 'social sanitation' designed to sweep the undesirables from the streets and place them in institutions away from public view (Welch, 1994). In England, workhouses seemed to be so effective that in 1576 Parliament instructed all British counties to construct a workhouse according to the vision of the Bridewell (Sellin, 1976). Soon Holland built its version of workhouses in 1596, and many other nations in Europe followed suit because they, too, were responding to failing economic conditions.

The fact that the interiors of the workhouses were out of public view, compounded with public apathy concerning them, led to the proliferation of horrible conditions. Disease, violence, and sexual assaults were common in the workhouses because the segregation of men from women, the young from the old, and the sick from the healthy was not always enforced. Another feature of the workhouses was a fee system by which food, blankets, and candles were made available only to those inmates who could purchase them from the keeper. During that period, criminals convicted of serious offenses were still being publicly whipped, transported, or executed. Thus those confined to the workhouses were primarily prostitutes, vagabonds, and those with no visible means of support (see Morris and Rothman, 1995).

Transportation: Banishment for Profit

In an attempt to rid itself of a growing underclass and ease overcrowding in prisons and gaols (jails), England began transporting rogues, vagabonds, and sturdy beggars to colonial lands in 1598. In those distant colonies (i.e. Australia and America), penal slaves would serve lengthy sentences in forced labor. A century later, the use of transportation expanded considerably: the Transportation Act of 1718 stated that the purpose of transportation was to deter criminals as well as to supply the colonies with labor (Shaw, 1966).

Eventually, transportation applied to more than thieves and vagabonds; it also served as a convenient method of deporting political undesirables and religious dissidents. The popularity of transportation spread throughout Europe. Russia made use of Siberia; Spain deported prisoners to Hispaniola, Portugal exiled convicts to North Africa, Brazil and Cape Verde; Italy herded inmates to Sicily; Denmark relied on Greenland as a penal colony; Holland shipped convicts to the Dutch East Indies.

England transported thousands of criminals to work in the American colonies. Following the American Revolution, between the years 1786 and 1867, approximately 134,000 prisoners were sent to Australia (Sutherland *et al.*, 1992). The transportation of prisoners remained popular for centuries, even until recent times. For instance, the infamous Devil's Island in French Guiana (as depicted in the novel and movie *Papillon*) was used by French authorities until 1953. Over the years, approximately 68,000 of the 70,000 prisoners on Devil's Island died before completing their sentence (Tappan, 1960).

Transportation should be viewed as a complex form of punishment. Beyond its obvious economic underpinnings, transportation boasted a form of banishment as well as the ritual of public humiliation. In London, men and women alike were placed in heavy chains and drawn in open carts through the local crowds, who jeered and terrorized them (Johnson, 1988). In Russia, over 850,000 convicts were exiled to Siberia between 1807 and 1899, and were forced to march between 4,700 and 6,700 miles while being chained together. The journey often lasted two to three years, contributing to high death rates (Sellin, 1976).

Although transportation was used for crime-control purposes by exporting hardened criminals, it also represented a form of social sanitation serving to rid urban centers of vagrants and other undesirables. Its success in England was affirmed when, in 1787, offenders sentenced to three or more years of imprisonment were eligible for transportation, and the penalty for an unauthorized return was execution. An estimated 2,000 prisoners annually (and a quarter of a million overall) arrived in America until the beginning of the Revolutionary War. At that time, England terminated transportation to the colonies, not wanting banished felons to be recruited as soldiers against their former homeland (Rusche and Kirchheimer, 1968 [1939]; Barnes and Teeters, 1946).

Transportation was essentially privatized through contracts, under which felons became the property of the ships' captains. Perhaps due to that contractual arrangement, convicts were subjected to horrible conditions aboard these vessels (known as 'floating hells'), and many died en route to the penal colony. Felons who survived the voyage were subsequently sold at a high price to American colonists, and they usually became indentured servants. Upon completion of their term, lasting from seven to 14 years, the banished felons were allowed to remain in the colony as free citizens. In some cases, indentured servants were awarded land by their owners (Barnes, 1968 [1939]).

As a result of the prevailing economic forces, transportation flourished as a method of securing slave labor for developing colonies. Changing economic forces later contributed to its demise. As immigrants migrated to the colonies, they campaigned for the abolition of penal slavery and transportation in order to secure higher wages for themselves (Rusche and Kirchheimer, 1968 [1939]).

Hulks: Prison Warehouses on the Waterfront

Among the motivating forces behind transportation was the need to ease prison and jail crowding, and after the American Revolution (when transportation to America was terminated), England again faced that problem. For a short period, one solution was to transform prisoners into soldiers to be sent to fight in West Africa. That plan, however, was abandoned because the convicts did not make good soldiers. In due course, England returned to a penal practice that was popular in the late fifteenth century. That is, old, unseaworthy vessels were converted into floating prisons. In the late 1400s, abandoned galley-powered vessels, which were replaced by sail ships, were used for imprisonment. By the late 1700s, officials relied on broken-down transportation ships, known as hulks, to house prisoners. Also, referred to as 'hell holds' or 'floating hells,' hulks were moored at river banks and harbors while serving as penal warehouses for men, women, and children who were subjected to disease-infested conditions without adequate food and sanitation. Prisoners were routinely flogged and forced to engage in degrading labor. At one time, the English hulk system consisted of eleven ships holding 3,552 prisoners (Barnes and Teeters, 1946).

During the Revolutionary War, American prisoners of war were held in hulks anchored in New York harbor. An estimated 12,000 prisoners of war died on those ships, their bodies simply thrown overboard, eventually drifting to the Brooklyn shore (Welch, 1991c). In the 1800s, California relied on hulks to house prisoners, and as recently as the 1970s, Louisiana, Maryland, Massachusetts, New York, and Washington considered the conversion of decommissioned warships into makeshift correctional facilities (ACA, 1983). Perhaps the most interesting replication of the hulks, though, existed recently in New York City. Between 1988 and 1993, the city housed jail inmates on the *Bibby Venture* and the *Bibby Resolution*—floating jail barges that previously served as English military barracks during the Falkland Islands War in Argentina in 1982 (Welch, 1991c).

As was the case with other makeshift innovations initially designed to serve as temporary solutions to overcrowding, the English hulks remained correctional fixtures until 1858. In fact, the last hulk remained in operation until 1875, when transportation to Australia ceased (Barnes and Teeters, 1946).

Box 13.2 CULTURAL PENOLOGY

Franz Schmidt: Famous Executioner

Perhaps the most renowned of Germany's executioners was Franz Schmidt, who bestrode Nuremberg's scaffold from 1573 to 1617. No record of his early life has survived but it is known that his father was executioner of the German town of Bamberg. Franz was his assistant there from 1573 to 1578 and when thoroughly proficient he moved to Nuremberg, where he became chief executioner. Franz's skills with the various tools of his trade were due in no small part to his interest in anatomy, knowledge of which he put to further use in the dissection of some of his victims. Hospitals were always in need of specimens for medical research and it was the hangman's duty in most countries to supply them (Abbott, 1991).

Not that he was inhumane; on the contrary, in 1580 he used his influence to have the penalty of drowning, which was inflicted on women guilty of infanticide, changed to the more merciful one of hanging or beheading. As in England, Germany's public executioners were feared and loathed by the populace—and this included their assistants—but despite society's rejection Franz performed his duties with impersonal efficiency and dedication. Unlike many of his calling he never drank strong liquor, and such had been his upbringing that his ability to write encouraged him to keep a detailed diary of his official activities, annotated accordingly where the felon had finally confessed his misdeeds. A contemporary picture portrays Schmidt as a tall well-built man, full bearded, in jerkin and knee-length hose. He could afford to dress well, for the pay was good. He received a fixed salary, with an extra fee per execution, and half that sum for each felon tortured. He and his assistant were also loaned to neighboring authorities whenever they lacked an executioner of their own, and a higher rate was then paid. The team even received some compensation in the event of a last-minute reprieve being granted to the condemned person (Abbott, 1991; Morris and Rothman, 1998).

Nor did Franz have any rent to pay, for he occupied an official residence provided by the city council, a tower house on the stone bridge that straddled Nuremberg's River Peginitz. Like their English counterparts, German executioners did a good trade in providing the superstitious with severed portions of their victims' corpses for use as revered relics, medicines, or lucky charms. In those days a macabre belief existed among the criminal fraternity of Europe that the severed hand of a hanged man, if prepared in accordance with the ancient recipes, possessed special powers (see Newman, 1978).

A German executioner's duties did not start on the scaffold, of course, but in the cells beneath the courtroom. There the executioner and his assistant would endeavor to coax a confession from the accused, utilizing the several instruments of torture provided by the authorities. If the thumbscrews didn't persuade, the 'ladder' might, stretching the bound victim to an agonizing degree. There was the 'fass,' a spiked cradle in which the victim was tied and rocked violently, hands bound behind him, or the 'gauntlets' whereby the accused, hands bound behind him, was hoisted aloft by the wrists, weights then being attached to his ankles.

As Franz entered in his diary in 1576: 'Hans Payhel, who committed three murders; two years ago I cut off his ears and flogged him; today I beheaded him at Focheim' (Abbott, 1991: 73). Schmidt served honorably during his 44 years in office and executed no fewer than 360 felons, at least 42 being women. His busiest year was 1580, when he performed 20 executions: 2 murderers who had to be broken on the wheel, 2 other murderers and 9 thieves hanged. All of which Franz performed with his usual expertise. Many such criminals received their due deserts at the hands of Franz Schmidt—floggings, brandings, amputation of fingers and ears—until finally, in 1617 he decided to retire and become a 'respectable' person again. He lived quietly in Nuremberg for a further 17 years until his death in 1634. The old executioner was given an honorable funeral, the burial service being attended by many of the city dignitaries as a mark of respect for his services to the community (Abbott, 1991; see Foucault 1977).

The Enlightenment and Its Enduring Impact on Corrections

The Enlightenment, or the Age of Reason, flourished during the mid-eighteenth century in Europe. At that time, great changes in social and scientific thought took place. Reason became a prevailing method of analyzing social life and the world around it. One source of inspiration for the Enlightenment was Isaac Newton's *Principia* (1687), which encouraged intellectuals to investigate social and scientific phenomena methodically and objectively. Another inspiration was John Locke's *Essay Concerning Human Understanding* and his *Second Treatise on Government* (both published in 1690). In those works, reason, complemented by humanitarianism and secularism, was applied to political theory and philosophy. That intellectual current made its mark on France, England, and America, where ideas of constitutionalism and limited political power quickly transformed those nations into independent republican governments (Johnson, 1988).

The Enlightenment was not without controversy. Among its major themes was the rejection of a school of thought dominated by institutional Christianity. That challenge to theological dominance gave rise to secular reasoning, in which social and scientific inquiries were no longer filtered through a religious perspective. Consequently, there was an enormous backlash from the Church. Montesquieu (in *Spirit of the Laws*, 1748) confronted religion and the historical role of the Church in the political arrangement of society. Drawing on the notion of utility, Montesquieu offered this question: What benefit does religion offer society? In the spirit of the Enlightenment, he maintained that 'Earthly institutions and societies were no longer to be judged by religious standards; rather, religion was to be measured by the new moral standard of utilitarianism: what good it did for mankind' (Johnson, 1988: 116–17). Montesquieu's critique of religion was considered subtle. Even so, he was confined to the Bastille in 1726; later his release stipulated that he leave France. In contrast to Montesquieu, Voltaire unswervingly attacked the Church in his writings, and he too was imprisoned. Similarly, Diderot, a French philosopher, was incarcerated for publishing his *Lettre sur les Aveugles* ('Letter on the Blind')—a scathing criticism of orthodox religion.

As the role of religion became less significant in social and scientific thought, ideas of crime and punishment were also transformed. Crime and punishment could now be conceptualized in a secular context, forcibly moving the concept of sin into the periphery of criminological debate. Accordingly, the focus of crime shifted away from a theological perspective and toward the consequences that crime had on other individuals and society. In response to that new focus of crime, punishment took a utilitarian approach. First and foremost was the idea of deterrence. The goal of punishment was to discourage individuals from engaging in crime, and it was assumed that this goal could be achieved by ensuring the certainty and swiftness of punishment. In sum, the Enlightenment thinkers contributed to the field of criminal justice by criticizing capricious sentencing and inhumane punishment, and by advocating the improvement of prison conditions.

Cesare Beccaria and Penal Reform

Among those strongly influenced by the notions of Montesquieu and Voltaire was the Marquis de Beccaria (1738–94), an Italian economist who published his *Essay on Crimes and Punishments* in 1766. The classic essay was originally published anonymously because he too feared persecution from the Church. Although Beccaria did avoid the Church's persecution, the essay was quickly condemned by the Church because of his disapproval of torture, a common method of punishment employed by the Church during the Inquisition (Maestro, 1973).

In his work, Beccaria borrowed heavily from the utilitarian perspective that served to formalize a theory of deterrence. He proposed that if laws (and penalties) were clearly written and fully understood, crime would subsequently decline. Beccaria further advanced the idea that the *certainty* and *swiftness* of punishment, not its *severity*, would prove to be the crux of deterrence. The social utility of punishment would be the deterrence of crime, but in doing so, it also would strengthen the bonds of society.

Beccaria was critical of arbitrary and unnecessarily harsh punishment. He believed that any penalty that was not intended to discourage crime or protect society was unjust and would interfere with the goal of deterrence. In fact, Beccaria opposed the death penalty on the grounds that it was excessive and that the protection of society could be achieved through banishment. He also opposed transportation of less serious offenders, because he felt that their punishment might go unobserved, thereby undermining the value of deterrence. Beccaria considered any excessive punishment meted out by the state as tyrannical.

In crusading for changes in the legal codes that would support his theory of utility and deterrence, Beccaria challenged the abuse of political power within the criminal justice system. Specifically, he attacked those magistrates who arbitrarily sentenced offenders, and he recommended that penalties be graduated to fit the severity of the crime.

Beccaria's utilitarian ideas on crime, punishment, and criminal law became known as the classical school of criminology. His major proposals for law reform, which remain an important contribution today, are briefly listed (Beccaria, 1981 [1764]):

1. The criminal law should be clear, so that all could know and understand it.

2. Torture to obtain confessions should be abolished.

3. Judges should be impartial, and the sovereign who makes the laws should determine guilt or innocence.

4. The accused should be allotted the time and resources necessary for their defense.

5. The death penalty should be abolished.

6. Secret accusations and royal warrants for the imprisonment of people without trial should be done away with.

7. Punishment should be quick, certain, and commensurate with the crime.

8. The true measure of crime should be the harm done to the rights and liberties of individuals in society, rather than vague standards of moral virtue.

Although Beccaria advocated specific reforms for the criminal justice system, the foundation of his school of thought was more conceptual in nature. At the heart of the classical school of criminology was the concept of free will. In brief, deterrence could be achieved if prompt and certain punishments were given to those who chose to commit crime. Operating from a highly rationalistic framework, Beccaria was criticized for assuming that all criminals would react in similar ways to the same penalty. His oversight of individual differences and the diversity in the motives of crime remain a limitation of his theory (Johnson, 1988).

Moreover, recent re-examinations of Beccaria's contributions have surfaced. Newman and Marongui (1990) assert that, for years, scholars have blindly worshipped Beccaria. Returning to Beccaria's work and its impact on liberal penology, Newman and Marongui argue that his contributions are vastly overrated. 'Many of the reforms that occurred during the eighteenth century can as easily be ascribed to social and political conditions as to Beccaria's work' (Newman and Marongui, 1990: 325). Furthermore, Newman and Marongui note that, by comparison, the contributions of Voltaire and Jeremy Bentham were more profound than Beccaria's writings. In contrast to the ritual adoration of Beccaria common among criminologists, Newman and Marongui contend that it was Bentham who advanced Beccaria's utilitarian notions and bolstered the classical school of criminology (see Chapter 4).

John Howard and Institutional Reform

Throughout history, the sheriff has functioned as the chief law enforcement official of a county as well as the top administrator of the jail. The term *sheriff* emerged in England, where each county or shire was assigned a political appointee, the reeve. The sheriff (or shire-reeve) collected taxes, kept the peace, and managed the county jail. John Howard (1726–90) remains one of the most famous sheriffs in history because of his lasting contributions to jail reform. Over the past few centuries, John Howard and institutional reform have become synonymous. Howard's European-wide reputation as a prison reformer began following his appointment as the sheriff of Bedfordshire in England in 1773. Perhaps Howard's interest in penology can be traced to his own capture and detention by pirates during a trip to Portugal in 1755 (Barnes and Teeters, 1946; Wines, 1895).

During his tenure as sheriff, Howard was appalled by the horrific conditions in jails and in the hulks, which led to his crusade to reform jails throughout England and Europe. Among his first achievements was abolishing the fee system in which prisoners were forced to pay jailers for their keep. Under this system, those without the necessary funds to pay their keeper were forced to remain in jail, even after being tried and acquitted. In solving this problem, Howard proposed that fees be eliminated and jailers be paid a salary. His book *State of Prisons* (1777), the product of hundreds of jail and prison inspections throughout England and Europe, exposed and systematically recorded the brutal conditions of imprisonment. However, during those inspections, Howard did witness some penal practices that were quite progressive and humanitarian, namely those in use at the Hospice of San Michele and the Maison de Force.

Howard's contributions were not limited to publishing his ideas. He drafted the Penitentiary Act, which was passed by the British Parliament in 1779. This act of legislation was built around four principles:

1. Elimination of fees.

2. Regular inspection of prisons and jails.

3. Provision of sanitary and healthful facilities.

4. Emphasis on the reformation of inmates.

Howard's institutional reform also included an element of religion. He thought that reformation could be achieved by assigning each inmate his or her own cell in which to sleep, thus creating an atmosphere of solitude and silence which would be favorable to reflection and repentance. Howard assumed that crime was associated with idleness and unemployment, and criminal tendencies could therefore be exacerbated in prison if mischief and rebellion went unchecked. Therefore Howard's reforms combined discipline and Christian charity with a humanitarian philosophy. But discipline remained an important component of his plan, which incorporated religious teaching, daily routine, and productive labor (Howard, 1929 [1777]).

Other specific reforms included the removal of the mentally ill from prisons and the separation or release of women and children. The gaol at Wymondham in Norfolk, England, in 1785, was among the first to incorporate Howard's recommendations. Howard died of jail fever (typhus) in 1790 while inspecting a prison in Russia: still, his legacy lives on (Barnes and Teeters, 1946). In his name, John Howard Societies in England and the United States continue to monitor prison and jail conditions today.

Jeremy Bentham, Utilitarianism, and the Panopticon

The contributions of Jeremy Bentham (1748–1832) are an important part of any discussion of the secular theme of crime and punishment and its impact on the classical school. In his major work, *An Introduction to the Principles of Morals and Legislation* (1789), Bentham elaborated on the concept of free will to further his utilitarian theory of hedonistic calculus, also known as the pleasure/pain principle. The central assumption in his theory was that human beings are motivated by pleasure while consciously avoiding pain. In advancing the deterrence model, Bentham proposed that penalties should sufficiently outweigh the gain that the offender would achieve in committing the crime. That framework was heavily psychological in nature because it assumed that crime could be deterred by addressing the rationality of those who commit such acts. The rational component of crime advanced the notion that if an individual chooses to act criminally, then he or she should embrace the responsibility for the act, and accept the punitive consequences (Bentham, 1995).

Bentham also was active in extending the reform of English criminal law. He supported the legal reform that called for graduated punishments that would fit the severity of the crime. One of his most notable contributions, however, was a product of his keen interest in architecture. He designed the panopticon, which became known as the 'ultimate penitentiary.' In the 1770s, the panopticon (from the Greek, meaning 'everything' and 'a place of sight') was proposed as a solution to the English correctional crisis during which horrific prison conditions and the hulks became major concerns for reformers. Bentham's inspiration to design the panopticon is traced primarily to English prison reformer John Howard.

The blueprints of the panopticon (also known as the 'inspection house') outlined its physical structure, which featured a column in the center of the floor plan to serve as an indoor guard tower. Several tiers of cells were arranged in a circular format that faced the guard tower. The design provided the guards with a complete and continuous view of the inmates confined to their individual cells (Bentham, 1995). One of the most detailed analyses of the panopticon was generated by French philosopher Michel Foucault. In his *Discipline and Punish: The Birth of the Prison* (1977), Foucault examines the subtleties of social control that he asserts distinguished the panopticon from other penal institutions. Foucault argues that the panopticon illustrated how

Figure 13.3 Postcard of an American panopticon: 'Interior view of cell house, new Illinois State Penitentiary at Stateville, near Joliet, Ill.'

Source: Scanned from the postcard collection of Alex Wellerstein and reprinted with permission. Copyright expired. See http://www. hks.harvard.edu/sdn/sdnimages/.

geometry can complement economics in an effort to enhance social control. The circular design of the institution would make the inmate population more visible, and thus lead to a decrease in the guard-inmate ratio, making supervision more efficient. Conceivably, only a few guards would be needed to maintain supervision over the entire prison population (see Alford, 2000; Lyon, 1991; Mathiesen, 1997).

Foucault contends that the key to inmate control is constant inspection, which represents power in two ways: it becomes both visible and unverifiable. 'Visible: the inmate will constantly have before his eyes the tall outline of the central tower from which he is spied upon. Unverifiable: the inmate must never know whether he is being looked at any one moment: but he must be sure that he may always be so' (1977: 201; 1996). Due to the central location of the guard tower, inmates could not always be sure whether or not they indeed were the objects of observation. Therefore Foucault notes that the target of social control is not so much the inmate's body, but the inmate's mind, in that constant surveillance creates a permanent presence in the mind (similar to the effects of surveillance cameras today). 'Hence, the major effect of the Panopticon: to induce in the inmate a state of conscious and permanent visibility that assures the automatic functioning of power' (1977: 201). Perhaps Aldous Huxley's insight best captures the essence of the panopticon when he called it the 'totalitarian housing project' (Johnston, 1873: 20).

Although the plans to construct a panopticon received serious consideration by some members of Parliament, it never won complete approval in England. However, similar circular prisons were built in Holland, Spain, and the Isle of Pines off Cuba. In America, the design of the panopticon was modified, as evidenced by the architecture of the Virginia Penitentiary, the Western Penitentiary (in Pittsburgh), and later, the Stateville Correctional Center (in Joliet, Illinois) (1919).

Inventing Make-Work Devices

As prisons in England became overcrowded, institutional jobs became scarce. Consequently, wardens had to find ways to keep other inmates busy, so many of them were assigned meaningless and repetitive tasks resembling work only in form or ritual. Emerging technological forces led to such innovative devices as the crank and the treadmill. Those devices served as methods of punishment that were monotonous, irksome, and dull, as well as degrading.

The crank, commonly referred to as a reform engine, resembled the starting device of early automobiles and was attached to a wall and a mechanical counter. The punishment involved forcing inmates to turn the crank, with a resistance of 4 to 11 pounds, as many as 1,800 revolutions per hour and 14,400 revolutions per day. The treadmill (also known as the treadwheel, or wind-grinding machine) was invented by eminent engineer Sir William Cubbit in 1818. The treadmill featured a short staircase of 24 steps. As the prisoner walked up the stairs, the steps collapsed in a manner that impeded progress (a task similar to trying to walk up a down escalator). In a given day, an inmate might climb anywhere from 7,200 to 14,000 feet (by comparison, it is estimated that a stiff mountain climb consists of 3,000 to 5,000 feet). The following describes the drudgery of the treadmill:

> The weariness of the employment results from two causes. First, the want of a firm footing for the feet—a want painfully experienced in walking through a deep soft snow; and secondly, the strength that is expended to keep the body from sinking with the step—which is equal to that required to lift a man's own weight, say 140 pounds ... No wonder that prisoners maim themselves or feign sickness (at the rate of 4,000 instances in a twelve-month) to escape such a brutal use of their bodies.
>
> (*Journal of Prison Discipline and Philanthropy*, 1857: 40,
> reprinted in Barnes and Teeters, 1946: 691)

The shot drill was another type of strenuous and degrading chore. The convict was forced to carry heavy cannonballs from one pile to another and back again. The repetitious and monotonous punishment kept the prisoner active because the task could never be completed. The introduction of such methods of punishment is subject to many interpretations, but it is clear that those exercises were designed to be boring and void of the satisfaction of accomplishing a task or manufacturing a product. According to Foucault (1973), those punishments mark a divorce of labor from utility and profit, meaning that the exercises took on a pure significance as punishment. That shift in the attitude toward punishment makes it apparent that the ideals of genuine rehabilitation were being replaced with the notions of retribution (Sellin, 1976)

Hospice of San Michele and Maison de Force

Two European institutions that helped shape the humanitarian philosophy in punishment and corrections were the Hospice of San Michele and the Maison de Force. Those institutions are remembered as notable contributions to the development of corrections because they systematically applied the concepts of reformation and rehabilitation. The Hospice of San Michele (Hospital of Saint Michael) opened in Rome in 1703 under the direction of Pope Clement XI. The hospice was commonly thought to be a training school for juvenile delinquents, housing about 60 boys, but it also opened its doors to orphans, as well as over 500 aged and infirm men and women (Sellin, 1926).

Among its contributions to the reformatory movement, the hospice advanced the use of individual prison cells as an alternative to large dormitories. In the course of separating inmates, individual cells provided a solitary space conducive to solitude, silence, religious meditation, and repentance: all of which were each considered necessary conditions for personal reform. Although they slept in their own cells at night, inmates worked together in silence during the day, producing items for the Vatican State. Hence reform meant combining labor with the development of the spiritual well-being of the prisoner. In the Hospice of San Michele, the monastic features of the design were joined with the mission of workhouses (Johnston, 1973). The driving force behind the program of the hospice was regarded as humanitarian in nature because it emphasized reform, not necessarily punishment. Today, after undergoing considerable changes, the hospice remains a reformatory for delinquent boys.

The Maison de Force (the Stronghouse) was founded in Ghent, Belgium, by Jean Jacques Philippe Vilain in 1773. Similar to the hospice, the Maison incorporated religion with silent work as a means of reform. Inmates were confined to private cells at night and involved in congregate work during the day. Consistent with the humanitarian approach was the provision of separate quarters for men, women, children, felons, misdemeanants, and vagrants. The Maison marked an early attempt by a large-scale penal institution to use architecture to enhance the treatment philosophy. 'The plan was in the form of a giant octagon formed by eight trapezoid-shaped units, each completely self-contained to allow for the separation of various classes of prisoners' (Johnston, 1973: 13). The combination of work with religious training and of architecture with institutional management continued in the emergence of American penitentiaries (see Chapter 3).

Conclusion

Looking at the social history of punishment provides clear reference points that improve our understanding of corrections. Taking a historical approach to corrections also provides evidence that the linear direction of history should not be equated with progress. Many advances and reforms in corrections were offset by a return to earlier and more barbaric forms of punishment. An important finding in the historical analysis of punishment is that the formulation and distribution of penalties developed in earlier times were vital components in the structure and maintenance of the social order. Although punishment has been used in the name of protecting society, it also has been viewed as protecting a particular arrangement of society (Michalowski, 1985).

The emergence of the prison as a form of punishment and rehabilitation took place gradually and not without the influence of such social forces as politics, economics, religion, and technology. The evolution of imprisonment can be interpreted in two interrelated ways: incarceration can be civilized as well as civilizing. As imprisonment becomes less brutal and more humane, it becomes more civilized. Furthermore, if imprisonment can achieve the purposes of both rehabilitation and reform, in the final analysis, it can also be regarded as civilizing (Johnson, 1987: Johnston, 2009).

Summary

Within a critical approach to corrections, a history of punishment can be understood according to the overlapping social forces that shaped it: politics, economics, religion, and technology. From that perspective, the chapter explores punishment from the time when formal and legal penalties were established, through ancient Greece, ancient Rome, the Middle Ages, the sixteenth and seventeenth centuries, and the Enlightenment. In early European history, several themes emerged, shedding additional light on the rationale for punishment. Especially in cases involving executions, criminals were viewed as purveyors of evil clearly illustrating the overlap between religion, crime, and punishment. Indeed, the death penalty was a means to ward off evil in the community, particularly when certain *apotropaic* rituals were carried out, such as the breaking of bones, the sacred use of the wheel and the magic circle, burning bodies, drawing and quartering, drowning, beheading, and hanging (Newman, 1978).

Another form of *apotropaic* ritual is found in collective punishments, such as stoning to death. As citizens vent their anger toward the offender, a cleansing effect is believed to occur as they rid the community of evil (Newman, 1978). The chapter also explains how, in light of the prevailing religious forces, the Church and institutional religion continued to shape punishment. Finally, punishment is presented in the context of economics (penal slavery and fines), politics (the class bias and such elitist methods of execution as banishment and poisoning), and technology (various devices for torture and execution).

Review Questions

1. What were some of the brutal methods of punishment that emerged throughout European history, and what was the rationale for them?

2. What role did institutional religion have in shaping punishment?

3. Explain the emergence of galley slavery and transportation. Which social force contributed most to their use?

4. What does the career of Franz Schmidt reveal about the social status of executioners in sixteenth—and early seventeenth-century Germany?

5. What is the historical relationship between urban poverty and the use of houses of correction?

Recommended Readings

Abbott, G. (1991) *Lords of the Scaffold: A History of the Executioner.* New York: St. Martin's Press.

Foucault, M. (1977) *Discipline and Punish: The Birth of the Prison.* New York: Vintage.

Morris, N. and Rothman, D. J. (eds) (1998) *The Oxford History of the Prison: The Practice of Punishment in Western Society.* New York: Oxford University Press.

Newman, G. (1978). *The Punishment Response.* New York: Lippincott.

Rusche, G. and Kirchheimer, O. (1968 [1939]) *Punishment and Social Structure.* New York: Russell & Russell.

Sellin, T. (1976) *Slavery and the Penal System.* New York: Elsevier.

References

Abbott, G. (1991) *Lords of the Scaffold: A History of the Executioner*. New York: St. Martin's Press.

Alford, C. F. (2000) 'What would it matter if everything Foucault said about prisons was wrong?' *Theory and Society*, 29: 125–46.

American Correctional Association (1983) *The American Prison: From the Beginning ... A Pictorial History*. College Park, MD: American Correctional Association.

Barnes, H. (1968 [1927]) *The Evolution of Penology in Pennsylvania*. Montclair, NJ: Patterson Smith.

Barnes, H. and N. Teeters (1946) *New Horizons in Criminology* (3rd edn). New York: Prentice-Hall.

Beccaria, C. (1981 [1764]) *On Crimes and Punishments*, trans. Henry Paolucci. Indianapolis, IN: Bobbs-Merrill.

Bentham, J. (1789 [1982]) *An Introduction to the Principles of Morals and Legislation*, ed. J. Burns and H. L. A. Hart. London: Methuen.

Bentham, J. (1995) *The Panopticon Writings*, ed. and intro. M. Bozovic. London: Verso.

Dobash, R. P. (1983) 'Labour and discipline in Scottish and English prisons: moral correction, punishment and useful toil,' *Sociology*, 17 (1): 1–25.

Foucault, M. (1973) *The Birth of the Clinic*. London: Tavistock.

Foucault, M. (1977) *Discipline and Punish: The Birth of the Prison*. New York: Vintage.

Foucault, M. (1996) 'The eye of power,' in S. Lotringer (ed.), *Foucault Live: Collected Interviews, 1961–1984*. New York: Semiotext(e), pp. 226–40.

Howard, J. (1929 [1777]) *State of Prisons*; reprinted by E. P. Dutton, New York.

Ives, G. (1970 [1914]) *A History of Penal Methods*. Montclair, NJ: Patterson Smith.

Johnson, H. A. (1988) *History of Criminal Justice*. Cincinnati, OH: Anderson.

Johnson, R. (1984) 'A life for a life?' *Justice Quarterly*, 1 (4): 569–80.

Johnson, R. (1987) *Hardtime: Understanding and Reforming the Prison*. Monterey, CA: Brooks/Cole.

Johnston, N. (2009) 'Evolving function: early use of imprisonment as punishment,' *Prison Journal*, 89 (1): 10S–34S.

Johnston, R. (1973) *The Human Cage: A Brief History of Prison Architecture*. New York: Walker.

Lea, H. C. (1969 [1887]) *The Inquisition of the Middle Ages*. New York: Harper & Row; originally published as Vol. I, *A History of the Inquisition of the Middle Ages*.

Lombroso, C. (2006) *Criminal Man*, trans. M. Gibson and N. H. Rafter. Durham, NC: Duke University Press.

Lyon, D. (1991) 'Bentham's panopticism: from moral architecture to electronic surveillance,' *Queens Quarterly*, 98 (3): 596–617.

Maestro, M. (1973) *Cesare Beccaria and the Origins of Penal Reform*. Philadelphia: Temple University Press.

Marteilhes, J. (1894) *Secrets of the Prison House*. London.

Mathiesen, T. (1997) 'The viewer society: Michel Foucault's "panopticon" revisited,' *Theoretical Criminology*, 1 (2): 215–34.

Mattick, H. W. (1974) 'The contemporary jails of the United States: an unknown and neglected area of justice,' in D. Glasser (ed.), *Handbook of Criminology*. Chicago: Rand McNally.

Michalowski, R. J. (1985) *Order, Law, and Crime: An Introduction to Criminology*. New York: Random House.

Morris, N. and Rothman, D. J. (1995) *Oxford History of the Prison: The Practice of Punishment in Western Society*. New York: Oxford University Press.

Newman, G. (1978) *The Punishment Response*. New York: Lippincott.

Newman, G. and Marongui, P. (1990) 'Penological reform and the myth of Beccaria,' *Criminology*, 28 (2): 325–46.

Norris, R. L. (1985) 'Prison Reformers and Penitential Publicists in France, England, and the United States, 1774–1847.' Unpublished dissertation, American University, Washington, DC.

O'Malley, P. (2009) 'Theorizing fines,' *Punishment and Society*, 11 (1): 67–83.

Olson, E. (2002) 'Fair penalties or torture? U.N. at odds with Saudis,' *New York Times*, May 19, p. A5.

Peck, H. T. (ed.) (1922) *Harper's Dictionary of Classical Literature and Antiquity*. New York: American Book Company.

Pièces originales et procedures du process fait à Robert-François Damiens, III, 1757.

Rothman, D. J. (1971) *The Discovery of the Asylum: Social Order and Disorder in the New Republic*. Boston: Little, Brown.

Rusche, G. and Kirchheimer, O. (1968 [1939]) *Punishment and Social Structure*. New York: Russell & Russell.

Sellin, T. (1926) 'Felippo Franci—a precursor of modern penology,' *Journal of Criminal Law and Criminology*, XXVII (May): 104–12.

Sellin, T. (1976) *Slavery and the Penal System*. New York: Elsevier.

Shaw, A. (1966) *Convicts and the Colonies*. London: Faber & Faber.

Spierenburg, P. (1984) *The Spectacle of Suffering: Executions and the Evolution of Repression*. New York: Cambridge University Press.

Strom, F. (1942) *On the Sacred Origin of the Germanic Death Penalties*. Stockholm: Wahlstrom & Widstraud.

Sutherland, E. H., Cressey, D. R., and Luckenbill, D. F. (1992) *Principles of Criminology* (11th edn). Dix Hills, NY: General Hall.

Tappan, P. (1960) *Crime, Justice, and Correction*. New York: McGraw-Hill.

Van der Slice, A. (1936–7) 'Elizabethan houses of correction,' *Journal of the American Institute of Criminal Law and Criminology*, XXVII: 44–67.

Welch, M. (1991c) 'The expansion of jail capacity: makeshift jails and public policy,' in J. A. Thompson and G. L. Mays (eds), *American Jails: Public Policy Issues*. Chicago: Nelson-Hall.

Welch, M. (1994) 'Jail overcrowding: social sanitation and the warehousing of the urban underclass,' in A. R. Roberts (ed.), *Critical Issues in Crime and Justice*. Thousand Oaks, CA: Sage.

Wines, F. H. (1895) *Punishment and Reformation*. New York: Crowell.

Wines, F. H. (1971 [1895]) *An Historical Sketch of the Rise of the Penitentiary System*. New York: Benjamin Blom.

CHAPTER FOURTEEN

Women and the Criminal Justice System

Historically, criminologists have failed to recognize the relationship between gender and crime, which has led to inaccurate assumptions about women in the criminal justice system as victims, offenders, and practitioners. Although researchers have long acknowledged the fact that crime is gendered, they persist in their assumptions that the gender is always masculine. In doing so, the field of criminology, criminal justice, and academia in general have consistently ignored female offending, female offenders, and women's potential as practitioners in the field of criminal justice.[1]

A major problem pertains to the idea that women do not engage in criminal activity, and that female victimization is more limited than that of men. Like many assumptions, these ideas are not without merit, and give rise to the continued obfuscation of the reality of women and crime. For example, crime rates for women have been, and remain, significantly lower than those of men. There is also the thinking that women are less likely than men to be crime victims, with a few important exceptions. The reality, however, and what traditionalists in the academy fail to recognize, is that female violent crimes are on the rise, along with women's participation in the criminal justice system at large.[2]

---

1   Eric W. Hickey, *Serial Murders and Their Victims*, 5th edition (Belmont, CA: Wadsworth Cengage Learning, 2010).
2   Eric W. Hickey, *Serial Murders and Their Victims*, 5th edition, 2010.

CHAPTER FOURTEEN

Women and the Criminal Justice System

Any Woman's Blues

A Critical Overview of Women, Crime, and the Criminal Justice System

By Dorie Klein and June Kress*

....

I. Introduction

The changing nature of women's position in the workforce and in the family has given rise to a new set of issues concerning women's participation in crime. Among these are increasing rates of and fluctuating patterns in women's offenses, and growing resistance both through the emergence of political movements and through rising militance in women's prisons. These developments, in turn, have stimulated not only the portrayal of a new "violent" woman by the media, but also a flurry of speculation among criminologists. However, the great majority of academic material has lacked serious consideration of the economic and social position of women, and consequently has been limited by a narrow correctionalist perspective.

Therefore, this article will present, in a more systematic and politically viable fashion, several key elements critical to a radical view of the phenomenon of female crime and experience with the criminal justice system. First, we will briefly critique the traditional criminological literature on

*   **Dorie Klein** completed her doctoral studies at the School of Criminology, University of California, Berkeley. She has maintained a longstanding interest in drug policy, women, and criminal justice. As a senior research scientist at the Public Health Institute in Berkeley, California, she has conducted research on substance use treatment of adolescents in California (email: doriek@publichealth.org). **June Kress** earned a doctorate from the School of Criminology in Berkeley. Her dissertation was on legal repression, resistance, and the federal grand jury. Currently, she is executive director of the Council for Court Excellence and for many years worked as a criminal justice policy analyst, researcher, program director, consultant, and academic, including many years at the US Department of Justice COPS Office and the Bureau of Justice Assistance. She has been active in community service on behalf of the homeless (email: kress@courtexcellence.org). Both authors were members of the Editorial Board of *Crime and Social Justice*. They thanked Suzie Dod, Judy Grether, and Tony Platt for their helpful and supportive comments at the time of initial publication. This article originally appeared in *Crime and Social Justice* 5 (Spring-Summer, 1976).

women and describe how such scholarship has been utilized in the formulation of criminal justice planning, and will introduce the basic tenets of radical criminology and the developing body of feminist literature that shape the parameters of our analyses. Second, we will briefly sketch a picture of the position of women in contemporary American society, a picture that we regard as essential to any analysis of women and crime. We will then focus on the criminal justice system itself as an instrument of control and how it reflects and reinforces the particular position of women as well as the ideology of sexism. This section of the article will include an outline of female offenses, and the responses of the police, courts, and prisons, integrating an analysis of the factors that come into play in the treatment afforded women by these institutions. Furthermore, we will incorporate a critical discussion of what has been referred to as chivalry and benevolence toward women offenders, and lay the groundwork for an alternative view of differential treatment of women with reference to their political and economic position. These ideas will be utilized to illustrate our main points about the exploitative character of American justice, and more important, to raise some of the relevant "burning questions" for future investigation and practice.

II. The Criminologist's Study of Women and Crime

Cried all, "Before such things can come.
You idiotic child.
You must alter Human Nature!"
And they all sat back and smiled.
—Charlotte Perkins Gilman, "Similar Cases"

A. Traditional Criminology: Serving the State

In order to locate the theoretical underpinnings of our critical overview of women and crime, it is first essential to summarize and critique the role that traditional criminology has played in service to the state. Criminologists have almost unanimously accepted the legal definition of crime[1] and have centered primarily on the individual offender, who has been regarded as abnormal, in fact as inherently pathological. The conclusions drawn are that ill-adjusted individuals in conflict with society, in other words "deviants," must be psychologically "rehabilitated" by the criminal justice system.

This ahistorical, individualistic approach of academic criminologists has contributed to and has been reinforced by their close relationships with the criminal justice system in policy formulation. These mutually reinforcing tendencies are evidenced by the kinds of research grants they receive (for example, from the Law Enforcement Assistance Administration), from the types of studies conducted in prisons at the invitation of the staff,[2] and by the rise of the number of criminal justice schools across the country that are training professional administrators.

As far as the subject of women and crime is concerned, its sparse body of literature has been written either by men or by women without feminist consciousness. Female criminality is viewed as the result of innate biological or psychological characteristics of women that are only marginally affected by social and economic factors. These writers have made universal, ahistorical assumptions about female nature in general, based on the reproductive role. Thus, sexuality becomes the key to understanding the deviance of a woman, since this is supposedly her primary social function.[3]

Specifically, women (and women offenders) have been characterized in the literature as devious, deceitful, and emotional (Pollak 1950), intellectually dull and passive (Thomas 1907, 1923), atavistic (closer to animals in evolution) and immoral (Lombroso 1920), lonely and dependent (Konopka 1966), and anxious to serve and be loved (Herskovitz, in Pollak and Friedman 1969).

Moreover, women offenders, the direct object of these studies, are treated with condescension. The Gluecks (1934) called them a pathetic lot. Quite recently, female deviants were described as:

> Increasing numbers of broken gears and bits of flying debris ... found leaping from bridges, wandering desolate city streets, and entering banks with pistols in their pockets. (Adler 1975, 24)

Women criminals have rarely been accorded even the grudging respect shown to male criminals, who at least are seen as a threatening force with which to be reckoned. Instead, women often have been the target of voyeuristic studies concerned only with their sexuality.[4] Further, delinquency is described as a symptom of homosexuality in girls (Cowie, Cowie, and Slater 1968), or unsatisfactory relationships with the opposite sex (Vedder and Somerville 1970). One author argues that, for a delinquent girl, "whatever her offense—whether shoplifting, truancy, or running away from home—it is usually accompanied by some disturbance or unfavorable behavior in the sexual area" (Konopka 1966,4).

Basing their work on the sexual theories of motivation, few traditional criminologists recognize sexist oppression itself as a causative factor or the need for its elimination. Their recommendations for rehabilitation impose standards of femininity, which are in fact ruling-class standards. One example of this is the imposition of certain conditions for parole, which we discuss later in the article. Thus, social control, not social justice, is the underlying thread of unity in this literature. And, more important, any attempts at reform have neither changed the balance of power within the criminal justice system, nor have they fundamentally altered the class-biased nature of that system.

As previously mentioned, these writers have definitely had an influence on the control of women by the criminal justice system. Studies of "violent" women prisoners and their menstrual cycles have been federally funded, with a suggestion being the chemical regulation of these women (see Austin and Ellis 1971; West 1973). That interest in the alleged new "violent" woman is high is evidenced both by sensationalized media stories and by academics eagerly publishing confirmations (see *Newsweek* 1975; Adler 1975). Yet academics did *not* note the upswing of violence *against* women perpetrated, for example, by the state in Vietnam (see Bergman 1974) or the continued, forced sterilization of women in this country (see Allen 1974; Maclean 1975). Consequently, one must look not to traditional criminology for an understanding of women and crime, but rather to the emerging movements of radical criminology and feminism.

B. Radical Criminology: Theory and Practice

One of the outcomes of popular struggles waged during the 1960s by women, students, Third World people, and various political organizations has been an ongoing transformation of the field of criminology. Taking its early direction from the ideas and writings of prisoners themselves, a radical analysis of crime and criminal justice was in fact created outside of the academic community and adopted by students and a small number of faculty.

Theoretically, radical criminology utilizes a multidisciplinary approach to examine the issues of crime and justice, emphasizing the study of political economy. Representing a sharp break from the traditional field, radical criminology has begun to challenge the dominant assumptions long held by academic practitioners and by workers within the criminal justice system. One such challenge is to the legal definition of crime. In contrast to the traditional definition, radicals see as a starting point the notion of human rights to self-determination, dignity, food and shelter, and freedom from exploitation. This perspective defines crime as a violation of these rights, whereby the focus is on specific systems of exploitation, or criminogenic systems, such as imperialism, racism, capitalism, and sexism, because they promote inherently repressive relationships and social injury. In this orientation, the solution to crime is predicated on a total transformation of society and its inequitable political and economic system. Thus, in its broadest theoretical sense, radical criminology involves a move toward a redefinition of crime and justice.

Coupled with this is an ongoing evaluation of the criminal justice system according to whether it meets people's needs. In challenging that system, we do not deny the existence of street crime such as rape or burglary, or consider that people who commit such crimes are totally victims of an unjust society. On the contrary, petty criminals do exploit working people, and street crime is a pressing problem that demands immediate attention. But a primary focus of our work is how the economic system *itself* promotes the conditions for typical criminal behavior (see Platt 1974b). This requires an analysis of the material basis of criminality, the illegal marketplace of goods and services, e.g., drugs and prostitution,[5] and the connections between exploitative social relations and economic foundations.

In drawing its main attention away from individual offenders, radical criminology concentrates on the social structure through its recognition of the criminal justice system as a class phenomenon; that is, as an instrument of the ruling elite to maintain a social system that is class-biased, racist, and sexist (see Balbus 1973; Wolfe 1973). Our work is guided by a perspective that views the state as serving certain segments of the population over others.[6] As one coercive arm of the state, the criminal justice system protects corporate and private property. While it brings full pressure to bear on petty property offenders from the poor sectors of the population, it virtually ignores major corporate crime and handles white-collar offenses through "wrist-slapping" civil procedures.[7] Thus, the legal apparatus is in effect a dual system of justice for the rich and against the poor.

In making the study of women and crime a priority, radical and progressive criminologists have begun to confront the economic, social, and political conditions that have a direct bearing on the incidence of crime. The historical and contemporary role of women in society is analyzed in order to account for the kinds of crimes that women commit. By attempting to break down oppressive sexual attitudes that surround women, radical criminologists incorporate a political view of justice. While our theoretical work emphasizes the need to eliminate sexism and ruling class standards of femininity, our political practice concentrates on strategies of resistance to bring about fundamental change, for example anti-rape groups that are now growing on a national scale. This developing body of literature on women is characterized by a high degree of feminist consciousness. Moving well beyond mere critiques of traditional approaches, radicals and progressives have begun to develop their own political analyses of female criminality and the institutions of criminal justice that act as agents of control.

For example, the "crime" of prostitution has been reinterpreted as a question of economic survival, as a crime with a victim—the prostitute herself—who is stigmatized by arrest, vulnerable to drugs and rip-offs, and faced with financial insecurity. Recent studies have concerned themselves with the class and racial hierarchy within prostitution (Sheehy 1971), the creation of a whole class of prostitutes by US imperialism in Vietnam in the 1960s (Bergman 1974), and with convincing arguments that call for the decriminalization of prostitution (Roby and Kerr 1972; Women Endorsing Decriminalization 1973).

Another concern addressed by these more progressive writers has been the phenomenon of rape, which is a terrifying metaphor for sexist oppression shaped by class and race. Rape has been redefined as a crime against women, rather than its historical importance as a crime against *any* man whose property, i.e., his woman, had been violated by another man. Rape is now being analyzed as a form of terrorism that functions to keep woman in her place (Griffin 1971; Brownmiller 1975), and to drive an entire population into subservience (Bergman 1974). Studies demystify long-held theoretical and legal assumptions about rape and rapists (Schwendinger and Schwendinger 1974b; Weis and Borges 1973), trace racial stereotypes back to the Civil War period (Lerner 1973; Davis 1975), and explore particular problems faced by rape victims in obtaining justice from the criminal law (DeCrow 1974).

Crimes against women that have not been legally sanctioned, particularly medical practices, have also become subjects of study: for instance, works on the politics of abortion reform (Humphries 1973), the brutality of forced sterilization (Maclean 1975; Allen 1974), and the newly improved techniques of behavior modification that have been refined for use on women defined as "deviant" (Klein 1973a).

Turning their attention to the criminal justice system, feminist writers have examined the juvenile court's selective treatment of female delinquents (Rush 1972; Chesney-Lind 1973, 1974). The issue of women in prison has also been a major undertaking, as evidenced by a growing body of feminist literature that exposes the deplorable conditions of incarceration and supports women in prison who are beginning to take control over their lives (Burkhart 1973; Hansen 1974; *Women: A Journal of Liberation* 1972). Additionally, the subject of women and mental illness is seen as a priority, mainly because mental hospitalization is another form of incarceration and because of the large numbers of women undergoing psychiatric commitment (see Chesler 1972; Roth and Lerner 1975).

While many of these studies lack theory or explicit strategies for political change, all of them do illustrate a deep concern for women offenders and victims. No longer can traditional correctionalist perspectives be taken for granted. More important, today women are refusing to be the *objects* of class-biased and male–dominated social science and are increasingly speaking out for themselves. It is to this developing feminism as well as to the budding movement of radical criminology that this article owes its existence.

III. The Position of Women

Man may work from sun to sun,
*But women's work is never done—*traditional verse

A. The Family

An understanding of the relationship between women and criminal behavior requires a brief examination of women's unique economic and social position in modern capitalist society, which is rooted in the sexual and maternal aspect of female life.

The economic position of women hinges on their location in the institution of personal survival, life support, and emotional refuge known as the family. Within it, women have historically been treated as the laboring property of their individual men-fathers and husbands—who themselves have mostly had to sell their labor to other men. Thus, women have been, in the words used to describe the double oppression of black women, the "slaves of slaves." In the shift from pre-industrialism to contemporary advanced capitalism, the economic role of the family in the US has changed from being a center of production, for exchange as well as use value, to being essentially a center of consumption, as the goods required for life-support, e.g., food and clothing, are increasingly mass-produced. Thus, women's work has changed, too (Rowbotham 1973, 107–8). In that the family consumes the goods, reproduces the workers, keeps them alive, and helps to inculcate children and adults alike with the values required to maintain the legitimacy of present arrangements, women's work bolsters capitalism.

The structure of the family itself is legitimated by the ideology of sexism, which assures us that the roles filled by women are their "natural" ones. Women are meant above all to be wives and mothers, either because of their physiology (not only do women bear children, they are soft and weak as well) or their psychology (women are passive, gentle, irrational, personal, expressive). Or, if one is a liberal sociologist who scorns such superstition, women are meant to be wives and mothers above all because they do it so well, and women's work is necessary work.

B. Women's Work

Below we shall briefly outline the separate, though interrelated, elements of women's work, and note the sexist ideology that reinforces the ensuing web of oppression.[8] First, women are unpaid house workers in the family, doing the vital chores that allow their husbands, fathers, sons, and daughters to leave home and do a full week's work at a job.[9] And although it might appear that technological advances and mass production would free women from much housework, it has been estimated that the average housewife spends 99.6 hours a week performing these tasks (Rowbotham 1973). The tyranny of housework partly stems from the fact that a woman's self-esteem is tied into it: a woman is judged by the appearance of her house, and the ideal of the good housekeeper is promoted by the mass media to sell products.

Second, women are nurturing agents. They raise children, emotionally care for men, do unpaid charity work, and generally act as softening agents in a harsh and competitive society.[10] Sexist notions that women should be gentle and passive keep women nurturing others at their own expense.

Third, women are the "sexual backbone" of society. Particularly when they are young, their worth is measured by men as sexual objects. It is their function to uphold moral standards and preserve monogamous marriage, which ensures a stable society. Many young women must hustle to earn a living through their looks, as waitresses or secretaries; for unskilled women particularly, access to security depends on sexual attractiveness, whether as wives or prostitutes.[11] Further, hegemonic standards of feminine beauty keep women insecure about themselves, vulnerable to consumer exploitation, and competitive with one another for male approval.

The fourth role that women play in the political economy is that of a reserve labor force, which is bolstered by the unequal work and power structure within the family and the sexist ideology previously outlined. Women are used as part-time labor, as poorly paid and unorganized clerical workers in offices, as factory help in competitive industries with low capitalization and low wages, and as extra workers when the demand is high, for example during World War II.[12] Domestic workers, who are primarily Third World women, are among the most poorly paid workers and are lower in occupational status than anyone, performing traditional "women's work" for other women.[13] For minority women in general, decent job opportunities have until recently been almost totally denied them, out of racial prejudice, inadequate education, and sexual barriers.

It is in the area of labor-force work where women are most sharply divided in their interests along class and racial lines. Female professors, for instance, do not have the same problems at work as female domestics. However, within each class, women find themselves in defined female roles with a sex-determined lack of opportunity and control. For most women, "class privilege" is fundamentally a male prerogative that a woman marries for and loses if she loses the man. Thus, a feminist analysis must be integrated within a class analysis of women's position in order to understand women's oppression and their particular treatment within the different stages of criminal justice.

IV. The Criminal Justice System: Controlling Women

I was, being human, born alone;
I am, being woman, hard beset;
I live by squeezing from a stone
The little nourishment I get.
—Elinor Hoyt Wylie, "Let No Charitable Hope"

A. Women and the Law

The legal system mirrors and upholds the sexist ideology that legitimates women's position. Historically, women have been first the legal chattel of their fathers and later of their husbands. Only recently have women acquired independent rights in Western countries, and these have been slow in coming.

The much-vaunted "chivalry" of the law has afforded certain dubious privileges to women in return for curtailment of their rights and restrictions on their activities. Two examples are special protection on the job and the exemption of wives from prosecution for criminal conspiracy with their husbands. In the first case, the rationale of the protective legislation has been to protect women because they are mothers, and hence, in the words of the US Supreme Court in the 1908 *Muller* v. *Oregon* decision, to protect the "well-being of the race." This decision paved the way for separate job protective legislation. This same rationale was used to keep women off juries, out of state-supported colleges, and forbidden to vote. While often well intentioned, this paternalism has been at a great cost to women, especially to poor and working women. They have been denied well-paying jobs because they are legally forbidden to work at night, to lift things, or to work overtime (see Murphy and Deller Ross 1970). In the example of conspiracy exemption, the argument used to justify lenient treatment for wives has centered on women's legal irresponsibility. Like minors and slaves, wives have been not quite full persons in the eyes of the law. While they may not have been prosecuted for conspiracy, they may also then not possess marital property rights: the sword cuts two ways. They have not had control over their husbands' income and have been at their mercy for household money. After a divorce, despite long years of housework at a man's service, wives are dependent on alimony, which is awarded in only 2 percent of the cases and even then it is usually defaulted on.[14]

Women have been "protected" in the sense that they are valuable property. For example, rape has been mentioned as historically a crime against a man whose property has been violated. Rape laws attempted to regulate male ownership of women's sexual capacity and to preserve female fidelity in the nuclear family, ensuring patriarchal reproduction and inheritance. It is telling that a man cannot legally rape his own wife, and that it is extremely difficult to win a conviction of rape against a man who rapes a prostitute—she does not *belong* to another man. During the slavery era, it was an everyday occurrence for black women to experience sexual assault by their owners, white men, which also was not legally rape (see Davis 1975).

Within the realm of female sexuality and marital responsibility, legal paternalism has been severe and restrictive. The function of the law in preserving premarital chastity and marital fidelity for women is evident in requirements that women furnish proof of freedom from venereal disease to marry, prohibition of intercourse for underage women, and the outlawing of prostitution and juvenile "promiscuity." Prostitution is both a challenge and an adjunct to the nuclear family, a Coney Island mirror of marriage itself, as previously mentioned.[15] Wifely submission has been controlled by the widespread ban on abortions and birth control, and by the legal definitions of a couple's domicile as the husband's and the handing over of property control to him. Women's rights over their children have been regulated and "unfit" mothers lose custody and risk forced sterilization.[16]

The techniques of legal control over women take on broader significance when examining the class character of the law, as it becomes apparent that protection of women's rights is not a priority. From a radical viewpoint, the most critical thing to understand and to investigate is actually the lack of criminal law to deal with activities most harmful to a great number of women: production of unsafe birth control devices, profitable medical experimentation, industrial pollution, military violence, and economic injustice. Understanding these realities is crucial to understanding the following discussion of women who commit offenses and are processed through the criminal justice system at the stages of arrest, court sentencing, and prison.

B. Women Arrested

The great majority of women arrested are petty offenders. Both in 1972 and in 1974, women and men were arrested in rank order for the offenses indicated in Table 14.1.

For both years, the women's and men's lists are fairly similar. Women are apparently being arrested for proportionately fewer "violent" offenses than men: 6.1 percent in 1972 and 3.8 percent in 1974 of female arrests (aggravated assault and other assaults) vs. 8.5 percent and 7.1 percent in 1974 of male arrests (aggravated assault, robbery, and other assaults). A relatively greater percentage of women are arrested for larceny and fraud (22.6 percent in 1972 and 25.5 percent in 1974), and of course women constitute almost all of the arrests for prostitution (which can be masked as "disorderly conduct"). By and large, a good number of these women and men are not a dangerous lot. If certain "victimless" offenses (prostitution, drug use, drunkenness, and juvenile running away) were decriminalized, the number of women arrested could drop considerably.

Women and men showed percentage increases for arrests in certain categories from 1960 to 1973 and from 1973 to 1974, as illustrated in Tables 14.2 and 14.3 below. Along with rape, these seven offenses constitute the FBI Index for which national data is collected.

Despite the increase in arrests for women, we must remember that they still comprise a small percentage of all arrests, although it is still growing. This is shown below in Table 14.4.

In studying the figures, it is obvious that arrests for women are going up, relatively and absolutely. However (see Tables 14.2, 14.3, and 14.4), over the last decade women's rate of increase for "violent"

Table 14.1 Rank Order of Offenses and Percent Arrested out of All Female and Male Arrests, 1972 and 1974

Rank	Women 1972: Offense	% Female Arrests	Men 1972: Offense	% Male Arrests
1	Larceny/Theft	20.2	Drunkenness	22.9
2	Drunkenness	9.8	Drunken Driving	9.0
3	Disorderly Conduct	8.5	Disorderly Conduct	8.5
4	Narcotic Drug Laws	6.0	Larceny/Theft	8.2
5	Other Assaults	4.1	Narcotic Drug Laws	5.8
6	Drunken Driving	3.8	Burglary	4.7
7	Prostitution	3.4	Other Assaults	4.5
8	Liquor Laws	2.7	Liquor Laws	2.9
9	Embezzlement/Fraud	2.4	Aggravated Assault	2.2
10	Aggravated Assault	2.0	Robbery	1.8
11	All Other Offenses	37.1	All Other Offenses	29.5
Total		100.0		100.0

Rank	Women 1974: Offense	% Female Arrests	Men 1974: Offense	% Male Arrests
1	Larceny/Theft	22.5	Drunkenness	16.3
2	Disorderly Conduct	11.2	Drunk Driving	10.9
3	Juvenile Runaways	8.8	Larceny/Theft	9.8
4	Drunkenness	6.6	Disorderly Conduct	8.3
5	Narcotic Drug Laws	6.5	Narcotic Drug Laws	7.5
6	Drunken Driving	5.0	Burglary**	6.2
7	Prostitution	4.1	Other Assaults	4.5
8	Other Assaults	3.8	Liquor Laws	3.1
9	Fraud*	3.0	Vandalism	2.6
10	Liquor Laws	2.9	Aggravated Assaults	2.6
11	All Other Offenses	25.6	All Other Offenses	28.2
Total		100.0		100.0

* Does not include embezzlement; ** Includes breaking and entering.

Sources: Simon (1975, 45) Federal Bureau of Investigation (1975, 189).

Table 14.2 Total Arrests for Men and Women, 1960–1973

	Percentage Increase	
	Males	**Females**
Murder	141	103
Robbery	160	287
Aggravated Assault	116	106
Burglary	76	193
Larceny	84	341
Auto Theft	59	155
Fraud	50	281
Narcotic Drug Laws	995	1,027

Source: Newsweek (1975, January 6, p. 35).

Table 14.3 Total Arrests for Men and Women, 1973–1974

	Percentage Increase	
	Males	**Females**
Murder*	5.6	1.2
Robbery	13.6	14.1
Aggravated Assault	9.9	14.6
Burglary/Breaking & Entering	20.5	20.1
Larceny/Theft**	25.6	23.0
Motor Vehicle Theft***	−2.9	3.8
Fraud	11.8	22.4
Narcotic Drug Laws	2.5	−.1

* Includes non-negligent manslaughter; ** Includes larceny under $50; *** Includes all kinds of motor vehicles.
Source: Federal Bureau of Investigation (1975, 190).

crimes without obvious economic motive (murder, aggravated assault) has not been as great as men's or as great as their (women's) rate of increase for property and drug offenses. Over the past 10 years, women's rate of increase *has* exceeded men's for robbery, burglary, auto theft, and fraud, although it is still true that in these categories women's actual number of arrests barely approaches that of men (see Table 14.4). Fraud has been one of the traditional "women's offenses." Women have also always been arrested for drug offenses. This stands in contrast to media reports and sociologists' warnings (see Adler 1975) that a new "violent" breed of female criminal is on the rise, and that women are becoming more aggressive. As Simon (1975, 46) states:

Table 14.4 Percentages of Females among All Arrests, 1953–1974

| Year | All Crimes | Serious Crimes* | |
		Violent**	Property***
1953	10.8	11.9	8.5
1954	11.0	11.6	8.2
1955	11.0	12.0	8.4
1956	10.9	13.5	8.0
1957	10.6	13.1	8.5
1958	10.6	12.0	9.3
1959	10.7	12.7	10.1
1960	11.0	11.8	10.8
1961	11.2	11.6	11.4
1962	11.5	11.5	12.6
1963	11.7	11.6	12.9
1964	11.9	11.6	13.9
1965	12.1	11.4	15.0
1966	12.3	11.3	15.6
1967	12.7	10.8	16.0
1968	13.1	10.3	16.1
1969	13.8	10.6	18.0
1970	14.6	10.5	19.7
1971	15.1	10.9	20.1
1972	15.3	11.0	21.4
1973	15.6	10.0	21.1
1974	16.1	10.2	21.2

* All those included in FBI Crime Index except rape; ** Homicide, robbery, aggravated assault; *** Burglary, larceny, motor vehicle theft.
Sources: Adapted from Simon (1975, 35, 38); 1973 and 1974 figures from Federal Bureau of Investigation (1975, 190).

In sum, the arrest data tell us the following about women's participation in crime: the proportion of female arrests in 1972 was greater than the proportion arrested one or two decades earlier; the increase was greater for serious offenses than it was for all Type I and Type II offenses combined.[17] The increase in female arrest rates among the serious offenses was owing almost entirely to women's greater participation in property offenses, especially larceny. In 1953, roughly 1 out of 7 arrests for larceny involved a woman; in 1972, the proportion was approximately 1 out of 3. Contrary to impressions that might be gleaned from the mass media, the proportion of female arrests for violent crimes has changed hardly at all over the past two decades. Female arrest for homicide, for example, has been the most stable of all violent offenses,[18]

A rise or decline in arrest rates does not necessarily indicate a rise or decline in real illegal activity. It may reflect the political situation in, or growth of, law enforcement circles, a different organization of the data, changes in arrest categories, or altered perceptions of women offenders by the police. (Not all offenders are equally vulnerable to capture. For example, rapists have often escaped being reported, and the high estimated rape rate is in contrast to the low arrest rate for charged rapists.) However, the arrest figures above do raise questions about women's participation in the illegal marketplace. As we have previously discussed, women are economically an underpaid group, and in a simplistic determinist view, we would expect very high rates of petty property offenses because of their economic situations. We do not agree with Pollak (1950) that women do commit as many offenses as men, but receive more lenient treatment and hence escape the law. There are other factors involved.

Due to women's historical position in the management of commodity production and distribution, including the competitive illegal marketplace of goods and services, e.g., drugs and prostitution, most women are not socially, psychologically, or economically in a position at this time to aggressively steal, nor do those with male providers have such a need. Women are traditionally just as timid and just as limited by male constrictions on their roles and male leadership within the arena of crime as they are "above ground." They are no more big-time drug dealers than they are finance capitalists. They are, however, first, petty offenders in the area of "consumerism," which reflects their position as house workers in "straight" society. They shoplift, use illicit drugs purchased from men—especially the less-threatening barbiturates and amphetamines, often over-prescribed—and pass bad checks. Second, they may act as accomplices to men in offenses such as robbery. Third, just as most women must sell themselves, in a sense, in marriage, so prostitution affords other women the opportunity to earn a living through their sexuality. To understand why women become prostitutes, then, one must look not only at their personal histories, but also at women's general condition. As surrogate wives and lovers, prostitutes serve the same functions of sexual work and nurturance that other women do. Fourth, women "on the streets" are harassed for vagrancy and drunkenness much as men in their situation are, chivalry not notwithstanding. Fifth, juvenile females are apprehended for status offenses, such as running away. And finally, women commit "crimes of passion," primarily against husbands and lovers, and strike out sometimes at children as well, which may reflect emotional frustration created by sexist roles.

Women's lack of participation in "big time" crime highlights the larger class structure of sexism that is reproduced in the illegal marketplace. Also reproduced is the structure of racism—for example, black streetwalkers are the worst-paid and worst-treated group of prostitutes, and young white call girls are the most highly privileged. Of course, black prostitutes have disproportionately high arrest rates; in New York City in the late 1960s, blacks were arrested on that charge ten times more frequently than whites were (Winick and Kinsie 1971, 43).

In the current economic crisis, with the likelihood that women—along with other non-favored groups such as Third World people and the young—will be the first fired, one may expect that women may begin to commit more "street offenses" as they are thrown out of work. Conversely, with the rise of job opportunities for certain classes of women, and the increased integration of women into the labor force partly due to the successes of the women's movement, women who *are* working may be more affluent and may also have more opportunities for the types of crimes that were once remote: white-collar offenses such as embezzlement. The change in the family structures and functions, such as women increasingly heading households, may also affect future patterns of illicit activity.

With these changes, does it mean that we will see a great change in women's crime rates? We do not have an answer to this question, but we can pose some hypotheses. First, the incorporation of women into the labor force does not mean the end of sexism. Women continue to be trained for low-paying "women's work" in roles that require submissiveness and compliancy; and sexist ideology continues, of course, to be legitimated and reproduced by the mass media and educational and cultural institutions. This may mean, then, that we can expect an increase in or at least the maintenance of the rate of traditional women's crime (accomplices to men, check writing, etc.). On the other hand, if the women's movement develops a class analysis of women's oppression and a program around which working-class women can be organized, then we may witness a decrease in women's individualism, self-destructiveness, competitiveness, and crime. Finally, what is the relationship between the deteriorating economic situation and women's crime rates? We can expect greater pressure on the wives and lovers of working-class men who are laid off from their jobs and perhaps an increase in crime-related activities such as welfare fraud and prostitution.

Whatever the outcome of this process, we are certain that the women's movement is not criminogenic. Freda Adler's book owes its popularity, no doubt, to the fact that it reinforces sexist stereotyping and is written by a woman. In contrast to her simplistic analysis of the roots of women's crime, we must look more deeply into the social relations under capitalism and to the systematic and special oppression that women suffer. Clearly, these relationships require further study.

C. Women and the Judiciary

At the second stage of the criminal justice system, the judiciary, women appear to fare better than their male counterparts in obtaining leniency. The following are 1972 figures for California:

Table 14.5 Percentage of Persons Charged Who Pleaded Guilty and Who Were Convicted, 1972

	Women				Men		
	Number Charged	Percent Pleading Guilty	Percent Convicted	Number Charged	Percent Pleading Guilty	Percent Convicted
All Crimes	6,394	69.2	83.2	49,567	72.1	87.6
Violent Crimes	797	59.3	80.7	8,762	63.5	87.0
Property Crimes	2,003	79.8	89.6	16,614	79.4	91.0

Source: Simon (1975,64–65).

One might assume a relationship between the percentage of each sex pleading guilty and the percentage convicted; however, women are particularly prone to receiving acquittal for "violent" crimes, especially murder, a crime for which almost the same proportion of women (42.2 percent) as men (42.5 percent) pleaded guilty, and for which only 77.6 percent of those women were convicted (in contrast to 86.3 percent of the men) (figures from ibid, not shown here). And even those crimes for which women pleaded guilty more frequently than men (property crimes), the bias of leniency toward women holds. In the case of "violence," part of the explanation for the clear-cut difference in the treatment afforded men and women may be due to the insignificant number of women charged with these offenses who come through court; in these rare cases, judges may tend toward leniency. Second, many women commit "crimes of passion" against spouses or lovers, as opposed to the more frequent random shooting of strangers or casual acquaintances among men (see Wolfgang 1958), and courts are traditionally forgiving in the former type of case. A factor that may operate across offense categories is that women charged are often accomplices in male-initiated crimes rather than the instigators, and hence are more likely to be acquitted.

In juvenile court, on the other hand, a different picture emerges. Girls have received *more* severe treatment than boys have, in that they are referred to the juvenile courts more frequently for minor offenses. The following are 1964 figures for the Honolulu Juvenile Court:

Table 14.6 Delinquency Referrals Made to the Honolulu Juvenile Court, 1964: Nature of Alleged Offense by Sex of Accused

	Male	Female
Part I (Type I) Offenses	52.8	17.5
Part II (Type II) Offenses	19.8	8.0
"Sex Offenses"*	1.8	11.4
Juvenile Offenses**	25.7	63.1
	100.0	100.0
	(2,191)	(537)

* Not including prostitution; ** Includes running away, curfew violations, and incorrigibility.
Source: Chesney-Lind (1973, 60–61).

Unlike male delinquents, girls are by and large brought to the attention of the court for offenses that would not be criminal were they committed by adults. This is borne out by the findings of the "Task Force Report: Juvenile Delinquency and Youth Crime" of the President's Commission on Law Enforcement and the Administration of Justice (1967), which found that over half the girls, but one-fifth of the boys, were referred to court for juvenile (non-criminal) activities.

Girls are also detained longer in institutions than boys are, despite the fact that their offenses are generally less serious. For example, in Honolulu in 1964, girls were detained an average of 19.3 days, compared to 8.9 days for the boys (Chesney–Lind 1973, 63).

Conversely, the frequency with which adult women are sentenced to imprisonment parallels their rate of conviction. Despite their proportional rise in arrests, women have barely risen as a percentage of prisoners. In California in 1952, women made up only 3.2 percent of the prisoner population; 20 years later, they still accounted for only 3.9 percent (Simon 1975, 75). Within each category of offense, women are more lightly sentenced, usually receiving a fine or probation. (They are also more frequently paroled once incarcerated.) The following are representative figures:

Table 14.7 California: Percentage of Convicted Persons Committed to Prison by Crime and Sex, 1969

	Women	Men
Homicide	34.4	59.1
Robbery	28.0	42.1
Assault	6.0	11.3
Burglary	7.4	11.8
Theft	16.6	28.8
Forgery/Checks	3.6	10.0
Narcotics	2.1	4.6
All Above Crimes	5.1	11.8
Violent Crimes	14.3	27.3
Property Crimes	6.2	14.0

Source: Simon (1975, 76).

However, there are differences in the leniency shown women for various offenses. They receive the relatively lightest sentences compared to men for traditional "nonviolent" female offenses: forgery and narcotics. Unlike the pattern of conviction, where "violent" women are disproportionately acquitted (see Table 14.5), those convicted receive less benign treatment in sentencing.

Differential court treatment for women and girls, both economic and sexual offenders, has been dismissed as evidence of chivalry in the male-dominated criminal justice system. However, it is fundamental to view the system as an instrument of control over people, and in the case of women, reflecting and reinforcing the sexism in society at large. Its class bias explains the phenomenon that has previously been attributed to chivalry.[19] The legal treatment of women offenders can only be understood in reference to the place of women in the economic and social structure. Because of their differences from men in production and reproduction, which we have outlined, women commit different sorts of offenses from men, as shown, and consequently are treated differently. That is, they are de facto penalized less harshly than men are at this time at various stages of the criminal justice system—particularly with reference to Third World men—when they commit certain economic or "violent" offenses. This has come about because, first, women comprise still a fraction of offenders in these categories; second, women are *seen* as economically marginal; and, in view of the previous factors and the stereotypes of female docility, women are not taken as serious threats to the social order. One may speculate that women's changing situation will create strains in the fabric of leniency.

In contrast to the benefit of the doubt shown women at the judicial level for certain offenses, they are penalized far more harshly than men are for crimes defined as sexual, such as prostitution, juvenile promiscuity, and incorrigibility. Again, this is comprehensible only in the context of women's central role in reproduction and the legal sanctions regarding their sexuality previously discussed. It is also the case that workers in the criminal justice system at various levels and stages tend to agree with the criminologists' tendency to view even female *property* offenders as sexually motivated deviants, due to sexist preconceptions. For example, scholars and psychiatrists see women shoplifters as women sublimating their sexuality (see Pollak 1950). Prostitution, which is most often an economically motivated activity, is legally defined as a sexual deviation, like child molesting, and women entering this field are seen as promiscuous (see Davis 1937). Consequently, prostitutes (and all female offenders) bear a social stigma connected to sexuality unshared by, say, thieves. (However, patronizing prostitutes and, to a lesser degree, pimping for them, is not regarded as equally depraved or "self-destructive," if one is a liberal.)

For example, girls brought to juvenile court for all sorts of offenses are routinely examined for virginity. Putting themselves *in loco parentis*, judges uphold standards of female chastity; in the name of sweet womanhood, girls are locked up for their own protection. Chesney-Lind (1973, 54) notes:

> Since female adolescents have a much narrower range of acceptable behavior, even minor deviance may be seen as a substantial challenge to the authority of the family, the viability of the double standard, and to the maintenance of the present system of sexual inequality. It is the symbolic threat posed by female delinquency to these values that best explains (1) why the juvenile court system selects out aspects of female deviance which violate sex role expectations rather than those that violate legal norms; and (2) why female delinquency, especially sexual delinquency, is viewed as more serious than male delinquency and is therefore more severely sanctioned.

In the case of adult women, on the other hand, it is contrary to the interests of society for large numbers of offenders to be incarcerated, given their nurturing and housekeeping functions. Women cannot care for children in prison; 38 percent of mothers incarcerated lose custody of their children, and this creates a burden for the state (Hansen 1974, 2). As the superintendent of the California Institute for Women (CIW) states:

> Almost all the women who come to prison have husbands and children. If a man goes to prison, the wife stays home, and he usually has his family to return to, and the household is there when he gets out. But women generally don't have family support from the outside. Very few men are going to sit around and take care of the children and be there when she gets back. So—to send a woman to prison means you are virtually going to disrupt her family. (Simon 1975, 77)

Yet women *are* sentenced to prison. In the final analysis, chivalry is above all a classist and racist notion that has been extended primarily to affluent white women. For those outside the pale—Third World women, poor whites, political rebels—chivalry is less reliable. Documentation of police beatings, court severity, and harsh imprisonment for female radicals throughout American history illustrates this (see Zinn 1964). As Sojourner Truth, a black woman born into slavery, eloquently declared:

> That man over there say that women needs to be helped into carriages, or over mud puddles, and to have the best place everywhere. Nobody ever help me into carriages or over ditches or gives me any best places ... and ain't I a woman? Look at me! Look at my arm! I have plowed and planted and gathered into barns, and no man could head me—and ain't I a woman? I could work as much as a man (when I could get it) and bear the lash as well—and ain't I a woman? I have borne five children and I seen them most sold off into slavery, and when I cried out with a mother's grief none but Jesus heard—ain't I a woman?

It is precisely women who are not "ladies" by ruling-class standards who are likely to be sentenced to prison, and to commit offenses in the first place, making them vulnerable to arrest. The racism in the judiciary is illuminated by various statistical reports. In the Washington, DC, correctional system, a study found 73 percent of the 3,000 women surveyed to be black, as opposed to 27 percent white. Of the blacks, 14 percent remained in jail over a month awaiting trial, as opposed to 8 percent of the whites. More strikingly, 83 percent of the blacks and only 17 percent of the whites were returned to jail following arraignment (charges not dropped, disposed of; bail not granted or paid). The black conviction rate was 60 percent, while the white rate was 40 percent (*Off Our Backs* 1973).

Each level of the criminal justice system discriminates against blacks and the poor, not only out of judicial prejudice, but also through procedures and standards that favor the affluent. Because of racism, poverty, and white cultural hegemony,[20] blacks may in fact *have* higher rates of "street crime." The tragic forced "emancipation" of black women into heading families and holding jobs

has created a great economic burden for them; thus, the gap between black women and men in the commission of crimes of survival is narrower than that between white women and men.

Poor women of all races are disproportionately sent to prison. A study of the Federal Reformatory for Women at Alderson, West Virginia (where, in fact, one might expect a more affluent group than in state or local institutions), showed the prisoners to be poorly paid and poorly educated in their backgrounds. Of the 600-odd women, one-third had been in service occupations. They were employed as laundry workers, hospital attendants, and beauticians; and more women did waitressing than any other occupation. About 10 percent each were domestics, housewives, factory operatives, and clericals. Only about 2 percent owned or managed small businesses of their own.

Half the population had only or less than a grammar school education, and only 28 women had gone to college (Giallombardo 1966).

The hierarchy within the illegal marketplace also affects a woman's chances within the criminal justice system. Within prostitution, for example, young or attractive white call girls can easily evade arrest and earn considerable money, whereas older, black and working-class streetwalkers are most vulnerable. Gail Sheehy (1971, 33–35) notes:

> Probably no vocation operates with such a fierce system of social distinction as prostitution. The streetwalker has nothing but slurs for those "lazy flatbackers," meaning call girls. The call girl expresses contempt for the "ignorant street hooker." The madam wouldn't be caught dead with a "diseased" street girl .... The street hooker is at the bottom of the blue-collar end of the ladder. She far outnumbers anyone in the business.

Streetwalkers are financially victimized by "revolving door" justice—the series of street cleanups that rarely result in lengthy imprisonment. The women are consequently at the mercy of pimps, corrupt police, lawyers, bail bondsmen, politicians, and racketeers, who prey on them. Their treatment can hardly be described as chivalrous.

D. Women in Prison

Within the third stage of the criminal justice system, the very insignificance of the volume of women prisoners—nationally 5,600 women out of a total of 196,000 inmates in 1970 (Simon 1975, 69)—adversely affects women who *are* incarcerated. First, there are few separate women's prisons and only the largest cities have makeshift quarters for women within men's facilities, such as the one that housed Joan Little.[21] Only 15 states have separate women's jails. In city jails, prostitutes and drug offenders spend a good deal of their time and there are few resources available to them. Second, in the women's prisons that do exist, few vocational or industrial programs comparable to men's (which are themselves inadequate) exist. While the average number of vocational programs in a men's prison is 10, the average number for women is 2.7. Similarly, the choice of vocations that women can train for is extremely limited: compared to the 50-odd programs for men, women get cosmetology, food service, clerical skills, keypunching, and nurse's aide training (ibid., 80–83).

A characteristic of the penal system for women is marked paternalism and false benevolence. Some prisons for women resemble school campuses, e.g., Alderson Federal Reformatory and the California Institute for Women. Inmates are treated in such a way as to reinforce their helplessness and dependence on authority. In other prisons, of course, such as the New York House of Detention, conditions are brutal and in no way campus-like.

In general, the rehabilitative ideal has fit nicely with the womanly ideal. Convicts are presented with the model of the lady, a hegemonic standard of conduct that speaks little to their own social and sexual needs. For example, "ladylike" behavior may be required as a condition of parole.[22] The standards imposed are those of sexual virtue, namely monogamous heterosexuality confined to the nuclear family.

The ubiquitous psychological view held by treatment personnel, which sees offenders as individually responsible for their misdeeds, diverts attention away from social and economic inequalities such as sexism and toward the psyche. This underscores the way in which women are generally isolated, both physically in the nuclear family (unlike men, who work and socialize freely) and emotionally, tending toward a conservative personalization of the world. The rehabilitative ideal strengthens privatism and attempts to deaden movements of political or collective activity. The rehabilitative failure is evidenced by the deep and justified cynicism among treatment personnel, which reflects the reality that they are regulating and not reducing criminal activity.

The developing medical model of rehabilitation, which defines crime as illness and the prisoner as patient in traditional liberal form, again reinforces women's childlike helplessness. Women are commonly child/patients under the male domination of doctors and husbands (see Chesler 1972; Roth and Lerner 1975). Historically "ideal" mental patients and medical guinea pigs, women convicted of "crimes"

now suffer the indignity of behavior modification and enforced therapies behind bars.[23] Women have been the targets of extreme technologies of control; the "father of psychosurgery" in the United States, Dr. Walter Freeman, contended that women made the best candidates for lobotomy, and cited one elderly housewife who "was a master at bitching and really led her husband a dog's life" until surgery made her into a model housekeeper. A contemporary neurosurgeon has estimated that up to 80 percent of his patients have been women (Klein 1973a, 7–8). Hospitalization and chemotherapy, less spectacularly, have been prime methods for controlling deviant women, who might have been imprisoned for their conduct had they been male. It is possible that high rates of mental hospitalization for women complement their low rates of imprisonment.

In sum, differential treatment of women in the criminal justice system has been based on the assumption that, treated paternalistically, women will not make trouble. They have not constituted a major problem so far, and the volume has been too small to trouble the state. Chivalrous treatment has been a double-edged sword, as our preceding arguments have made clear:

> Women are not oppressed in the same way as black people, for example; they are not at the bottom of many scales and at the top of none. There is a pedestal—they are respected and praised for many things, for greater sensitivity, for moral fortitude, for modesty .... In some sense, then, one might say that the job of bringing up children has high status, but the status of a different kind than most. It is sex-specific, it is compulsory, and the price is too high. (Quick 1972, 13)

V. Conclusion

In this article we have critically reviewed the position of women with respect to the criminal justice system in the United States. We have indicated that the special oppression of women by that system is not isolated or arbitrary, but rather is rooted in systematic sexist practices and ideologies that can only be fully understood by analyzing the position of women in capitalist society. However, there are changes occurring in the position and activities of women—in their participation in the labor force, in educational opportunities, political activity, and family roles. Consequently, all of this has had repercussions in the legal system: witness such upheavals as the inadequacy of rape laws that are currently being challenged, and the debate around the overcriminalization of prostitution.

The same conditions that are at the root of the sexist oppression of women are also responsible for the rise in recent years of a revitalized women's movement, which has changed women's consciousness and has been organizing around the right to abortion, the decriminalization of prostitution, and the needs of prisoners. Although a full discussion is outside the scope of this article, it is in this arena that we view the potential for struggles of resistance. For example, the emergence of a viable women's prisoners' movement in places such as New York, California, and Washington, DC, has created concrete links between women inside and outside. This has encouraged organizing for improved prison conditions and creating alternatives such as halfway houses and prison education programs with substantive content. Self-defense and self-help groups against rape have evolved into strong supportive mechanisms for victimized women. In cities across the country, these groups have exerted pressure on police and hospitals to treat women with respect instead of condemnation. Furthermore, the struggle to decriminalize prostitution has been carried out by prostitutes' unions (COYOTE in San Francisco, ASP in Seattle, PONY in New York) that, in the face of incredible social stigma, have fought creatively and successfully to educate people and win legitimacy.

These political activities, together with the increasingly active role played by women in militant organizations (see, for example, the number of women on the FBI's "Ten Most Wanted" list), have brought women's groups under repressive fire from the government. Moreover, one can observe a trend toward the use of more blatant techniques of control in women's prisons previously reserved for men. The myth of the "violent female criminal" has conveniently appeared in the popular media when women are asserting themselves. Repression does not only take the form of clubs and guns. Its ideological forms can be just as devastating in the long run. Clearly, women can no longer argue for special treatment, although activism has set in motion the dynamics of repression. We see these continued struggles against repression as the best way to work toward the creation of a more humane system of justice.

Notes

1. Fora discussion of the legal definition of crime vs. radical alternatives, see Herman Schwendinger and Julia Schwendinger (1970).

2. For a discussion of "agency-determined research," see Tony Platt (1974a); see also Herman Schwendinger and Julia Schwendinger (1974) for a lengthy treatment of the technocratic perspective in general.

3. See Dorie Klein (1973b) for a substantive discussion of the traditional criminological views on women.

4. An example of this is Ward and Kassebaum's study (1965) of the California Institute for Women, which is primarily concerned with inmate lesbianism.

5. We are indebted to the Schwendingers for introducing us to this concept.

6. See Ralph Miliband (1969) for an analysis of the role of government in capitalist society and economic and state elites.

7. An excellent analysis of corporate crime may be found in David Gordon (1971).

8. Fora fuller discussion of the elements of women's work, see Juliet Mitchell (1969), Margaret Benston (1969), and Paddy Quick (1972).

9. In discussing housework under capitalism, Paddy Quick (1972, 67) notes:

   If it admitted that the family is maintained at the expense of women, capitalism would have to devise some other way of getting the work done. Although this is not inconceivable, and housework could be socialized within capitalism, the political and social consequences as well as the economic cost would be considerable. At present it would seem to be more profitable for the capitalist system to continue to "preserve the family."

10. See Tony Platt (1969) for an historical analysis of women reformers.

11. It is still true that only marriage offers a woman any kind of economic security, as the following figures show. These are 1968 median earnings of fulltime workers (Quick 1972, 6):

	Women	Men
Year-round workers	$4,818	$8,226
Unrelated individuals	2,239	4,086
Families headed by*	4,477	9,096

   * With wife working, $10,686; with just men working, $8,215.

12. During that time, four million women joined the labor force while the men were overseas. Their occupations put the myths to rest about what women could do; "Women became welders and shipbuilders; they built airplanes and produced ammunition; they made complicated electrical equipment and riveted the sides of tanks. By the end of the war, women were working in almost all areas of manufacturing" (Trey 1972, 44). Within a month after the war's end, however, 600,000 women were fired, and those women who did maintain jobs were often demoted to lower-paid "women's jobs" within factories.

13. Nonwhite women suffer particularly within the labor force, as the following figures show. These are wages for 1967 (Beal 1970, 345):

White men	$6,704
White women	3,991
Nonwhite men	4,277
Nonwhite women	2,861

14. See Karen DeCrow (1974) for a fuller discussion of women and the law.

15. The law, by creating a "bad" class of women, sanctifies only one form of sex-as-barter: marriage (see Goldman 1970). Yet marriage and prostitution are inextricably linked. Simone de Beauvoir (1961, 523–24) has written:

> It has often been remarked that the necessity exists of sacrificing one part of the female sex in order to save the other and prevent worse troubles. One of the arguments in support of slavery advanced by the American supporters of the institution was that the Southern whites, being all freed from servile duties, could maintain the most democratic and refined relationships among themselves; in the same way, a caste of "shameless women" allows the "honest woman" to be treated with the most chivalrous respect.

It is the irony of the legal system that it punishes individual prostitutes and in no way challenges the inevitability of prostitution in a society plagued by male sexual consumerism and female economic impoverishment. While prostitution may not be eradicated under capitalism, the well-being of women demands that it be decriminalized.

16. For example, "in the U.S. over the last few years, an estimated 100,000 to 150,000 low-income persons have been sterilized annually under federally funded programs" (Maclean 1975, I). In Puerto Rico, by 1965 "34% of the women of child-bearing age had been sterilized in so-called 'family planning' programs paid for and controlled by the U.S. Department of Health, Education and Welfare" (Allen 1974, 6).

17. Type I offenses are the FBI Index Crimes, Type II offenses are, for example, non-aggravated assault, fraud, forgery, narcotics laws, and prostitution.

18. In 1953, women comprised 14.1 percent of homicide arrests; by 1972, they were still only 15.6 percent (Simon 1975, 40).

19. See Walter Reckless and Barbara Kay (1967) for a summary of this view.

20. Bias is shown, for example, in the prohibition of leisure activities widespread among minorities: gambling, use of certain drugs (see Helmer 1975).

21. For a discussion of this case, see Angela Davis (1975).

22. At CIW, several hundred operations for plastic surgery were performed on prisoners in 1974. A good appearance was a condition for release (Angell 1975).

23. "The Management Cottage at CIW has about 40 women who were completely segregated from the rest ... the behavior modification was where inmates were trained to police each other 6 hours a day of group (therapy). They wouldn't allow a person to come out .... Put into this unit were always dissenters" (*Off Our Backs* 1975).

References

Adler, Freda 1975. *Sisters in Crime: The Rise of the New Female Criminal.* New York: McGraw-Hill.

Allen, Barbara 1974. "Stop Forced Sterilization." *Sister-West Coast Feminist Newspaper* (November).

American Friends Service Committee 1971. *Struggle for Justice.* New York: Hill and Wang.

Angell, Catherine 1975. "Sex Role Stereotyping and Women in the Criminal Law System." Paper presented at the 70th Annual Meeting of the American Sociological Association, San Francisco (August).

Austin, Penelope and Desmond Ellis 1971. "Menstruation and Aggressive Behavior in a Correctional Center for Women." *Journal of Criminal Law. Criminology and Police Science* 62(3) (September).

Balbus, Isaac D. 1973. *The Dialectics of Legal Repression.* New York: Russell Sage Foundation.

Beal, Frances 1970. "Double Jeopardy: To Be Black and Female." In *Sisterhood Is Powerful,* edited by Robin Morgan. New York: Vintage.

Beauvoir, Simone de 1961. *The Second Sex.* New York: Bantam Books

Benston, Margaret 1969. "The Political Economy of Women's Liberation." *Monthly Review* (September).

Bergman, Arlene Eisen 1974. *Women of Viet Nam.* San Francisco: People's Press.

Boggs, Carl 1972. "Gramsci's Prison Notebook." *Socialist Revolution* 11 & 12 (September-October and November-December).

Brownmiller, Susan 1975. *Against Our Will: Men, Women and Rape.* New York: Simon and Schuster.

Burkhart. Katherine W. 1973. *Women in Prison.* New York: Doubleday and Company.

Chesler, Phyllis 1972. *Women and Madness.* New York: Doubleday and Company.

Chesney-Lind, Meda 1973. "Judicial Enforcement of the Female Sex Role: The Family Court and the Female Delinquent." *Issues in Criminology* 8(2) (Fall).

_____. 1974. "Juvenile Delinquency: The Sexualization of Female Crime." *Psychology Today* (July).

Cleaver, Eldridge 1968. *Soul on Ice,* New York: McGraw-Hill.

Cowie, John, Valerie Cowie, and Eliot Slater 1968. *Delinquency in Girls.* London: Heinemann.

Dalla Costa, Mariarosa 1972. "*Women and the Subversion of the Community.*" London: Failing Wall Press.

Davis, Angela 1971. *If They Come in the Morning.* New York: Signet Books.

_____. 1974. *An Autobiography.* New York: Random House.

_____. 1975. "Joan Little—The Dialectics of Rape." *Ms. Magazine* (June).

Davis, Kingsley 1937. "The Sociology of Prostitution." *American Sociological Review* 2(5) (October).

DeCrow, Karen 1974. *Sexist Justice.* New York: Random House.

Federal Bureau of Investigation 1975. *Uniform Crime Reports, 1974.* Washington, DC: U.S. Government Printing Office.

Firestone, Shulamith 1971. *The Dialectic of Sex.* New York: William Morrow.

Giallombardo. Rose 1966. *Society of Women: A Study of a Women's Prison.* New York: John Wiley and Sons.

Glassman, Carol 1970. "Women and the Welfare System." In *Sisterhood Is Powerful,* edited by Robin Morgan. New York: Vintage.

Glueck, Eleanor and Sheldon 1934. *Four Hundred Delinquent Women.* New York: Alfred Knopf.

Goldman, Emma 1970. *The Traffic in Women and Other Essays on Feminism.* New York: Times Change Press.

Gordon, David 1971. "Class and the Economics of Crime." *Review of Radical Political Economics* 3(3) (Summer).

Griffin, Susan 1971. "Rape: The All-American Crime." *Ramparts* (September).

Guettel, Charnie 1974. *Marxism and Feminism.* Toronto: The Women's Press.

Hansen, Donna 1974. "Mothers in Prison." *Sister-West Coast Feminist Newspaper* (November).

Helmer, John 1975. *Drugs and Minority Oppression.* New York: Seabury Press.

Humphries, Drew 1973. "The Politics of Abortion: A Case Study of New York's Abortion Law." Unpublished doctoral dissertation. School of Criminology, University of California, Berkeley.

Kittrie, Nicholas 1973. *The Right to Be Different.* Baltimore: Penguin Books.

Klein, Dorie 1973a. "Notes on the Center for the Study and Reduction of Violence." Pacific News Service (August).

_____. 1973b. "The Etiology of Female Crime: A Review of the Literature." *Issues in Criminology* 8(2) (Fall).

Konopka, Gisela 1966. *The Adolescent Girl in Conflict.* Englewood Cliffs: Prentice-Hall.

Lerner, Gerda (ed.) 1973. *Black Women in White America: A Documentary History.* New York: Vintage.

Liazos, Alex 1972. "The Poverty of the Sociology of Deviance: Nuts. Sluts and Preverts." *Social Problems* 20(1) (Summer).

Lombroso, Cesare 1920. *The Female Offender* (translation). New York: Appleton. Originally published in 1903.

Maclean. Pam 1975. "Sterilization Hearings." *Plexus* 2(4) (June).

Marcuse, Herbert 1968. *One-Dimensional Man.* Boston: Beacon Press.

Miliband, Ralph 1969. *The State in Capitalist Society.* New York: Basic Books.

Mitchell, Juliet 1969. "The Longest Revolution." In *Masculine-Feminine,* edited by Betty and Theodore Roszak. New York: Harper & Row.

Murphy, Jean and Susan Deller Ross 1970. "Liberating Women—Legally Speaking." In *With Justice for Some,* edited by Bruce Wasserstein and Mark J. Green. Boston: Beacon Press.

New York Radical Feminists 1974. *Rape: The First Sourcebook for Women.* New York: New American Library.

Off Our Backs 1973. "Prisons." (January).

_____. 1975. "Interview: Women Ex-Cons." (April-May).

Pearce, Frank. 1972. "Crime, Corporations and the American Social Order." In *Politics and Deviance,* edited by Ian Taylor and Laurie Taylor. London: Penguin.

Platt, Tony 1969. *The Child Savers.* Chicago: University of Chicago Press.

_____. 1974a. "Prospects for a Radical Criminology in the United States." *Crime and Social Justice* 1 (Spring-Summer).

_____. 1974b. "Problems in the Development of Radical Criminology." Paper presented at the 69th Annual Meeting of the American Sociological Association, Montreal (August).

Pollak, Otto 1950. *The Criminality of Women.* Philadelphia: University of Pennsylvania Press.

Pollak, Otto and Alfred Friedman (eds.) 1967. "Task Force Report: Juvenile Delinquency and Youth Crime." Washington, DC: U.S. Government Printing Office.

_____. 1969. *Family Dynamics and Female Sexual Delinquency.* Palo Alto: Science and Behavioral Books, President's Commission on Law Enforcement and the Administration of Justice.

Quick, Paddy 1972. "Women's Work." *Review of Radical Political Economics* 4(3) (July).

Quinney, Richard 1974. *Critique of Legal Order: Crime Control in Capitalist Society.* Boston: Little, Brown and Company.

Reckless. Walter and Barbara Kay 1967. "The Female Offender." Report to the President's Commission on Law Enforcement and the Administration of Justice. Washington, DC: U.S. Government Printing Office.

Roby, Pamela and Virginia Kerr 1972. "The Politics of Prostitution." *Nation* (April 10).

Roth, Bob and Judith Lerner 1975. "Sex-Based Discrimination in the Mental Institutionalization of Women." *California Law Review* 62.

Rowbotham, Sheila 1973. *Woman's Consciousness, Man's World.* London: Pelican Books.

Rush, Florence 1972. "The Myth of Sexual Delinquency." *Women: A Journal of Liberation* 3(3).

Schwendinger, Herman and Julia Schwendinger 1970. "Defenders of Order or Guardians of Human Rights?" *Issues in Criminology* 5(2).

_____. 1973. "A Report to the European Group at the Florence Conference." Paper presented at the First Conference of the European Group for the Study of Deviance and Social Control, Impruneta. Italy (September).

_____. 1974a. *Sociologists of the Chair.* New York: Basic Books.

_____. 1974b. "Rape Myths: In Legal, Theoretical and Everyday Practice." *Crime and Social Justice* 1 (Spring-Summer).

Sheehy, Gail 1971. *Hustling.* New York: Dell Press.

Simon, Rita James 1975. *Women and Crime.* Lexington: D.C. Heath and Company.

Taylor, Ian, Paul Walton, and Jock Young 1974. *The New Criminology.* New York: Harper & Row.

Taylor, Ian, Paul Walton, and Jock Young (eds.) 1975. *Critical Criminology.* London: Routledge & Kegan Paul.

Thomas, W.I. 1907. *Sex and Society.* Boston: Little, Brown and Company.

_____. 1923. *The Unadjusted Girl.* New York: Harper & Row.

Trey, Joan Ellen 1972. "Women in the War Economy—World War II." *Review of Radical Political Economics* 4(3) (July).

Vedder, Clyde and Dora Somerville 1970. *The Delinquent Girl.* Springfield: Charles C. Thomas.

Ward, David and Gene Kassebaum 1965. *Women's Prison: Sex and Social Structure.* Chicago: Aldine.

Weis, Kurt and Sandra S. Borges 1973. "Victimology and Rape: The Case of the Legitimate Victim." *Issues in Criminology* 8(2) (Fall).

Werkentin, Falco, Michael Hofferbert, and Michael Baurmann 1974. "Criminology as Police Science or: 'How Old Is the New Criminology?'" *Crime and Social Justice 2* (Fall-Winter).

West, Louis J. 1973. *Proposal for the Center for the Study and Reduction of Violence.* Neuropsychiatric Institute, UCLA (April).

Winick, Charles and Paul Kinsie 1971. *The Lively Commerce: Prostitution in the US.* New York: Signet Books.

Wolfe, Alan 1973. *The Seamy Side of Democracy.* New York: David McKay.

Wolfgang, Marvin E. 1958. *Patterns in Criminal Homicide.* Philadelphia: University of Pennsylvania Press.

Women: A Journal of Liberation 1972. Issue on Women in Prison 3 (3).

Women Endorsing Decriminalization 1973. "Prostitution: A Non-Victim Crime." *Issues in Criminology* 8(2) (Fall).

Zinn, Howard 1964. *SNCC: The Student Non-Violent Coordinating Committee.* Boston: Beacon Press.

CPSIA information can be obtained
at www.ICGtesting.com
Printed in the USA
FSHW011805200820
73157FS

9 781516 530151